D1599381

Ethnicity and Identity in Ancient Israel

Ethnicity and Identity
in
Ancient Israel

Prolegomena to the Study of Ethnic Sentiments
and Their Expression in the Hebrew Bible

Kenton L. Sparks

Eisenbrauns
Winona Lake, Indiana
1998

BS
1199
.E84
S63
1998

Library of Congress Cataloging-in-Publication Data

Sparks, Kenton L.
    Ethnicity and identity in ancient Israel : prolegomena to the study of ethnic sentiments and their expression in the Hebrew Bible / Kenton L. Sparks.
       p.   cm.
    Rev. ed. of the author's thesis (University of North Carolina—Chapel Hill, 1996).
    Includes bibliographical references and indexes.
    ISBN 1-57506-033-7 (cloth : alk. paper)
    1. Ethnicity in the Bible.   2. Bible. O.T.—Social scientific criticism.
3. Jews—Identity—History.   I. Title.
BS1199.E84S63   1998
221.8'3058—dc21   98-44816
                                                           CIP

To Clive Staples Lewis
(1898–1963)

Though he died in the year of my birth,
the fruit of his work freed me from a wearisome agnosticism.

Contents

Abbreviations

AB	Anchor Bible
ABD	*Anchor Bible Dictionary*
ACEBT	Amsterdamse Caheirs voor Exegese en Bijbelse Theologie
AEL	M. Lichtheim, *Ancient Egyptian Literature*
AfO	*Archiv für Orientforschung*
AJA	*American Journal of Archaeology*
AJSL	*American Journal of Semitic Languages and Literature*
AnBib	Analecta Biblica
ANET	*Ancient Near Eastern Texts*, 3d ed. (ed. J. B. Pritchard)
AOAT	Alter Orient und Altes Testament
ARAB	*Ancient Records of Assyria and Babylon* (ed. and trans. D. D. Luckenbill)
ATD	Das Alte Testament Deutsch
BA	*Biblical Archaeologiest*
BARev	*Biblical Archaeology Review*
BASOR	*Bulletin of the American Schools of Oriental Research*
BBB	Bonner Biblische Beiträge
BDB	Brown, Driver and Briggs Hebrew Lexicon
BHS	*Biblia Hebraica Stuttgartensia* (ed. K. Ellinger and W. Rudolph)
Bib	*Biblica*
BibOr	*Biblica et Orientalia*
BR	*Biblical Research*
BT	*The Bible Translator*
BZAW	Beiheft zu Zeitschrift für die Alttestamentliche Wissenschaft
CAD	The Assyrian Dictionary of the University of Chicago
*CAH*³	*Cambridge Ancient History*, 3d edition
CBQ	*Catholic Biblical Quarterly*
ConBOT	Coniectanea Biblica, Old Testament Series
Dtr	Deuteronomistic History
DD	*Dor le Dor*
EDB	*Eerdmans Dictionary of the Bible* (forthcoming)
ER	*Encyclopedia of Religion* (ed. by M. Eliade)
ErIsr	*Eretz-Israel*
EA	El Amarna
FRLANT	Forschungen zur Religion und Literatur des Alten und Neuen Testaments
HAT	Handbuch zum Alten Testament
HKAT	Handkommentar zum Alten Testament

HSM	Harvard Semitic Monographs
HSS	Harvard Semitic Studies
HTR	*Harvard Theological Review*
HTS	Hervormde Teologiese Studies
HUCA	*Hebrew Union College Annual*
ICC	International Critical Commentary
IEJ	*Israel Exploration Journal*
JANES	*Journal of the Ancient Near Eastern Society*
JAOS	*Journal of the American Oriental Society*
JARCE	*Journal of the American Research Center in Egypt*
JBL	*Journal of Biblical Literature*
JCS	*Journal of Cuneiform Studies*
JEA	*Journal of Egyptian Archaeology*
JJS	*Journal of Jewish Studies*
JNES	*Journal of Near Eastern Studies*
JNSL	*Journal of Northwest Semitic Languages*
JSOT	*Journal for the Study of the Old Testament*
JSOTSup	Supplements to the Journal for the Study of the Old Testament
KAT	Kommentar zum Alten Testament
KHAT	Kurzer Hand-commentar zum Alten Testament
LCL	Loeb Classical Library
LdÄ	*Lexikon der Ägyptologie*
NCBC	New Century Bible Commentary
OBO	Orbis Biblicus et Orientalis
Or	*Orientalia*
OrAnt	*Orients antiquus*
OTL	Old Testament Library
OTS	*Oudtestamentische Studiën*
PRU	*Le Palais royal d'Ugarit* (eds. C. F. A. Schaeffer & J. Nougayrol, Paris)
REJ	*Revue des études juives*
RIMA	Royal Inscriptions of Mesopotamia, Assyrian Periods
RIME	Royal Inscriptions of Mesopotamia, Early Periods
RLA	*Reallexikon der Assyriologie*
SB	Sources bibliques
SBL Monographs	Society of Biblical Literature Monograph Series
SBLDS	Society of Biblical Literature Dissertation Series
SAA	State Archives of Assyria (Helsinki)
SSEA	Society for the Study of Egyptian Antiquities
SBT	Studies in Biblical Theology
SBT2	Studies in Biblical Theology, Second Series
SEÅ	*Svensk Exegetisk Årsbok*
SJOT	*Scandinavian Journal of the Old Testament*
SSEA	Society for the Study of Egyptian Antiquities
TLZ	*Theologische Literaturzeitung*
TRE	*Theologische Realenzyklopädie*

TB	*Tyndale Bulletin*
TWAT	*Theologisches Wörterbuch zum Alten Testament*
UF	*Ugarit-Forschungen*
UUA	*Uppsala Universitets Arsskrift*
VT	*Vetus Testamentum*
VTSup	Supplements to Vetus Testamentum
WBC	Word Biblical Commentary
WMANT	Wissenschaftliche Monographien zum Alten und Neuen Testament
YNER	Yale Near Eastern Researches
ZAH	*Zeitschrift für Althebräistik*
ZAW	*Zeitschrift für die Alttestamentliche Wissenschaft*
ZDPV	*Zeitschrift des deutschen Palästina-Vereins*

Preface

This monograph is a thoroughly reworked version of a dissertation completed under the direction of John Van Seters at the University of North Carolina–Chapel Hill in spring of 1996. I have added a new chapter on the early sources (the Merneptah Stele and the Song of Deborah) and have reconsidered a number of more subtle issues. But the essential trajectory of the work remains the same as in the original. For the most part, I have attempted to approach the text from a "minimalist" perspective, in part because I find it to be a heuristically valuable enterprise and in part because of certain sympathies that I share with the so-called "minimalist school." But the results of my analysis suggest to me that there is a good bit more that can be gleaned from the Hebrew sources than some of the minimalists are wont to admit.

As will become clear, I have attempted to integrate into my work some of the research done in the field of ethnicity studies, an effort that has proved very profitable in many instances. I am, however, unable participate in the post-modern discourse that prevails in that field of study because I strongly disagree with its most fundamental notion, namely, that our realities are nothing more than linguistic constructions that do not—in fact, cannot—correspond with a world that is "out there." Although I respect the erudition of so many scholars that share the post-modern perspective and acknowledge some of the important contributions that have emerged from the post-modern dialogue, about the more virulent brands of post-modernism I can only say with the apostle Paul, φάσκοντες εἶναι σοφοὶ ἐμωράνθησαν.

One issue that was recently raised to me, too late for discussion in this volume, is the problem of ethnic mechanism: how did the ancients explain the obvious transference of physical and cultural features from one generation to the next? Benjamin Braude expressed it to me via email in this way, "Unconciously, I feel, you have adopted modern notions of biological inheritance. To transfer the modern concept of ethnicity to a pre-Mendelian and pre-Darwinian world is to neglect the fundamental differences between the old and new concepts of inheritance." I believe that he was particularly concerned with language like "genetic heritage," which in his view necessarily assumes modern notions about the mechanism of phenotypical transference. In my view, such language does not presume such a modern perspective, and I can stress here that by "genetic" I mean: "pertaining to the origin or development of something," as one popular English dictionary defines it. But I do feel that he raises an important issue that I have not dealt with and which requires additional attention at some future point.

As is generally the case with works such as this, those who deserve my thanks are numerous. Most of the intellectual assistance was rendered by my *Doktorvater*, Professor John Van Seters, who has proved himself to be an ideal mentor. Thanks are also due to Professor Jack Sasson, who served on my dissertation committee and also counseled me during parts of the revision process. The other committee members, Profs. David Halperin, Laurie Mafley-Kipp, and Carl Ernst, provided valuable feedback as well. Words of appreciation are due especially to those that lent a hand well beyond what is normally expected in such efforts, particularly in the cases of Dana Pike (BYU), Philip Stadter (UNC Classics), and Janet Johnson (Oriental Institute, Chicago). The whole effort ultimately goes back to a conversation with Hector Avalos, now at Iowa State University, who provided me with an initial bibliography that got things started. To all of these, and especially to my fellow graduate students at UNC, many thanks.

So far as publishers go, the scholarship, flexibility, and professionalism of Jim Eisenbraun and his staff has been enumerated by others on countless occasions, and here I can only reconfirm these acclamations. Special thanks should be extended to my copy-editor, Bev Fields, who did all that she was able—short of rewriting the piece—to make the volume free from grammatical infelicities and from rhetorical ambiguity.

Special thanks are reserved for my family and for my family of faith. The members and staff of my home institution, Providence Baptist Church, have been supportive in so many ways during the revision process and this has been a special source of encouragement. Even more important has been the life-long encouragement of my Mom and Dad and also of my brother, Caelius Secundus. But my surest debts have been accrued to my wife, Cheryl, and my two daughters, Emily and Cara Ellen. One of the most amazing things about life is that they have already canceled those debts, just as was done for me more completely so long ago by the one who receives this concluding word: *Soli Deo Gloria!*

Chapter One

Introduction

When we speak of ethnicity, we bring into view a particular kind of sentiment about group identity wherein groups of individuals view themselves as being alike by virtue of their common ancestry. It is something of a truism to point out that ethnicity has played an important role in the history of Judaism, both in the postbiblical era and prior to it.[1] In this case it is the early historical period that is of interest to me, specifically the period of Israelite history before the exiles returned to Palestine in 538 B.C.E. The reason for this interest is twofold. First, in virtually every discipline of the humanities there seems to be a general unhappiness with the superficial way that scholars have handled the issues of culture and identity. More specifically with respect to ancient Israel, recent biblical scholarly activity—both literary and historical—has raised serious doubts about the supposed origins and antiquity of Israelite ethnicity.[2] So there is a growing consensus that these issues need to be revisited. But before we address them in detail, a more thorough-going definition of ethnicity is in order.

Ethnicity has been called an "extraordinarily elusive concept" that is "very difficult to define in any precise way,"[3] and by way of illustration we need look only at two definitions to show, first, that both are heuristically difficult to employ, and second, that they are not the same kind of definitions. If the reader will brook a bit of telescoping from

1. M. G. Brett, "Interpreting Ethnicity," in *Ethnicity and the Bible* (ed. M. G. Brett; Biblical Interpretation Series 19; Leiden: Brill, 1996) 11; H. G. M. Williamson, "The Concept of Israel in Transition," in *The World of Ancient Israel* (ed. R. E. Clements; Cambridge: Cambridge University Press, 1989) 141–61.

2. See, for instance, M. Skjeggestad's "Ethnic Groups in Early Iron Age Palestine: Some Remarks on the Use of the Term 'Israelite' in Recent Research," *SJOT* 6 (1992) 159–86.

3. T. Parsons, "Some Theoretical Considerations on the Nature and Trends of Change in Ethnicity," in *Ethnicity: Theory and Experience* (ed. N. Glazer and D. P. Moynihan; Cambridge: Harvard University Press, 1975) 53.

the *Dictionary of Race and Ethnic Relations,* according to E. Cashmore ethnicity is:

> . . . the term used to encapsulate the various types of responses of different groups . . . the ethnic group is based on a commonness of subjective apprehensions, whether about origins, interests or future (or a combination of these) . . . material deprivation is the most fertile condition for the growth of ethnicity . . . ethnicity may be used for any number of purposes, sometimes as an overt political instrument, at other times as a simple defensive strategy in the face of adversity.[4]

We may profitably compare this definition with the one adopted by F. W. Riggs, who has concluded that ethnicity involves:

> . . . an ascriptive, genetically self-perpetuating mode of social relations treated as an alternative to, or complement of, other forms of social organization, in the context of a larger society.[5]

If we examine these two definitions closely, the resulting comparison brings (among other things) two important differences to the surface. First, while some theorists view the concept of common ancestry—kinship—as an essential component of ethnic identity (Riggs), this is not a requirement of ethnicity as defined by Cashmore, and it is this theoretical contrast that points us to the second difference between the two.[6] Ethnic theorists in the tradition of Cashmore are especially interested in the problems faced by peripheral groups when they experience the oppressive dominance of other sociopolitical modalities and also in the effects that this peripheral experience has on identity. Because common ancestry may or may not figure in the "basic group identity" of the subjects they study,[7] the concept of common ancestry would be a

4. E. Cashmore, *Dictionary of Race and Ethnic Relations* (3d ed.; London: Routledge, 1994) 106.
5. This definition is taken directly from F. W. Riggs (ed.), *Ethnicity: Concepts and Terms Used in Ethnicity Research* (International Conceptual Encyclopedia for the Social Sciences 1; Honolulu: COCTA, 1985) 4.
6. For an introduction to the theoretical discussion about kinship, see R. Fox, *Kinship and Marriage* (Cambridge Studies in Social and Cultural Anthropology 50; Cambridge: Cambridge University Press, 1984).
7. I am referring to H. Isaacs's well-known summary of the fundamental components of group identity. See his "Basic Group Identity," in *Ethnicity: Theory and Experience* (ed. N. Glazer and D. P. Moynihan; Cambridge: Harvard University Press, 1975) 29–52.

particularly limiting factor for these theorists. On the other hand, although Riggs no doubt shares many theoretical concerns with Cashmore, his definition stands more closely to the questions raised by the literature of ancient Israel, particularly the question of how Israel's concept of a common genealogical ancestry originated and how this ancestral tradition developed and changed over the course of time. So my work is of a somewhat different character than what sometimes goes on in the field of ethnicity studies, especially in its "politically-motivated" garb. This does not mean that the observations and "assured results" of that field's research are irrelevant to my work, as will become clear. But it does mean that my definition of ethnicity, with its primary interest in notions of common ancestry, is semantically narrower than—but certainly within—the broader definition of ethnicity used by Cashmore and others. One might say that we are examining ethnic groups that meet Cashmore's definition and that also use kinship as an organizing principle of group membership or as a model for conceptualizing other groups. Or to put it in terms of the data from the Hebrew Bible, we are researching ethnic kinship when it serves as: (1) a concept of sociocultural integration ("*we* are the children of Abraham"); (2) as a tool for sociocultural delimitation ("*they* are not children of Abraham"); and (3) as a model for explaining the origins of other peoples ("*they* are the children of Lot").

Returning to the thorny problem of definition, most theorists would in large measure agree with the general parameters offered by F. Barth, that ethnicity is a social boundary that partitions population groups on the basis of one or more of the following distinctions: (a) genealogical characteristics; (b) cultural traits such as language, religion, customs, shared history; and (c) inherited phenotypical characteristics,[8] *with the first of these three being the primary carrier of ethnic sentiment.* Certain "anchors" or "ethnic markers" appear in conjunction with these "ethnic sentiments" (distinctive identities rooted in perceived genealogical connections between people) and become the primary indicators of those who are in an ethnic group and those who are outsiders.[9] These anchors can range from the obvious physical

8. F. Barth, *Ethnic Groups and Boundaries* (Boston: Little, Brown, 1969).
9. We must be careful to distinguish between cultural characteristics and ethnic markers. For instance, when D. Edelman suggests that we might use architecture, pottery, or site layout as Israelite "ethnic markers," she implies that these features functioned in Israelite society as symbols of their ethnic identity. But it seems to me that, in

characteristics that we more readily associate with ethnic identities, such as skin tone, to more subtle types of markers, such as the ability to participate in the community's in-group discourse. Similar anchors help to define cultural boundaries in general, but one must take care not to confuse ethnicity with the closely related term *culture*. When we speak of culture, we should think about groups of people who share common intragroup systems, behavior patterns, language, and, generally speaking, a specific territorial unit.[10] When attention is given to this definition of culture, it becomes clear that ethnic behavior is always one aspect of culture but that a given culture may or may not exhibit pronounced displays of ethnic behavior.[11] Some confusion may arise here because the terms "culture" and "ethnic group" have become largely synonymous within the *Geisteswissenschaften*, but this situation should not obscure the fact that culture is semantically broader than ethnicity as I have defined it, so that, contrary to some work already done, the archaeological identification of a given material culture cannot easily demonstrate that the culture displayed ethnic sentiment and behavior.[12] Ethnic sentiment and behavior is closely related to (but

the event that we find ourselves able to distinguish Israelite pottery from Canaanite pottery, it would probably be more precise to view it as a characteristic of Israelite culture, since we have no idea that the Israelites would have viewed pottery as a symbol of their common identity or as a feature that distinguished them from Canaanites. See D. Edelman, "Ethnicity and Early Israel, in *Ethnicity and the Bible* (ed. M. G. Brett; Biblical Interpretation Series 19; Leiden: Brill, 1996) 42–7.

10. This is something of an oversimplification, since there are various categories that may fall under the rubric of the term *culture*. Here I am thinking specifically about culture as an object of study for those in the field of cultural anthropology and ethnography. For a summary of the issues involved in defining the term *culture* and the variety of referents related to the term, see S. J. Knudson, *Culture in Retrospect* (Boston: Waveland, 1985) 84–95.

11. For instance, any attempt to isolate and identify ethnic groups with the archaeological data is (very nearly) doomed to failure because distinctive pottery types and other similar kinds of evidence cannot tell us whether ethnic ancestry served an important role for the modality in question. In the end the archaeological data only isolates peripheral sociocultural modalities that may or may not have embraced ethnic sentiments. For a recent attempt to isolate and identify cultural groups through ethno-archaeology, see G. Emberling, *Ethnicity and the State in Early Third Millennium Mesopotamia* (Ph.D. diss, University of Michigan, 1995).

12. Note especially the work of T. Özgüç, excavator at Kültepe, who has pointed out that without the cuneiform texts and seal impressions the Assyrian merchant communities there are not archaeologically distinguishable from their Hittite hosts ("An Assyrian Trading Outpost," *Scientific American* 208 [1963] 101–2). Recent studies that

hardly synonymous with) culture because the latter does not necessarily include social identities that are rooted in a perceived genealogical connection between the group's members.

As one might guess, there is a healthy debate surrounding the issue of how ethnic sentiments arise, and the various perspectives on the subject have been conveniently summarized by R. Thompson.[13] Some would argue that ethnic behavior is innate and biological while others would view it more as a product of specific sociohistorical circumstances.[14] A somewhat different but related theoretical debate pits those who view ethnicity as a natural extension of kinship ("primordialists") against those who consider ethnicity to be a tool used to further political and economic interests ("instrumentalists"). We will pick up this issue a little later, but for now we may state that everyone seems to agree that the emergence of ethnic sentiments and the social boundaries that they produce are related to the question of "otherness" that has received so much recent attention.[15] The most frequently cited example of "the other" as a human experience is the response of the colonial West to the cultures it encountered as the European presence

---

attempt to focus on isolating ethnic groups in the ancient Near Eastern context fail precisely because they are identifying cultural distinctives rather than evidence of ethnic sentiment. See W. G. Dever, "Cultural Continuity: Ethnicity in the Archaeological Record and the Question of Israelite Origins," *ErIsr* 24 (1993) 22–33; K. A. Kamp and N. Yoffee, "Ethnicity in Ancient Western Asia during the Early Second Millennium B.C.: Archaeological Assessments and Ethnoarchaeological Prospectives," *BASOR* 237 (1980) 85–104.

13. Richard H. Thompson, *Theories of Ethnicity: A Critical Appraisal* (New York: Greenwood, 1989). See also the very useful volume by M. Banks, *Ethnicity: Anthropological Constructions* (London: Routledge, 1996).

14. In her recent study Edelman leaves the impression that the biological model has been rejected by ethnicity scholarship, and this is not the case. Rather, some of the more recent theorists are emphasizing the genesis of ethnic sentiments only within specific kinds of circumstances, and this is not the definitive conclusion of ethnicity studies but rather one view within a rather factious debate. See Edelman, "Ethnicity and Early Israel," 25–26.

15. See especially the following: Charles H. Long, "Primitive/Civilized: The Locus of a Problem," and "Freedom, Otherness and Religion: Theologies Opaque," *Significations: Signs, Symbols and Images in the Interpretation of Religion* (Philadelphia: Fortress, 1986) 79–96, 185–99; J. Z. Smith, "What a Difference a Difference Makes," *"To See Ourselves as Others See Us": Christians, Jews, "Others" in Late Antiquity* (ed. J. Neusner and E. S. Frerichs; Scholars Press Studies in the Humanities; Chico, Calif.: Scholars Press, 1985) 3–48. See also the entertaining critique of scholarship's preoccupation with "otherness" by P. W. Kroll, "Us and Them," *JAOS* 113 (1993) 457–60.

spread into new regions. This prompted Western societies to establish clear social and cultural boundaries between themselves and the "new" peoples.[16] These boundaries included strong ethnic sentiments that naturally followed from the West's genealogical conception of a world populated by the posterity of Noah's sons, Ham, Shem, Japeth. At certain points, Westerners became so preoccupied with preserving an ethnic identity distinct from these new peoples that *polygenesis* became popular.[17] Now I do not wish to belabor the rather obvious fact that new and different stimuli (as in "the other") often elicit interesting responses from human beings, nor is it my goal to catalog the imperial West's encounter with the rest of the world. Rather, apart from the apparent connection between "otherness" and the issue of ethnicity, the more important connection between "otherness" and ancient Israel is the extent to which, in a given case, "the other" represented a concrete referential entity (as in "ancient Israel really fought the Canaanites") or a socially constructed entity (that is, "the Canaanites were the *literary* opponents of Israel"). As one might imagine, scholars tend to line up on either side of this question, and I will certainly take a look at this and related issues before my work is done. But at this point there are more pressing introductory issues that will have to be addressed.

Israel's Ethnic Identity: Issues and Problems

Israelite ethnicity represents a special problem in biblical studies at this point. In decades past, the "American school" in the Albright tradition,[18] the "German school" in the Alt tradition,[19] and the "Socio-

16. Edward Said provides a useful analysis of this process in *Orientalism* (New York: Vintage, 1979).

17. B. G. Trigger, *A History of Archaeological Thought* (Cambridge: Cambridge University Press, 1989) 111–12. By *polygenesis* I am referring to the belief that various ethnic groups were created separately by the deity and were not, therefore, genetically related.

18. See, for example, W. F. Albright, *Yahweh and the Gods of Canaan* (London: University of London Press, 1968; reprint, Winona Lake, Ind.: Eisenbrauns, 1978) and F. M. Cross, *Canaanite Myth and Hebrew Epic* (Cambridge: Harvard University Press, 1973).

19. For Alt and scholars accepting his amphictyonic model of early Israel, the tribal groups involved stood in opposition to native Canaanite peoples: "These neighbors were the inhabitants of Palestine before the Israelite settlement. We shall refer to them here, for the sake of brevity, as the Canaanites, without distinguishing between the different elements in the population" (Alt, *Essays on Old Testament History and Religion* [Garden City, N.Y.: Doubleday, 1968] 125).

logical school" associated with G. E. Mendenhall[20] could, despite their important differences, suggest a Sitz im Leben for the emergence of Israelite ethnic sentiments. For the American school, the Israelites represented the conquering outsider who, upon entrance into Palestine, met a foreign culture that could be viewed as ethnically distinct from Israel. In the case of the German school, the popular "amphictyony hypothesis" suggested a united Israel that stood over against the surrounding peoples, again a context of "otherness" suitable for ethnic sentiment to emerge.[21] For Mendenhall and Gottwald, the original opposition pitted village dwellers against residents of the Palestinian city-states. However, literary studies of the Hebrew text and archaeological work in Palestine have raised considerable problems for all of these paradigms over the last few decades.

With respect to the amphictyonic context, one of the first systematic criticisms of the hypothesis came in G. Fohrer's 1966 article,[22] which pointed out that the book of Judges portrays a number of disparate tribes rather than a previously unified Israel and that Dtr's picture of Saul's rise shows little evidence of an "all Israel" sentiment. Furthermore, the idea of an early covenant was motivated, Fohrer suggested, more from theological interest in covenant than from unquestionably early textual evidence. A more thorough criticism of the amphictyony was published in C. H. J. de Geus's *Tribes of Israel*,[23] which reiterated a number of Fohrer's arguments but made two important additions: (1) "amphictyony" is a misnomer, since an amphictyony was not a strictly religious but a political institution; and (2) no

20. G. E. Mendenhall, "The Hebrew Conquest of Palestine," *BA* 25 (1962) 66–87; idem, *The Tenth Generation* (Baltimore: Johns Hopkins University Press, 1973); N. K. Gottwald, *The Tribes of Yahweh: A Sociology of the Religion of Liberated Israel, 1250–1000 B.C.* (Maryknoll, N.Y.: Orbis, 1979).

21. For a discussion of the Greek evidence, see F. Cauer, "Amphiktyonie," *Pauly-Wissowa Real-Encyclopedie* 1 (1894) 1904–35; J. M. Cook, *The Greeks in Ionia and the East* (London: Thames and Hudson, 1962); J. Penrose-Harland, "The Calaurian Amphictyony," *AJA* 29 (1925) 160–71; R. de Vaux, *The Early History of Israel* (Philadelphia: Westminster, 1978) 697–700.

22. G. Fohrer, "Altes Testament: 'Amphiktyonie' und 'Bund'?" *TLZ* 91 (1966) 801–16, 893–904.

23. C. H. J. de Geus, *The Tribes of Israel: An Investigation into Some of the Presuppositions of Martin Noth's Amphictyony Hypothesis* (Studia Semitica Neerlandica 18; Assen: Van Gorcum, 1976); for a very brief outline of important criticisms, see M. L. Chaney, "Ancient Palestinian Peasant Movements and the Formation of Premonarchic Israel," in *Palestine in Transition: The Emergence of Ancient Israel* (Sheffield: Almond, 1983) 41–44.

early central cult or shrine (around which the Israelites unified) can be isolated in the sources. In defense of the amphictyony hypothesis, von Rad had suggested that, despite the apparent lateness of Deuteronomic thought, early credal statements from the amphictyonic period could be isolated within the later Dt/Dtr corpus.[24] But this argument has been soundly dismissed by B. Childs, W. Richter, and others, who point out that these creeds are too colored by Deuteronomistic influence to be unquestionably early.[25] In sum, there is no longer convincing evidence for an early amphictyonic Israel and, therefore, such a context for the appearance of a distinct, Israelite ethnic identity can no longer be confidently maintained.[26]

The conquest model as a context for the emergence of ethnic Israel has faced a similar fate, not only because of the literary problems that we have already mentioned (i.e., that there is no early united Israel) but also because of recent archaeological work. First, archaeological studies have failed to uncover evidence for a unified conquest of Palestine that could be connected with a group of Israelites. As J. M. Miller has noted, "were we dependent upon archaeological and other non-biblical evidence alone, we would have no reason even to suppose that such a conquest ever occurred."[27] True, there is evidence of widespread destruction associated with Late Bronze Age Palestine, but this evidence

24. Particularly Deut 6:20–24 and Josh 24:2b–13. See G. von Rad, "The Form Critical Problem of the Hexateuch," *The Problem of the Hexateuch and Other Essays* (trans. E. W. T. Dickens; Edinburgh: London: Oliver and Boyd, 1966).

25. B. S. Childs, "Deuteronomic Formulae in the Exodus Tradition," *Hebräische Wortforschung: Festschrift zum 80. Geburtstag von Walter Baumgartner* (VTSup 16; Leiden: Brill, 1967) 30–39; W. Richter, "Beobachtungen zur theologischen Systembildung in der alttestamentlichen Literatur anhand des 'kleinen geschichtlichen Credo,'" in *Wahrheit und Verkündigung: Festschrift M. Schmaus* (2 vols.; ed. W. Dettloff et al.; Munich: Schoningh, 1967) 1.175–212.

26. For other arguments against the amphictyony hypothesis, see H. I. Irwin, "Le sanctuaire central israélite avant l'établissement de la monarchie," *RB* 73 (1965) 161–84; A. D. H. Mayes, *Israel in the Period of the Judges* (Naperville: Allenson, 1974); H. M. Orlinsky, "The Tribal System of Israel and Related Groups in the Period of the Judges," *OrAnt* 1 (1962) 11–21; R. de Vaux, "Le thèse de l'amphictyonie Israélite," *HTR* 64 (1971) 415–36. A recent article by H. E. Chambers has suggested that ancient Sumerian "leagues" might provide the comparative context for an original Israelite amphictyony at Shiloh. But this proposal is based on the flawed suggestion that the biblical sources reflect such an amphictyony, which is not the case ("Ancient Amphictyonies, Sic et Non," *Scripture in Context II: More Essays on the Comparative Method* (ed. W. W. Hallo, J. C. Moyer, and L. G. Perdue; Winona Lake, Ind.: Eisenbrauns, 1983) 39–59.

27. J. M. Miller, "Israelite History," in *The Hebrew Bible and Its Modern Interpreters* (ed. D. A. Knight and G. M. Tucker; Philadelphia: Fortress, 1985) 11.

cannot be uniformly characterized as the result of military action, and the sites show no correlation to the biblical sites conquered in Dtr. Because of this situation, some scholars now choose to begin their Israelite histories with later, more concrete periods, such as the United Monarchy.[28] The questions raised by the archaeological evidence extend beyond the question of the conquest to later periods in Israel's history because, to this point, the evidence derived from the sources has failed to provide any clear distinction between a supposed Israelite material culture and competing material cultures that might be identified with other ethnic groups.[29] Even those who might attempt to identify certain early settlement features as "Israelite" must admit that "defining a distinctively 'Israelite' material culture is a difficult venture."[30]

Despite support in some quarters, the "peasant revolt" model of the sociological school has also been heavily criticized. From a theoretical standpoint, the model is informed by a modern sociological scheme that is of highly questionable value, particularly in its tendency to use comparative "ideal types" in the analysis of quite disparate social and historical contexts.[31] Another major problem with the theory is its

---

28. For example, J. A. Soggin, *A History of Ancient Israel* (Philadelphia: Westminster, 1984). There are a growing number of scholars who question the referential status of Israel's United Monarchy, but I cannot agree with their skepticism. For a recent discussion and defense of its referential status, see G. N. Knoppers, "The Vanishing Solomon: The Disappearance of the United Monarchy from Recent Histories of Ancient Israel," *JBL* 116 (1997) 19–44.

29. See chapter three of G. W. Ahlström's *Who Were the Israelites?* (Winona Lake, Ind.: Eisenbrauns, 1986). Supporting this position are most theorists. See also N. Lemche, *Early Israel: Anthropological and Historical Studies on the Israelite Society before the Monarchy* (VTSup 37; Leiden: Brill, 1985) 386–406; J. M. Miller and J. H. Hayes, *A History of Ancient Israel and Judah* (Philadelphia: Westminster, 1986) 72; Soggin, *A History of Ancient Israel,* 361–64.

30. A. Mazar, *Archaeology of the Land of the Bible: 10,000–586 B.C.E.* (New York: Doubleday, 1992) 353. See also I. Finkelstein, *The Archaeology of the Israelite Settlement* (Jerusalem: Israel Exploration Society, 1988) 27–28.

31. For a brief example of this sociological philosophy in action, see N. K. Gottwald, "Early Israel and the Canaanite Sociological System," *Palestine in Transition: The Emergence of Ancient Israel* (ed. D. N. Freedman and D. F. Graf; Sheffield: Almond, 1983) 25–37. In this article Gottwald, aware of criticisms that European medieval feudalism is unsuitable for comparative purposes, attempts to position Canaanite society within an "Asiatic mode of production model" developed by Marx and Engels. The speculative nature of the endeavor is reflected by the fact that this model assumes a basic socioeconomic correlation between Indian, Chinese, Mesopotamian, Egyptian, and Islamic societies, a perspective that is intuitively simplistic and that has been much criticized in Said's monograph, *Orientalism.*

questionable use of the Hebrew sources. Although there are some correspondences between the peasant revolt model and the biblical text,
B. Halpern has correctly pointed out that there is very little agreement
between them.[32] The sociological school is also generally careless with
the biblical sources—on the one hand ignoring biblical testimony that
does not fit the scheme and on the other uncritically accepting evidence when it does. The model also requires that the *Ḥapiru* of the
Amarna letters and the emergence of Israel represent the same phenomenon, which in the first place is a much-debated problem,[33] in the
second place erroneously assumes that the biblical sources come from a
very early period, and in the third place fails to recognize that, as I will
show, the development of the term עברי ('Hebrew') is probably to be
associated with the late biblical period many centuries after the
Amarna period (see below, pp. 245–248).

But by far the most scathing criticism of the sociological school is
that it has utterly failed to comprehend the ecological situation in Palestine during the period in question, though it is at this point that the
sociological school has tended to be most confident.[34] Finkelstein
points out that Gottwald's assumptions about rainfall, settlement patterns, irrigation and agricultural technology, animal husbandry, and
material culture can all be proven erroneous. This is primarily because,
as he put it, "Gottwald's fundamental error is that he took a body of
data from North Syria at the beginning of the second millennium and
applied it, without the slightest reservation or hesitation, to the Land of
Israel at the end of the second millennium—heedless to the totally different geographical and historical settings involved."[35] But all of this
said, the fundamental problem with the sociological school (as with so
many discussions about the "origins" of Israel) is that it holds to the
now questionable assumption that the biblical narrative traditions
about early Israel—particularly the pentateuchal J/E sources—are quite
old and that these sources provide us with an ancient account of Israel's
second-millennium emergence in Palestine. It is precisely this, among
other things, that must be addressed before our work is done here.

32. B. Halpern, *The Emergence of Israel in Canaan* (SBLMS 29; Chico, Calif.:
Scholars Press, 1983) 7.
33. See especially Weippert's criticism in *The Settlement of the Israelite Tribes in
Palestine: A Critical Survey of Recent Scholarly Debate* (2d ed.; SBT 28; Naperville, Ill.:
Allenson, 1971) 63–74.
34. Finkelstein, *The Archaeology of the Israelite Settlement*, 306–14.
35. Ibid., 309; see also comments by Lemche, *Early Israel*, 162.

Because of the serious questions surrounding the amphictyonic hypothesis, the conquest model, and the peasant-revolt theory, we are left without a convincing historical context that could produce or foster ethnic distinctions between ancient Israelites and other groups. The question then remains how and why ethnic sentiments became such a powerful form of identity in ancient Israel. Furthermore, the matter is complicated by the fact that, despite an overarching concern for ethnic identity in the Hebrew sources, the sentiments are not uniform in character, as several examples show. While certain sources are preoccupied with the patriarch Abraham, Jacob dominates the discussion in early prophetic literature. In the case of Israel's twelve-tribe ancestry, the biblical picture is clouded by the fact that tribal combinations vary in both name and number in the materials. And why do some texts urge foreigners into Israel's religious fold and others exclude them from the community? How do we explain Abraham's relationship with Hagar when we juxtapose it with Ezra's rejection of foreign women? In other words, we must remember that the problem is not limited to the nature of "Israel" and how its ethnic boundaries were defined but with "Israelites" (and "Judeans") and how their various definitions of ethnic identity played out on the stage of history.

Although the three reconstructed contexts—conquest, peasant revolt, and amphictyony—have provided the ground from which Israelite distinctiveness supposedly emerged, the supposed demise of these historical theories is only now beginning to affect our views of Israelite identity and of the origins of its ethnic sentiment. For the most part, scholarship has continued to assume the essentially ethnic nature of ancient Israel, primarily because the fundamental statement of Israelite ethnic identity, the patriarchal narratives, is thought to reflect very ancient circumstances. But the assumption that the pentateuchal sources are very early has been strongly challenged, beginning especially with the efforts of J. Van Seters and H. H. Schmid in the mid-seventies.[36] The writings of these scholars, which propose that the tetrateuchal sources are rather late, were at first viewed as eccentric but have now

36. H. H. Schmid, *Der sogenannte Jahwist: Beobachtungen und Fragen zur Pentateuchforschung* (Zurich: Theologischer Verlag, 1976); John Van Seters, *Abraham in History and Tradition* (New Haven: Yale University Press, 1975). See also the somewhat different contribution of T. L. Thompson, *The Historicity of the Patriarchal Narratives: The Quest for the Historical Abraham* (BZAW 133; Berlin: de Gruyter, 1974). Subsequent works by these and other scholars only seem, in my opinion, to raise even more questions.

gained greater support than was anticipated at the time. Since then, the pentateuchal narratives, or at least many of the pentateuch's components, have been increasingly viewed as literary products from the late monarchy, the exile, or even from the Persian era. And even if one is not fully convinced of such a late date for the materials, D. A. Knight is certainly correct that "it is now difficult to hold to an early date with unshaken confidence."[37] Neither an amphictyonic context, nor the conquest model, nor a supposed patriarchal age can be established with any certainty, and so they cannot serve as a stable context for the emergence of a distinct ethnic identity in ancient Israel.

As in the case of Israelite literature and history, the religion of ancient Israel is being conceptualized with new paradigms. In decades past, both the "American school" in the Albright tradition[38] and the "German school" in the Alt tradition[39] could, despite their important differences, endorse the idea that the Israelites stood in contrast to Canaanite religion. But presently the observation of M. Coogan that Israelite religion "should be viewed as a subset of Canaanite religion" is becoming the rule rather than the exception.[40] M. Smith echoes this sentiment that "the varied forms of Yahwistic cult [reflect] Israel's Canaanite background."[41] Recent archaeological finds, such as the discoveries at Kuntillet Ajrud and Deir 'Alla,[42] and our growing under-

37. D. A. Knight, "The Pentateuch," *The Hebrew Bible and Its Modern Interpreters* (ed. D. A. Knight and G. M. Tucker; Philadelphia: Fortress, 1985) 281–22.

38. For example, see Albright, *Yahweh and the Gods of Canaan*; Cross, *Canaanite Myth and Hebrew Epic*.

39. For Alt and those accepting his amphictyonic model of early Israel, the tribal groups involved stood in opposition to native Canaanite peoples: "These neighbors were the inhabitants of Palestine before the Israelite settlement. We shall refer to them here, for the sake of brevity, as the Canaanites, without distinguishing between the different elements in the population" (see *Essays on Old Testament History and Religion*, 125).

40. M. D. Coogan, "Canaanite Origins and Lineage: Reflections on the Religion of Ancient Israel," in *Ancient Israelite Religion* (ed. P. D. Miller; Philadelphia: Fortress, 1987) 115–6. Similarly, in the same volume (pp. 249ff.) J. Holladay's "Religion in Israel and Judah under the Monarchy: An Explicitly Archaeological Approach" suggests that we should conceptualize Israel as fundamentally similar to the other Syro-Palestinian states nearby.

41. M. S. Smith, *The Early History of God* (San Francisco: Harper, 1990) 146.

42. There is a very large body of literature that addresses the finds at Kuntillet Ajrud and the related finds at Khribet el-Qom. A good starting place is W. G. Dever, "Asherah, Consort of Yahweh? New Evidence from Kuntillet Ajrud," *BASOR* 255 (1984) 21–37. A more recent work is S. A. Wiggins, *A Reassessment of "Asherah": A*

standing of other features such as cults of the dead[43] suggest that this trend is not misguided. Just as the newer conceptions of Israelite literature have raised questions about Israel's ethnic distinctiveness so also the net result in the realm of Israelite religion seems to be that Israelite religion is, in many respects, "Canaanite" religion, or perhaps better, "West Semitic religion." These circumstances in essence raise the question of how one should speak properly of the "Israelites" in contrast to the "Canaanites" and other peoples in the region.

Clearly then, the present situation in the study of Hebrew literature, Syro-Palestinian archaeology, and Israelite religion runs counter to the standard contexts that older scholarship has suggested for the emergence of an ethnically distinct Israel. Nevertheless, the very sources that we are wont to question contain some of the most pronounced expressions of ethnic sentiment that human literature has produced. An attempt to clarify this paradoxical situation must necessarily break with the three dominant conceptual models of Israel's ethnic distinctiveness (amphictyony, conquest, peasant-revolt) and begin to ask new questions of the materials. If we cannot get a clear picture of Israelite origins and hence of its nascent sense of identity, then a better set of queries should set aside the somewhat misguided preoccupation with Israel's nebulous origins and focus on the more tangible literary sources and historical periods. Our interrogatories in this task are three: (1) What varieties of ethnic sentiment and definition played important roles in ancient Israel's literature? (2) What does the literary discussion tell us about the origin and history of these identities? (3) What roles do other modes of identity (e.g., religious, political, etc.) play in relation to the various conceptions of ethnic identity?

As I pursue these three questions I will be guided by three sets of data and their relationship to each other. First, it is necessary that a *theoretical base* be established with respect to ethnic studies proper.

Study according to the Textual Sources of the First Two Millennia B.C.E. (AOAT 235; Neukirchener-Vluyn: Neukirchener Verlag, 1993). Regarding Deir ʿAllâ, see J. A. Hackett, *The Balaam Text from Deir ʿAlla* (HSM 31; Cambridge: Harvard University Press, 1980).

43. T. J. Lewis, *Cults of the Dead in Ancient Israel and Ugarit* (HSM 39; Atlanta: Scholars Press, 1989); B. B. Schmidt, *Israel's Beneficent Dead: Ancestor Cult and Necromancy in Ancient Israelite Religion and Tradition* (Forschungen zum Alten Testament 11; Tübingen: Mohr, 1994). Schmidt's work was recently reprinted by Eisenbrauns (1996).

This should provide the necessary ground rules that will circumscribe and give shape to my work, especially with respect to the kinds of issues that are brought to the materials in question. On the other hand, what I am proposing is to use only those conclusions from ethnic studies that enjoy the broadest base of support. I will studiously avoid using "off the shelf" theoretical models offered by ethnicity studies to accomplish my task, since such models are themselves subject to the concrete data presented by the evidence and are inevitably based on some hotly-debated presuppositions. Second, a *comparative base* of materials must be collected and evaluated, this being accomplished through both primary and secondary sources that address ethnicity and ethnic issues among Israel's ancient neighbors. Specifically, I am thinking here about Egypt, Assyria, and Greece. Finally, these first two corpora of data must be integrated with my *primary research base*, which is composed of the materials available to us from the Hebrew Bible along with a few extrabiblical sources.

Due to the complexity of these sources and the difficulties that accompany their use in historical reconstruction, it is necessary that I briefly explain the strategy that will guide my examination of the archaeological and biblical sources. Although I will refer to the archaeological evidence when relevant, the difficulties associated with ethno-archaeology dictate that my point of departure will be the Hebrew text, since it is, despite obvious limitations, our best window into the ancient Israelite context.[44] The assumptions that will govern my handling of these biblical materials are as follows. The "new orientation" in biblical studies has its appeal for a number of reasons.[45] To defend this position fully here is unnecessary, but I can offer a brief synopsis to explain its attractiveness. One perplexing issue in scholarship of the Hebrew Bible during the last few decades has been the enigma of von Rad and Noth: scholarship has tended, in a contradictory way, to embrace both Noth's tetrateuch and von Rad's hexateuch simultaneously by agreeing that the first four books of the Hebrew Bible stand apart from Dt/Dtr and yet also agreeing that the first four books cannot exist

---

44. Classicists face a similar archaeological problem in their ethnic research. See J. M. Hall, *Ethnic Identity in Greek Antiquity* (Cambridge: Cambridge University Press, 1997) 128–9.

45. The "new orientation" views the Hebrew historical works, basically the Pentateuch and Dtr, as later works that might tell more about the period in which they originated (the late monarchy and the exilic period) than about Israel's earlier history.

without Dtr's conquest narrative. A very natural way to account for this has been suggested by Van Seters, who argues that Dt/Dtr existed first, followed by the addition of J and then P (he eliminates the Elohist).[46] In this scenario, J and P never existed without the conquest narrative, and the literary distinctions between J[E?]P and Dt/Dtr are preserved.

There are, of course, other solutions that have been suggested to address these problems, and the works of Rendtorff and Blum, among others, come immediately to mind.[47] And of course the nature of Dtr has been very much questioned in recent years, including its very existence, and so the simple sketch that I have offered above is not intended to stake out a position. Rather, the major point here is that the supposed antiquity of the pentateuchal sources (if indeed they are sources) has now been questioned from several directions, so that the dating and nature of the those sources must now become another element within our continuing debate. As a result, it is methodologically questionable to begin a traditiohistorical inquiry with the pentateuchal materials. The more appropriate starting place is with the sources that can be dated with greater certainty, or at least with relative certainty. Our primary and most substantive sources would naturally become the eighth-century prophetic collections of Amos, Hosea, and Isaiah, to be followed chronologically with the materials in Jeremiah, Ezekiel, Deutero-Isaiah, and so forth. Deuteronomy can also be added to the list, since its association with the late Judean monarchy is secure (although it is important to recognize that it contains older materials). There remain several sources that are of unquestionable antiquity, namely the Merneptah Stele and the Song of Deborah, and I would be misguided to address the question of Israelite ethnicity apart from them.

I have come to view this work as "prolegomena" rather than as a complete analysis of ethnic sentiments throughout the history of Israel.

---

46. The status of the "Elohist" document and its implications for the dating of the pentateuchal traditions is not always fully appreciated. Any appraisal of E must conclude that we have only a few fragments of the source, and it is certainly debatable that the source exists at all. Without an E source, we no longer possess "Northern" (E) and "Southern" (J) versions of the pentateuchal stories, and it precisely these versions that have for so long implied to us that the traditions hark back to the United Monarchy.

47. E. Blum, *Die Komposition der Vatergeschichte* (WMANT 57; Neukirchen-Vluyn: Neukirchener Verlag, 1984); *Studien zur Komposition des Pentateuch* (BZAW 189; Berlin: de Gruyter, 1990); R. Rendtorff, *Das überlieferungsgeschichtliche Problem des Pentateuch* (BZAW 147; Berlin: de Gruyter, 1977).

From a literary standpoint, an extended analysis of ethnicity in the tetrateuchal traditions and in the Deuteronomistic History will not be offered. From the historical perspective, with the exception of a few brief comments on the postexilic period, my work will end with the exile. Nevertheless, I think that the implications of my work are substantial for both the excluded literary sources and for the postexilic period which it does not cover.

The Role of Ethnicity Studies

Concerning my first task, that of establishing a theoretical base from ethnic theory, attention must be given to three separate issues within ethnic studies: focus, paradigm, and terminology. The question of focus refers to the various foci of ethnic behavior that can absorb one's theoretical attention. By foci I mean, for instance, that theorists interested in political aspects of ethnicity will be preoccupied with an analysis of the associated political structures, while theorists interested in the psychological aspects of ethnicity will concern themselves with the inner realities of ethnic affiliation, the human psyche. In this case I am interested in ethnic identity as a corporate experience of the Israelite community/communities, both in terms of the ethnic ideas that most Israelites shared and also in terms of the ideas that separated them into distinct ideological parties. I am particularly interested in how ethnicity became an important component of Israelite national identity when, as I will show, ethnicity appears to have played a relatively minor role in the national identity of the surrounding ancient Near Eastern states. But because ethnic identity is often intertwined with other modes of identity—for instance, religious identity—our discussion cannot elude these aspects of identity. So while our primary concern will be ethnic identity, especially as it relates to national identity, three commonly related modes of identity will necessarily fall within the purview of this study: the political, the religious, and the sociocultural. This effort will necessarily be clouded by two facts: first, that our sources are often the work of one person (and hence one perspective), and second, by the fact that the sources may reflect only one of several competing communities or parties within ancient Israel. There is precious little that can be done about this source limitation, but an awareness of it may prevent us from taking speculative turns and from making unwarranted assumptions.

The preliminary discussion of paradigm and terminology can be handled together. The question of paradigm in relation to ethnic studies is a sticky one, in part because the field is presently influenced by rather strong sociopolitical motivations that (in my view) often preempt objective scholarship.[48] Despite my personal convictions about the questions of race, ethnicity, and social justice, I do not think that our discussion of theoretical paradigms can be debated at the level of social consciousness that permeates the field. Such a discussion requires that we offer value judgments based on our economic, religious, philosophical, and anthropological assumptions, and this would itself require several monographs to address and defend. I have no intention of entering the discussion at that level. But this problem aside, the question of paradigm has ethnic theorists in quite a debate about which conceptual models successfully account for the origins of ethnic sentiment and explain or predict ethnic behaviors. Some theorists argue that ethnic sentiments originate as an extension of kinship, some maintain that they originate in "oppressive" social contexts, and still others adhere to a geographic paradigm.[49] On another level there is the debate between the "primordialists" and the "instrumentalists" over whether ethnic sentiments are an avoidable social outcome.[50] All of this needs to be addressed.

While I whole-heartedly agree that attention must be given to theoretical issues, I have not adopted any particular "system" of ethnic behavior, despite the fact that R. Thompson has enthusiastically criticized theoretical eclecticism.[51] True, no one can argue with the point that a holistic theory of ethnic behavior is a suitable ideal, but I am uncomfortable with approaches that tend to overburden the heuristic side of the model-data dialectic—and this is precisely what seems to happen when theorists adopt a particular ethnic model. In the discussion below I will provide one example from the anthropological data (the

48. I say this with all due respect to scholars who doubt the possibility of objective scholarship. But to them I must say that the question is not whether we can *actually* succeed in our efforts to be objective but, rather, should we make the *effort* to be objective nonetheless?

49. For a summary of the various paradigms, see Riggs, *Ethnicity: Concepts and Terms Used in Ethnicity Research* 30–37; Thompson, *Theories of Ethnicity.*

50. This debate can be put in other terms: "ascriptive theorists" versus "situationists," or "genetics" versus "environment." See Riggs, *Ethnicity: Concepts and Terms Used in Ethnicity Research,* 11–29.

51. Thompson, *Theories of Ethnicity,* 1–19.

Tiv kinship tradition) to illustrate the difficulties that are associated with choosing a particular model of ethnic behavior and also the reasons for the methodological debate. This methodological disagreement among ethnicists can hardly be solved in a cross-disciplinary work such as mine; eclecticism seems entirely appropriate, provided that one does not, in his or her eclecticism, embrace two or more contradictory principles. Thus I hope to take up several theoretical conclusions with which most agree and to utilize these within an eclectic paradigm. The reader might cry "foul" rather quickly, given that my work seems already to have adopted Riggs's definition of ethnicity over Cashmore's,[52] but the two definitions are in fact quite similar and differ mainly on this point: whether kinship is an integral part of ethnicity, and to this I am saying "yes." But this hardly breaks my commitment to eclecticism, and I believe that the reader will find that the methodological principles outlined below stand, not alongside the definition of ethnicity that I have adopted, but as a clarification of it.

To begin, we should first recognize that ethnicity is one of the many varieties of human behavior and is perceptible only in certain cultural contexts. For instance, if a particular a group should take action against a perceived threat, this action would be understood as "ethnic" only if the group's action were related to their ethnic sentiment. Since F. Barth's seminal work, anthropological thinking has moved away from ethnicity defined as a cultural unit to ethnicity as the organizing principle of that unit, with these organizing principles usually called "ethnic boundaries."[53] This implies that our comprehension of a given ethnic community is achieved primarily as we come to identify its discursive strategies of self-definition and also as we understand the devices it uses to distinguished itself from other communities.

Second, ethnicity as we have defined it here is a phenomenon of genetic perception, that is, it includes the idea that the group in some way shares a common ancestry, and this is quite apart from the question of whether the individuals in the group are actually related.[54] In

---

52. See pp. 1–2, but for convenience repeated here: "Ethnicity involves an ascriptive, genetically self-perpetuating mode of social relations treated as an alternative to, or complement of, other forms of social organization, in the context of a larger society" (Riggs, *Ethnicty: Concepts and Terms Used in Ethnicity Research,* 4).

53. Barth, *Ethnic Groups and Boundaries.*

54. Although the genetic component is deemed essential by most sources, the confusion associated with the definition of ethnicity is evident from W. Sollors' article,

this respect, ethnicity would seem to be an extension of kinship, but I would not necessarily limit it in this way as some would.[55] Unlike this genetic component of identity, other factors, such as language, culture, religion, and history contribute to but are not, alone, indicators of ethnic sentiment.[56] These other features often complement and contribute to ethnic modes of identity (or vice versa, ethnicity to them), which means that our discussion cannot move very far from these other aspects of identity. It is precisely for this reason that my title reads "ethnicity *and identity.*"

Third, ethnic sentiments do not arise in a vacuum but as distinctive behaviors in contrast to other social groups, and both the members and nonmembers usually recognize these sentiments.[57] This distinctive identity is intensified (and some would say created) by competition,[58] either between ethnic groups or between an ethnic group and other social modalities. In particular, Wallerstein has argued that imperialist, colonial structures tend to create ethnic groups in order to justify exploitation of them.[59] This contention that imperialism creates ethnicity

---

which states that ethnicity is "differentiation based on nationality, race, religion, or language." See "Literature and Ethnicity," *Harvard Encyclopedia of American Ethnic Groups* (ed. S. Thernstrom; Cambridge: Harvard University Press, 1980) 648.

55. In the work of P. L. van den Berghe, for example, ethnicity is fundamentally an extension of kinship behavior, and this is a genetically induced reality (*The Ethnic Phenomenon* [New York: Elsevier, 1981]). See also C. Geertz, "The Integrative Revolution: Primordial Sentiments and Civil Politics in the New States," *The Interpretation of Cultures* (New York: Basic Books, 1973) 255–310; E. Shils, "Primordial, Personal, Sacred, and Civil Ties," *British Journal of Sociology* 8 (1957) 130–45.

56. Although Harold Isaacs's now famous article on "group identity" suggests that a number of these items are integral to the establishment of ethnic identity ("Basic Group Identity") 29–52.

57. I say "usually recognize" because ethnic sentiments can arise in a number of different combinations. For example, early ethnographers classified newly encountered peoples along the ethnic lines inferred from Genesis 10, and this was quite apart from any ethnic sentiments that the new peoples themselves may have had.

58. As all scholars would agree. See especially Susan Olzak's *Dynamics of Ethnic Competition and Conflict* (Stanford: Stanford University Press, 1992); M. Banton, *Racial and Ethnic Competition* (Cambridge: Cambridge University Press, 1983).

59. I. Wallerstein, *The Capitalist World-Economy* (Cambridge: Cambridge University Press, 1979). See also his earlier work, *The Modern World System: Capitalist Agriculture and the Origins of the European World-Economy in the Sixteenth Century* (New York: Academic, 1974); for a discussion of this theory and the suitability of its application to ancient societies, see K. Ekholm and J. Friedman, "Capital Imperialism and Exploitation in Ancient World Systems," in *Power and Propaganda: A Symposium on Ancient*

is much debated in ethnicity studies and is closely tied to a question
that we have already raised, the question of primordial and instrumental theories of ethnicity.

A brief digression into the anthropological data is sufficient to
bring some order to this debate about core, periphery, primordialism,
instrumentalism, and the like. Some time ago L. Bohannan offered her
genealogical study of the Tiv people of northern Nigeria.[60] Although
for some theorists the mere fact that they were "studied" will make the
Tiv subject to Western imperialism, the historical and sociocultural
context makes it quite inappropriate to describe the Tiv as a colonial
subject on the periphery of an overbearing core civilization. Yet the Tiv
have a very pronounced notion of kinship and ethnicity, as is reflected
by their belief in a common ancestor (named Tiv), by their conception
of eponymous ancestors for each segment of Tiv society, and by their
use of genealogy to explain Tiv relationships with non-Tiv tribes
nearby.[61] The kinship links defined by the Tiv genealogies are relatively important because they define who the Tiv can marry, who will
help in time of need, who can bewitch them, and who can protect
them from witchcraft. Tiv genealogies are relatively stable but can exhibit marked fluidity when it becomes necessary to match the genealogies to changing circumstances. In such cases Tiv ethnicity is not so
much instrumental (used to effect changes in political and economic
status) as it is useful to reinforce or explain changes that have already
taken place. On the other hand, on one occasion Tiv elders appear to
have invented a genealogical relationship between two groups for the
purpose of avoiding participation in a border conflict, and this is very
much in keeping with the instrumental model of ethnicity.

This example is sufficient to demonstrate that we cannot limit ethnicity to imperial core/periphery contexts (as Wallerstein suggests) and

---

Empires (ed. M. T. Larsen; Mesopotamia 7; Copenhagen: Akademisk, 1979) 41–59;
S. N. Eisenstat, "Observations and Queries about Sociological Aspects of Imperialism
in the Ancient World," *Power and Propaganda*, 21–33.

60. L. Bohannan, "A Genealogical Charter," *Africa* 22 (1952) 301–15. A. Malamat recognized the relevance of Bohannan's research for our study of ancient Israel in
"Tribal Societies: Biblical Genealogies and African Lineage Systems," *Archives europé-
ennes de sociologie* 14 (1973) 126–36.

61. W. R. Smith observed similar uses of female eponyms among the Arabians.
See *Kinship and Marriage in Early Arabia* (Cambridge: Cambridge University Press,
1885) 27–34.

also that we unduly simplify our theoretical problems when we try to choose between primordial and instrumental ethnic models. The primordialists are right that kinship structures, and frequently ethnicity with them, are extremely common social modalities that can hardly be explained as mere "instruments" of socio-economic manipulation. They are instead the natural result of human affections for family and the extension of these affections to those who are (or appear to be) like us.[62] But there is also little doubt that these kinship models are frequently manipulated or created for ulterior (instrumental) purposes, and in the absence of compelling evidence one way or the other it is only proper that we recognize both the primordial and the instrumental aspects of ethnicity.[63] Turning again to Wallerstein's core/periphery thesis—although I cannot agree with it all the way, I can agree with the premise that ethnicity arises, or at least becomes more salient, in the context of multicultural contact and also with the notion that ethnic sentiments intensify when "peripheral" groups live under the domination of a powerful "core" civilization.

Leaving aside the Tiv example and returning to our discussion of essential ethnic principles, the fourth principle that we should emphasize is that phenotypical characteristics[64] often play an important role as ethnic *indicia* used to make ready judgments about individual group membership (although we should stress that numerous other indicia are possible). Such indicia are to be distinguished from *criteria*, which are used to define the boundaries of group identity (= "ethnic boundaries"). Although we have said this, it is generally agreed that phenotypical characteristics cannot have played an important role in distinguishing Israel from the surrounding West Semitic peoples, particularly from any supposed "Canaanites" or "Amorites," and this reminds us to examine the evidence for more subtle types of indicia and also to note any difficulties that we have in recognizing them. Such a

---

62. For other helpful discussions of kinship, see M. Fortes, *The Dynamics of Clanship among the Tallensi* (London: Oxford University Press, 1945); H. I. Hogbin, *Kinship and Marriage in a New Guinea Village* (London: Athlone, 1963); G. K. Nukunya, *Kinship and Marriage among the Anlo Ewe* (London: Athlone / New York: Humanities, 1969); E. E. Evans-Pritchard, *Kinship and Marriage among the Nuer* (Oxford: Clarendon, 1969);

63. With respect to ethnic origins, my feeling is that the primordial character of ethnicity is primary and the instrumental character secondary.

64. I.e., inherited physical features.

difficulty might imply the absence of ethnicity (or at least of intense ethnicity) because functional indicia are necessary ingredients in the effort to preserve or emphasize ethnic distinctiveness.

Fifth, to the extent that it is possible, ethnicity must be considered in its political, social-structural, and economic setting to be fully apprehended, with special care given to the issue of its relation to social and class structures. This is a natural inference from the observation that various kinds of competition contribute to and intensify ethnic sentiments because politics and economics are frequently (some would say always!) the causes of group competition. This is particularly relevant for any inquiry into Israelite society because class struggles, in particular, show up at numerous points in the biblical evidence.

And finally, as ethnic theorists frequently point out, ethnic identities are highly fluid, and attention must be given to the kinds of changes that occur in a given, concrete historical situation. These changes take place according to several recognized patterns, as summarized by D. Horowitz.[65] On the one hand, differing social groups may join by either of two types of assimilation: "amalgamation" or "incorporation." On the other hand, existing groups may differentiate, creating new social and cultural units, as in the case of "division" or "proliferation."[66] But as M. M. Gordon has pointed out, we must guard against the assumption that these four dynamic processes *necessarily* effect a change in group ethnicity, since similar social patterns can be observed quite apart from ethnicity itself.[67] Moreover there are many types of changes that can take place within an ethnic group that do not correspond to any of these terms or patterns, particularly when in-group changes are made to preserve the status quo in the face of increasing pressures on group identity. Consequently, the issue of ethnicity is a complicated one, and this is all the more true when we realize that it is but one of many products (and ingredients!) of the complex dialectic through which cultures make individuals and individuals create culture. This is a human process that scholars of every discipline are apt to struggle with for a long time to come.

65. D. Horowitz, "Ethnic Identity," in *Ethnicity: Theory and Experience* (ed. N. Glazer and D. P. Moynihan; Cambridge: Harvard University Press, 1975) 111–140.

66. One might illustrate these patterns with the following formulas: "amalgamation" (A+B = C); "incorporation" (A+B = A); "division" (A yields B+C); and "proliferation" (A yields A+B).

67. M. M. Gordon, "Toward a General Theory of Racial and Ethnic Group Behaviors," in *Ethnicity: Theory and Experience,* 84–110.

Chapter Two

Ethnicity and Identity in Israel's Ancient Context

The range of anthropological and sociological materials from which comparative data might be drawn is considerable. In the previous chapter, I believe that a sufficiently broad theoretical base—itself tied to these extensive sources—was established to serve as a general framework against which to evaluate the present study. This general theoretical summary of the data is of limited use, however, in a detailed comparative endeavor, and it is for this reason that I will now provide a more thorough examination of materials from three of Israel's ancient neighbors: Assyria, Egypt, and Greece. Given the many potential alternatives, my choice of comparative sources requires some explanation. Assyria and Egypt were chosen because Palestine, and Israel with it, lay on the periphery of these two great centers of civilization. The Egyptian and Assyrian materials therefore do us a twofold service in that they tell us not only about Egyptian and Assyrian identity but also about the perspective of these peoples regarding Israel and its environs. Assyrian texts are of particular importance because many of our Hebrew sources originated during the period in which Neo-Assyrian dominance was emerging in the Levantine region.

Greece is another matter and is of importance for different reasons. Archaeologists of both classical and oriental stripe have become increasingly aware that the exchange of ideas between East and West was much more active in the ancient world than previously supposed. Although scholars have gradually become aware that this exchange took place prior to the collapse of Mycenaean civilization and, of course, during the relatively late Hellenistic period, they have been hesitant to discuss how soon contacts were restored in the aftermath of the Mycenaean age. The evidence has been carefully evaluated by W. Burkert, who has shown that contacts between the Greeks and Phoenicians increased markedly during the eighth century B.C.E. and afterward.[1] Although there is very little evidence of direct cultural exchange between Israel and Greece during this period, Israel's close ties to Phoenicia—linguistic, cultural and economic—represented a potential avenue of influence from the West. Furthermore, if one adheres to or is open to a somewhat late dating of the pentateuchal sources, then much of Israel's literature was composed during the eighth, seventh, and sixth centuries B.C.E., and this is precisely the period in which Greek contacts with the East mushroomed.[2] As we will see, the Greek and Hebrew sources share many common elements that are either less prominent in or missing from the other ancient Near Eastern materials.

The textual witnesses from these three ancient contexts are quite extensive, so our discussion must be limited to several representative samples. One of the curious features of Israel's ethnicity is that, at least in the later historical periods, it was linked with Israelite national and religious identity. Given this feature, a helpful parameter is that our comparative texts ought to reflect a state perspective (or at least reflect on state perspective). In the case of Assyria, the most natural selections would then come from the royal inscriptions and king-lists, with the king-list tradition being especially important because it leads to a discussion of some important Old Babylonian evidence for ethnicity in ancient Mesopotamia. The same kinds of materials would seem to be appropriate for our study of Egyptian identity, but two modifications are necessary. First, the perspective of the Egyptian king-list tradition is quite close to the perspective of the royal inscriptions and, unlike the Assyrian king-lists, it will not lead us to any new data that is particu-

1. W. Burkert, *Die orientalisierende Epoche in der griechischen Religion und Literatur* (Heidelberg: Carl Winter Universitätsverlag, 1984) . Burkert's work is also available in translation as *The Orientalizing Revolution* (Cambridge: Harvard University Press, 1992); See also O. Murray's recent edition of *Early Greece* (2d ed.; Cambridge: Harvard University Press, 1993) 80–101; G. Markoe, "The Emergence of Orientalizing in Greek Art: Some Observations on the Interchange between Greeks and Phoenicians in the Eighth and Seventh Centuries B.C.," *BASOR* 301 (1996) 47–67; D. Harden, *The Phoenicians* (London: Thames and Hudson, 1963) 24, 55–56, 84, 192–93. A somewhat different but very interesting study is *Israel and Hellas* by J. P. Brown (BZAW 231; Berlin: de Gruyter, 1995).

2. Cultural exchange between Greece and Israel's coastal neighbor, Phoenicia, was especially active during the period between 750 and 650 B.C.E. (Murray, *Early Greece*, 80–101).

larly relevant to our study.[3] Second, by all accounts one of the more important texts relating to Egyptian identity is the Middle Kingdom "Tale of Sinuhe," particularly because it brings Egyptian and Asiatic identity into close literary quarters. Therefore we will add this Egyptian literary piece to our study.

The concept of "national identity" is something of a problem in Greece, since the notion of a Greek nation is not relevant during the archaic and classical periods that interest me. The *Histories* of Herodotus, however, are very much concerned with the problems of politics and national conflict; I can think of no better source for our inquiry. The thoughtful reader who is interested primarily in Israel will no doubt characterize Herodotus as a rather "late" source, chronologically speaking. But I will introduce my discussion of Herodotus with several earlier Greek texts and in the process hope to show that the so-called "father of history" is a suitable representative of earlier periods in Greek literary history.

Ethnicity and Identity in Neo-Assyria

To foreshadow the results of this portion of my work, I would like to state at the outset that one of the more important features of the Assyrian materials is how little they reflect ethnic sentiment on the part of the Assyrians, either in terms of their own identity or in terms of their conceptions about other groups. If we must attach labels to Assyrian identity in the form of the modalities that we have discussed already, then it would be most accurate to describe it as a religious and political identity. The Assyrian aim was to construct a sense of identity for itself and for its imperial subjects in which its national policies seemed "right" and, in doing so, the Assyrian ruling class hoped to motivate its subjects to cease their resistance to its expansionist program.[4] After we have looked at a number of relevant texts, I will attempt to describe how these modes of identity promoted this effort, and I will also attempt to explain why ethnic sentiments are missing within the texts. The texts are handled chronologically, with the first selection dating to

3. For a discussion of the Egyptian king-lists, see D. B. Redford, *Pharaonic King-Lists, Annals and Day-Books* (SSEA Publication 4; Mississauga, Ontario: Benben, 1986).

4. M. Liverani, "The Ideology of the Assyrian State," *Power and Propaganda: A Symposium on Ancient Empires* (ed. M. T. Larsen; Mesopotamia 7; Copenhagen: Akademisk, 1979) 297–317.

the ninth century, from the reign of Aššurnaṣirpal, and the last selection dating to the seventh century, from the reign of Assurbanipal.[5]

Assyrians and Non-Assyrians in the Days of Aššurnaṣirpal II (883–859)

When Aššurnaṣirpal began his reign, the core area administered directly from the Assyrian capital included seven nearby provinces and comprised about 75 miles square, about half of which was either mountainous terrain or unirrigated territory.[6] The text that interests me is from the king's annals, Year 2, and describes the rebellion of "Assyrians," along with their governor and the "land of Nirbu," in a region just northwest of this core territory. The most relevant feature of the text for our purposes is that it outlines some of the criteria that were used to distinguish Assyrians from other surrounding peoples.[7]

The first example differentiates the rebel Assyrians (*nišê* ^māt^*Aššurai*) from their cohorts, the 'troops of the land of Nirbu' (*ṣābê ša* ^māt^*Nirbi*), which raises the question of how such a distinction was made in a region outside of Assyria proper, where geography was useless as a distinguishing criterion. Contextually speaking, the Assyrians mentioned are rebel inhabitants of the city of Ḫalzi-luḫa, their governor being Ḫulai. They were Assyrians by virtue of the fact that Shalmaneser I had settled Assyrians in the region several centuries earlier. The rebellion was met in the characteristic way: Aššurnaṣirpal gathered his armies, traveled to the region, set up a statue of himself, took supplies from nearby

---

5. One might argue that Neo-Assyrian epistolary texts would provide a better window into Assyrian identity, but this is not the case. We are interested primarily in ethnicity as a component of national identity, and this is best examined in the monarchic inscriptions. Furthermore, S. Parpola has convincingly shown that the epistolary corpus adds little to our inscriptional evidence. See his "Assyrian Royal Inscriptions and Neo-Assyrian Letters," in *Assyrian Royal Inscriptions: New Horizons in Literary, Ideological and Historical Analysis* (ed. F. M. Fales; Rome: Istituto per l'Oriente, 1981) 117–42.

6. A. T. Olmstead, *History of Assyria* (New York: Scribners, 1923) 81.

7. I am following D. D. Luckenbill's translation from *Ancient Records of Assyria and Babylon* [hereafter *ARAB*] (2 vols.; Chicago: University of Chicago, 1926–27) 1.145–48. For text with transliteration, see E. A. W. Budge and L. W. King, *Annals of the Kings of Assyria* (2 vols.; London: Longmans, 1902) 1.288–98. See also A. K. Grayson, *Assyrian Rulers of the Early First Millennium BC: I (1114–859 BC)* (RIMA 2; Toronto: University of Toronto Press, 1991) 200–202. For a discussion of the chronology of the inscriptions, see W. de Filippi, "The Royal Inscriptions of Aššur-naṣir-apli II (883–859 B.C.E.): A Study of the Chronology of the Calah Inscriptions," *Aššur* 1 (1977) 123–69.

peoples (in this case, from those of Isala), and then proceeded with the destruction of city. The "Assyrian" identity of the people did not protect them from the usual cruelties that awaited rebel vassals:

> Ḫulai, their governor, I captured alive. Their corpses I formed into pillars; their young men and maidens I burned in the fire. Ḫulai, their governor, I flayed, his skin I spread upon the wall of the city of Damdamusa [a royal city in the region]; the city [of Ḫalzi-luḫa] I destroyed. . . .

Joining in the rebellion were the non-Assyrian people of Nirbu, who received a similar punishment:

> Many captives from among them I burned with fire, and I took living captives. From some I cut off their hands and their fingers, and from others I cut off their noses, their ears, and their fingers, of many I put out the eyes. I made one pillar of the living, and another of heads, and I bound their heads to posts round about the city.

The punitive measures taken against the Assyrians of Ḫalzi-luḫa were therefore comparable to the punitive measures taken against the non-Assyrian people of Nirbu. In the case of rebellion, it would seem, there was no distinction between the Assyrian and non-Assyrian.

The question of Assyrian identity is here linked to the origins of the particular group of people in question, that is, to the cities or regions that kings had previously colonized with Assyrian people.[8] This of course begs the question somewhat, since we know nothing about the original group settled in Ḫalzi-luḫa by Shalmaneser. However, it is clear that groups surrounding Assur were viewed as non-Assyrian, which implies that the distinction between Assyrians and non-Assyrians was partially related to the supposed origins of the local population. If this was so, then a vital component of Assyrian identity, at least among groups distant from Assyria proper, was the recognition that a group had been settled amid foreigners by Assyrian imperial policy. And as a corollary of this, a vital component of Assyrian identity at home would have been the necessity and importance of spreading, via conquest and settlement, an Assyrian presence throughout the known world. So we should conclude that Assyrian identity, at home or

---

8. There is a very valuable study of Old Assyrian imperialism and colonialism in M. T. Larsen, *The Old Assyrian City-State and Its Colonies* (Mesopotamia 4; Copenhagen: Akademisk, 1976).

abroad, was closely related to the idea of dynastic rule and the imperialist expansion of the empire.[9]

A second reference to the *nišê* [māt]*Aššurai* occurs after the conquest of Nirbu by Aššurnaṣirpal when he traveled to the nearby city of Tušḫa.[10] The city had apparently seceded in sympathy with Governor Ḫulai, so that Assyrians in the Tušḫa region were forced farther north into the environs of Shuprê (south of Lake Van).[11] In classic imperialist fashion, Aššurnaṣirpal restored the city (*ana eššute aṣbat*), erected an image of himself along with a victory inscription, constructed a palace for himself, and fortified the city with a new foundation and wall. Disenfranchised Assyrians, who had withdrawn to the environs of Shuprê to find food, were resettled by Aššurnaṣirpal in Tušḫa and provided with foodstuffs and other resources from the land of Nirbu. In the case of Tušḫa, then, we see quite different population patterns than in the previously discussed city of Ḫalzi-luḫa. In Ḫalzi-luḫa, the city itself was viewed as Assyrian, having been established long ago by Shalmaneser. But in Tušḫa, the Assyrian population represented a military and bureaucratic minority that fled from the city's non-Assyrian inhabitants during the rebellion.[12] However, the difference between population patterns in Ḫalzi-luḫa and Tušḫa should not obscure the obvious fact that in both cases the term *nišê* [māt]*Aššur* carries the same sense: new additions to the regional population via Assyrian imperial policy.

While it appears clear enough that the texts distinguish between Assyrians and non-Assyrians and that this distinction hinged on the Assyrian origins of the former, certain features in the royal inscriptions

9. A policy driven perhaps as much by commercial interests as by ideological perspectives. For the suitability of the term *imperialism* with respect to Assyria, see R. J. van der Spek, "Assyria and History: A Comparative Study of War and Empire in Assyria, Athens, and Rome," *The Tablet and the Scroll: Near Eastern Studies in Honor of William H. Hallo* (ed. M. E. Cohen et al.; Bethesda, Md.: CDL, 1993) 263–64.

10. In this second case the gentilic form is not used, but I see no reason to make anything of it.

11. Olmstead, *History of Assyria*, 88.

12. The difference may also center on the formal distinction of citizenship. The best textual example comes from Sennacherib's annals, which distinguish between citizens of Babylonian cities and other groups within those cities: "The Arabs, Arameans, and Chaldeans, who were in Uruk, Nippur, Kish, etc., together with the citizens of those cities responsible for the revolt (*adi* DUMU.MEŠ *āli bēl ḫitti*)." See CAD N/1 315 and D. D. Luckenbill, *The Annals of Sennacherib* (OIP 2; Chicago: University of Chicago Press, 1924) 25.

modify this perspective. From the time of Tiglath Pileser I (1114–1076 B.C.E.) until Sargon II (721–705 B.C.E.), a stereotyped phrase was used of the non-Assyrian peoples who succumbed to Assyrian rule: 'with the people of Assyria I considered them' (*ana/itti nišê* ᵐᵃᵗ*Aššur amnû-šunūti*). Aššurnaṣirpal (883–859 B.C.E.) used a somewhat different phrase in his inscriptions, 'I considered them with the people of my land' (= *ana nišê mātîa amnu*),[13] but it is difficult to suggest that this phrase is meaningfully different, since the older stereotyped phrase resurfaces after his reign. Although the first texts that we examined knew of the distinction between Assyrians (*nišê* ᵐᵃᵗ*Aššur*) and non-Assyrians, this tendency to use inclusive language in describing the non-Assyrian shows that the barriers that separated the two were quite permeable. One should properly deduce that *ana/itti nišê* ᵐᵃᵗ*Aššur amnûšunūti* was not only a formula that extolled imperial expansion but also an invitation to cultural assimilation—to embrace the Assyrian way. But this inclusive tendency should not be associated with the Neo-Assyrian epoch as a whole, as our examination of Sargon II's royal inscriptions will show.

Foreigners in the Eyes of Sargon II (721–705)

Several features in Sargon's royal inscriptions make them a uniquely valuable source for the study of Assyrian identity.[14] They reflect a time after Samaria had succumbed to Assyrian rule and when Palestine's environs began to feel more direct pressure from Assyrian imperialism. In addition to their excellent literary quality, the texts offer a number of opportunities to probe into the issues of ethnicity and identity, particularly into the issue of how the Assyrians viewed the peoples they conquered. Also significant is the fact that Sargon's annalists were the last to use the stereotyped phrase *ana/itti nišê* ᵐᵃᵗ*Aššur amnûšunūti*, so that the

13. Budge and King, *Annals of the Kings of Assyria*, 1.181, 195, 217. The change in terminology used by Aššurnaṣirpal might reflect a new tendency to distinguish between Assyrian and non-Assyrians.

14. One related (but hard to appraise) difficulty is that Sargon II is usually viewed as a usurper, seizing the throne from his predecessor, Shalmaneser V. The major evidence for this is: (1) the obscurity of Sargon's rise to power; (2) he called himself Sargon, after the founder of the dynasty of Akkad; and (3) he founded a new capital at Dûr-Sharrukin. However, these circumstances could equally well by explained if Sargon II was one of Shalmaneser V's brothers. Cf. G. Roux, *Ancient Iraq* (2d ed.; New York: Penguin, 1980) 287.

reign of Sargon represents a transitional period in the development of
Assyrian identity. Three texts will be examined, one each from the "Let-
ter to Assur," from the Nineveh prism inscriptions, and from the Dûr-
Sharrukîn cylinder inscription. I will also discuss the terms *Hittite* and
Amorite, focusing primarily on the history of the terms and their use in
the inscriptions.

Among the four main forms of Assyrian royal inscriptions is the
"letter to the god."[15] This subgenre is the least attested of the four, and
its most famous example is Sargon's "Letter to Assur." The text includes an interesting ethnographic notice that is quite unusual within a
royal inscription. The text is dated to the eponym of Ištar-dûri, 714
B.C.E., and describes the peoples of Zaranda, an Urartian district, as
follows:

> The people who live in the district are without equal in all of Urartu
> in their knowledge of riding-horses. For years they had been catching
> the young colts of (wild) horses, native to this wide land, and raising
> them for the royal army [of Urartu]. But they are not caught as far
> over as Sûbi, a district which the people of Urartu call Mannean
> country, nor are their herds seen there. They do not saddle them, but
> (whether) going forward, turning to one side, or turning around, (as
> the tactics) of battle require, they are (never) seen to break the yoke
> (i.e., to become separated from their team).[16]

The text reminds one much more of Herodotus's *Histories* than it does
of Assyrian literary traditions.[17] This glimpse into the author's perspective demonstrates that Assyrian scholars probably harbored much more
interest in the customs and practices of Assyrian imperial subjects than
we might suppose on the basis of extant Neo-Assyrian texts.[18] And,

15. A. K. Grayson, "Assyrian Royal Inscriptions: Literary Characteristics," *Assyrian Royal Inscriptions: New Horizons in Literary, Ideological and Historical Analysis* (ed.
F. M. Fales; Rome: Istituto per l'Oriente, 1981) 36.

16. Luckenbill, *ARAB* 2.84.

17. This similarity has also been noted by A. L. Oppenheim, "The City of Assur,"
JNES 19 (1960) 133–47.

18. Another example of such ethnographic interest is found in Sennacherib's palace reliefs, which depict in illustrations how Judean commoners wrapped their heads in
turbans. See M. Wäfler, *Nicht-Assyrer neuassyrischer Darstellungen* (2 vols.; AOAT 26;
Neukirchen-Vluyn: Neukirchener Verlag, 1975) 1.67. On foreign depictions during
the reign of Assurbanipal, see J. Reade, "Ideology and Propaganda in Assyrian Art,"
Power and Propaganda: A Symposium on Ancient Empires (ed. M. T. Larsen; Mesopotamia 7; Copenhagen: Akademisk, 1979) 329–43.

although it would be quite unwarranted to extrapolate from this short text the existence of an Assyrian "Herodotus,"[19] the text suggests that other ethnographic materials probably existed in the Neo-Assyrian libraries, despite the fact that so few examples have come our way. This alerts us to the somewhat limited perspective that we gain from the sources at our disposal, especially in our attempts to understand how Assyrians viewed the various peoples around them.

Despite these limitations, the royal inscriptions do provide us with a window into the Assyrian view of the ancient Near East and its peoples. One example comes from Sargon's prism inscription at Nineveh, which probably mirrors the Assyrian view of Western Asia that was current during his reign:

> The wicked Hittites . . . the kings of the lands of Piliste (Philistia), Iaudi (Judah), Edom, Moab, who dwell by the sea, payers of tribute [and] tax to Assur, my lord , (they sent) numberless inflammatory and disdainful (messages) to set them at enmity with me, to Pir'u, king of Egypt, a prince who could not save them, they sent their presents (bribes) and attempted to gain him as an ally.[20]

In comparison with the other royal inscriptions, there is nothing particularly unusual about the text's description of these Western nations. They are collectively referred to as "Hittites," which at once shows us that Assyrians viewed the West, at least discursively, as more homogenous than Westerners themselves did. In one sense this demonstrates how misleading evidence can be, since our Assyrian source claims that the Judeans *were* Hittites. The fact that these Hittites are also described as "wicked" is another matter that I will address in a moment. Although we might venture to identify the Levantine nations listed here as ethnic entities (at least in some cases), for the Assyrians these nations were political modalities ruled by "kings," and this is, after all, the predominant notion of Assyrian identity in the sources at our disposal. So the Assyrians have not gone very far in their efforts to understand these foreign peoples, and this brings us to an important issue.

If *we know* that the Assyrians have erred in joining these diverse groups under the rubric of a single name, it is important to ask this:

19. The uniqueness of Herodotus lies in the unusual combination of various genres in his work, including ethnography, genealogy, mythology, and history. The road from ethnography to Herodotus may therefore be quite a long one.

20. Luckenbill, *ARAB* 2.105.

Why did they "carelessly" link these nations together with the "Hittite" label? An answer to this question requires a brief digression into some related issues. In the Assyrian view of things, the "Hittites" in our text shared a common status as vassals, in this case rebel vassals who were under revenue obligations. There is a sense in which these tax obligations contributed to the cultural assimilation of non-Assyrians: 'Tribute, tax, I imposed upon them as upon Assyrians' (= *biltu maddattu kî ša Aššuri ēmssunūti*).[21] However, the idea that imperial subjects became "fully Assyrian" through taxation is mitigated by the strong negative language used by the inscription to describe these "wicked Hittites." Furthermore, the phrase in Sargon's annals, *biltu maddattu kî ša Aššuri ēmssunūti*, is at variance with the old stereotyped phrase used in the annals of his Assyrian predecessors, *ana/itti nišê* [māt]*Aššur amnûšunūti*. The new phrase and its employment of simile (*kî*) seems to reflect a discourse strategy aimed at generating firmer boundaries between Assyrian identity and that of its vassals.[22] B. Oded has pointed out that after Sargon II, the phrase *ana/itti nišê* [māt]*Aššur amnûšunūti* disappeared entirely from the inscriptions of Sennacherib, Esarhaddon, and Assurbanipal.[23] Oded explains this phenomenon as follows:

> The impressive victories of Tiglath-pileser III and Sargon II, in the course of two generations (745–705), gradually fostered a sense of superiority of the Assyrian people over other nations. The old ideology of Assyrian domination of the whole world, *šar kiššati šar kibrāt erbettim*, started to become an apparent reality during the eighth century B.C. . . . This deep-rooted feeling of superiority led to a sterner attitude towards deportees, and sharpened the differentiation between Assyrians (*mârê/nišê* [kur]*Aššur*) and non-Assyrians. . . . This is, we believe, one of the underlying reasons for the disappearance of the formula *itti nišê* [mātu]*Aššur amnûšunūti*.[24]

This evidence suggests that the reign of Sargon represented a transition in the Assyrian perspective of its imperial subjects. Prior to Sargon, the inclusive phrase *ana/itti nišê* [māt]*Aššur amnûšunūti* was commonly used

---

21. Ibid., 2.2.

22. Although the new phrase is used in Sargon's annals, his other inscriptions tend to use the stereotyped phrase, *ana/itti nišê* [māt]*Aššur amnûšunūti*. See, for instance, in the inscription published by C. J. Gadd, "Inscribed Prisms of Sargon II from Nimrud," *Iraq* 16 (1954) 179. See also the "Letter to Assur," in Luckenbill, *ARAB* 2.98

23. B. Oded, *Mass Deportations and Deportees in the Neo-Assyrian Empire* (Wiesbaden: Reichert, 1979) 81–91.

24. Ibid., 89–90.

in the annals. But during his reign, although this phrase was retained in some royal inscription, it was used alongside the new and more differentiating phrase, *biltu maddattu kî ša Aššuri ēmssunūti*. Following Sargon's reign, phrases that equate imperial subjects with Assyrians are lacking entirely and were replaced with a marked tendency to describe conquered peoples as foreign booty or as a source of corvée labor (e.g., *šallatiš amnu, nišê mâšâte kišitti nakiri, ḫubut qašti, sitti nišê . . . šallatiš amnu*).[25]

So, returning to our original question, it comes as no surprise, that Sargon would describe a number of disparate entities with the same "Hittite" terminology. In the view of eighth-century Assyria, the smaller nations to the west were nothing more than a group of inferior vassals, and to make them discursively all of a kind was very easy and very convenient. This is certainly one part of the explanation for the Assyrian tendency to speak of the "wicked" and "evil" Hittites, or to describe the Hittites as "plotters of iniquity" who "did not fear the name of the gods." But this cultural contempt for vassals and this literary sense of convenience does not entirely explain the "Hittite" rhetoric of the annals. It is still important to ask why the name *Hittite* was chosen to serve in this way and also whether there is any truth to the Assyrian notion that these Hittite groups, despite their differences, shared common cultural connections that might have "fooled" the Assyrians into thinking of them as a single group.

The lands of Hatti and Amurru are basically synonymous in Sargon's annals and describe a region west of Assyria that stretched from Asia Minor to Egypt, north–south, and from the Euphrates to Palestine, east–west. The very general employment of these two terms reveals a later development of each, since in earlier times *Hatti* referred to the empire of the Anatolian Hittites and *Amurru* variously referred to the "West" in general, or to nomadic groups in the Syrian desert, or to the second-millennium kingdom of Amurru in central Syria.[26]

---

25. Ibid., 90.

26. For a summary discussion of the terms *Hittite* and *Amurru* in the ancient Near Eastern sources, particularly in the Neo-Assyrian sources and in the Old Testament, see J. Van Seters, "The Terms 'Amorite' and 'Hittite' in the Old Testament," *VT* 22 (1972) 64–81. For a catalogue of the evidence on the Amorites, see R. Zadok, "On the Amorite Material from Mesopotamia," *The Tablet and the Scroll: Near Eastern Studies in Honor of William W. Hallo* (ed. M. E. Cohen et al.; Bethesda: CDL, 1993) 315–33; A. Haldar, *Who Were the Amorites?* (Monographs on the Ancient Near East 1; Leiden: Brill, 1971).

This means that in the Neo-Assyrian sources, the "land of the Hittites" and the "land of Amurru" represented, not ethnopolitical designations, but general archaic designations employed to simplify references to the vast array of western social and political modalities.

On the basis of what we have been saying, it would at first seem that the terms "Amorite" or "Hittite" denoted very little in terms of specific cultural characteristics or qualities, and it is for this reason that we catch ourselves criticizing the Assyrians for their lack of cultural sensitivity. But there are reasons to believe that the Assyrians attached more concrete notions to the terms *Amorite* and *Hittite* than we might at first suppose, primarily because they associated a number of common features with the peoples of this region. The Assyrian sources consistently refer to the language of the Hittites and Amorites, a notion that obviously fails to comprehend the various dialectal differences but that nonetheless correctly groups together the West Semitic tongues. The Hittites were known for their shipbuilding and seafaring, so that Tyrians, Sidonians, and Cypriote sailors were all, despite their differences, "Hittite people."[27] Likewise, certain architectural styles were considered quite worthy of Assyrian imitation, being labeled as the 'Hittite pattern' (*tamšil ekal* [māt]*Ḫatti*) rather than the 'Assyrian pattern' (*epišti* [māt]*Aššur*[ki]).[28] We also know that, despite their differences, much of the West shared a cultural affinity in the areas of lifestyle, religious tradition, and political modalities. These linguistic and cultural similarities, coupled with the fact that these people were "outsiders" living in the same general region west of Assyria, suggests that the Assyrian perspective of the "Hittite" and "Amorite" was more specific and stereotyped than we might suppose. By joining together various groups under the rubric *Hittite*, the Assyrians gradually created a "rhetorical other" that shared a language, lived in a common region, and followed common cultural patterns, and this is quite apart from our perspective that these generalizations about "Hatti" were quite misleading. That the "Hittites" were not a homogenous cultural unit is obvious; less obvious is whether the Assyrians tended, nonetheless, to perceive them as such.

Up to this point, the Neo-Assyrian materials have revealed that Aššurnaṣirpal, Sargon II, and their followers sometimes distinguished

27. Luckenbill, *ARAB* 2.145.

28. I am of course refering to the *bît-ḫilâni* structures mentioned often in the royal inscriptions (for example, Luckenbill, *The Annals of Sennacherib*, 132–33).

Assyrians from non-Assyrian and at other times rhetorically joined them as a single unit. But in either case, there is an assumed Assyrian identity from which one is either distinguished or to which one is joined, and this raises the question of how we should understand the Assyrian identity that this entire discussion has been presupposing. A text from Sargon's Dûr-Sharrukîn cylinder inscription will help us fashion a clearer view on this question:

> Peoples of the four regions of the world, of foreign tongue and divergent speech, dwellers of mountain and lowland, all that were ruled by the light of the gods, the lord of all, I carried off at Assur, my lord's command, by the might of my scepter. I unified them (made them of one mouth) and settled them therein. Assyrians, fully competent to teach them how to fear god and the king, I dispatched to them as scribes and sheriffs (superintendents). The gods who dwell in heaven and earth, and in that city, listened with favor to my word, and granted me the eternal boon of building that city and growing old in its midst.[29]

The task given Sargon by Assur was to unify the world, to make peoples of "divergent speech" a people "of one mouth." The text speaks clearly about this as a process of cultural assimilation, which included the deportation of foreigners to Assyria, where they became people "of one mouth," and also the dispatching of Assyrian leaders and teachers to conquered regions so that they might "fear god and the king," that is, be good citizens.[30] The text depicts two levels of assimilation based on a uniquely Assyrian sense of identity that was founded, not on ethnic sentiments, but on certain fundamental criteria of community membership. For those transplanted in Assyria, this would have included acquisition of the Akkadian language (probably symbolic of cultural assimilation as a whole), but for all peoples in the empire, the primary requirement was political assimilation: reverence for the god Assur and for his high priest (*šangû*), the king.[31] This assimilation

29. Luckenbill, *ARAB* 2.65–66.

30. The social status and position of deportees within their homeland was not uniform, as Oded has shown. Deportees included those of the royal house, landowners, agricultural workers, craftsmen, scholars, artisans, businessmen, etc. Generally speaking, these deportees were considered "freemen" and were not used as force labor, although this pattern changed somewhat during and after the reign of of Sargon II. See Oded, *Mass Deportations and Deportees in the Neo-Assyrian Empire*, 75–115.

31. Note well the comment of Liverani ("Ideology of Assyrian Kinship," 301): ". . . it would be incorrect to speak of the Assyrian king as a 'non-absolutist' in so far as

process was encouraged during most of Assyria's history. It was only after Sargon II that Assyria forged so great a rift between itself and its imperial subjects as to eliminate the idea that non-Assyrians might become Assyrians.[32] But this rift must have been discursive and highly rhetorical, and we should assume that assimilation processes continued much as they had in earlier periods of Assyrian history.

Although the texts that I have examined show that the most outstanding feature of Assyrian identity was its preoccupation with political and monarchic concerns, the prominence of political identity should not distract us from the possibility that ethnic sentiments may have played a minor role in the Assyrian conception of identity. Specifically, I am thinking of the Mesopotamian phrase *black-headed men*, which turns up in one of Sennacherib's undated building inscriptions:

> The queen of the gods, the goddess of procreation . . . watched over my conception, while Ea provided a spacious womb, and granted (me) keen understanding, the equal of Master Adapa's. Assur, father of the gods, brought in submission to my feet the whole race of *blackheaded men*, raised aloft my head to be ruler of land and people, gave me a righteous scepter which enlarges my land and put into my hands an unsparing sword for the overturn of my enemies [italics mine].[33]

According to Luckenbill, the term 'blackheaded men' (*ṣalmat qaqqadi*) in this inscription is referring not to men in general but to Assyrians.[34] He does not give a reason for this analysis, but I would guess that he has been influenced by the term itself, which tends to conjure up ideas

---

he acts in the name and stead of the god Assur, since Assur is precisely the hypostasis of the Assyrian kingship." Liverani is certainly correct in part, but he seems to miss the point that each monarch has successively inherited the Assyrian tradition from the previous regimes and so becomes as much a product of the tradition as he (and his party) were creators of it.

32. I am thinking here about the tendency to view conquered peoples as slave labor and booty. See Luckenbill, *The Annals of Sennacherib*, 28, 38, 52, 95, 117; R. Borger, *Die Inschriften Asarhaddons: Königs von Assyrien* (AfO Beiheft 9; Graz: Published by the editors, 1956) 20, 59, 106, 116; A. C. Piepkorn, *Historical Prism Inscriptions of Assurbanipal* (Chicago: University of Chicago Press, 1933) 53, 70; M. Streck, *Assurbanipal und die letzten assyrischen Könige bis zum Untergange Niniveh's* (3 vols.; Vorderasiatische bibliothek 7; Leipzig: Hinrichs, 1916) 2.44, 88. See also Oded's discussion in *Mass Deportations and Deportees in the Neo-Assyrian Empire*, 56–58, 81–99.

33. Luckenbill, *The Annals of Sennacherib*, 117.

34. Ibid., 130.

related to phenotypical characteristics and thus to ethnic conceptions of identity. The phrase originated with the Sumerians, and they used it regularly in descriptions of themselves.[35] But even in the ancient Sumerian context it cannot have served a purely ethnic role, since it could equally well refer to humanity as a whole:

> Father Enki . . . on the earth he set up cities and hamlets, multiplied the *Black Heads*, supplied them with a king for "their shepherdship," raised him high for "their princeship," and made the king go out to all the lands as a steady light [italics mine].[36]

This precludes the idea that the phrase itself had ethnic connotations. In the Neo-Assyrian documents, it is best to understand *ṣalmat qaqqadi*, not as a reference to discrete groups within Mesopotamia, but as an ancient archaic term for the people of Mesopotamia.[37] Despite the obscurity of the term's etiology, it appears that, just as Sargon II reached back into history and identified with the ancient Sumero-Akkadian figure of Sargon the Great, so too the Assyrians seem to have viewed themselves as the descendants of the Sumerians, the "black-head peoples." Whether they understood themselves as political descendants or as ethnic descendants is a another matter, but the former seems much more likely.

To summarize, although the annals clearly distinguish between Assyrians and non-Assyrians, the textual evidence shows that for most of the nation's history these foreigners could become "Assyrians" through cultural assimilation. At the very least, they could become "Assyrians" through political assimilation when they submitted to the sovereignty of the Assyrian overlords. In the latter case, it would seem that they were "counted with the people of Assyria" but that they also retained a certain cultural independence that distinguished them from the Assyrians living in their midst, as reflected in the texts from Aššurnaṣirpal II. The only prospect for an ethnic component in Assyrian identity is their use of the ancient Sumerian designation, the *black-headed people*. It is now clear, however, that this was probably not an ethnic term but a general reference to the Mesopotamian peoples.

35. S. N. Kramer, *The Sumerians* (Chicago: University of Chicago Press, 1963) 285–86.
36. S. N. Kramer and J. Maier, *Myths of Enki, the Crafty God* (New York: Oxford University Press, 1989) 87.
37. CAD S 75–76.

Esarhaddon's Succession Treaty (680–669)

Despite the bellicose impressions of imperial ideology in the annalistic sources, the primary formal mechanism of Assyrian expansion was the treaty, both its text and its ceremonial accoutrements.[38] Political deals were often struck with foreign rulers or pro-Assyrian "would-be" rulers, and in many cases this preempted the need for military action.[39] The oaths (*adê nīš ilāni*) administered in these ceremonies are recorded in Esarhaddon's vassal treaties, along with the names of some of those who took the oath. The vassals swore allegiance to Esarhaddon and to Assurbanipal and were prohibited thereby from concluding similar treaties with Assyria's competitors. They also accepted the obligation to report acts of treason and promised to protect the treaty document itself. These promises were made in the context of the ritual event and in the presence of divine witnesses, who would enact the appropriate curses for a lapse in vassal fidelity. As has been noted by S. Parpola and R. Frankena, these formal features are very similar to those found in the eighth-century Sefîre treaties and also in the book of Deuteronomy.[40]

Esarhaddon's succession to the throne was among the more difficult in Assyrian history, and it is not surprising that he attempted to preclude similar problems for his son, Assurbanipal. Assurbanipal records this effort in the Rassam Prism, which dates to the eponym of Shamash-daninanni, that is, sometime between 644 and 636 B.C.E. The text reads:

38. For a related study on other peaceful strategies used by the Assyrians (in this case after military conquest, however), see B. N. Porter, "Conquest or Kudurrus? A Note on Peaceful Strategies of Assyrian Government," *The Tablet and the Scroll: Near Eastern Studies in Honor of William W. Hallo* (ed. M. E. Cohen et al.; Bethesda: CDL, 1993) 194–97.

39. S. Parpola and K. Watanabe (eds.), *Neo-Assyrian Treaties and Loyalty Oaths* (SAA 2; Helsinki: University of Helsinki Press, 1988) xxiii.

40. See R. Frankena, "The Vassal-Treaties of Esarhaddon and the Dating of Deuteronomy," *OTS* 14 (1965) 122–54. For the bulk of these texts, see D. J. Wiseman, *The Vassal-Treaties of Esarhaddon* (London: The British School of Archaeology in Iraq, 1958). See also new and closely related texts published by A. K. Grayson, "Akkadian Treaties of the Seventh Century B.C.," *JCS* 39 (1987) 127–59. S. Parpola, *Neo-Assyrian Treaties and Loyalty Oaths*, xxx. The diffinitive publication of the Sefîre texts is J. A. Fitzmyer, *The Aramaic Inscriptions of Sefîre* (BibOr 19; Rome: Pontifical Biblical Institute, 1967). I understand that there is a new edition of Fitzmyer's work, but I have not yet seen it.

Esarhaddon, king of Assyria, the father who begot me, respected the word of Assur and Bêlit-ilê (the Lady of the Gods), his tutelery (divinities), when they gave the command that I should exercise sovereignty; in the month of Airu, the month of Ea, the lord of mankind, the twelfth day, an auspicious day, a feast day of Gula, at the sublime command which Assur, Bêlit, Sin, Shamash, Adad, Bêl, Nabû, Ishtar of Nineveh, queen of Kudmuri, Ishtar of Arbela, Urta, Nergal, Nusku, uttered, he gathered together the people of Assyria, great and small, from the upper to the lower sea. That they would accept (lit., guard) my crownprinceship, and later my kingship, he made them take oath by the great gods, and (so) he strengthened the bonds (betweeen them and me).[41]

Although the Assyrian monarchs often concluded vassal treaties with new subjects, in the case of this succession treaty, all subjects of the empire were included. We cannot be certain about the antiquity of this succession tradition, but we do know that Esarhaddon was not the first to do this for his crown-prince. His father Sennacherib appears to have done the same for him in 683–682 B.C.E.[42] Although the stock of Neo-Assyrian treaties that predate Sennacherib is scant, it would not be surprising to find that this tradition dates back to the eighth century or even earlier. The treaty renewal ceremony probably served two purposes, the first being a show of solidarity and strength to preempt thoughts of rebellion during the tenuous succession period. But just as important was the symbolic gathering of peoples "from the upper to the lower sea." One of the primary roles of the Assyrian monarch was that of a warrior-king who was charged both with preserving and also with extending the sovereign domain of Assur to the "ends of the earth" (see below, pp. 41–42). The assembly of vassals described in this text demonstrates that the Assyrian vision of Assur's universal dominance was becoming a reality. And the Assyrians would be followed in this imperial ideology by the Babylonians, who would in turn be followed by the Persians.[43]

M. Weinfeld has pointed out that ancient Near Eastern terms for treaty and pact concentrate in two semantic fields, oath/commitment and grace/friendship, both of which are commonly present in ancient

41. Luckenbill, *ARAB* 2.291.
42. For a discussion of this text, see S. Parpola, "Sennacherib's Succession Treaty," *JCS* 39 (1987) 160–78.
43. See *ANET* 307, 316–17.

treaty texts. It is interesting that the latter semantic field is lacking in Esarhaddon's treaties and in other seventh-century Neo-Assyrian treaties while, on the other hand, our earlier, less-complete sources reflect both semantic fields.[44] Furthermore, it is only in these seventh-century treaties that vassals are required to accept Assur as god: "In the future and forever Aššur will be your god, and Assurbanipal, the great crown prince designate, will be your lord."[45] Taken together, these facts reflect a more hostile stance toward imperial subjects than in previous periods of Neo-Assyrian history, which is not surprising in light of what we have discerned from the sources thus far, namely, that following Sargon II, there was a decidedly negative turn in the way that Assyrians viewed their imperial subjects.

Another interesting feature of the text is Assurbanipal's claim that "the people of Assyria, great and small, from the upper to the lower sea," were summoned to this succession ceremony. Who were these 'people of Assyria' (*nišê* mat*Aššur*)? I have pointed out that the sources after Sargon II tend to discursively separate Assyrians and their non-Assyrian subjects, so that one would at first expect that "people of Assyria" would be used in a restrictive sense; but this is not the case. The texts usually cited as relevant are the treaty texts unearthed at Nimrud in 1955, which include fragments of at least nine separate vassal treaties concluded by Esarhaddon with cities to the east and northeast of Assyria proper.[46] S. Parpola has argued, I think correctly, that these text are only a small part of the puzzle, since these texts actually reflect newly acquired vassals rather than a loyalty oath imposed on the whole empire. The situation that Assurbanipal's text describes included not just these new vassals, but all political modalities under Assyrian domination. The not-so-surprising fact is that, while elsewhere Sennacherib, Esarhaddon, and Assurbanipal discursively excluded imperial subjects from the cultural entity they called "Assyria," Assurbanipal felt free to include them when the objective was to portray the extent of Assyrian domination. This semantic juggling is evidenced by the fact that Assurbanipal calls his subjects the "people of Assyria" while the associated

44. Weinfeld, "Covenant Terminology in the Ancient Near East and Its Influence on the West," *JAOS* 93 (1973) 190; Parpola and Watanabe, *Neo-Assyrian Treaties and Loyalty Oaths*, xviii.

45. Ibid., 44.

46. For the complete texts, see Wiseman, *The Vassal-Treaties of Esarhaddon*.

texts from Esarhaddon's treaties distinguish between the 'citizens of As-syria' (dumu ᵐᵃᵗ*Aššur*) and the 'foreigners' (dumu ᵐᵃᵗ*šanitim*).[47]

Borders and Boundaries in the Days of Neo-Assyria

Given the imperialistic bent of Assyrian rulers, it is not surprising that a preoccupation with borders and boundaries can be discerned in the Neo-Assyrian materials.[48] Many texts highlight the expansion of Assyrian imperialism and control, in some cases, as in this text from the reign of Aššurnaṣirpal, enumerating borders in a style reminiscent of the Hebrew sources (cf. Deuteronomy 3):

> Aššurnaṣirpal . . . subdued (the territory stretching) from the oppo-site bank of the Tigris to Mount Lebanon and the Great Sea, the en-tire land of Laqû, (and) the land Suḫu including the city Rapiqu. I brought within the boundaries of my land (the territory stretching) from the source of the River Subnat to the passes of Mount Kirruru (and) to the land Gilzânu, from the opposite bank of the Lower Zab to the city Tîl-Bâri which is upstream from the land Zaban, from the city Tîl-ša-Abtâni to the city Tîl-ša-Zabtâni, (and) the cities Hirimu (and) Harutu (which are) fortresses of Karduniaš. Finally, I have gained dominion over the entire extensive lands of Nairi.[49]

This concern for political boundaries is actually evidence of a certain agenda that the Assyrian monarchs had adopted for themselves, namely, the effort to extend Assyrian influence to the ends of the earth.[50] And there is strong evidence that, late in Neo-Assyrian history, its monarchs began to see this agenda realized:

> The Bir'ai I brought in submission to my feet. The Mese'ans and Te-means, the Sabe'ans, the Haiappeans, the Badaneans, the Hatteans,

47. Parpola and Watanabe, *Neo-Assyrian Treaties and Loyalty Oaths*, 37, 42. The two groups are distinguished by their identities but are presented on equal footing as potential rebels.

48. M. Liverani has provided an extended theoretical discussion about the issue of borders and boundaries in the ancient Near East in *Prestige and Interest: International Relations in the Near East ca. 1600–1100 B.C.* (History of the Ancient Near East 1; Padova: Sargon, 1990) 33–112.

49. See Grayson, *Assyrian Rulers of the Early First Millennium BC, I (1114–859 BC)*, 320.

50. P. Garelli, "L'État et la légitimité royale sous l'empire assyrien," *Power and Propaganda: A Symposium on Ancient Empires* (ed. M. T. Larsen; Mesopotamia 7; Copenhagen: Akademisk, 1979) 319–28, esp. 323.

Idibaileans . . . which are on the border of the lands of the setting sun, whom no one knew of, and whose abode is far off. . . .[51]

The king of Meluhha (Ethiopia), who in the midst of . . . an in-approachable region . . . whose fathers since the far-off days of the moon-god's time (era), had not sent messengers to the kings of my fathers, to bring their greetings . . . brought him [the fugitive Ia-manî) before me into Assyria, (after) a most difficult journey.[52]

Upêri, king of Dilmun, who lives . . . like a fish 30 *bêru* ("double hours") away in the midst of the sea of the rising sun, heard of Assur . . . and sent him gifts. And seven kings of Ia', a district of Iatnana (Cyprus) whose distant abodes are situated a seven days' journey in the sea of the setting sun, and the name of whose land, since the far-off days of the moon-god's time (era), not one of the kings, my fa-thers who (ruled) Assyria and Babylonia, had heard, (these kings) heard from afar, in the midst of the sea, of the deeds which I was per-forming in Chaldea and the Hittite-land, their hears were rent, fear fell upon them . . . gold, silver, furniture . . . they brought before me . . . and they kissed my feet.[53]

Guggu (Gygus), king of Lydia, a district of the other side of the sea, a distant place, whose name, the kings, my fathers, had not heard, As-sur, the god, my creator, caused to see my name in a dream. "Lay hold of the feet of Assurbanipal, king of Assyria and conquer thy foes by calling upon his name." Upon the day that he beheld this vision, he dispatched his messenger to me. . . . From the day that he laid hold of my feet, he overcame, by the help of Assur and Ishtar, the gods, the Cimmerians, who had been harassing the people of his land, who had not feared my fathers, nor had laid hold of my royal feet.[54]

It is quite evident that from the Assyrian perspective the dream of king-ship over "the four corners of the world" was becoming a reality during the reigns of Tiglath-Pileser III, Sargon II, and afterward. Kings from "distant lands," from the very edges of the world, had "kissed the royal feet," kings and kingdoms of which previous Assyrian kings had no knowledge. Assur and his *šangû*, the kingly high priest, now ruled the

51. From Tiglath-pilerser III's inscriptions (Luckenbill, *ARAB* 1.293).
52. From Sargon II's inscriptions (ibid., 2.32).
53. Ibid., 2.36.
54. From the inscriptions of Assurbanipal (ibid., 2.298).

entire world.[55] This period of tremendous Assyrian optimism and un-precedented domination of the Near East is the same period from which our earliest Israelite prophetic works come. So our discussion of the early prophetic materials must presuppose that both Israel and Judah were functioning as "peripheral" communities under the "core" domination of the Assyrian empire. Even if one does not agree with the Wallerstein School's claim that this core/periphery situation creates ethnic sentiments, the ethnic theorists are quite right when they tell us that among peripheral groups any existing ethnic boundaries tend to become more solid and sentiments of distinction more intense. If ethnic sentiments did exist among eighth-century Israelites, we would therefore expect them to become quite pronounced in the early prophetic literature.

There was a time, of course, when Assyria's geographical boundaries were not so far-reaching, and I should not leave the topic of "borders and boundaries" without some mention of the well-known "Synchronistic History" from the end of Adad-nerari III's reign (810–783 B.C.E.). The text is a narration of Assyro-Babylonian relations from the reign of Puzur-Aššur III (fifteenth century B.C.E.) until that of Adad-nerari III. In the account, the author argues that an ancient border had long existed between Assyria and Babylon and that each Babylonian encroachment of this territory had ended in Assyrian victory. As A. K. Grayson has noted, the most obvious historical context for the work is immediately after the death of Adad-nerari III, when a weakened Assyria was threatened by Urartu in the north and Babylon to the south.[56] Although the text is clearly based on original inscriptions of Assyrian kings and is careful to mention only Assyrian kings who had dealings with Babylon—thus contributing to the perceived legitimacy of the document—in the final analysis, it is clear that the author is quite selective with the data and at points fabricates Assyrian victories out of Assyrian defeats. The idea that Assyria and Babylon shared a long-standing border agreement recorded on a frontier stela

55. See comments by M. T. Larsen, "The Tradition of Empire in Mesopotamia," in *Power and Propaganda: A Symposium on Ancient Empires* (ed. M. T. Larsen; Mesopotamia 7; Copenhagen: Akademisk, 1979) 90–91.

56. For text and discussion, see A. K. Grayson's *Assyrian and Babylonian Chronicles* (Texts from Cuneiform Sources 5; Locust Valley, N.Y.: Augustin, 1975) 50–56, 157–70.

between the two states was an invented tradition, one that the Assyrians were more than happy to ignore a few decades later.

The Assyrian King-Lists

To preempt any speculation on the reader's part, I can report that we will not find much evidence of Assyrian ethnicity in its king-list tradition, and this conforms with the evidence that we have already examined from the royal inscriptions. On the other hand, I have alluded already to the fact that certain features of the Assyrian king-lists make them a thoroughfare to the discussion of ethnicity during the Old Babylonian period, and this probably comes as no surprise. No examination of ethnicity in the ancient Near East would be complete without discussion of the Old Babylonian evidence, especially when this evidence has commonly been associated with the ethnic character of ancient Israel.[57]

According to W. Röllig, the Assyrian king-lists (AKL) come to us in three formal varieties (A, B, and C), and it is the so-called "A" variety that interests us, primarily because it includes genealogical features that are not found in the synchronistic tradition (B) or in the simple list tradition (C).[58] R. R. Wilson has been relatively successful in identifying the modus operandi behind the composition of the list and also in reconstructing the text's form-critical and intertextual relationships with other list traditions, particularly the Babylonian king-lists (BKL) and the Genealogy of the Hammurabi Dynasty (GHD).[59] The earliest exemplar of the AKL-A text tradition dates to the tenth century,[60] and its last major witness was composed in 722 B.C.E.[61] The text is divided

57. See, for instance, A. Malamat, *Mari and the Early Israelite Experience* (Schweich Lectures; Oxford: Oxford University Press, 1984), esp. 27–52; Gottwald, *The Tribes of Yahweh*, 293, 435–42; J. T. Luke, *Pastoralism and Politics in the Mari Period: A Re-examination of the Character and Political Significance of the Major West Semitic Tribal Groups of the Middle Euphrates, ca. 1828–1758 B.C.* (Ph.D. diss., University of Michigan, 1965) 4–5; G. E. Mendenhall, "The Hebrew Conquest of Palestine," *BA* 25 (1962) 66–87;

58. W. Röllig, "Zur Typologie und Entsetehung der babylonischen und assyrischen Königslisten," *lišān mithurti: Festschrift Wolfram Freiherr von Soden* (ed. M. Dietrich and W. Röllig; AOAT 1; Kevelaer: Butzon & Bercker, 1969) 265–77.

59. Wilson, *Genealogy and History in the Biblical World*, 86–114.

60. E. Nassouhi, "Grande Liste des rois d'Assyrie," *AfO* 4 (1927) 1–11.

61. I. J. Gelb, "Two Assyrian King Lists," *JNES* 13 (1954) 209–30.

into four sections, but I am interested primarily in the first portion of the text that registers the earliest kings of Assyria:

> Tudiya, Adamu, Yangi, Kitlamu, Harharu, Mandaru, Imsu, Harsu, Didanu, Hanu, Zuabu, Nuabu, Abazu, Belu, Azarah, Ushpiya, Api-ashal—Total: 17 kings living in tents.[62]

Rather than discuss this excerpt at length, I would prefer to focus our attention on just one of its component features, that according to the list Ḫanu was one of the earliest Assyrian kings who lived during a no-madic period of Assyria's early history. The reference to Ḫanu, like the other names in this first section of AKL-A, does not follow the genea-logical convention ("PN son of PN") used in most of the text but in-stead lists the names without any notice of their relationship to each other.[63] The names in this first section of the list were of much greater antiquity than in the other sections of the list, and the scribe(s) that composed AKL-A no doubt lifted them from an earlier source that lacked the genealogical notations. This being the case, some time ago J. J. Finkelstein raised the question whether this Ḫanu could be profit-ably connected or related to the much earlier Ḫeana (or Ḫana) tribal groups that are so well known from the Mari documents of the Old Babylonian period.[64] In a detailed comparison of AKL-A with the Old Babylonian GHD, which also mentions the name Ḫeana, Finkelstein identified several correspondences between AKL's list of "kings who lived in tents" and the earliest names listed in GHD, for instance, Mandaru (= *ma-da-ra*), Ṭudiya (= *tu-ub-ti-ya*), Yangi (= *ya-am-qú-us*), Didanu (= *di-ta-nu*), and so forth. While the similar names argue that a common source or tradition lay behind the two documents, this should not distract us from the fact that the two texts diverge from each other in a number of important respects. However, these differ-ences will become clear only if we leave Neo-Assyria for a brief foray into the Old Babylonian period, a context separated from our first ex-emplar of AKL-A by nearly a millennium.

The so-called "Genealogy of the Hammurabi Dynasty" would be more properly cited as the "Genealogy of Ammiṣaduqa," who was the

---

62. *ANET* 564.

63. With the exception of Apiashal, who is made out to be the son of Ushpiya in section two of the list.

64. J. J. Finkelstein, "The Genealogy of the Hammurapi Dynasty," *JCS* 20 (1966) 95–118.

great-grandson of Hammurabi. Equally imprecise is our identification of the text as a genealogy, since it is actually a "kinship list" that includes no genealogical formulas whatsoever. Its presumed status as a genealogy stems from the fact that the list includes (for the most part) the kith and kin of Hammurabi, and it is this kinship feature that has prompted scholars to connect it with the notion of genealogy. While it is superficially similar to texts from the Mesopotamian king-list tradition, its intrinsic genre is rather different from AKL-A. Unlike most ancient Near Eastern king-lists, which were composed to provide historical legitimation for monarchic officeholders, GHD functioned in an entirely different sphere as the invitation list for Ammiṣaduqa's *kispum* ceremony, in which he offered food and libation to his deceased relatives.[65] It seems that a similar list stood behind the first few sections of AKL-A, which were likely composed for Šamši-Adad to legitimate his usurpation of the Assyrian throne.[66] This would account for the similarities between GHD and this section of AKL-A, since both were composed during the Old Babylonian period and shared Amorite origins.[67] The *kispu* ritual has been much discussed and we will not explore it any further here (although we should remind ourselves that this ancestor cult has been connected with certain aspects of Israelite religion). More important for our purpose is the kinship aspect of the text, which we can explore by returning to our Ḥanean example.

We know from the Mari documents that the Ḥaneans were an important component within the sociocultural context of that city-state, both as assimilated village dwellers and also as part of the seminomadic population in its territorial periphery.[68] We also know that they were but one of several well-known sociocultural entities living in the Old Babylonian context that used kinship structures as an important in-

<hr>

65. The inclusion of "all persons from East to West," as well as the Gutians, demonstrates that the ceremony hoped to include every "shade" that might create trouble for the family dynasty, and this was quite apart from the question of whether these groups were members of Ammiṣaduqa's dynastic tradition (Malamat, *Mari and the Early Israelite Experience*, 99).

66. The first few sections of AKL-A include: (1) 17 nomadic kings; (2) 10 ancestor kings; (3) 6 early kings; (4) 6 Old Assyrian Kings; (5) the usurper Šamši-Adad.

67. M. T. Larsen, *The Old Assyrian City-State and Its Colonies*, 34–40. Larsen is summarizing a number of conclusions culled from Finkelstein, Landsberger, and Kraus, whose works we will refer to as we go along.

68. M. Anbar, *Les tribus amurrites de Mari* (OBO 108; Freiburg: Universitätsverlag / Göttingen: Vandenhoeck & Ruprecht, 1991) 77–82, 209–16.

strument of political and social organization.[69] In the case of the Haneans this included segmented kinship structures of seven to nine distinct
clans and a common identity as Hanean "brothers."[70] Most relevant for
our inquiry is the fact that GHD seems to have conceptualized these
Haneans as the progeny of a single eponymous forefather, *Ḫe-a-na*, as
it did in the case of other groups mentioned in its list of early dynastic
"rulers." This is at variance with AKL-A, in which the names were understood as dynastic kings only, no doubt because the tribal connections were long forgotten by the Neo-Assyrian period. But returning to
the Old Babylonian context, it is somewhat difficult to identify the
source of the eponymous figures listed in GHD, whether we should
view them as scribal inventions or as traditions inherited by the scribe
from the tribal groups themselves. The fact that the Haneans made extensive use of kinship structures and that they viewed themselves as
"brothers" makes the second option more likely, in my view, and the
comparative data certainly lends support to this conclusion (see my
discussion of the Tiv people in chapter 1 above).

The fact that this ethnic data is connected with the royal dynastic
tradition suggests one way that ethnic sentiments might become associated with a national sense of identity. Specifically, it suggests that when
rulers or peoples rise to power they will naturally tend to carry with
them any preexisting ethnic sentiments and affective notions of kinship. In the case of the dynasty of Hammurabi, this included a special
sense of connection with the ethnic Haneans and also with the "Amorites," who were probably viewed as an ethnic entity as well (if we may
extrapolate from the Hanean evidence).[71] These observations about
ethnicity in the Mari context are satisfactory for my purposes, and if
the reader wishes to explore it further, I would recommend the work of
M. Anbar that I have already cited. But in doing so I would caution
that, although certain theoretical paradigms mentioned in chapter 1
might suggest that the core/periphery context of ancient Mari created
the nearby ethnic communities that we are discussing, such a conclusion is premature, because the origins of the tribal groups themselves is
hotly debated. On the other hand, the documentary evidence certainly

69. Ibid., 77–157. Other examples include the "Bini-Yamina," "Bini-Simʾāl," and
"Sutûm."
70. Ibid., 80–83.
71. See GHD lines 29–30.

shows that tensions were often high between the urban culture of Mari and these ethnic cultures on its periphery,[72] and it was no doubt this sense of ecological and political competition that intensified the ethnic sentiments of the groups and thereby made them so visible to us in the ancient textual evidence.

There is another example from the same second-millennium time frame that brings some refinement to our discussion of Assyrian identity. In the inscription of a certain Puzur-Sin (ca. 1700 B.C.E.),[73] the Assyrian monarch disparaged Šamši-Adad I (and his deposed dynasty) as "a man of foreign seed, not of Assyrian blood," which was no doubt a swipe at the usurper's Amorite origins. The broken state of the text makes the translation of "seed" somewhat speculative, but even in Grayson's more careful (and accurate) translation, the essential message is the same: the Amorites were "a foreign plague, not of the flesh of the city of Aššur." This discursive strategy is markedly different from what we see in Neo-Assyrian texts and, unlike the king-list tradition, it lays stress quite clearly on the ethnic pedigree of the ruler rather than on his status as the legitimate royal heir. In this respect, the text is unusual (we might even say idiosyncratic) and we should probably ask why its sentiments appear to be a rather isolated case in the context of the Assyrian literary corpus. To speculate a bit, for theorists that espouse Wallerstein's core/periphery model of ethnicity the answer would be fairly straightforward: it was a context of political competition between the "core" Amorite dynasty and the "peripheral" Assyrians that created this ethnically charged polemic, with the appeal to ethnic kinship being a suitable instrument in the effort to fuse political support for the Assyrian side of the controversy. When the Assyrian political hegemony eventually became more secure, its core status gradually eliminated the instrumental importance of ethnic sentiment, particularly among its more elite classes. To continue in the theoretical vein, this situation also reminds us of A. D. Smith's thesis that nation-states fre-

72. As reflected in M.2802, which describes Yaḫdun-Lim's expedition against the Bini-Yamina and the Ḫaneans.

73. This text provides the only evidence that the otherwise unknown Puzur-Sin ruled Assyria and that he did so by deposing a successor of Šamši-Adad I. For a discussion of the identity of Puzur-Sin as well as a text and translation of his inscription, see B. Landsberger "Assyrische Königsliste und 'dunkles Zeitalter,'" *JCS* 8 (1954) 31–33; A. K. Grayson, *Assyrian Rulers of the Third and Second Millennium BC (to 1115 BC)* (RIMA 1; Toronto: University of Toronto Press, 1987) 77–78.

quently begin as ethnic communities.[74] But our resources for reconstructing this early period of Assyrian history are somewhat limited, particularly with respect to the question of ethnicity and its relative importance, and this means that we are in no real position to say categorically whether the circumstances behind this text lend genuine support to the theories of either Wallerstein or Smith. Nevertheless, although in historical terms we cannot confirm (or, I think, disconfirm) that the Assyrians actually shared "blood ties" in some meaningful way during the Old Assyrian era, our text confirms that at least some people from this early period believed that they did.

Returning again to the Neo-Assyrian period, I have already remarked in passing that the AKL-A phrase, "17 kings living in tents," points to the Assyrian notion that its earliest kings were nomadic. What is interesting about this is that the evidence we have examined above confirms that the second-millennium Ḥaneans, as well as a number of other groups listed in the early section of AKL-A, turn out to have been nomadic (or seminomadic) just as AKL-A has suggested. That AKL-A seems to have preserved this nomadic tradition is somewhat remarkable, given the long chronological interval that separated the Neo-Assyrian context from the Old Babylonian tribal groups.[75] There can be little doubt that this nomadic "tent-tradition" was subjected to reinterpretation during its historical trek between the two time frames, and it seems that in the Neo-Assyrian context it probably connoted a model of social progress from an early nomadic life to a relatively urban context (for the monarchs, at least). But the unavoidable necessity of reinterpretation during the tradition's history in no way detracts from the important observation that the Mesopotamian scribal tradition can transport meaningful (though distorted) sociological information over a rather long time period.

To summarize our discussion of the Assyrian evidence, the Assyrians had forged a national identity based on imperialistic expansion of the kingdom of the god Assur and his high priest, the king. This national identity was, of course, political and monarchic rather than ethnic, and it was forged at the expense of many non-Assyrians in the

74. A. D. Smith, *The Ethnic Origins of Nations* (Oxford: Oxford University Press, 1986) 129–52.

75. Landsberger long ago suggested that the *Grundstock* of the text tradition originated during the time of Šamši-Adad I ("Assyrische Königsliste und 'dunkles Zeitalter,'" 109).

ancient Near East. On the one hand, boundaries could represent the successful expansion of the empire and, at other times, as in the Synchronistic History, the concept of boundary was used to protect the nation in its weakness. During the course of Assyria's history, great pride was often taken in the process of making non-Assyrians become Assyrians through territorial expansion and political control. As the texts from Aššurnaṣirpal reveal, there was a perceived difference between the new imperial subjects, those "counted as Assyrians," and true Assyrians more closely associated with Assyrian politics, rule, and culture, but this distinction did not preclude the use of the term *Assyrian* to refer to these new subjects. However, as the Assyrian goal of universal domination seemed to become reality, that is, during and after the reign of Sargon II, the concept of *new Assyrians* seems to have waned and been replaced with a more negative view of imperial subjects, so that derogatory expressions like *wicked Hittites* began to appear and imperial subjects became *booty*, not *Assyrians*. It was during this period of Assyrian hubris that Israel's early prophetic literature appeared. Any analysis of these Israelite materials must account for the influences such an oppressive force must have exerted upon the authors of the Hebrew literature.

Assyrian preoccupation with the origins and preservation of kingship and with the expansion of monarchic rule absorbed much of its literary attention. This is not to say that Assyrians had no interest in a topic like ethnography or that they were unaware of ethnic concepts of identity. A few scattered sources, some of which I have mentioned (Sargon's "Letter to the God" and Sennacherib's palace reliefs), show that such an interest did exist within the Assyrian scribal community. However, this interest seems to have been precluded and truncated by monarchic interests, so that the formal attention given to such inquiry was minimal. As we will see, this was not the case in Greece.

Only in the case of the second-millennium monarch Puzur-Sin did we find any evidence of Assyrian ethnicity, and this single example was multiplied when we expanded our comparative materials to use some of the Old Babylonian evidence. In the GHD and in the ethnographic data that we derive about tribal groups from the Mari texts, it is clear that the second-millennium context included many instances of ethnic awareness among both peripheral groups and also among the monarchic rulers. The most interesting point is that this ethnic awareness was not preserved in the royal inscriptions of the Amorite monarchs but rather in a ritual list associated with the *kispu* ceremony, which demonstrates that ethnicity can play an important role within one's identity and still remain quite apart from one's sense of national or political identity.

Ethnicity and Identity in Archaic and Classical Greece

I have chosen Herodotus's *Histories* as the primary source material for exploring the notions of ethnicity and identity in ancient Greece. One might fault this because Herodotus's fifth-century date is somewhat distant, chronologically speaking, from most of Israel's literature. As the growing penchant for comparative anthropological data shows, however, chronological proximity is by no means a prerequisite for comparative significance. Moreover, Herodotus is not so distant from the Hebrew sources when one considers the possibility that much of the biblical text is later than usually supposed and when it is acknowledged that Herodotus is a suitable representative of those who preceded him—particularly Homer, Hesiod, and Hecataeus—because his work is nearly a compendium of their various genres and interests. It is because of this motley, form-critical appearance that, before I turn to questions of ethnicity and identity in Herodotus, I will offer a few introductory comments on the genre, literary features, and historicity of the *Histories*. A primary goal of this introduction will be to determine whether the work's ethnographic sections provide accurate information about other peoples or, on the other hand, furnish mainly hellenized representations of them. If the latter is the case—and I will argue that it is—then the materials from Herodotus will serve us most adequately, not as a witness to various foreign identities, but rather as a representative of Greek notions about identity and ethnicity.

In spite of my caveat about our preoccupation with chronological proximity, I suppose that it is significant for us to determine the extent to which we might expect features in Herodotus to provide a *direct* explanation for features in the Hebrew Bible (or vice versa). So before I introduce our study of Herodotus, the onus is upon me to show more convincingly that he is a suitable representative of the older Greek materials, and, therefore, of the historical periods that are closer to the time in which many of our Hebrew sources were composed. I must also suggest the cultural path that these traditions may have followed on their trek from Greece to Israel. All of this can be done through a brief examination of Homer, Hesiod, and Hecataeus.

The Predecessors of Herodotus: Homer, Hesiod, and Hecataeus

For many classical scholars, the story of Greek historiography begins with Homer's epics,[76] and this is because there is a certain organic connection between the epic tradition and the historiographers, particularly Herodotus.[77] There are a good many things that we could say about the epics, but if we want to examine the supposed connection between Homer and Herodotus, I would suggest that we start with this question: what Homeric purposes lay behind the composition of the *Iliad* and how do they compare with those of Herodotus? Certainly one purpose was to provide a good story for the entertaining bards of ancient Greece. Hornblower has directed us to two excerpts from the *Iliad*, however, that suggest a more serious motive for this epic composition. In the first example Achilles sings about "the glorious deeds of men," and in the second Helen explains to Hector that trouble had befallen her "so that in times to come we may be sung about by people yet unborn."[78] While we cannot expect a transparent purpose statement in epic poetry of the sort we might find in historiography, these comments certainly stand close to the stated aims of Herodotus: "so that things done by man [will] not be forgotten in time."[79] So the generic differences that separate Homer from Herotodus cannot be translated into entirely disparate purposes, for the two writers shared very similar interests in the human past and in preserving it for posterity. They were interested in history.

Not only do their purposes overlap to an extent, but Homer's scope of interest is also similar to that of Herodotus. The two major concerns of the *Iliad* and the *Odyssey* are warfare and genealogy, and these are also important themes in the *Histories* of Herodotus. On the

---

76. Along with most classical scholars, I am presuming a "unitarian" position regarding Homer and the epics, that is, that he was the author of both the *Iliad* and its sequel, the *Odyssey*. See "Homer," *The Oxford Companion to Classical Literature* (2d ed.; ed. M. C. Howatson; Oxford: Oxford University Press, 1989) 283.

77. See, for instance, S. Hornblower's introduction to *Greek Historiography* (ed. S. Hornblower; Oxford: Clarendon, 1994) 7–9.

78. Ibid., 7; Cf. *Iliad* 9.189, 6.357. See also in the *Odyssey* 8.580: "that there might be a song for those yet to be born."

79. Herodotus *Histories* 1.1.

other hand, as we will see, while the connections between genealogy and ethnicity are made very explicit in Herodotus, this simply is not the case in Homer, a fact that has caused Hall in a recent study of Greek ethnicity to devote very little attention to him.[80] Nevertheless, Hall does see in the poet a subtle awareness of ethnicity, and I think that we can both explain the paucity of ethnic concepts in Homer and, if we read between the lines, identify discrete instances of ethnicity in his epic tales.

The paucity of ethnic genealogies is best explained by the fact that Homer is preoccupied with the pedigree of his characters, and in this regard the ethnic origins of Odysseus (that he is by lineage from the city of Ithaca) are of much less interest than the fact that he was the son of Deucalion and grandson of Zeus.[81] Because of this, Homer's genealogies are primarily linear and familial, and they are not used as tools for establishing the origins or collective nature of ethnic entities. But when Odysseus warned Penelope not to inquire about his "race" and "native land," and then later, when he finally explained to her that "by lineage he came from Ithaca" and that "his own father was Laertes"— all this does seem to imply an ethnic understanding of Ithacan identity. Similarly, Telemachus says, "of Ithaca I am by birth, and my father is Odysseus."[82] And in 6.35 Nausicaa, daughter of King Alcinous, is reminded that she has "suitors in the land, the noblest of all the Phaecians, from whom is thine own lineage." These texts seem to connect collective identities (Ithacans, Phaecians) with ancestral lineage, and when this connection is made, we are dealing with ethnicity. So while ethnicity was not a preoccupation of Homer, this eighth-century source provides subtle evidence that ethnic modes of identity were already current during the early Greek archaic period. But there is at least one example of ethnicity in Homer that is not subtle—the figure Hellen. There can be little doubt that he was already the eponymous ancestor of the Hellenes that figure so prominently in Homer's work, and this tradition was subsequently picked up by later authors, as we will see.

When we consider the Hesiodic corpus, more pronounced expressions of Greek ethnicity appear, particularly in the later "pseudo-

---

80. Hall, *Ethnic Identity in Greek Antiquity,* 42.
81. Cf. *Odyssey* 24.269 and 19.116, 164–89.
82. *Odyssey* 15.267

Hesiodic" *Catalogue of Women*. But before turning to the *Catalogue*, we should briefly discuss Hesiod's *Works and Days* and his *Theogony*. The introductory portion of *Works and Days* speaks of mortal history as comprised of five successive races, and while this conception is not, strictly speaking, ethnic in the common sense of the term, it does reflect the tendency to explain human identity in terms of ancestry and lineage.[83] But we should recognize that the agricultural concerns of *Works and Days* are not of the sort that would emphasize ethnic issues. Thematic concerns also appear to have precluded ethnic concerns in Hesiod's *Theogony*. But while the poem does not discuss human genealogies, it is very interested in divine genealogies. Genealogy and kinship are therefore not in the least foreign to Hesiod's work. And the fact that these genealogical concerns have natural affinities with ethnicity is confirmed by the *Catalogue of Women*, which was composed as a sequel to the *Theogony* and features pronounced notions of ethnicity.

The *Catalogue of Women* was composed at least a century after Hesiod, during the sixth century B.C.E., and has accordingly been dubbed "pseudo-Hesiodic." According to Hall, this text is the real starting point for any serious study of Greek ethnicity because it provides a series of genealogies that trace the Hellenic race back to a common ancestor.[84] The most noteworthy example comes from a fragment that says, "from Hellen the war-loving king sprang Dorus and Xuthus and Aeolus," to which we may add a recently discovered fragment that makes Xuthus the forefather of "Akhaios and Ion." That is, Hellen was the forefather of the Dorians, Aeolians, Achaians, and Ionians, among others.[85] This use of ethnic eponymy is a part of the tradition that Herodotus and later Greek writers inherited (and used), and it is also quite close to what we see at certain points in the Hebrew Bible.

Hall has done us a great service in sorting out the history of Greece's genealogical tradition, and I refer the reader to his study for

83. *Works and Days*, 110–80. Here and elsewhere, our study of the Hesiodic corpus is based on H. G. Evelyn-White's translation in the Loeb edition, *Hesiod: The Homeric Hymns and Homerica* (Cambridge: Harvard University Press, 1982).

84. Hall, *Ethnic Identity in Greek Antiquity*, 42.

85. See fragment 4 in the Loeb edition of the *Catalogue*. This is labeled fragment 9 in M. L. West's text, and the newly discovered text he labels fragment 10. See *The Hesiodic Catalogue of Women: It's Nature, Structure and Origins* (Oxford: Oxford University Press, 1985).

more detail on the subject.[86] In sum, what he describes is the process by which the genealogical tradition was often edited (or new elements invented) to support certain political and social agendas. On the one hand, we can point to what Hall calls *aggregative* tendencies in Greek ethnicity, which sought to connect various peer groups with each other and in doing so created the tradition that the various Greek peoples stem from a common ancestor, Hellen.[87] In this sense Hellenic genealogy was etiological and sought to explain the ethnic order by means of an evolution from ethnic homogeneity to ethnic diversity. On the other hand, we can speak of *oppositional* ethnicity, in which traditions were modified to distinguish one group from other Greeks or from barbarian populations. A case in point is Athens, which found it expedient to trace its lineage back to the Ionians, and then later on, during the sixth-century reforms of Kleisthenes (and at a time of anti-Ionian sentiment), replaced their Ionian forefathers with eponymous heroes and a new "tribal" structure.[88] During the fifth century, when their claim to the land took an autochthonous turn, one of these eponymous heroes, the earth-born Erekhtheus, became a much more prominent figure in the Athenian origin tradition. So ethnicity played a very important role in ancient Greek identity.

How early can we date these ethnic traditions and how directly can we connect them with Herodotus? According to West, the genealogical tradition behind the Hesiodic *Catalogue* dates no later than the eighth century B.C.E.,[89] and Hall's conclusion that an ethnic consciousness is already present in our earliest sources from the eighth and seventh centuries squares with this perspective. Moreover, Hall suggests that these ethnic demarcations probably became rather pronounced during the eighth century, when a new sense of identity was emerging with the concept of "citizen" communities.[90] So there is evidence of the ethnic tradition in the eighth-, seventh-, and sixth-century sources. It is unfortunate that the genealogical work of Hecataeus of Miletus is lost to

86. There is also a very detailed study of Greek genealogy by Broadbent, but her primary focus is in the direction of royal and family genealogies rather than Greek ethnicity and identity (M. Broadbent, *Studies in Greek Genealogy* [Leiden: Brill, 1968]).

87. On the oppositional and aggregative character of Greek ethnicity, see Hall, *Ethnic Identity in Greek Antiquity,* 47.

88. Ibid., 53–54.

89. West, *Hesiodic Catalogue of Women,* 1–11, 164.

90. Hall, *Ethnic Identity in Greek Antiquity,* 58–59, 65.

us, since he was the immediate predecessor of Herodotus and would have served as a partial bridge to the earlier period. But even in his absence there are many connections between Herodotus and the ethnic traditions and tendencies of the Homeric and Hesiodic materials, and it is a safe assumption that the ethnic traditions passed from the early archaic sources through Hecataeus (and others) to Herodotus. Thus there are many reasons to believe that the ethnic traditions in Herodotus are representative of the earlier archaic period, and I believe that this makes the comparative value of Herodotus more attractive—if we can be convinced that there are sufficient reasons to postulate a path of cultural exchange between archaic Greece and ancient Israel.

The argument for this path of exchange may be summarized as follows: I have already mentioned Burkert's study, which confirms a marked increase in the contacts between the Greeks and Phoenicians during the eighth century B.C.E. and afterward.[91] Now we have recently been warned by J. C. Waldbaum that, while pottery sherds and the like can confirm ongoing trade patterns, these patterns do not necessarily translate into an active cultural exchange.[92] There are nevertheless several reasons for postulating a cultural connection between Israel and Greece during the archaic period. First, we know from both historical and prophetic texts that Israel had extensive contacts with the Phoenicians, and this was no doubt facilitated by their proximity to each other and by their common language. This means that we can establish Phoenicia as a possible arbiter of the process of cultural exchange, since the Phoenicians had on-going relations with both Greece and Israel.[93] Second, as Penglase's recent study demonstrates, there were extensive cultural exchanges between the Near East and Greece during the archaic period, because Homer and Hesiod reflect strong influences from the Near Eastern traditions.[94] Whether this influence moved in both directions and in equal magnitudes is difficult to say, but it certainly makes West-to-East influence more probable. Third, and perhaps most important, not only have we confirmed extensive economic trade between Greece and Phoenicia but we also have an eighth-century Phoenician

91. Burkert, *Die orientalisierende Epoche in der griechischen Religion und Literatur* (= *The Orientalizing Revolution*).

92. J. C. Waldbaum, "Greeks *in* the East or Greeks *and* the East? Problems in the Definition and Recognition of Presence," *BASOR* 305 (1997) 1–18.

93. Ibid., 4.

94. C. Penglase, *Greek Myths and Mesopotamia: Parallels and Influence in the Homeric Hymns and Hesiod* (London: Routledge, 1994).

text from Karatepe that reflects an awareness of Greek traditions about the founding of the Danunian royal dynasty by a certain מפש, which Gibson has profitably compared to the Greek tradition about a seer named Mopsos who was associated with the same region.[95] It is somewhat unclear what is going on in the text and how it relates to the Greek traditions, and Gibson is very cautious to avoid drawing hasty conclusions. But it does provide tentative evidence that Greek ethnic and royal traditions were know to those using the Phoenician language. What all of this implies is that although there is very little evidence of direct cultural exchange between Israel and Greece during the archaic period, Israel's close ties to Phoenicia—linguistic, cultural, and economic—represented a potential avenue of cultural influence from the West. But I would caution that these circumstances will make it very hard to prove that Greek–Israelite similarities stem from one influencing the other, since this circumstance might equally arise because of their common influence from the Phoenicians.

An Introduction to Herodotus

In classical antiquity, Herodotus became known as the "Father of History," a title that has doggedly followed him up to the present, when his work is generally regarded with great admiration. To encapsulate his work within the genre of *history* is somewhat misleading, since his work includes features from other genres of the period, particularly genealogy, mythology, and ethnography.[96] Before we discuss why his work displays this curious combination of literary features, I want briefly to explore questions that arise from Herodotus's own statement of purpose in the *Histories*.

> What Herodotus the Halicarnassian has learnt by inquiry is here set forth: in order that so the memory of the past may not be blotted out from among men by time, and that great and marvelous deeds done by Greeks and foreigners and especially the reason why they warred against each other may not lack renown.[97]

95. J. C. L. Gibson, *Textbook of Syrian Semitic Inscriptions* (3 vols.; Oxford: Clarendon, 1971–82) 3.44.

96. C. W. Fornara lists the standard designations used by classical scholarship for genres closely related to history (*The Nature of History in Ancient Greece and Rome* [Berkeley: University of California Press, 1983] 2–45).

97. Herodotus *Histories* 1.1. Here and elsewhere, all quotations are taken from the A. D. Godley's Loeb translation, *Herodotus* (4 vols.; LCL; Cambridge: Harvard University Press, 1982).

Here and elsewhere, Herodotus indicates that the reader ought to believe what he has to say, often asserting that extensive research lies behind his claims. In this sense, he claimed to be doing something akin to what modern historians do: to evaluate critically various sources and lines of evidence and to arrive at a conclusion about what probably happened.

Scholars have tended to believe that Herodotus did this rather well, but this was not always the case. In antiquity, Herodotus had acquired the reputation of being "unreliable, biased, parsimonious in his praise of heroes, and mendacious."[98] Such bad press came from the likes of Thucydides, Aristotle, Cicero, Josephus, Plutarch, Manetho, and Libanius.[99] He has especially been criticized for his "lack of scientific spirit" and his "gullibility."[100] It was a little over a century ago that two scholars with ties to our own period joined the ranks of these ancient writers.[101] Nevertheless, this perspective on Herodotus has generally been ignored until D. Fehling's comparatively recent study reopened the debate. Fehling claimed that in only one case could he verify an authentic source behind Herodotus's work.[102] Unlike those before him, Fehling did not examine the external evidence and then test Herodotus's account against it. Instead, he argued that the internal features of the *Histories* themselves discredit Herodotus. For instance, Herodotus writes:

> I saw there a strange thing . . . the bones of those slain on either side [the Persians vs. the Egyptians] in this fight scattered separately . . . the skulls of the Persians are so brittle that if you throw no more than a pebble it will pierce them, but the Egyptian skulls are so strong that a blow of a stone will hardly break them. And this, the people said (which I for my own part readily believed), is the reason for it: the Egyptians shave their heads from childhood, and the bone thick-

98. J. A. S. Evans, *Herodotus* (Boston: Twayne, 1982) 162–63.

99. See Aristotle *Poetica* 23; Cicero *de Legibus* 1.1.5; Josephus *Contra Apion* 1.3; Libanius *Against Herodotus*; Manetho *Against Herodotus*; Plutarch, *On the Malignity of Herodotus*; Thucydides *History of the Peloponnesian War* 1.20–21.

100. B. Baldwin, "How Credulous was Herodotus?" *Greece and Rome* 11 (1964) 167.

101. A. H. Sayce, *The Ancient Empires of the East: Herodotus I–III* (New York: Scribner's, 1884); H. Panofsky, *Quaestionum de historiae Herodoteae fontibus pars prima* (Ph.D. diss., University of Berlin, 1885).

102. D. Fehling, *Die Quellenangaben bei Herodot* (Berlin: de Gruyter, 1971) 110. This volume is now available in English as *Herodotus and His Sources* (ARCA Classical and Medieval Texts, Papers, and Monographs 21; Leeds: Francis Cairns, 1989).

ens by exposure to the sun. This is also the reason why they do not grow bald; for nowhere can one see so few bald heads as in Egypt.[103]

To this text Fehling responds (and I must agree) that it is clear that both observations Herodotus makes cannot have a basis in reality.[104] He claims to be an eyewitness to something that simply cannot be true.

Similarly, R. Rollinger has examined Herodotus's description of Babylon, particularly his depiction of its fortifications, riverworks, bridges, and city gates. He finds that there is little correlation between the *Histories* and the archaeological data. Furthermore, Rollinger has found that those who would assert the reliability of Herodotus's Babylonian account—P. Panitschek, for instance—are often guilty of using Herodotus as a basis for their reconstruction of ancient Babylon, so that their assertions are actually circular and turn out to compare Herodotus with Herodotus rather than Herodotus with the archaeological record.[105] Rollinger's conclusion is that Herodotus was not very familiar with Babylon and, in my view, it is fair to say that his observations and also those of Fehling are rather important for our evaluation of Herodotus.

W. K. Pritchett has recently taken up a defense of Herodotus's veracity, particularly in his response to Fehling. However, in doing so he has failed to offer a serious challenge to Fehling's arguments. Pritchett criticizes Fehling because he "openly scorns at citing archaeological and topographical publications," but this shows that Pritchett has failed to appreciate Fehling's central argument, which claims that it is the evidence *within* the *Histories* that raises questions about Herodotus's reliability.[106] Furthermore, in his handling of the text cited above (Herodotus *Histories* 3.12), Pritchett counters Fehling's arguments by postulating that Egyptians were of black heritage, the Persians of white heritage, and that "physical anthropologists . . . put some stock in the thickness of the skull in racial classifications [italics mine]."[107] Pritchett's argument cannot be sufficient, since it is based on questionable

103. Herodotus *Histories* 3.12.
104. Fehling, *Die Quellenangaben bei Herodot*, 23.
105. R. Rollinger, *Herodots babylonischer Logos: Eine kritische Untersuchung der Glaubwürdigkeitsdiskussion an Hand ausgewählter Beispiele* (Innsbrucker Beiträge zur Kulturwissenschaft 84; Innsbruck: Instituts für Sprachwissenschaft der Universität Innsbruck, 1993) 92. Cf. P. Panitschek, *Babylon bei Herodot und Ktesias* (Ph.D. diss, University of Graz, 1986) 1–22.
106. W. K. Pritchett, *The Liar School of Herodotus* (Amsterdam: Bieben, 1993) 10.
107. Ibid., 29–30.

anthropological data and because, even if there were some osteological distinctions between Egyptians and Persians, it hardly seems likely that Egyptian skulls would be impervious to a serious blow while Persian skulls were easily pierced by "pebbles."

Despite my sympathy for the arguments put forth by Rollinger and Fehling, I agree with Pritchett that Fehling fails to account for some of the more important secondary literature and that, on occasion, he is also guilty of excessive "rationalism."[108] Moreover, the blanket skepticism that Rollinger and Fehling espouse is perhaps unwarranted.[109] A. B. Lloyd's commentary on Herodotus presents a good deal of evidence that, especially in terms of Egyptian chronology, Herodotus worked from actual sources and that he made a serious effort to reconstruct the past.[110] Likewise, J. M. Balcer has compared Darius's autobiography from the Bisitun texts to Herodotus's parallel description in the *Histories*. In the end, Balcer has concluded that Herodotus's work "is a collection of Persian and Egyptian tales, myths, fables, and other stories, reworked by Herodotus into Ionian prose, and influenced by East Greek rationalism."[111] Thus, in both the Persian and Egyptian narratives (which have come to be viewed as Herodotus's least trustworthy accounts) there is evidence that he made a serious effort to perform the task of a historian. But all of this said, the question that remains is why such a serious effort to uncover the truth was so often colored by liberties taken with source material and by occasional tendencies toward invention.

P. Levi has postulated an answer to this question by suggesting that Herodotus was a story-teller by profession, a collector of anecdotes and tales.[112] This profession was common in the classical world, and Levi's

108. Ibid., 12–14, 16. So, for instance, Pritchett criticizes Fehling's conclusion that local traditions cannot survive through several generations when scholaship is under the spell of a "Romantic movement."

109. For instance, compare Fehling's comments on Herodotus *Histories* 2.104 with the observations of A. B. Lloyd's commentary on the same text (*Herodotus, Book II: Commentary 99–182* [3 vols.; Études préliminaires aux religions orientales dans l'Empire romain 43; Leiden: Brill, 1975–88] 3.21–25).

110. Ibid., 185–94.

111. J. M. Balcer, *Herodotus and Bisitun* (Stuttgart: Franz Steiner, 1987) 12. Balcer's conclusions are in agreement with the previous work of D. Hegyi, "Historical Authenticity of Herodotus in the Persian LOGOI," *Acta antiqua academiae scientiarium hungaricae* 21 (1973) 73–87.

112. P. Levi, *A History of Greek Literature* (New York: Viking, 1985) 153–66.

hypothesis makes sense of the *Histories*, because the most consistent feature of Herodotus's work was his desire for a good story. Because of this, truth and invention, myth and history provided equally appropriate material for his work. Whenever history served this purpose, Herodotus could be counted on to tell us about it. However, it seems that he was equally willing to sacrifice the truth for a good story.[113] And it must be remembered that even when Herodotus does give us "the truth," Balcer is right that his most serious efforts are thoroughly colored by his Greek identity. In sum, with respect to our inquiry about ethnicity and identity, we should probably expect to find the perspectives of Herodotus in the *Histories* more often than the perspectives of the various peoples with whom he supposedly had contact.

The World of Herodotus

The definitive work in the area of ethnicity and identity in Herodotus was authored by F. Hartog, who argued that Herodotus's perspective was greatly influenced by his conceptual model of the world.[114] Although Hartog examined the *Histories* in earnest, several observations escaped his attention, and several potential subjects were left unexplored. Because of this, I offer here a brief discussion of the issue. My discussion is particularly interested in Herodotus's understanding of regions to the extreme southwest (Ethiopia), east (India), and north (Europe) of the Greek homeland.

Herodotus seems particularly aware of the world's extremities, saying that "the distant parts of the world . . . have those things which we deem best and rarest," in this case referring to the copious amounts of gold found in the north of Europe (3.116). As in this northern extreme, so too the Indians, who dwell at the "sunrise of all the nations of Asia," and the Ethiopians, who dwell toward the sunset, have gold

---

113. This would account for the mottled literary character of Herodotus's work compared to the much more consistent historical works of his near contemporaries, Thucydides and Xenophon.

114. F. Hartog, *The Mirror of Herodotus: The Representation of the Other in the Writing of History* (The New Historicism: Studies in Cultural Poetics 5; Berkeley: University of California Press, 1988) 12–33. W. K. Pritchett, whom I have already mentioned in connection with D. Fehling, is equally critical of Hartog. However, once one becomes convinced that Herodotus is as much a storyteller as a historian, then Pritchett's arguments are not persuasive.

in abundance. The Indians and Ethiopians lived in hot, desert regions and were "black-skinned." Herodotus does not suggest a climatic reason for this (as does Hippocrates)[115] but surmises that both the Indians' and the Ethiopians' genital seed was "not white like other men's, but black like their skin."[116] Ethiopians, that is, black-skinned peoples, lived not only southwest of Asia but also to the extreme east of Asia, in a region that Herodotus identified as the seventeenth province of Persia. As Herodotus explains it, these Ethiopians differed from those of Africa only in "speech and hair," with the former having straight hair and the latter being "woolly-haired."[117] The Asian Ethiopians apparently lived nearer to India than to Africa, since India lay in the twentieth province of Persia and African Ethiopia lay to the south of Egypt, the fifth province. Thus, we see that the extremities of Herodotus's world, to the south, west, and east, were populated by black-skinned groups, ethnic groups in the sense that Herodotus understood their identity, at least with respect to their phenotypical characteristics, an identity associated with genetic heritage.

To the north of Herodotus's homeland lay Europe, which included the Scythians and a number of strange and exotic groups farther north. Scythia stood at the edge of this extremity, serving as a boundary between Asia and the northern limits, while its schematic counterpart, Egypt, stood between Asia and the southern extreme in Ethiopia. The Scythians were the "youngest of all peoples" and the Egyptians the oldest.[118] For Hartog, this means that Scythia and Egypt were "antitypes" in Herodotus's understanding of the world. However, a closer inspection reveals that Herodotus's perspective was not as schematically consistent as Hartog suggests, since Scythia clearly lay on the periphery of the world and Egypt most certainly did not. On the contrary, the Scythians did not reflect the stability of Egypt but the multifarious character of other peripheral peoples. Both the Indians and Scythians were nations (εθνοι) on the periphery, and each was characterized by diversity, particularly due to the fact that in each group some lived as nomads and others did not.[119] Just as there were 'many Indian nations'

115. Hippocrates *Airs, Waters, Places* 13–17.

116. Herodotus *Histories* 3.101.

117. F. M. Snowden, *Before Color Prejudice: The Ancient View of Blacks* (Cambridge: Harvard University Press, 1983) 46; Herodotus *Histories* 7.7.

118. Hartog, *The Mirror of Herodotus*, 28; Herodotus *Histories* 2.2; 4.5.

119. Herodotus *Histories* 3.98–99, 4.18–20.

(εστι δε πολλα εθνεα Ινδοων), so too there were nomadic Scythians, sedentary Scythians, and even "Royal Scythians."[120] However, despite the differences among them, the Scythians remained a people ethnically distinct from those nearby: 'to the north dwell the Blackcloaks, who are of another and not of Scythian stock' (αλλο εθνος και ου Σκυθικον).

One of the more interesting features of Herodotus's ethnographic work is his attempt to describe regions beyond the periphery of Scythia, India, and Libya. His narration of Ethiopian culture mentions little about the regions beyond them—not even a confession of ignorance. In comparison to this, Herodotus seems rather uncomfortable describing the peripheral regions beyond Scythia, India, and Libya:

> As far as India, Asia is an inhabited land; but thereafter all to the east is desert, nor can any man say what kind of land is there. (4.40)

> These then are the most distant parts of the world in Asia and Libya. But concerning the farthest western parts of Europe I cannot speak with exactness. . . . (3.15)

> Above the Royal Scythians to the north dwell the Blackcloaks . . . and beyond the Blackcloaks the land is all marshes and uninhabited by men, so far as we know. (4.21)

> Aristeas . . . visited the Issedones [north and east of Scythia]; beyond these . . . dwell the one-eyed Arimaspians, beyond whom are the griffins that guard gold, and beyond these again the Hyperboreans, whose territory reaches to the sea. Except for the Hyperboreans, all these nations ever make war. . . . (4.13)

> In that country [beyond Libya] are the huge snakes and the lions, and the elephants and bears and asps, the horned asses, the dog-headed men and the headless that have their eyes in their breasts, as the Libyans say, and the wild men and women. . . . (4.191)

In these texts Herodotus seems quite aware that his quest for understanding faced formidable obstacles. If one agrees that he was indeed a storyteller as much as a historian, then it should come as no surprise that the paucity of his sources about these distant regions did not prevent him from offering rather lengthy descriptions of them. Because Herodotus lacked first-hand sources from these regions, it makes sense

120. The Royal Scythians represented a group that deemed all other Scythians as "their slaves." They were supposedly the "best" and "most in number" among the Scythian groups.

that his lengthy narrations about the peoples therein would reflect much more his own cultural expectations than any concrete realities. If this is so, then we should expect that his descriptions of peripheral peoples will display a certain rhetorical pattern. And this, as I will show, is precisely how the evidence unfolds.

The Rhetoric of "Otherness" in Herodotus

F. Hartog, whose work I have already mentioned, has thoroughly investigated the *Histories'* portrayal of foreign peoples, particularly the rhetorical patterns and rationale that guided Herdotus' descriptions of them. However, because his work was limited to Herodotus's description of the Scythians, there are certain patterns within the *Histories* that Hartog does not address. I am thinking at this point about Herodotus's propensity to tell us that peripheral peoples practice (a) cannibalism, (b) human sacrifice, (c) sexual perversion and promiscuity, (d) nomadism, and (e) strange cultic rites. In his descriptions of such practices, Herodotus tends to provide, as J. Z. Smith has noted, the "observer's vision without apparent analytical mediation."[121] My view is that this analytical silence is more of a rhetorical device than an early example of *epoché*. We are as much dismayed by Herodotus's seeming objectivity as we are aghast at the described cultural *faux pas*. When Herodotus writes that the Indians "have intercourse openly like cattle," he reveals implicitly his appraisal of Indian social mores, that they are the mores that one more readily associates with animals than with people. So it is hardly appropriate to begin our study of Herodotus with the notion that he tended to be "objective," especially in light of recent studies that argue for the strong influence his own identity exerted on his work.[122] And with these introductory comments out of the way, we can begin our discussion of Herodotus's ethnographic work, starting with the place of "cannibalism" in his history.

Of the Indian peoples, Herodotus writes that "when any of their countryfolk male or female are sick, a man's closest friends kill him . . . though he denies that he is sick, yet they will not believe him, but kill

---

121. J. Z. Smith, "Adde Parvum Parvo Magnus Acervus Erit," in *Map is Not Territory: Studies in the History of Religions* (Leiden: Brill, 1978) 247.

122. W. Burkert, "Herodot als Historiker fremder Religionen," in *Hérodote et les peuples non-grecs* (ed. G. Nenci and O. Reverdin; Entretiens sur l'antiquité classique, 35; Vandoeuvres-Genève: Hardt, 1990) 1–39; J. Gould, "Herodotus on Religion," in *Greek Historiography* (ed. S. Hornblower; Oxford: Clarendon, 1994) 91–106.

and eat him (3.99)." Likewise, when an Issodeone father dies, "all the nearest of kin bring beasts . . . and having killed these and cut up the flesh, they cut up also the dead father . . . and set out all the flesh mingled together for a feast (4.26)." The name of the *Androfagoi* ('man-eaters'), a people to the north of Scythia, is self-explanatory and provides an additional example of cannibalism among the groups that the *Histories* describes for us (4.106). These three groups—the Indians, Issodeones, and "Man-eaters"—share a common status as peripheral peoples, and it is not a coincidence that they are viewed as cannibals, while Assyria, Greece, Persia and Egypt are free of the practice. For obvious reasons, cannibalism is used in the *Histories* as a stereotyped characteristic of peripheral, uncivilized peoples. One might argue that Herodotus is only citing his sources and that he held no such stereotyped view of the periphery, but it seems rather clear that, whether from Herodotus or from his cultural milieu, there was a decided tendency in Greek thought to view marginal peoples in this way.

Within the broad scholarly pursuit that we call "History of Religions," it is a common observation that cannibalism is often closely related to human sacrifice, with both practices evoking a natural horror among "outsiders."[123] This close association is maintained in the *Histories*, which are as likely to portray marginal peoples as sacrificing humans as they are to point out that they also ate them. Herodotus writes of the Scythians, Getae, and Tauri peoples, respectively:

> Of all their enemies that they take alive, they sacrifice one man in every hundred, not according to their fashion of sacrificing sheep and goats, but differently. . . . They pour wine on the men's heads and cut their throats . . . they carry the blood up on the pile of sticks and pour it on the scimitar . . . they cut off all the slain men's right arms and hands and throw these into the air. . . .

> Once every five years they choose by lot one of their people and send him as a messenger to [the god] Salmoxis . . . and this is their manner of sending . . . three lances are held by men thereto appointed; others seize the messenger to Salmoxis by his hands and feet, and swing and hurl him aloft onto the spear-points. If he be killed by the cast, they believe that the god regards them with favor; but if he be not killed, they blame the messenger himself, deeming him a bad man, and send another messenger in place of him whom they blame.

123. D. Carrasco and K. A. Read, "Human Sacrifice," *ER* 6.515–23.

Among these, the Tauri have the following customs: all ship-wrecked men, and any Greeks whom they take in their sea-raiding, they sacrifice to the Virgin goddess . . . after the first rites of sacrifice, they smite the victim on the head with a club . . . they then throw down the body from the cliff whereon their temple stands, and place the head on a pole.[124]

When it is recognized that human sacrifice is, by definition, the ritual killing of a human being, then several of the above incidents of cannibalism may be added to these three examples of human sacrifice, creating a final list of Indians, Scythians, Issedones, Getae, and Tauri—all participants in the cult of human sacrifice—all peripheral peoples within Herodotus's conceptual model of the world. The core civilizations, represented by Persia, Egypt, and Greece, were quite excluded from this cultic activity (with the fleeting exception of Iphigenia) and are to be distinguished from the uncivilized peoples of the earth's extremities. Interestingly, several classical scholars have noted that in Greek thought cannibalism was also associated with the primeval period of human history.[125] This may indicate that, for Herodotus, the contemporary uncivilized peoples represented a "survival" from the primeval period.

In the *Histories*, uncivilized peoples practiced cannibalism and human sacrifice; they also practiced various forms of sexual perversion and promiscuity. Of the Agathyrsi and Nasamones, Herodotus writes, "Their intercourse with women is promiscuous," and of the Indians, Machlyes, and Auseans, he says that they "have intercourse openly like cattle." Gindane women proudly displayed anklets that marked the progress of their promiscuity (4.176). Similarly, the *Histories* tell us that Amazon women were prone to wander about so that young Scythian men might lay hold of them. When this occurred, "the woman made no resistance but suffered him to do his will . . . she signed with the hand that he should come on the next day to the same place."[126] So we see that Scythians were apt to commit rape, and the Amazons were

124. For these descriptions of the Scythians, Getae, and Tauri, see Herodotus *Histories* 4.62, 72; 4.93–94; 4.103.
125. S. Blundell, *The Origins of Civilization in Greek and Roman Thought* (London: Croom Helm, 1986) 186; W. K. C. Guthrie, *In the Beginning: Some Greek Views on the Origins of Life and the Early State of Man* (Ithaca: Cornell University Press, 1957) 95.
126. Herodotus *Histories* 3.101; 4.104, 113.

inclined to like it.[127] Generally speaking, the practices of these peripheral peoples were weighed against Greek mores and found wanting. Rape was a crime, but the Scythians committed the crime. Normal women struggle against a rapist, but the Amazons asked for more. Sexual intimacy was for the bedroom, but Indians performed the act in public view. From the perspective of Herodotus and his thought world, the peripheral peoples were quite barbarous in their sexual promiscuity, just as they were in their cannibalism and sacrificial cult.

Peripheral peoples are cannibals, practice human sacrifice, and participate in sexual promiscuity. They are also nomads. To the north, Scythia was partially nomadic, and the Massagetae, Budinin, and Man-eaters were nomads. To the south and west were found both Libyan and Ethiopian nomadic groups. In the east, some Indians were nomadic, and various groups (γενεα, αριστοι) on the Persian periphery— the Dai, Mardi, Dropici, and Sagartii—were also nomadic.[128] This mode of life was, of course, distinct from the settled life of Greek civilization and was associated with more primitive peoples. It is interesting that, among the four Scythian origin traditions Herodotus knew, it was the nomadic origin tradition that he preferred. It is probably not a coincidence that Herodotus viewed the Scythians both as the youngest of peoples and as nomadic in origin. This probably stemmed from his theoretical understanding that nomadism represented an early stage in the development of human civilization, a perspective that is not unlike what we saw in the Assyrian king-list tradition.

The final point to be made in this portion of my work concerns Herodotus's depiction of cultic rites and religion. Both W. Burkert and J. Gould have pointed out his tendency to focus on the cult as the primary expression of religion, as it was in Greece, so that in the *Histories* he frequently fails to appreciate the religious subtleties of his ethnographic subjects.[129] So after listing the deities that the Scythians acknowledged, Herodotus proceeded to point out that the Scythians generally avoided building shrines and altars and that they also eschewed libations and burnt offerings (4.59–60). I. M. Linforth recognized long

127. Hartog argues that this scene is "in no sense one of rape" because the Amazons do not resist. However, this reading of the text misses the point: the Scythians think it rape, but the Amazons enjoy it (F. Hartog, *The Mirror of Herodotus*, 221).

128. Ibid., 194.

129. Burkert, "Herodot als Historiker fremder Religionen," 4–5; Gould, "Herodotus on Religion," 98.

ago that the exceptional feature of the Scythian pantheon (and of all the "uncivilized" pantheons in the *Histories*) is that it included so few deities in comparison with the Greek pantheon.[130] In other words, Herodotus was chiefly concerned with pointing out the unusual characteristics of the non-Greek cults. This is why he tells us that the Hyperboreans sacrifice "wheat-straw" (4.35) and that the Libyans "cut the victim's ear off and throw it over the house" (4.188). So we see that in the *Histories*, the general rule was that the cult of the peripheral peoples differed markedly from standard Greek practice. In the event that this general rule did not hold, an explanation was required. For instance, although the city of Gelonus was situated in the midst of the Budini people and claimed by them, this did not square well with the fact that the Geloni followed Greek fashion in their images, altars, and festivals. Herodotus therefore tells us that the Geloni were, after all, Greeks:

> the Greeks call the Budini too Geloni; but this is wrong. . . . For the Geloni are by their origin Greeks, who left their trading ports to settle among the Budini. They speak a language half Greek and half Scythian.

In their religious life as well as in all other aspects of life, the peripheral peoples had proved themselves to be, at least in Herodotus's eyes, uncivilized. And when the cultic activities of these peripheral peoples paralleled the features of the more advanced cultures, as was the case with the Geloni, the explanation could only be that they originated in a more civilized context.

Aside from the features I have pointed out—cannibalism, human sacrifice, sexual promiscuity, nomadism, and cultic irregularity—the *Histories* are replete with descriptions of cultural "barbarism." For instance, the Indians and Budini, who are guilty of all of the vices above, are also vulgar in that they "eat raw flesh." The Scythians are similarly crude when they drink the blood of their war victims. As S. Blundell has noted, this reflects the Greek attitude that cooking was responsible "for the human race's rise from unruly cannibalism to their present condition of urban association."[131] Such descriptions of uncivilized barbarism stand in stark contrast to Herodotus's description of the

---

130. I. M. Linforth, "Greek Gods and Foreign Gods in Herodotus," *University of California Publications in Classical Philology* 9 (1926) 6–7.

131. Quoting from Athenaeus *Deipnos* 14.660–61. See also Blundell's related discussion in *The Origins of Civilization in Greece and Roman Thought*, 165–86.

quite civilized Egyptians, as illustrated by this quotation from the *Histories*:

> They are beyond measure religious, more than any other nation; and these are among their customs; They drink from cups of bronze, which they cleanse out daily; this is done not by some but by all. They are especially careful ever to wear newly-washed linen raiment. They practice circumcision for cleanliness' sake; for they set cleanliness above seemliness. . . . [With respect to the priests] sacred food is cooked for them, to each man is brought every day flesh of beeves and geese in great abundance.[132]

The Origins of Peoples in Herodotus

One of the more important components in a group identity answers the question of how and when the group originated. The *Histories'* most extensive inquiry into this question is found in Book 4 (4.1– 12), where Herodotus explores the various theories of Scythian origins. He identifies the sources of these four competing origin traditions as (1) the Scythians, (2) the Black Sea Greeks, (3) Aristeas of Proconnesus, and (4) an unnamed λογος. Given the problems that I have cited in my introduction to Herodotus, it becomes difficult to know whether these represent authentic sources or fabrications, and I must again caution that we are more apt to learn about the perspective of Herodotus than of any supposed Scythian sources. This is certainly the case with the Scythian account, which begins in a peculiar fashion.

According to the Scythians, says Herodotus, their forefather, Targitaus, was a son of Zeus. This is of course an unlikely claim for the non-Greek Scythians to make, although it is possible that here Herodotus has interpreted the chief Scythian deity as Zeus. But even if this was the case, it shows how quickly Herodotus resorted to representing foreigners in categories more in tune with his Greek identity.[133] The Scythian source claims that Targitaus fathered three sons—Lipoxaïs, Arpoxaïs, and Colaxaïs—who were in turn the forefathers of the four Scythian clans (γενος).[134] As F. Hartog has noted, the curiosity in this arrangement is that the youngest son, Colaxaïs, turned out

132. Herodotus *Histories* 2.37.
133. Despite my point here, G. Dumézil has argued that certain features of the story do reflect authentic Indo-European sources. See his *Romans de Scythi et d'allentour* (Bibliotheque historique; Paris: Payot, 1977) 172. It would seem that here, as elsewhere, Herodotus's work is a combination of authentic traditions and Greek ideology.
134. This three-son pattern is common in both Greek and Israelite literature.

to be the forefather of the royal clan of Paralatae.[135] As we might expect, this cannot have happened under the usual circumstances and was instead prompted by a divine choice of Colaxaïs over his brothers. The will of the gods was made known by the fact that Colaxaïs alone was permitted to take hold of the golden implements that "fell down from the sky." This divine preference for the younger son over the older ones is a motif found elsewhere in Herodotus (cf. 4.10, 8.137) and reminds us of the Jacob/Esau story and of other traditions in the Hebrew Bible. As I have said, it is difficult to know where the Scythian source ends and Herodotus begins in this tradition, but whatever we may make of it, Herodotus claimed not to believe it: εμοι μεν ου πιστα λεγοντες (4.5). But this should not divert our attention from the fact that genealogical traditions played an important role in the work of Herodotus.

The second origin tradition, told by Greeks living near the Black Sea (4.8–10), claimed that Scythian origins should be sought in the person of Heracles, a claim not so distant from the Scythian claim when it is remembered that Heracles was a son of Zeus. If we assume that there is some truth behind the Scythian tradition, then we might construe this as a Greek effort to weaken the Scythian pedigree by replacing Zeus with Heracles. Moreover, this tradition is much less flattering than the first one. According to this tradition, Heracles had intercourse with a creature, "half damsel and half serpent," in return for information about his missing livestock. Once again, three sons resulted from this union, and the youngest, Scythes, became the eponymous ancestor of the settled Scythians. The two older brothers became the forefathers of the nomadic Scythian groups. Despite the peculiarities of this origin tradition, it shares several things in common with the Scythian version, no doubt a result of the Greek tendency to introduce their own mythology into regions where they settled.[136] First, in both cases the youngest son's position superseded that of his older brothers because of divine intervention, in this story by the intervention of semidivine Heracles. Second, in both traditions an important component of identity was ethnic sentiment, since the claim in each case was that the Scythians originated from a common genealogical stock. But

135. Hartog, *Mirror of Herodotus*, 21.
136. W. W. How and J. Wells, *A Commentary on Herodotus* (reprint; 2 vols.; Oxford: Oxford University Press, 1989) 305.

perhaps most important is that both traditions paint the Scythians as autochthons and therefore as having a unique claim to their homeland. Taken together, these similarities suggest that we are perhaps dealing with a somewhat distorted Scythian story about their own origins followed by a Greek reworking of the same by the Black Sea Greeks. But we are really in no position to test out this theory.

At this point we should distinguish among several aspects of kinship that are reflected in these first two Scythian origins traditions. In the first place, both of the traditions place an emphasis upon genealogical pedigree, so that the people of Scythia are legitimated by their divine (Zeus) and semidivine (Heracles) origins.[137] As is well known, this kind of genealogical interest is widely attested in many cultures, Mesopotamia and Egypt being no exceptions.[138] However, while in Mesopotamia and Egypt this pedigree was used primarily to validate royalty and the priesthood, in the traditions cited by Herodotus the pedigree was extended to the people as a whole. This brings us to a second kind of kinship that is closely connected with ethnicity. In this case kinship is used by etic observers (outsiders) to provide an ethnographic explanation for both the origins of other cultural entities and also for the intercultural relationships that characterize those groups. So, for instance, from the Greek source we learn not only that the people of Scythia originated as the sons of Scythus but also that the close relations between these sedentary Scythians and the nomadic groups nearby stem from their common connection with Heracles. As the comparative materials show, this etic use of genealogy appears primarily when the "scholars" of a given (usually literate) culture contemplate and speculate about the origins and histories of other peoples.[139] We do not want to suggest that this kind of etic genealogical activity is found only among literate cultures, as our Tiv example in chapter 1 shows (p. 20). But in the case of Greece we have numerous and lengthy literary sources that illustrate a strong propensity to use ethnic kinship to explain both Greek and non-Greek origins.[140]

---

137. For a discussion of genealogical pedigree, see B. A. Van Groningen, *In the Grip of the Past: Essay on an Aspect of Greek Thought* (Leiden: Brill, 1953) 47–61.

138. R. R. Wilson, *Genealogy and History in the Biblical World* (YNER 7; New Haven: Yale University Press, 1977) 54–55, 132–35.

139. Ibid., 18–55; West, *The Hesiodic Catalogue of Women*, 11–30.

140. Note the use of "Graecus" as the forefather of Greece in the *Catalogue of Women*, 1–3.

As C. W. Fornara has pointed out, the kind of ethnographic interest that we see in Herodotus is invigorated by specific historical contexts, particularly when, as in the case of archaic and classical Greece, a culture is experiencing frequent contacts with other peoples through imperial expansion or increasing trade.[141] This means that serious ethnographic literature is the product of several important cultural and historical factors which make the number of contexts that can give rise to it somewhat limited. It is profitable to ask why ethnographic work prospered in Greece but not in the Assyrian sources that we have examined. In a few isolated cases, the Assyrian materials do exhibit a degree of scholarly ethnographic interest. Therefore we would be amiss, I think, to believe that Assyrians were less "inquisitive" than the Greeks. It is perhaps more correct for us to postulate that, because much of Assyria's scribal activity took place in a monarchic context, the monarchic concerns precluded the development of a full-blown ethnographic genre in Mesopotamia. This is not, of course, because the Assyrians produced only annalistic pieces. Rather, it stems from the fact that, although the annals were the most appropriate place to deal with Assyria's new imperial subjects, their thematic preference for royal achievement left no room for ethnography. On the other hand, the historiographic products of Greek literary activity were almost certainly intended, at least in the case of Herodotus, for the consumption of the "common folk," and this meant that the thematic choices of Herodotus were constrained only a little. There can be little doubt that this is what permitted his numerous ethnographic digressions.

Although the ethnographic genre came to the fore only in the fifth century B.C.E., I have already pointed out that Greek interest in ethnography and genealogy was much older than this and harked back to the eighth-century influences of Hesiod and Homer.[142]

The remaining Scythian origin traditions are quite different from these first two, which were primarily genealogical. According to Aristeas of Procannesus, says Herodotus, Scythian origins stemmed from a forced migration. The Arimaspians displaced the Issedones, who in turn displaced the Scythians, so that the Scythians forced the Cimmerians out of their homeland. Although Herodotus did not think much

141. Fornara, *The Nature of History in Ancient Greece and Rome*, 12–16.

142. Ibid. Homer reveals an interest in foreign lands, while the Hesiodic corpus, particularly in the *Catalogue of Women*, concerns itself with genealogies, forefather traditions, and the like.

of this migration tradition, he tells us that "there is yet another tale, to the tradition whereof I myself do especially incline (4.11)." This tradition is also a migration tradition and goes as follows. The Scythians were a nomadic people who inhabited Asia. When pressed in war by the Massagetae, the Scythians migrated across the river Araxes and displaced the Cimmerians. Several lines of evidence seem to have contributed to Herodotus's preference for this tradition over the others. First, Herodotus noted the presence of certain geographical and cultural features in the Scythian territory that bore the name Cimmeria. This reveals that the tradition is clearly etiological and seeks to explain in one fell swoop both the presence of the Scythians and the supposed Cimmerian features in the same region. Second, while Herodotus identified his sources for the other origin traditions as either Greek or foreign, of this last tradition he says, "I have now related this other tale, which is told alike by Greeks (Ελλήνων) and foreigners (Βαρβάρων) (4.12)." Herodotus seems to have preferred this origin tradition because it was derived from opposing sources, and although this seems a quite sensible conclusion, we have already pointed out that Herodotus has confirmed an impossible tale on the basis of opposing Persian and Egyptian sources (see Herodotus *Histories* 3.12 and above, pp. 58–60). In that case, and perhaps here as well, the best explanation may be the invention of sources rather than the use of authentic source traditions. But putting aside the question of the tradition's authenticity, it is important to recognize that the migration tradition described here should be distinguished from another type of migration that is often found in the Greek sources. Although in this story the Scythian migration was forced by the Issedones and Massagetae, the other type of tradition is an autonomous migration. The autonomous migration traditions are associated with the origins of higher cultures, as in the case of the Phoenicians, who settled in their Levantine homeland after an overseas migration (*Histories* 1.1). Similar migration traditions are a common element in the classical literary traditions and also in the biblical sources.[143]

In his discussion of Scythian origins, Herodotus considered two different types of origin traditions: genealogical origin traditions and migration traditions. While the genealogical tradition is readily identified

143. See J. Van Seters, *Prologue to History* (Louisville: Westminster/John Knox, 1992) 211–12.

with ethnic sentiments, it seems quite probable that the migration traditions are equally ethnic in scope, since they presume the same group of Scythian people. But more specifically, both types of origin traditions were part of a larger attempt to provide ethnographic data to the reader, albeit couched in the storytelling rhetoric of Herodotus, and similar kinds of literary activity were characteristic of Greek literature well before the *Histories*. Although there are some similarities between these Greek traditions and the Old Babylonian evidence that we have examined, the Greek material contrasts sharply with our Neo-Assyrian sources, which leave questions of ethnography and ethnic genealogy largely unexplored.

Defensive Military Leagues in Herodotus

Although we have raised serious questions about the amphictyonic hypothesis for early Israel's origins, the Greek amphictyonies nevertheless share some similarities with the biblical account of early Israelite history. Two texts from the *Histories* are suitable representatives of this "league" tradition, one an effort to repel Persian invaders and the other, more akin to the amphictyonies, to protect a newly established cult shrine. The texts read as follows:

> The Scythians, reckoning that they were not able by themselves to repel Darius's army in open warfare, sent messengers to their neighbours, whose kings had already met and were taking counsel, knowing that a great army was marching against them. Those that had so met were the kings of Tauri, Agathyrsi, Neuri, Man-eaters, Black-cloacks, Geloni, Budini, and Sauromatae. (4.102)

> . . . but the twelve cities aforesaid glorified in this name [Ionian], and founded a holy place (iron) for themselves which they called the Panionion, and agreed among them to allow no other Ionians to use it. (1.143)

With respect to comparative issues, the most relevant feature of these texts is numerological. A total of ten groups joined the anti-Persian coalition and twelve cities participated in the protection of the holy site.[144] These two numbers are often associated with social and mili-

---

144. Fehling notes that both *ten* and *twelve* are commonly used by Herodotus. For his discussion of numerology in the *Histories*, see *Die Quellenangaben bei Herodot*, 155–67.

tary organizations in the Greek sources, the most familiar example being the twelve-member religious league from sixth-century Delphi.[145] In the anti-Persian coalition, Herodotus uses this "standard" numbering scheme even when describing the non-Greek Scythians, Tauri, and others. And if the question occurs to us why the Ionian league should choose to include only twelve cities, it also occurred to Herodotus. He suggested that the Ionians would admit no more cities because "there were twelve divisions of them when they dwelt in Peloponnesus, just as there are twelve divisions of the Achaeans who drove the Ionians out."[146] The Ionian league was essentially religious, but the name of its cult site, Panionion (Πανιωνιον 'all Ionia'), shows that a central purpose of the arrangement was to promote Ionian unity. These traditions have many affinities with the traditions in the Hebrew Bible, and they will be discussed in the following chapter. Although we must stress that early Israel was probably not an amphictyony, it remains possible that the similarities between the Greek and Israelite traditions are not coincidental.

The features that we have outlined in this section of our study include only selected aspects of the complex thought-world reflected in the various Greek sources, and for every point that we have made here, there is assuredly a source one might adduce that would raise questions about it in some way. Nevertheless, I believe that this sketch of the properties and emphases in the *Histories* of Herodotus, along with our examination of earlier Greek materials, suitably represents some of the key trajectories in ancient Greek thought about ethnicity. In my view, it is obvious that, with respect to ethnicity, the Greek (and Old Babylonian) materials stand much closer to those in the Hebrew Bible than do the sources from Neo-Assyria.

Ethnicity and Identity in Egypt

The contribution of the Egyptian sources to this study are perhaps less important than one might at first suppose because, during the Egyptian late period, the period that coincides with much of Israel's

---

145. For bibliography on the Greek amphictyonies, see above, p. 7 n. 21. Another example of the ten-tribe organization scheme is found in Kleisthenes' Athenian reforms at the end of the sixth century B.C.E. See O. Murray, *Early Greece*, 275.

146. Herodotus *Histories* 1.145.

biblical literary activity, Egypt's political and social climate was troubled.[147] The era of Egypt's greatest influence on Palestine was well before most of the biblical materials made their appearance, so one should expect less direct Egyptian influence than from either Assyria or Babylon. In fact, the Egyptian presence in the biblical text, excepting the Exodus event, is very much in the background when compared to the presence of the Mesopotamian states. Nonetheless, it is quite true that Egypt maintained a continuing and influential presence in Palestine for most of the region's history, so much so that A. Mazar has been able to demonstrate a quite direct correlation between Egyptian success and the undulating rise and fall of Palestinian civilization.[148] However, our discussion of Egyptian imperialism in Palestine must keep in mind the point, ably brought out by P. J. Frandsen, that Egyptian policy was not uniform in every theater of its influence. While the Egyptians waged a very successful campaign to exert cultural influence in Nubian regions, its expansion in Syria–Palestine was devoted more specifically to economic and political issues.[149]

For the most part, this study of the Egyptian sources will focus on the earlier historical periods, when Egyptian influence in Palestine was more pronounced. Our first task is an examination of the well-known Middle Kingdom story about Sinuhe. After this we will study representative texts from the New Kingdom (especially those of Thutmose III) and also from later royal inscriptions that bring us relatively close to the period in which the first Israelite literary prophets worked. We will complete our review of the Egyptian sources with a few brief comments about the Persian and Hellenistic periods, first because these periods represent a peripheral sociological experience for the Egyptians, and second, because the comments will demonstrate that a sense of continuity existed between earlier Egyptian thought and the thought of the Persian and Ptolemaic periods. To summarize this in another

---

147. I regret that repeated attempts to acquire a copy of A. Loprieno's volume, obviously relevant to this study, have failed. Perhaps the reader will have more success. See *Topos und Mimesis: zum Ausländer in der ägyptischen Literatur* (Ägyptologische Abhandlungen 48; Wiesbaden: Harrassowitz, 1988).

148. Mazar, *Archaeology of the Land of the Bible: 10,000–586 B.C.E.* (New York: Doubleday, 1992). See also the historical survey of D. B. Redford, *Egypt, Canaan, and Israel in Ancient Times* (Princeton: Princeton University Press, 1992).

149. P. J. Frandsen, "Egyptian Imperialism," in *Power and Propaganda: A Symposium on Ancient Empires* (ed. M. T. Larsen; Mesopotamia 7; Copenhagen: Akademisk, 1979) 167–90.

way, in this section I hope to clarify early Egyptian perspectives on identity via the tale of Sinuhe and then to show that, in subsequent periods, this Egyptian notion of identity was rather stable, despite its historical permutations.

The Story of Sinuhe

Whether intentional or incidental to the story, the tale of *Sinuhe* provides one of the better descriptions of Egyptian attitudes and perspectives toward the Asian cultures, and this necessarily has importance for the whole question of Egyptian identity.[150] Although a fair bit of work has been done on the various texts and a number of translations are available including Koch's relatively new critical edition,[151] with the exception of a few recent comments from J. Baines, little has been done to explore the issue of Egyptian identity as revealed in *Sinuhe*.[152] The value of the story for this purpose is naturally tied to the question of genre, and there are at least three major schools of thought about this. For those who embrace a rather straightforward reading of the text, it is either a genuine autobiographical text about Sinuhe himself[153] or a piece of political propaganda in support of Senwosret I.[154] For others it is to be viewed primarily as a piece of narrative fiction whose ultimate aims are quite beyond the ostensible context of the story, and this view is preferable to me for several reasons.

150. My discussion is based on Lichtheim's translation, and the references to *Sinuhe* will utilize her line numbers (M. Lichtheim, *Ancient Egyptian Literature* [3 vols.; Berkeley: University of California, 1973–80] 1.222–35). For the text, see R. Koch, *Die Erzählung des Sinuhe* (Bibliotheca Aegyptiaca 17; Brussels: Fondation Égyptologique Reine Élisabeth, 1990); and also A. M. Blackman, *Middle Egyptian Stories: Part I* (Bibliotheca Aegyptiaca 2; Brussels: Fondation Égyptologique Reine Élisabeth, 1932).

151. Koch, *Die Erzählung des Sinuhe.*

152. The study of Baines is of limited use here because his definition of ethnicity does not feature kinship, as does mine: "Contextualizing Egyptian Representations of Society and Ethnicity," in *The Study of the Ancient Near East in the Twenty-First Century: The William Foxwell Albright Centennial Conference* (ed. J. S. Cooper and G. M. Schwartz; Winona Lake, Ind.: Eisenbrauns, 1996) 355–56.

153. See, for instance, J. W. B. Barnes, "Sinuhe's Message to the King: A Reply to a Recent Article," *JEA* 53 (1967) 6–14.

154. G. Posener, *Littérature et politique dans l'Égypte de la XIIe dynastie* (Bibliothèque de l'École des Hautes Études 307; Paris: Champion, 1956) 87–115. It might also be suggested that *Sinuhe* represents propaganda for the "established order" of ancient Egypt, but as Baines has pointed out, a similar case can be made for most of Egypt's literature (J. Baines, "Interpreting *Sinuhe*," *JEA* 68 [1982] 38).

In the first place, the focus of the narrative is not so much Sinuhe as it is the tragic situation of an Egyptian who is "forced" to leave his homeland and culture, with special emphasis on the problem of his exile from society and his reintegration to it. Of course, as the story tells us, this happened only because Sinuhe has misunderstood the situation at home and therefore acted rather brashly, which is all the more tragic. The fact that years of Asiatic assimilation can be expunged by a wash and a change of clothes (as we will discuss below) certainly points to the quite fictive character of the story. So we are not dealing with an autobiography but with a fictive narrative that draws upon the features of Egyptian funerary autobiographies.[155]

Moreover, we are probably not dealing with political propaganda. Although the importance of the king (and kingship) plays a considerable role in the framework of the piece, one can hardly reduce the aims of its narrative core to a political agenda. If this were its aim, we should have expected much more from both the departure narrative and the account of Sinuhe's return, for these are the points at which the king could play the most prominent role. But the narrative core of the story is Sinuhe's conquest of a difficult Asian territory, and the purpose behind this must be thematically associated with the superiority of Egyptian identity (of which kingship is an important element) rather than with dynastic rule itself. Furthermore, the fact that the story was probably composed after the death of the kings involved suggests that its function was not overtly political.[156] Consequently, in spite of any political overtones, we should deal with the story as a literary piece composed for other purposes, and I would propose that the primary purpose was to promote the value of Egyptian identity.

If the story is to exalt Egyptian identity, it must do so by rhetorically contrasting Egyptian and foreign identities, and in this comparative role, the Asiatics serve as the literary foil in our story. The Asiatics

---

155. Baines's study of *Sinuhe* identifies a number of points at which the story departs from the formal character of a funerary autobiography. First, its introduction includes the death of Ammanemes I. Second, the narrative is not about an achieved career recounted in a "timeless fashion," but rather, it ends with a "discreet allusion" to the death of Sinuhe. Third, the extended narrative character is much more complex and introspective than the standard funerary texts. Other examples could be mentioned (ibid., 31–44).

156. Baines, "Contextualizing Egyptian Representations of Society and Ethnicity," 355.

of *Sinuhe* are quite the antithesis of Egyptian identity, as reflected in these comments from the protagonist himself:

> I do not know what brought me to this country; it is as if planned by god. As if a Delta-man saw himself in Yebu, a marsh-man in Nubia.
>
> No Asiatic makes friends with a Delta-man. And what would make papyrus cleave to the mountain?[157]

The rhetoric of the text focuses on the geographical and physical features of the foreign lands and uses them to represent the cultural distance the separates Egyptians from Asiatics. Egyptians (in this case "marsh-men") live in the marshes of the Delta while Asiatics ("barbarians") live in the mountains.[158] And although the bedouin *Lebensart* had little in common with the settled highlanders, in the rhetoric of *Sinuhe* both groups become Asiatics (a pattern reminiscent of the Assyrian tendency to paint all Westerners with "Hittite" colors). The rift between Egyptians and Asiatics could be expressed in no better terms than in the words of Sinuhe, that "no Asiatic makes friends with a Delta-man." This is a gap that only the narrative would be able to cross.

Despite the rhetorical and cultural distance, in the story nothing is more certain than the fact that the Egyptian Sinuhe becomes an Asiatic nomad and sandfarer.[159] He marries an Asiatic and begets Asiatic children. He rules his own tribe (*whyt*), as do his sons after him.[160] He commands Asiatic troops and "wins the heart" of his fellow Asiatics. Finally, when his victory over the native champion of Retenu is realized, Sinuhe becomes the most powerful force in the Asiatic theater.[161] So the narrative is not in the least content with the idea that an Egyptian merely "survived" a difficult Asiatic experience, nor is it content with the notion that Sinuhe was nothing more than an Asiatic peer.

---

157. *Sinuhe*, 40–45, 120–25. J. L. Foster properly translates *Yebu* as 'Elephantine'. Despite the fact that neither Elephantine or Nubia are in Asia, they represent foreign lands and suitably make the point that an Egyptian more properly belongs in an Egyptian environment (see Foster, *Thought Couplets in the Tale of Sinuhe* [Berlin: Peter Lang, 1993] 43).

158. Here the Egyptian term is the more general *pdtyw* 'barbarian, foreigner'.

159. In fact, G. Maspero has argued that Sinuhe is a play on the word Simaḥi ('son of the North'), because he had resided for a long time in the country situated to the north of Egypt (see his *Les Mémoires de Sinouhit* [Cairo: Institut Français d'Archéologie Orientale, 1908] 154).

160. I will discuss the use of the term *whyt* below.

161. Foster, *Thought Couplets in The Tale of Sinuhe*, 119.

Only when Sinuhe became the ruler of his foreign hosts did he become quite convinced that the angry god who made him an Asiatic would restore him to his Egyptian homeland, or, to put it another way, Sinuhe's stay in Asia ends when the superior character of Egyptian identity is illustrated by his life success. His victory is essential because, as Baines has put it, "Sinuhe stood for Egyptians as a whole."[162]

The choice to look homeward at this high point in the narrative is an important one, for it reaffirms the notion that a modest position in Egypt is better than an exalted one in Asia.[163] This perspective is reinforced, I think, by the narrative treatment of Sinuhe's departure from his tribal home. Although we want to believe that he wrestled with powerful affections for his Asiatic family, the curt description says, "I was allowed to spend one more day in Yaa, handing over my possessions to my children." So Sinuhe's cultural identity as an Egyptian is much stronger than the natural kinship ties that he shares with the Asiatics. Egypt is his home.

The affections of Sinuhe's heart do not mask his Asiatic appearance, as is given dramatic force in the response of the royal ladies to his arrival in Egypt:

> "Here is Sinuhe, come as an Asiatic, a product of nomads!" She [the queen] uttered a very great cry, and the royal daughters shrieked all together. They said to his majesty: "Is it really he, O king, our lord?"

Initially the "victorious" Sinuhe was nothing more than an object of pity. There seems to be some tension here because, while we get the impression that the Asiatics were uncouth, sand-covered nomads in Egyptian eyes, and while Sinuhe's hymn praises the king as the smiter of Asiatics, the story has cast the Asiatic friends of Sinuhe in a rather positive light. We should remember that the story was composed prior to the Hyksos experience, after which Egypt's view of Asia became increasingly suspicious, even to a neurotic degree. But in our story there is room for two camps of Asiatics, those who supported Egyptian rule (and befriended Sinuhe) and those who resisted Egyptian rule (and were defeated by him). So we are not dealing with strong antipathies toward Asiatics but with strong antipathies toward *rebellious* Asiatics.

At any rate, to our narrator even friendly Asiatics are quite inferior to Sinuhe's Egyptian roots, and so his Asiatic status has to be set aright:

162. Baines, "Interpreting *Sinuhe*," 37.
163. Ibid.

> I left the audience-hall. . . . We went through the great portals, and I was put in the house of a prince. In it were luxuries: a bathroom and mirrors. In it were riches from the treasury; clothes of royal linen, myrrh and the choice perfume of the king and of his favorite courtiers were in every room. Every servant was at his task. Years were removed from my body. I was shaved; my hair was combed. Thus was my squalor returned to the foreign land, my dress to the Sand-farers. I was clothed in fine linen; I was anointed with fine oil. I slept on a bed. I had returned the sand to those who dwell in it, the tree-oil to those who grease themselves with it.

Here the narrative makes too easy a process that would have been, in genuine circumstances, more difficult. Although our protagonist appears to have assimilated to Asiatic culture, which would be necessary for marrying and rearing children, the narrative treats this foreign experience in the most superficial way. The markers of Egyptian identity are cleanliness and refinement, and these are easily reacquired. But above everything else, reintegration into Egyptian society required the king's embrace.

The importance of kingship and of the king's rule in foreign lands is evident even in the core narrative about Sinuhe's stay in Asia. Despite the good-natured portrayal of Sinuhe's Asiatic friends, Asia was nonetheless a region of foes and a domain to be conquered. He speaks of the "walls of the ruler," made to "repel the Asiatics and to crush the Sand-farers." Likewise in his praise of the king, Sinuhe says that Pharaoh is "the enlarger of frontiers . . . made to smite the Asiatics and tread on Sand-farers!" This notion of foreign conquest is not just discursive but is also acted out by our protagonist:

> Every hill tribe against which I marched I vanquished, so that it was driven from the pasture of its wells. I plundered its cattle, carried off its families, seized their food, and killed people by my strong arm, by my bow, by my movements and my skillful plans.

In the end, Sinuhe was an Egyptian "vizier" who conquered Asia, taking territory, booty, and captives in the process. Such was the standard imperial practice among Middle Kingdom pharaohs, who consistently employed "epithets constructed around claimed victories over Asiatics."[164] It is this view of Asia that finally emerged when Sinuhe said, despite his Asian family and people, that Retenu belonged to the

---

164. Redford, *Egypt, Canaan and Israel in Ancient Times*, 77, 71–97.

king "like his dogs." Similarly, Senwosret I was extolled as the "throat-slitter of them that are in Asia." For Middle Kingdom Egyptians, Asia represented a peripheral region marked for territorial expansion and conquest, and it was the king who led the conquest. Assyrian superiority was secured by the god Assur and by his *šangû*, the king; Egyptian superiority rested with the god Horus, who was the king.

While it appears that the tale of *Sinuhe* tells us a good bit about Egyptian identity, it reflects a somewhat hazy view of Asian social organization, a circumstance that is easily explained. First, the writer of *Sinuhe* may have been much less aware of Asian society than seems to be indicated by the text. A. H. Gardiner has pointed out that in the tale, Sinuhe departed through the desert and arrived by land-route to the one place familiar to Egyptian seafarers: Byblos.[165] What of Lachish, Gezer, and Megiddo? And why run to the city where he is most likely to be found?[166] Actually, the story reflects much more familiarity with nomadic Asian groups on Egypt's immediate periphery than it does with conditions in northern Syria. Even in this view, there are points of confusion. Why was Sinuhe sometimes portrayed as an Asiatic bedouin nomad and, at other times, depicted as a mountain-dwelling, landed fellow with figs, grapes, wine, honey, and oil?[167] In light of these facts, the reference to Byblos is more likely a literary device. I must say, along with Gardiner, that I am skeptical that the writer was very familiar with the Asian regions to the north and east. Sinuhe's Asiatic identity is best understood as the eclectic construction of a scribe who combined a number of disjointed impressions into one cultural entity.

Nevertheless, whether accurate or not, the tale does present a rather consistent picture of Asian social organization. Whether speaking of "Asiatics," "Men of Retenu," or "Sand-farers," *Sinuhe* customarily tells us that these groups were composed of smaller social units, *whyt*, and this has traditionally been translated by the term 'tribe'. There is,

---

165. The presence of "Byblos" in the original text has been debated. G. Maspero has argued that the Berlin Papyrus (B) of Sinuhe is superior to the Ramesseum Papyrus (R), and B appears to read *Kpni* rather than *Kpnj* (= Byblos), as in R. However, in all other cases *Sinuhe* refers to quite familiar place-names, and the reading *Kpni* does not correspond to this pattern of familiarity. Furthermore, Gardiner has shown that R is superior to B both textually and orthographically. See Maspero, *Les Mémoires de Sinouhit*, xlii–xliii; A. H. Gardiner, *Notes on the Story of Sinuhe* (Paris: Champion, 1916) 21–22.

166. Ibid., 167.

167. See *Sinuhe*, 75–85.

of course, an on-going debate about the use of anthropological terms like 'tribe', the most common objection being that such a term cannot possibly describe the many varied sociological and cultural contexts to which it is applied.[168] On the other hand, it seems to me that J. W. Rogerson is quite right when he points out that in English the word *tribe* has, from the outset, "designated groups of people whose social organization was not known." It seems useless to criticize a term as "imprecise" when its semantic purpose turns out to be imprecision. This problem is not, of course, limited to English. The meanings of מטה and שבט in Hebrew, φυλη in Greek, and *whyt* in Egyptian are equally obscure and for the same reasons. In each case, the terms could be applied to social organizations about which the authors had quite limited knowledge. Anthropological terms such as *tribe* readily appear when literate cultures attempt to describe little-understood social phenomena within other cultures or, as was the case in Israel and Greece, when they attempt to describe their remote history. So it stands to reason that we may find it difficult to clarify the tale's impression of these 'tribes', an exercise that we will nevertheless undertake.

First, we can say that in each case the tribal units were led by a single individual variously represented in the literature as "chief," "sheik," "prince," or "ruler." There seems to be a degree of precision here, since the nomadic *mtn* ('sheik'?) who befriends Sinuhe rules one tribe, while the 'princes' of Retenu, both the friend of Sinuhe and his chief antagonist, are consistently identified as rulers over groups of tribes. The Egyptian perception of Asian social organization would therefore seem to include a two-tiered understanding of Asian authority structures: tribes ruled by "sheiks" and groups of tribes ruled by 'princes'. However, even if this is an accurate assessment of the tale's perspective, it is an Egyptian model of Asian society that probably fails to do justice to the sociological complexities that existed there.

Because the open-ended notion of *tribe* is commonly associated with ethnic sentiments, it is natural to ask whether the evidence from Sinuhe reflects an ethnic understanding of Asian tribal organization. Sinuhe's hasty rise to tribal leadership in this foreign context would seem to argue against such an ethnic understanding of identity, since it is difficult to imagine an ethnic social modality that would so easily

168. For a summary of the debate, see J. W. Rogerson, *Anthropology and the Old Testament* (Growing Points in Theology; Atlanta: John Knox, 1979) 86–101.

accept the authority of a foreigner. But we are dealing with a fictive document, and there are several features in the text that make kinship, and with it perhaps ethnicity, an important concept in the story's view of Asiatic identity. Both Sinuhe and his sons become leaders of their own tribes, and Sinuhe's departure from Asia reads as follows:

> I was allowed to spend one more day in Yaa, handing over my possessions to my children, my eldest son taking charge of my tribe; all of my possessions became his—my serfs, my herds, my fruit, my fruit trees.[169]

Here we have Asiatic social modalities that were controlled by powerful overlords who perpetuated their family rule along kinship lines. Although in certain respects this stands close to pharaonic notions of royal succession and inheritance, the fact that each of Sinuhe's sons became the "master of his tribe" suggests a segmented (as opposed to a linear) structure. This seems to indicate that the Egyptians fully appreciated the important role of kinship in tribal Asiatic societies (and the reader will recall that the comparative ethnographic data outlined in chapter 1 demonstrates the close connection between kinship and ethnicity).

The ongoing popularity of the story of *Sinuhe*, which comes to us from texts as late as the first millennium, suggests that the Egyptian view of Asiatics found therein probably outlasted the Middle Kingdom. As is well known, this negative view of Asiatics intensified markedly during the Hyksos experience that followed the Middle Kingdom's decline, as seen in this famous quote from Kamose (1550–1524 B.C.E.), founder of the 18th Dynasty:

> Let me understand what this strength of mine is for! (One) prince is in Avaris, another in Ethiopia, and (here) I sit associated with an Asiatic and a Negro! . . . My wish is to save Egypt and to smite the Asiatics!

The "Asiatic" mentioned here is, of course, the last of the Hyksos rulers in Egypt.[170] For nearly a century the Egyptians had suffered under foreign rule and were now on the verge of ending it. Kamose found it a noble task to restore self-rule and also to confront the Nubian threat to the south, thus bringing an end to Egypt's first "peripheral" experience. Although it is sometimes contended by ethnicity scholars that

169. *Sinuhe*, 235–40.
170. See Redford, *Egypt, Canaan, and Israel in Ancient Times*, 98–122.

such a core-periphery situation will create ethnic sentiments within the affected peripheral population, the evidence shows that this did not occur among the Egyptians in response to the Hyksos experience. However, as the New Kingdom sources show, the nonethnic boundaries that defined Egyptian identity intensified markedly after the Hyksos experience, and antipathy toward Asiatics, Nubians, and all foreigners increased proportionally.

Egyptian Identity during the Time of Thutmose III and Afterward

In turning to Thutmose III, we pass from the Middle Kingdom through the Hyksos Intermediate period to the imperial epoch of Egyptian history. Although prior to this period Egypt had engaged in occasional military operations to the north and east, as J. A. Wilson has pointed out, the Hyksos experience permanently changed the disposition of Egypt toward this northern periphery.

> The old placid introspection and concentration on matters within the Nile Valley had been replaced by a vision of effective frontiers far away in Asia and Africa. It was no longer enough to exhibit to foreign countries the superiority of Egyptian culture and thus to harvest a favorable trade. These foreigners were no longer subjects to be patronized for their own good and for the good of Egypt; they had shown themselves to be "rebellious." Pharaoh must take the time to teach them effective lessons of discipline in their own lands.[171]

The inscriptions of Thutmose III (1479–1425 B.C.E.) are suitable representatives of this new strategy which, despite its virulent military tone, shared a good deal of continuity with Middle Kingdom views of the Asian perimeter. The perspective of Thutmose III and the quite thorough sources he has left us may be summarized in two quotations from his inscriptions: "to slay the countries of the wretched Retenu," and "to extend the frontiers of Egypt."[172] During the Middle Kingdom and intermediate period, and now during the New Kingdom, the Egyptians viewed Asiatics as inferior peoples suited for domination. This sense of continuity should not obscure the obvious effects of the

171. J. A. Wilson, *The Culture of Ancient Egypt* (Chicago: University of Chicago Press, 1965) 167. Cf. A. B. Knapp, *The History and Culture of Ancient Western Asia and Egypt* (Chicago: Dorsey, 1988) 171; Redford, *Egypt, Canaan and Israel in Ancient Times*, 129.

172. *ANET* 234–35.

foreign Intermediate period, however, because the New Kingdom texts feature a more heated rhetoric toward the "wretched" targets of imperial ambition. As Thutmose's Karnak inscription tells us, not only Asiatics, but the Shasu "border people," "Nubians," "easterners," "westerners," "highlanders," and "lowlanders"—all peripheral peoples—were the objects of Egyptian wrath.[173] We can see that the ideological boundaries that separated Egypt from its peripheral peoples intensified markedly after the Middle Kingdom period. For the *Tale of Sinuhe*, these boundaries were represented primarily by an attitude of cultural disdain and comparative superiority. In these New Kingdom texts, however, cultural disdain has been replaced by an active and aggressive policy of military annihilation and domination.

While Assyrian successes caused them to view the "Hittites" as contemptible, it was Egypt's defeat by the Hyksos that engendered their hated for "Asiatics." Despite the different circumstances that caused the intensification of both Assyrian and Egyptian identities as distinct from their peripheral territories, there are two notable similarities between the national policies that arose in these disparate contexts. First, Assyria after Sargon II had conquered most of the known world and viewed its previous policy of territorial expansion and world domination as largely realized. This is close to what we see in the Egyptian sources after the Second Intermediate period. Thutmose III's promise "to extend the frontiers of Egypt" was no idle threat, and it was repeated in different words on several occasions. As the god Amen-Re said of Thutmose, "You trod all foreign lands with joyful heart. . . . I came to let you tread on the earth's limits . . . for I bestowed on you the earth, its length and breadth."[174] The New Kingdom objective was nothing less than complete control of its periphery, and this periphery extended symbolically to the ends of the earth.

As this objective was more or less realized, the Egyptians, like the Assyrians after them, tended to view imperial subjects as sources of booty and slave labor. Thutmose III enumerates the booty that he captured,[175] and much larger numbers of captives are attested in New

173. See the poetic portions of Thutmose's "Political Stela" in Lichtheim, *Ancient Egyptian Literature*, 2.37.

174. Lichtheim, *Ancient Egyptian Literature*, 2.36–37.

175. "Now the army [of his majesty] carried off . . . 1,929 cows, 2,000 goats, and 20,000 sheep . . . 84 children of the enemy and of the princes who were with him, 5 maryanu belonging to them, 1,796 male and female slaves, as well as their children . . ." (see *ANET* 237; Lichtheim, *Ancient Egyptian Literature*, 2.34).

Kingdom texts, as this booty list of Amenhotep II shows: "princes of Retenu: 127; brothers of princes: 179; Apiru: 3,600; living Shasu: 15,200; Kharu: 36,300; living Neges: 15,070; the adherents thereof: 30,652; total: 89,600 men."[176] The purpose of these captives, as Thutmose III stated, was "to fill (Amun's) workhouse, to be weavers and make for him byssos, fine white linen . . . and thick cloth, to trap and work the fields, to produce grain to fill the granary of the god's offering."[177] Such a policy fostered close contact between Egyptians and Asiatics, so that a delicately positive shift in perspective is sometimes noticeable in the sources. As with the Assyrians, who greatly admired "Hittite" handiwork and architectural design, the Egyptians also, in spite of their distaste for Asiatics, came to appreciate Asiatic skills in metalwork, shipbuilding, and construction.[178]

The imperialist policy that we have outlined here was followed throughout the New Kingdom, with lackluster attempts to duplicate it even in the late period by the likes of Sheshonq (945–913 B.C.E.).[179] The inscriptions of Thutmose III are therefore representative of later periods in Egyptian history. Subsequent kings down to the end of the 13th century—Amenhotep II, Seti I, Ramses II, and Merneptah, for instance—harbored the same negative sentiments toward the "wretched" Asian population.

> *From Amenhotep II*: [the destroyer of] Naharin, the one that laid waste Khatte, viol[ator of the] Babylonian [women], the Byblian maid, the little girl of Alalakh and the old crone of Arrapkha! And the Takjsians are nothing at all!—really what are they good for?

> *From Seti I*: penetrating into the mass of Asiatics and making them prostrate, crushing the princes of Retenu . . . the wretched foe who is in the town of Hamath is gathering himself to many people.

> *From Ramses II*: How can these wretched Asiatics think [of taking] their [arms] for further disorder?

---

176. *ANET* 247.

177. Kurt Sethe (ed.), *Urkunden der 18. Dynastie* (5 vols.; Urkunden des ägyptischen Altertums 4; Leipzig: Hinrichs, 1906–58) 742. English translation from Redford, *Egypt, Canaan, and Israel in Ancient Times*, 223.

178. W. Helck, *Die Beziehungen Ägyptens zu Vorderasien im 3. und 2. Jahrtausend v. Chr.* (2d ed.; Ägyptologische Abhandlungen 5; Wiesbaden: Harrasowitz, 1971) 356–57.

179. *ANET* 263–64.

From Merneptah: The wretched enemy prince of Rebu has fled in the depth of the night, by himself. No feather was on his head; his feet were unshod. His women were taken before his face . . . The great Lord of Egypt is powerful; victory belongs to him. Who can fight, knowing his unhindered stride? Foolish and witless is he who takes him on! He who transgresses his frontier knows not for himself the morrow.[180]

This perspective outlasted even these New Kingdom representatives, so that the much later Piye (753–713 B.C.E.) would claim that "the grandeur of his majesty attained the Asiatics and every heart trembled before him," even in the unimpressive context of his own struggle to control Egypt itself.[181] In such a circumstance, this self-edifying remark served only Piye himself, since the Asiatics had long since escaped the oppressive context of Egyptian rule and were instead facing extreme pressure from Assyrian expansion. Only during the idiosyncratic reign of Akhenaton (1365–1349 B.C.E.) do we find a universalistic sentiment that would seem to place Egyptian identity on a par with Asiatics (= Kharu):

Thou [Atum] didst create . . . the foreign lands of Kharu and Kush and the land of Egypt, thou hast put every man in his place, thou hast provided their needs, each one with his food and a reckoned lifetime and tongues different in speech; likewise their nature and skin colors are distinguished.[182]

Despite Akhenaton's ideological uniqueness, the text he has left us suitably represents many other Egyptian texts that use the term 'Kharu' (*ḫ3rw*) to refer to the Syro-Palestinian region. What makes this interesting is that Kharu (= Hurru) originally derived from the Hurrians who appeared as part of the Palestinian cultural amalgam near the end of the 16th century B.C.E. and grew to comprise a significant presence in the region.[183] The Hurrians are perhaps better known as the founders of

180. See the following sources, respectively: Redford, *Egypt, Canaan and Israel in Ancient Times*, 301 (cf. W. Helck, "Eine Stele des Vizekönigs Wśr-Śt.t," *JNES* 14 [1955] 22–31); *ANET* 253, 255, 377.

181. Lichtheim, *Ancient Egyptian Literature*, 3.71.

182. M. Sandman, *Texts from the Time of Akhenaton* (Bibliotheca Aegyptiaca 8; Brussels: Fondation Égyptologique Reine Élisabeth, 1938) 94–95.

183. According to Glock's estimate (based on very slim evidence), the Hurrian and Indo-Aryan populations of Palestine represented 17 and 22%, respectively (A. Glock, "A New Taʿannek Tablet," *BASOR* 204 [1971] 30).

Mitanni, the nation-state that prospered between 1500 and 1350 B.C.E. The curious thing is that even before a distinctive Hurrian presence passed from the historical scene, Thutmose III and Amenhotep II applied the term Kharu to the Palestinian population in general, as did their successors.[184] One must conclude, then, that just as in Assyria the referent of Hatti evolved from the Hittite empire to the more general regions west of Assyria, so too in Egypt the referent for Kharu moved from the Hurrian peoples to the more general Syro-Palestinian area. The importance of this observation rests in the fact that the biblical materials often speak of the Horites as part of the indigenous population of Palestine. In light of the Egyptian evidence, this use of "Horite" more likely reflects a general exonym borrowed by Israelite literature than it reflects a particular population group within Palestine. By the time the biblical materials were composed, the original Hittites and Horites had long since departed from the stage.

Egyptian Identity during the Persian and Hellenistic Periods

Before summarizing our work in this chapter, I think that it would be useful to take a brief look at the Persian and Hellenistic periods, primarily because of Egypt's peripheral sociological experience at the time. We are fortunate to have a recent study of Egyptian identity during the Persian period by J. H. Johnson and, as one might expect, the sources reflect Egyptian and Persian efforts to adjust to each other and to handle their various cultural and linguistic differences.[185] There is no evidence, however, that the Egyptians identified themselves ethnically or that the Persians utilized ethnicity in the prosecution of their imperial efforts. Moreover, although the Egyptian effort to describe the minority foreign communities dwelling among them is rather frequent and sometimes heated, even here there no evidence that the Egyptians conceptualized foreign identity in terms of ethnic genealogy. Instead, during the Persian period and, as we will see, during the Hellenistic period, the Egyptians continued in their attempt to restore the traditional national identity that centered on the person of the king.

---

184. Redford, *Egypt, Canaan, and Israel in Ancient Times*, 137.

185. J. H. Johnson, "Ethnic Considerations in Persian Period Egypt," *Gold of Praise: Studies on Ancient Egypt in Honor of Edward F. Wente* (ed. E. Teeter and J. A. Larson; Chicago: Oriental Institute, forthcoming).

This spirit of Egyptian self-confidence and distinctive national identity is clearly typified by the Ptolemaic era "Demotic Chronicle." The text is hardly a chronicle and was more properly described by E. Revillout as *prophéties patriotiques*. Translation of the text is notoriously difficult and interpretation even more so, but several things seem clear. The text is organized into several "chapters," each consisting of a series of oracular statements followed by relevant commentary. The commentary explains the text in terms of Egyptian political developments during the period of Persian rule, the Ptolemaic period, and the brief Egyptian autonomy in between.[186] Theologically speaking, the text argues that each short-lived king of Egypt failed to adhere to the divine ordinances ("law") and subsequently received a truncated tenure because of it.[187] This dynamic was equally the cause of foreign oppression under the Persians and Greeks.[188] The chronicler wanted the reader to believe that he was living under the rule of King Tachos (362–361 B.C.E.) and used *vaticinium ex eventu* to "predict" a series of events in Egyptian history. His final oracle, however, predicted the unrealized hope that Ptolemaic rule would end at the hands of "a man of Heracleopolis" who would rule after the Ionians.[189]

Despite its Ptolemaic date, the ideas reflected in the chronicle had their origins in the Persian period, when "each enemy of Persia was automatically an ally of Egypt."[190] As the chronicle shows, the Egyptians abhorred foreign rule of any kind, as much under the Persians and Greeks as under the Hyksos many centuries earlier.[191] Form-critically,

186. J. H. Johnson, "The Demotic Chronicle as a Historical Source," *Enchoria* 4 (1974) 1–3.

187. This is not surprising given that, as Redford points out, the text was produced by the Egyptian priesthood (*Pharaonic King-Lists, Annals, and Day-books*, 295–96). The ideology of the text is very close to that of the Deuternomistic History.

188. C. C. McCown, "Hebrew and Egyptian Apocalpytic Literature," *HTR* 18 (1925) 387–92.

189. "Demotic Chronicle" 2.25 in W. Spiegelberg, *Die sogenannte demotische Chronik* (Demotische Studien 7; Leipzig: Heinrichs, 1914).

190. F. K. Kienitz, *Die politische Geschichte Ägyptens vom 7 bis 4 Jahrhundert vor der Zeitwende* (Berlin: Akademie, 1953) 79.

191. J. H. Johnson has recently argued that the "Chronicle" was "anti-Persian" but not "anti-Greek." Her reasoning is that the "Chronicle" was concerned primiarily with legitimate kingship, not with the problem of foreign domination (Johnson, "The Demotic Chronicle as a Statement of a Theory of Kingship," *SSEA Journal* 13 [1983] 61–72). But these concerns are not necessarily exclusive, as the Deuteronomistic History shows.

the apocalyptic genre of the text has been compared with the book of Daniel, and for good reason. In each case the prophetic figures promote confidence in their contemporary message that the "evil" of foreign rule would end. Both texts utilized extensive apocalyptic imagery, with Daniel's symbolism being somewhat less cryptic. The chief difference from our vantage point is that Daniel originated in a community with powerful ethnic sentiments, while the "Demotic Chronicle" does not, even though some ethnic theorists tell us that ethnic identity arises in just such an oppressive context. Egyptian identity in the chronicle was monarchic and nonethnic; while Daniel looked forward to the independence of his people and the establishment of divine kingship, the chronicle looked forward to the restoration of native Egyptian kingship. Despite this difference, the similarity of genre and argument shows that two quite disparate modes of identity can function in very similar ways to create a sense of community and to generate a sense of distinction between the group and outsiders. With the "Demotic Chronicle" this chapter has come full circle, since now both Egyptians and Jews live as oppressed peripheral peoples under the thumb of the Hellenistic powers.

Summary

Concepts of ethnic identity reflected in the sources we have examined reveal a general similarity between the Assyrian and Egyptian sources and, at the same time, a perspective that is quite different from Greek concepts. The Assyrian and Egyptian sources harbored quite a negative view of Palestine and its peoples, eyeing them as subjects of conquest and, many times, as sources of slave-labor. This harsh (and frequently arrogant) attitude naturally intensified as conflicts with the peripheral groups heightened and as imperial power over the conquered regions increased. Although the pictographic evidence sometimes hints otherwise, rarely do the Egyptian and Assyrian texts reflect any kind of ethnographic interest, which turns out to contrast rather obviously with Greek ethnographic interests. For the Egyptians and Assyrians, identity was political and cultural, not ethnic, and was linked with kingship, the king's relationship to the deity, and the deity's role in extending the national borders and the native empire to the "ends of the earth." Palestine became the object of these imperialist leanings, first under the thumb of Egypt and then, much later, under pressures from the Neo-Assyrian Empire. Palestine therefore endured a peripheral social experience during both the Egyptian and Assyrian periods of domination and, if the ethnic theorists are right, it stands to reason that these periods of oppression should be reflected in any Israelite literature that heralds from the respective periods. The rather militant circumstances associated with these contexts suggests that we can expect from Israel a rather severe and reactionary response, with any existing ethnic sentiments intensifying proportionally.

Two of the Egyptian sources, the story of *Sinuhe* and the "Satirical Instruction Letter," yielded interesting results in our study. The story of *Sinuhe* revealed that Middle Kingdom Egyptians probably defined Asiatic tribal structure in terms of kinship, and this certainly dovetails with the anthropological evidence examined in chapter 1 and also with the Old Babylonian evidence examined in this chapter. Egypt's non-urban periphery in Asia was like the periphery of Mari, where kinship played an important role in the organization and structure of the peripheral societies and (if we can guess about Egypt's periphery on the basis of the Mari evidence) where this sense of kinship produced a corresponding awareness of ethnicity as a broader organizing cultural principle. In all cases—Egypt, Assyria, Babylon, and Greece—the effort to describe this periphery gave rise to vague "tribal" terminologies, and this was necessitated by their relatively meager knowledge of the peripheral modalities in question.

The "Satirical Instruction Letter" depicted the Asiatic region as a dangerous territory inhabited by giant bedouin, a tradition that should be compared with similar traditions in the Greek materials and also in the Hebrew Bible. Because there were, no doubt, differences in physical stature among some peoples in the ancient world, this characterization of the bedouin may have stemmed from collective memories of actual but exaggerated contacts with "the other," but it is equally possible that we are dealing with invented traditions. The major distinction between this tradition and the Greek/Hebrew tradition is that the Egyptian giants lived on their territorial periphery, while the Greek/Hebrew giants lived on their historical periphery.

Greek identity as reflected in our sources was quite distinct from both of its ancient neighbors, being primarily concerned with ethnic varieties of social identity and with various standards of "civilized" behavior. Greek interest in the surrounding peripheral groups was more ethnographic than imperialistic, which is why we have quite a nice collection of materials that describe foreign traditions, customs, and geography. But in spite of the supposed efforts by Greek authors to provide "objective" reports, these peripheral peoples were frequently described in standard jargon as nomadic, impious, sexually perverse, ritually backward, and cannibalistic. In this respect, then, the Greeks thought little more of peripheral peoples than did Assyria or Egypt. The Greeks were interested in the origins of these peripheral groups and, generally speaking, in the origins of humanity and in how these earlier time-frames made a nexus with the present. Particularly popular were notions that, on the one hand, a "Golden Age" men once enjoyed had been lost and, on the other hand, that human culture was in a state of constant progress. Within the various schemes offered to explain human origins, certain features emerged in the sources, particularly the belief that the primeval period of history featured super-human figures (such as giants, demi-gods, and heroes) and that human population groups originated via eponymous ancestors or territorial migration. Also relevant for our discussion were the military coalitions described by Herodotus, whose ten- and twelve-group organization schemes compare to the tribal organization described in the Hebrew Bible.

Perhaps the most interesting feature of the Greek materials is their effort to account for the origins of political modalities in terms of ethnic ancestors like Dorus, Akhaios, Ion, and the like. The best explanation for this is that the pan-hellenic ideology was a relatively late development in Greece and as a result, unlike the Mesopotamians and Egyptians, the Greeks had to frequently wrestle with tension between their obvious cultural affinities with each other and their nonetheless frequent conflicts. The use of segmented ethnic genealogies was a useful model that explained both their common heritage and their differences. Only as common external threats grew, especially from Persia, did these differences wane to make room for a new sense of collective Hellenic identity. As I hope the reader recognizes already, our examination of the biblical materials will show that the Greek materials have the greatest affinity with the Hebrew Bible.

Chapter Three

Merneptah's Stele and Deborah's Song

If there is no consensus about the origins of ancient Israel and, therefore, about a specific historical circumstance that gave rise to its ethnic distinctiveness, can anything be said about the antiquity of these ethnic sentiments? How far back can we trace the notion of Israelite ethnicity? We have generally come to expect, in answer to this question, another extended discussion of the anthropological, archaeological, demographic, and ecological data from Late Bronze Age Palestine, along with an analysis of the Amarna correspondence and a treatment of the questions raised by the presence of the *Ḥapiru* in Palestine and the *shasu* nomads in the Negev and Sinai regions. But as is becoming clear, these sources of data are notoriously difficult to interpret and have given rise to every sort of theory and speculation about Israel's ancient history and, along with that, about its ancient ethnic context.[1] While I would not quibble in the least about the appropriateness of the endeavor to provide a detailed reconstruction of Israel's origins and ancient history, the idea of identifying and distinguishing ethnic groups through the use of mostly archaeological sources—ethnoarchaeology—remains an important problem. And it is precisely this that is necessary when one attempts to find Israel in the artifacts. Therefore, I find it helpful to proceed with an analysis of the most straightforward early sources about Israel, the Merneptah Stele and the Song of Deborah, and to carry on the discussion somewhat apart from

---

1. B. Halpern's transparency on this point is refreshing: "Under these circumstances, any explanation of Israel's origins will be an exercise in speculation . . . to some extent self-indulgent: it is less a work of scholarship than of sortition, less a work of history than of fancy" (*The Emergence of Israel in Canaan* [SBLMS 29; Chico, Calif.: Scholars Press, 1983] 81).

other materials, keeping in mind that the results of such an inquiry must ultimately dialogue with other avenues of research. We will begin with an analysis of the Merneptah Stele followed by an examination of the Song of Deborah, in each case looking for evidence of Israelite ethnic sentiments or, if not that, for evidence of a historical context that might make some sense of its ethnic sentiment.[2]

Israelite Identity and the Merneptah Stele

Broadly speaking, it is probably fair to say that there are two major schools of thought about the depiction of Israel in the "Israel stele." On the one hand, the majority "traditional school," regardless of its permutations, sees a rather direct link between Merneptah's Israel and the Israel of the Hebrew Bible. True, there was and is quite a difference in how the "German School" and the "American School," for instance, view the Hebrew Bible, both in terms of its compositional history and in terms of the referential history that lies behind it. But for virtually every stripe of scholar the essential antiquity of the biblical traditions has served as an underlying assumption, and it is precisely this that makes the equation that links Merneptah's Israel and the biblical Israel so appealing and, to many, so self-evident.[3] In recent years the so-called "minimalist school" has questioned the antiquity of the biblical traditions, and this has necessarily raised questions about our interpretation of the Merneptah text. If much of the biblical text dates to the exilic and even post-exilic periods, as is suggested by this school of

2. I will not address the debated Ugaritic text published in 1965 (PRU 5, 97 = RS 18.30), which may refer to Israel. See O. Margalit, "On the Origin and Antiquity of the Name 'Israel,'" *ZAW* 102 (1990) 226–27.

3. Among those who see a rather straightforward connection are G. W. Ahlström, *The History of Ancient Palestine from the Palaeolithic Period to Alexander's Conquest* (JSOTSup 146; Sheffield: JSOT Press, 1993); R. Albertz, "Israel," *TRE* 16.369–79; R. B. Coote, *Early Israel: A New Horizon* (Minneapolis: Fortress, 1990); W. G. Dever, "How to Tell a Canaanite from an Israelite," in *The Rise of Ancient Israel* (ed. H. Shanks; Washington, D.C.: Biblical Archaeological Society, 1992) 26–56; M. G. Hasel, "*Israel* in the Merneptah Stela," *BASOR* 296 (1994) 45–61; K. A. Kitchen, *Ancient Orient and Old Testament* (Downers Grove, Ill.: InterVarsity, 1966; A. Mazar, *Archaeology in the Land of the Bible 10,000–586 B.C.E.* (New York: Doubleday, 1990); L. E. Stager, "Merneptah, Israel and the Sea Peoples: New Light on an Old Relief," *ErIsr* 18 (1985) 56–64; F. J. Yurco, "Merneptah's Canaanite Campaign," *JARCE* 23 (1986) 189–215.

thought, how can one "connect the dots" between a thirteenth-century B.C.E. source like the Merneptah Stele and biblical sources written nearly half a millennium later? Even the earliest of the extrabiblical texts that mention Israel post-date Merneptah by several centuries.[4] In such a scenario are we not dealing, practically speaking, with two quite different "Israels?"[5] Although I am not necessarily espousing here a minimalist approach, when we heuristically set aside most of the Hebrew narrative sources, as I am attempting to do, then we face the limitation that our oldest remaining sources, primarily the eighth-century prophets, date some four centuries after the Israel stele. We must avoid the eisegesis of positing a connection between Merneptah's Israel and the biblical Israel when we examine this Egyptian source.

The victory stele of Merneptah dates to the end of the thirteenth century B.C.E. and was inscribed in two places, on a stele in Merneptah's mortuary temple (a stele that had previously belonged to Amenhotep III) and on a stele in the temple at Karnak.[6] The poetic text is largely concerned with Merneptah's victory over the Libyans but near its end mentions a number of different regions, peoples, and cities, including 'Israel' (*ysry³l*), and in doing so it provides us with several clues regarding the nature of this Israel and its relationship to the other sociopolitical modalities mentioned in the text. The relevant part of the stele reads as follows, according to L. E. Stager:[7]

> The princes are prostrate, saying, "Peace!"
> Not one is raising his head among the Nine Bows.
> Now that Tehenu (Libya) has come to ruin,
>> Hatti is pacified;
>> The Canaan has been plundered into every sort of woe:

---

4. Shalmaneser III's inscription (ca. 850 B.C.E.; *ANET*), the Mesha Stele (ca. 840 B.C.E.; *ANET*), and the ninth-century B.C.E. Tel Dan stele fragment published by A. Biran and J. Naveh, "An Aramaic Stele Fragment from Tel Dan," *IEJ* 43 (1993) 81–98.

5. As far as I know, only two scholars discount entirely the relationship between the Merneptah stele and biblical Israel: Margalit, "On the Origin and Antiquity of the Name 'Israel,'" 225–37; A. Nibbi, *Canaan and Canaanite in Ancient Egypt* (Oxford: DE, 1989). We should not follow Margalit's suggestion that the text may be read as 'Jezreel' instead of 'Israel'. We are dealing with an *³alep* here, not an *ʿayin*.

6. Miriam Lichtheim, *Ancient Egyptian Literature* (3 vols.; Berkeley: University of California Press, 1973–80) 2.73.

7. According to Stager, he is following E. F. Wente's translation and structure (Stager, "Merneptah, Israel and the Sea Peoples," 56–64).

> Ashkelon has been overcome;
> Gezer has been captured;
> Yano'am is made non-existent.
> Israel is laid waste and his seed is not;
> Hurru is become a widow because of Egypt.

As many have done before him, Stager has suggested a hymnic reading of the text in the hope that it might clarify the rather vague impression that the text gives us concerning the conquered regions.[8] Is "Canaan" the name of an Egyptian province, a particular geographical region, or a more general designation for Syria–Palestine? Does "Hurru" include North Syria only or also the regions closer to Egypt? Is Israel parallel to Hurru, parallel to Canaan, or an entity within one of the two (or within both)?[9] These questions and the answers that we posit for them have determined to a large extent what we think the text means when it refers to "Israel."

Apart from the name "Israel," the term "Canaan" has stimulated more discussion than any other toponym in the text, so it is perhaps best to begin with it. How one views Canaan is particularly significant, because the Hebrew sources frequently pit the Israelites and Canaanites against each other, and we would like to know the relative antiquity of these antagonistic sentiments. We are fortunate to have two recent monographic studies of "Canaan/Canaanite" terminology, by A. Nibbi and N. P. Lemche, respectively, with each providing a survey of the second-millennium materials and their use of the terms "Canaan" and "Canaanite."[10] Lemche's work has prompted quite an active debate, so for the most part we will deal with his thesis and with several responses to it.

---

8. For alternative hymnic readings, see G. Ahlström and D. Edelman, "Merneptah's Israel," *JNES* 44 (1985) 59–60; M. G. Hasel, "*Israel* in the Merneptah Stela," *BASOR* 296 (1994) 45–61.

9. Parallel to Hurru, as Stager suggests here; parallel to Canaan, as suggested by G. W. Ahlström, "The Origin of Israel in Palestine," *SJOT* 2 (1991) 19–34; an entity within one of the two (or within both), according to F. J. Yurco, "3,200-Year-Old Picture of Israelites Found in Egypt," *BARev* 16/5 (1990) 20–38.

10. N. P. Lemche, *The Canaanites and Their Land: The Tradition of the Canaanites* (JSOTSup 110; Sheffield: JSOT Press, 1991); Nibbi, *Canaan and Canaanite in Ancient Egypt*. Despite its many useful observations, Nibbi's study is particularly weak in its uncritical handling of the biblical text and also arrives at some rather idiosyncratic conclusions, most notably that "Canaan" included the northern coastline of Egypt.

With the exception of a few texts from Mari,[11] a report from the reign of Amenophis II,[12] and a few brief references in texts from Alalaḫ, most notably King Idrimi's fifteenth-century autobiographical text,[13] the oldest unambiguous references to "Canaan" and the "Canaanites" are found in the Amarna Letters, mostly communiqués between Levantine vassals and their Egyptian overlords written during the fourteenth century B.C.E.[14] According to Lemche, these letters show us that Canaan was a somewhat amorphous territory with no clearly defined borders and that, roughly speaking, during this period the most certain thing that we can say about Canaan is that it was a part of Egypt's empire in western Asia.[15] W. L. Moran similarly suggests that Canaan lay "from north to south, between Amurru and Egypt, and from east to west, between ill-defined borders and the Mediterranean."[16] The degree of certainly about the term "Canaan" in the Amarna correspondence

11. Only one published text from Mari mentions the Canaanites, referring to *ḫabbātum* and *Kinaḫnum*, that is, 'thieves and merchants?/Canaanites?' Chronologically, the text is somewhat isolated from other uses of the term and its meaning in that eighteenth-century B.C.E. context is somewhat unclear, although Na'aman suggests that already in this early period we have evidence of "Canaanite" identity. Charpin tells us that, in addition to this text, there are several unpublished texts from Mari that also mention Canaanites. See G. Dossin, "Une mention de Cananéens dans une lettre de Mari," *Syria* 50 (1973) 277–82; D. Charpin, "Mari entre l'est et l'ouest: Politique, culture, religion," *Akkadica* 78 (1992) 1–10; N. Na'aman, "The Canaanites and Their Land: A Rejoinder," *UF* 26 (1994) 398.

12. See *ANET* 246. This text lists a number of captive groups taken by Pharaoh during a fifteenth-century Asiatic campaign. According to Nibbi, who follows Maisler, with the exception of the "Canaanites," all of the groups listed in the source are social classes of people rather than ethnic or cultural groups. So here the term "Canaanite" is best understood as a nonethnic category, with the translation 'merchants' often suggested. See Nibbi, *Canaan and Canaanite in Ancient Egypt*, 30–31; B. Maisler [Mazar], "Canaan and Canaanites," *BASOR* 102 (1946) 7–12.

13. S. Smith, *The Statue of Idri-mi* (Occasional Publications of the British Institute of Archaeology in Ankara 1; London: British Institute of Archaeology in Ankara, 1949). See translation in *ANET* 557–58. See also the discussion in M. Dietrich and O. Loretz, "Die Inschrift der Statue des Königs Idrimi von Alalaḫ," *UF* 13 (1981) 199–269. On the other Alalaḫ texts, see Lemche, *The Canaanites and Their Land*, 41. To summarize, the Alalaḫ texts refer to the "city of Canaan" (AT 48), "a son of the land of Canaan" (AT 181), and "the land of Canaan" (Idrimi's statue text). This reflects what is clear from later texts, namely, that there was a region in the Levant called Canaan whose status as a geographical point of reference was quite stable.

14. See W. L. Moran, *The Amarna Letters* (Baltimore: Johns Hopkins University Press, 1992).

15. Lemche, *The Canaanites and Their Land*, 43.

16. Moran, *The Amarna Letters*, 389.

varies from scholar to scholar, and this has naturally given rise to various points of contention. For instance, Lemche notes a particular disagreement between himself and A. F. Rainey: Lemche takes the letter of Abi-milku from Tyre (EA 151, see text in n. 17 below) as evidence that Ugarit lay within Canaan, while Rainey views this as unlikely, since, in a different text from Ugarit, a foreign merchant visiting the city was called a "Canaanite."[17] Rainey suspects that Abi-milku was asked by Pharaoh to report what he had heard from his Tyrian vantage point in Canaan (*ištu Kina^{c}ni*) about the surrounding territories (including non-Canaanite Ugarit), an interpretation which is altogether different from Lemche's view. Lemche reads Ugarit as being one of the cities on a list of Canaanite locales from which Abi-milku was hearing news. Although to a certain extent I think that the evidence supports Rainey's view, especially in light of his recent response to Lemche,[18] if we set aside the issue of Ugarit, Canaan, and the like, what this kind of debate actually demonstrates is how difficult it can sometimes be to understand and pin down the precise meaning of geographical terms in these ancient texts.[19] According to Rainey and also N. Na'aman, however, these difficulties with respect to ancient Canaan are not as pronounced as Lemche supposes; they both argue that the term *Canaan* signified a rather clearly defined geopolitical entity during the second millennium.[20] The primary argument of both scholars is that second-millennium scribes from various sites were quite familiar with "the land of Canaan" and with its inhabitants, whom they variously

17. See A. F. Rainey, "Ugarit and the Canaanites Again," *IEJ* 14 (1964) 101. The relevant text from EA 151 reads as follows:

> The king, my lord, wrote to me, "Write to me what you have heard in Canaan." The king of Danuna died; his brother became king after his death, and his land is at peace. Fire destroyed the palace at Ugarit; (rather), it destroyed half of it and so hal⟨f⟩ of it *has disappeared*. There are no Hittite troops about. Etakkama, the prince of Qid_u, and Aziru are at war; the war is with Biryawaza.

18. For his response on this text, see A. F. Rainey, "Who Is a Canaanite? A Review of the Textual Evidence," *BASOR* 304 (1996) 9–11.

19. As noted by Nibbi, "we do not yet have a precise understanding for most of the names which the ancient Egyptians used for the foreign areas along its ancient borders: Kharu, Retenu, Naharin and Djahy, to mention only a few" (*Canaan and Canaanite in Ancient Egypt*, 7). In light of this, works such as those of Ahituv can be very useful but must also be read with a very critical eye (S. Ahituv, *Canaanite Toponyms in Ancient Egyptian Documents* [Jerusalem: Magnes, 1984]).

20. Rainey, "Who Is a Canaanite?"; Na'aman, "The Canaanites and Their Land."

identified as "sons of Canaan," "men of Canaan," "kings of Canaan," or, on occasion, as "Canaanites." While in certain generic contexts (such as poetry) one might argue, with Lemche, that these references are "vague," "imprecise," and "ambiguous," this supposedly "muddy" terminology could not have been very useful in legal, administrative, and epistolary contexts—and this is precisely where "Canaan" turns up in a number of places. This makes it very difficult to sustain the argument that Amarna-age Canaan was nothing more than a vague geographic convention used by second-millennium scribes. On the other hand, this whole discussion seems to suppose that a concrete entity like Canaan can only have existed if we are able to demonstrate that it possessed firm boundaries and that it existed as a political entity within the Egyptian empire. This seems entirely unnecessary. Even if the supposed boundaries of Canaan were obscure in antiquity, as they are to us, in my view, such a circumstance could hardly have prevented scribes from knowing where Canaan was and who lived there. That Palestine's coastal plain was located in Canaan was not at all affected by the question of Canaan's borders since, wherever they were, the coastal plain clearly lay within them. To go beyond the obvious geographical status of Amarna-age Canaan we must ask a different question: was Canaan a political province of Egypt?

There has been a tendency on this question to follow the lead of W. Helck, who suggested some time ago that Canaan was the southernmost province of Egypt's Asiatic empire, governed from the city of Gaza.[21] As W. T. Pitard has pointed out, this suggestion is somewhat speculative because it rests on Helck's belief that the term *rābiṣu* should be understood as a technical term for 'governor', a view complicated by the fact that it is used quite elastically in the Amarna correspondence and also by the fact that, as Redford has pointed out, the titles used by the Canaanite leaders for the Egyptian "supervisors" were simply the closest Canaanite or Akkadian terms that they could find to designate an official whose rank was actually unknown to them.[22] Furthermore, EA 162 appears to include Amurru within Canaan, and this too is at variance with the proposal of Helck, who suggested that Amurru, like

21. Helck, *Die Beziehungen Ägyptens zu Vorderasien*, 246–55.
22. W. T. Pitard, *Ancient Damascus: A Historical Study of the Syrian City-State from the Earliest Times until Its Fall to the Assyrians in 732 B.C.E.* (Winona Lake, Ind.: Eisenbrauns, 1987) 59–60; D. B. Redford, *Egypt, Canaan, and Israel in Ancient Times* (Princeton: Princeton University Press, 1992) 201.

Canaan, was an Egyptian province.[23] But these problems should not distract us from other evidence that might support the thesis that Canaan was an Egyptian province, provided that in examining this evidence we avoid a potential snare. That Egypt controlled Canaan in the Amarna period is not to be doubted, or that it had garrisons and administrative centers in the region.[24] But one cannot necessarily equate Egyptian rule in Canaan with Canaan's provincial status, as is frequently done.[25] This is because provincial rule implies to many scholars that we are dealing with a clearly defined district, with a relatively complex administrative bureaucracy, and with a name (in this case Canaan) used by imperial rulers to designate the particular district. Such provincial entities are created with a view to organizing and integrating conquered territories into the political matrix of the imperial power, in this case Egypt. But as the Amarna correspondence shows, the Pharaohs do not appear to have harbored much concern about preserving either the political structure or the social order in Canaan, with most of the regional power being wielded by local city-state kings.[26] So perhaps we ought to consider Egypt's "occupation of Canaan" rather than Egypt's "province of Canaan." In light of this, the question of Canaan's Amarna-age provincial status should be approached with caution.

There are two important texts that suggest that Canaan may have been an Egyptian province, but special problems accompany both of them. In the first instance, it has been suggested for some time, most recently by Rainey, that a letter from Alashia (EA 36:15) includes the phrase *piḥati ša kinaḥi* 'the province of Canaan'.[27] Moran argues against this for several reasons, first, because it requires reading the WA sign as *pi-* (in *pi-ḥa-ti*) and, second, because the reading 'Canaan' is also dubious in this very broken text.[28] To this Rainey has countered with evidence from another letter that the WA sign was known to have a *pi-* value by Alashian scribes. While this is possible, in my view the

23. See lines 39–41 in Moran, *The Amarna Letters*, 249.
24. The following discussion is concerned only with the question of Canaan's provincial status, not with whether there were two, three, or four Egyptian provinces in the Asiatic regions occupied by Egypt. For bibliography and discussion on the question of the Egyptian presence in Asia, see Helck, *Die Beziehungen Ägyptens zu Vorderasien*, 248; Pitard, *Ancient Damascus*, 63, and Moran, *The Amarna Letters*, xxvi.
25. See, for instance, Na'aman, "The Canaanites and Their Land," 402.
26. Pitard, *Ancient Damascus*, 63.
27. Rainey, "Who Is a Canaanite?" 7–8.
28. Moran, *The Amarna Letters*, 109–10.

unfortunate state of the text prevents us from reaching a definite conclusion, and Na'aman, Moran, Redford, and Lemche are convinced, against Rainey, that we are not dealing with evidence of Canaan's provincial status in this text.[29] In addition we must also deal with the possibility that, even in the event that Rainey's reading of the text is correct, the "Cypriot" scribe of Alashia might have referred to Canaan as an Egyptian province without it's actually being true; a letter from Egypt or Canaan would be more noteworthy. The Alashia letter is slim evidence in support of the thesis that Canaan was an Egyptian province, especially when the Amarna Letters reflect such a weak Egyptian hold on Canaan.

The other important text adduced by Rainey in this regard is a (post-Amarna) judicial report from Ugarit that brings us closer to the time-frame of Merneptah's "Israel stele."[30] According to Nougayrol, the text tells us about an indemnity payment due to the "sons of Canaan" from the "sons of Ugarit," a penalty that was probably incurred when a Canaanite merchant was slain in Ugarit. As Rainey sees it, the litigant status of Canaan's citizens in this text necessarily implies that Canaan was a political entity during the second millennium, despite Lemche's arguments to the contrary. The major problem with this reading of the text is that the text is quite broken and fragmentary, as is clear from the fact that the word 'litigation' (*di-ni?*) is a guess. It is also unclear whether the restitution would have gone to "Canaan" as a payment from one political entity to another or, rather, to an individual or town within Canaan. It is quite possible that references to the "sons of Ugarit" and "sons of Canaan" are nothing more than convenient ways to avoid minor details of the case, if that is indeed what we are dealing with. As is now clear, I cannot place much stock in this text and its supposed value in establishing the political identity of Canaan in the second millennium. But in spite of my disagreement with Rainey at certain points, I find that his useful study is certainly right about this: the city of Ugarit was not in Canaan.

29. Lemche, *The Canaanites and Their Land*, 29–30; N. Na'aman, *The Political Disposition and Historical Development of Eretz-Israel according to the Amarna Letters* (Ph.D. diss., Tel Aviv University, 1975) 2 [Hebrew]; D. B. Redford, *Egypt and Canaan in the New Kingdom* (Beer-Sheva 4; Beer-Sheva: Ben Gurion University of the Negev, 1990) 35

30. The text, RS 20.182 A+B, is published as text 36 in *Textes suméro-accadiens des archives et bibliothéques privées d'Ugarit* (ed. J. Nougayrol et al.; Ugaritica 5; Paris: Geuthner, 1968) 111.

The evidence for Canaan's provincial status is not very convincing, and the Amarna correspondence strongly argues against it. But the fact is that the word *province* can easily trap us in a game of semantics that obscures the results of our discussion. The real point, which I think Redford brings out nicely, is that: (1) we cannot speak of Egyptian provinces in the same way that we speak of the Roman Empire and its provinces; and (2) when the Egyptians referred to their northern empire, they still spoke of "the land of Canaan" or the "land of Hurru" rather than the "province of so-and-so,"[31] and this makes it is very unlikely that we are dealing in the second millennium with a monolithic people called "Canaanites" who lived in a political entity called "Canaan" and who harbored a strong sense of common national identity. The fact that the residents of Canaan knew that they lived in Canaan and that, on occasion, someone called them "Canaanites" or "sons of Canaan" (or that they called themselves by these names) does not change this.

Our observations have been focused largely on the Amarna age, but the 19th-Dynasty Merneptah Stele is a bit later than the Amarna correspondence, and some attention must be given to the question of how Canaan was understood during the intervening years. Although the term was used frequently during the period, the use of "Canaan" terminology remains somewhat ambiguous, as it was in the Amarna correspondence. One of the more interesting texts from this period is the well-known Papyrus Anastasi I, sometimes called the "Satirical Instruction Letter," in which an Egyptian official belittles a scribal colleague because of his ignorance of Asiatic regions.[32] According to Lemche, the text seems to understand "Canaan" somewhat differently from previous texts, as a more restricted region along the coast of Palestine, and for him it is likely that this same narrow sense is intended by the use of the term "Canaan" in the Merneptah Stele. This is primarily because, in Lemche's view, Merneptah's "Hurru" was a designation for the entire Asiatic theater, which would make Canaan the last in a toponymic list that leads the reader from Asia to Egypt (that is, Canaan lay in the southwestern extreme of the Asiatic empire).[33] But the on-going

31. Redford, *Egypt, Canaan, and Israel in Ancient Times*, 201.
32. *ANET* 475–79. See also the text and translation in A. H. Gardiner, *Egyptian Hieratic Texts* (Literary Texts of the New Kingdom 1; Hildesheim: Olms, 1964) 1–30.
33. Lemche, *The Canaanites and Their Land*, 47–48.

debate reflected in scholarly discussions of the text shows that this conclusion is far from certain.

All of our discussion up to now points in the same direction. The confusion about Canaan's boarders and political status shows that "Canaan" was primarily a geographical designation, and this is precisely the kind of evidence one expects to find when dealing with geographical entities: it is very easy to know what lies within them but it is frequently difficult to find their edges.[34] This also explains why very few Asiatics (if any) were interested in calling themselves "Canaanites," since to do so was to identify only one's connection with a geographical region.[35] The natural preference would have been one's town, city, or family, and this is precisely the most common convention.[36] It is therefore reckless to conclude that there was a national or ethnic modality in Late Bronze Asia that identified itself as "Canaan" or as "Canaanite." On the other hand we can in no way go as far as Lemche does when he says that the term "Canaanite" "always designated a person who did not belong to the scribe's own society or state, while Canaan was considered to be a country different from his own."[37] In saying this he seems to be suggesting that "Canaan" was a scribal technical term for "the other," and the evidence does not support this conclusion. The Asiatics of Palestine knew that they lived within a region that the Egyptians called "Canaan" and also that the inhabitants of Canaan were sometimes identified as "Canaanites." So unless we are prepared to expect very little from them, we must imagine that they understood themselves to be, at least in some sense, "Canaanites."

34. Nibbi agrees with the view that Canaan was geographical rather than political (*Canaan and Canaanites in Ancient Egypt*, 59).

35. Rainey suggests that the inhabitants of Canaan did call themselves "Canaanites" and cites as evidence their registration in Alalaḫ as "sons/men from the land of Canaan." He comments, "The scribes undoubtedly asked the foreigners where they came from and each one replied that he was from Canaan." But this is a speculative reconstruction of their conversation and, even if true, hardly indicates that these men viewed themselves primarily as "Canaanites." I should also comment on Rainey's contention that "the land of Canaan" ought to be understood just like the geopolitical entities of "the land of Mugiš," "the land of Niʾi," and "the land of Amaʾe," since, as he points out, Canaan occurs in parallelism with them. In my mind it is very difficult to take this as evidence that Canaan was a nation in the same sense as, say, Alalaḫ's kingdom of Mugiš (Rainey, "Who Is a Canaanite?" 3–4).

36. Cf. EA 8, 14, 30, 109, 110, 131, 137, 145, 151, 162, 367. As a cursory reading of these texts shows, no one in the Amarna correspondence calls himself a "Canaanite."

37. Lemche, *The Canaanites and Their Land*, 52.

But beyond the geopolitical and ethnic questions, the question of how the term "Canaan" should be understood in relation to the other toponyms in the text is an important one, especially in regard to our view of Merneptah's Israel. If we set aside Tehenu and Hatti as less relevant for our discussion, then we are dealing with these toponyms: Ashkelon, Gezer, Yano'am, Hurru, and Israel. Fortunately, scholarly consensus has identified Ashkelon, Gezer, and Yano'am as city-states lying within Canaan proper, and this makes our work somewhat easier. Similarly, there is a consensus that "Hurru" is a term semantically broader than "Canaan" that refers to the Asiatic theater in general. Which brings us to Israel. Normally the debate about Merneptah's Israel seems to hinge on one of two interpretations. On the one hand, Israel is sometimes understood as one of four entities within Canaan, so that Ashekelon, Gezer, Yano'am, and Israel share a common geographical space in Canaan. On the other hand, Israel can be understood as a geographical or sociological modality existing alongside the three Canaanite cities and could therefore be viewed as a "non-Canaanite" entity. But as we have pointed out already, the continuing debate stems precisely from the fact that both interpretations of the text are possible, and in my view there is really no way to assert one over the other. But this impasse is not particularly limiting from an ethnic point of view because what we are looking for initially is contrasting identity, and there is an additional feature in the text that suggests that Israel's identity did contrast with some of its neighbors.

As is frequently noted, the Egyptian text provides a determinative before the name of each toponym, and in every case but one the same determinative is used. The exception is Israel, which is preceded by the determinative for "people" instead of "land." Although the accuracy of these determinatives has been questioned by some,[38] it appears that Merneptah's scribe was rather careful and consistent in his use of determinatives in this unit,[39] and from this we should conclude that he intentionally distinguished the "people of Israel" from the other modalities, most notably the city-state populations. Thus, regardless of whether the scribe viewed Israel as living within Canaan or inland from it, we should grant that, at least in the eyes of an Egyptian, we have a context in which a distinctive Israelite identity existed in contrast to the

38. For instance, Ahlström and Edelman, "Merneptah's Israel," 59.

39. Hasel, "*Israel* in the Merneptah Stela," 52; A. Rainey, "Reply to D. Edelman," *BARev* 18/2 (1992) 73–74.

identity of city-state populations in Palestine. The problem, of course, is that Egyptian terminology frequently joined rather disparate groups of people within a single rubric for sociological reasons, such as a common *Lebensart*, as was the case with various bedouin "Shasu" peoples.[40] Therefore one cannot recklessly assume that these "Israelites" understood themselves, even in general terms, as the single unit that our scribe perceived. Such a hypothesis needs to be tested, and there is a way to do it.

Why do scholars tend to believe that the Shasu represent a sociological class rather than a single cultural or ethnic community? There are two major reasons. The first is that the Shasu people are widely distributed in a number of rather disparate geographical venues stretching from the Negev to Syria–Lebanon, and this makes it difficult (but not impossible) to imagine them as a single cultural unit.[41] The second and more important reason is the name "Shasu." Although its derivation is debated, it is generally agreed that the term comes from either the Egyptian word 'to wander' or the West Semitic root 'to plunder'.[42] Although the argument for Egyptian origin seems a bit stronger, in my view, in either case the name "Shasu" probably originated as an exonym used by outsiders to describe the various wandering groups on the periphery of Egyptian and urban Asiatic culture. It is of course true that cultural groups sometimes adopt exonyms and begin to use them when referring to themselves. But it is most likely that the "Shasu" represent an Egyptian social construct that joins the various Bedouin groups within an artificially unifying rubric on the basis of their common lifestyle and dress. One might say, then, that the Egyptians created the "Shasu" in much the same way that the Neo-Assyrians created the "Hittites."

If we ask similar questions of Merneptah's "Israel," what do we find? First, unlike the Shasu, Israel appears to inhabit a rather restricted region either in or near Canaan, and this suggests its potential status as a cohesive cultural unit. The more important question is Israel's name: what does it mean and what can it tell us about the people called "Israel"? First, "Israel" is not an Egyptian term and therefore can under no circumstance be viewed as an exonym of Egyptian origin. It is

40. See W. W. Ward, "Shasu," *ABD* 5.1165–66.
41. Ibid.
42. R. Giveon, *Les Bédouins Shosou des documents égyptiens* (Documenta et Monumenta Orientis Antiqui; Leiden: Brill, 1971) 259–64.

clearly West Semitic and must be either a name that Israel used for itself or an exonym coined by other West Semites to identify the group
called "Israel." Scholars are in general agreement that the name "Israel"
is the combination of the theophoric element 'El' along with a verbal
form, probably *śārâ* ('to fight/prevail') or *śrr* ('to rule'), but also perhaps *yšr/'šr* ('to be upright'). Although Hosea (12:4ff.) apparently took
the divine name as the object rather than subject of the resulting construction "He [Jacob] struggles [with] El," Albright long ago pointed
out that in West Semitic nomenclature the divine element is normally
the subject; that is, we should translate *Israel* as 'El persists', or 'El
rules', or something along these lines.[43] Although we might imagine a
scenario that prompted outside groups to coin such a name for Israel, it
is more likely that here we are dealing not with an exonym but with an
endonym, that is, *Israel* was the name that the people called themselves.[44] And it naturally follows from this that Israel represented a
sociocultural unit that shared some common sense of identity. While
this is not very much to go on and affords us very little perspective on
the content and parameters of this early "Israelite" identity, on the basis of the name itself we would suppose that this identity included a
common sense of religious identity (as El worshipers)[45] and also, perhaps, a propensity for warfare.

If Merneptah's Israel did share a sense of common identity, as
seems to be more probable than not, then it is quite possible that the
people of Israel expressed this polarity, rhetorically speaking, as a polarity between "Israel" and their neighbors, the inhabitants of "Canaan."[46]
Such cultural differentiation suggests that our rather early poetic source
reflects a context in which ethnicity could have emerged or intensified

43. W. F. Albright, "The Names 'Israel' and 'Judah', with an Excursus," *JBL* 46
(1927) 151–68. For other possibilities, see also the interesting, if controversial, study
by Margalit, "On the Origin and Antiquity of the Name 'Israel,'" 225–37.

44. Exonyms generally focus on some distinguishing feature of the named group
as viewed from the "etic" perspective (the outsider's point of view). Especially frequent
in these names is a focus on geographic distinctiveness (as in the case of the *Sea-peoples*
described in Egyptian texts) or on cultural distinctiveness, as seen in the case of the
Shasu, a name coined with reference to their nomadic lifestyle (if Egyptian in origin) or
to their vandal tendencies (if West Semitic in origin).

45. By way of example, note the Ishmaelites, who appear in the Hebrew Bible as a
sociocultural entity and also as devotees of El/Yahweh.

46. Especially given the propensity, identified by Lemche, for other people in the
region to call them "Canaanites."

as an Israelite mode of identity. But the text is too brief and sketchy to serve as proof of Israelite ethnicity in twelfth-century Palestine. So while I must generally agree with K. van der Toorn's assertion that "there is no proof" of the ethnic unity of the inhabitants of the hill country during the Early Iron Age, I cannot agree with his conclusion that we have "*no evidence*" [italics mine] of religious unity among them.[47] The probable use of the name "Israel" by the people of Israel can reasonably imply two things: both a common cultural identity and a shared devotion to the god El. I would state, therefore, that a judicious evaluation of Merneptah's text does provide some evidence that a sociocultural unity existed among a people called "Israel," and it also seems that it included common religious sentiments. Even after saying this, we must nevertheless entertain one other possibility.

The present skepticism about an early Israelite tribal confederation makes me hesitant to raise the issue, because I do not want to appear to be "looking" for a tribal confederation in our text. It is clear, however, that my presumptions about the sociocultural status of Merneptah's "Israel" rest on two key points—on the scribe's use of the determinitive for "people" and the conjunction of this evidence with the endonymic status of the name "Israel." These assumptions are reasonable but not beyond suspicion. If the Egyptian scribe was not clear on the nature of the entity he called "Israel," knowing only that it was "different" from the surrounding modalities, then we can imagine something other than a sociocultural Israel. It is possible that Israel represented a confederation of united, but sociologically distinct, modalities that were joined either cultically or politically via treaties and the like. This interpretation of the evidence would allow for the unity implied by the endonymic evidence and also give our scribe some latitude in his use of the determinitive. Although this interpretation is possible, I think it less likely than the sociocultural interpretation that I have outlined above.

There is one additional piece of evidence that ought to be discussed before we move our attention to the Song of Deborah. Several

---

47. Van der Toorn's volume is contradictory on this point: he suggests that Merneptah's Israel "constituted a group of nonurbanized people named presumably after their eponymous ancestor, Israel," i.e., Early Iron Age Israel was an ethnic community (K. van der Toorn, *Family Religion in Babylonia, Syria and Israel: Continuity and Change in the Forms of Religious Life* [Studies in the History and Culture of the Ancient Near East 7; Leiden: Brill, 1996] 185, 281).

years ago, F. Yurco, on the basis of cartouche evidence, made the now well-known observation that the reliefs accompanying Ramesses II's treaty text at Karnak should probably be associated with his successor, Merneptah.[48] The reliefs depict four battle scenes, three including walled cities and one open-terrain battle scene. In addition, one of the walled cities is labeled Ashkelon. From this Yurco concluded that the reliefs correspond to the four antagonists on Merneptah's stele, namely, Ashkelon, Gezer, Yano'am, and Israel, with Israel represented in the open-terrain battle scene. D. Redford has offered a modification of this reading in which he preserves the association of the reliefs with Ramesses but views them as the inspiration behind Merneptah's fictitious victories.[49] In this scenario, Merneptah's "Israel" might well be associated with the "Shasu" depictions left behind by the scribes of Seti I and Ramesses II.[50] While all of this is somewhat speculative, it is true that, if there is a connection between the relief depictions and Merneptah's stele, then the depictions would provide pictorial evidence for the sociocultural distinctions that the text already suggests between Israel and the nearby city-states of Canaan.

The Song of Deborah (Judges 5)

As in the case of the Merneptah Stele, there is a strong tendency to find characteristics of Israel in the Song of Deborah that are not necessarily there—namely, a united league of tribes who are covenanted with Yahweh and each other in defense of a central cultic shrine. The problem with this reading is that, apart from a few objections to the contrary, this song is often regarded as the oldest text of the Hebrew Bible and should not necessarily be read in light of the other texts that

48. See F. Yurco, "Merneptah's Palestine Campaign," *JSSEA* 8 (1978) 70; idem, "3,200-Year-Old Picture of Israelites Found in Egypt," 20–38.

49. Ahlström takes the Amada Stele as evidence that Merneptah's conquests were not literary fictions (*Who Were the Israelites?* 38). On the Amada Stele, see R. O. Faulkner, "Egypt: From the Inception of the Nineteenth Dynasty to the Death of Ramses III," *CAH*, volume 2 / part 2: *The Middle East and the Aegean Region c. 1380–1000 B.C.* (3d ed.; Cambridge: Cambridge University Press, 1970) 234.

50. For a complete explanation, see D. Redford, "The Ashkelon Relief at Karnak and the Israel Stela," *IEJ* 36 (1986) 188–200. For more on the Shosu and Israel, see R. Giveon, *Les Bédouins Shosou*, 267–71; van der Toorn, *Family Religion*, 283; M. Weippert, "Semitische Nomaden des zweiten Jahrtausends: Über die der ägyptischen Quellen," *Bib* 55 (1974) 265–80, 427–33.

depict a united Israel and reflect a strong covenantal ideology. On the other hand, I have little sympathy for the so-called "criteria of dissimilarity" so often employed in New Testament research and consequently do not feel that it is incumbent upon us to force a contrast between Deborah's Israel and Israel as depicted in the remaining portions of the historical books and the Pentateuch. We should, nevertheless, begin with a clear notion of what might reasonably be derived from the song as an independent source before we proceed to consider how it might "connect" with other sources in the Hebrew Bible.

As I have said, there is a strong consensus that Judges 5 is rather old, but this has not always been true. Around the turn of the century M. Vernes argued, on the basis of supposed Aramaic influence and late features in the Hebrew of the text, that the Song of Deborah (SDeb) was an archaized piece produced no earlier than the fifth century B.C.E.[51] So, for instance, in 5:7 the song twice employs the relative pronoun –שֶׁ, rather than אֲשֶׁר, a feature common in late Biblical and Mishnaic Hebrew. Similarly the term עֲמָמִים ('peoples') rather than עַם in 5:14 is explained as a late form resulting from Aramaic influence. G. F. Moore commented soon afterward that Vernes did not offer sufficient grounds for dating the song late and for good reason. In the case of –שֶׁ, for example, it has long been thought that the form is rather archaic in the Northern Hebrew dialect and was used alongside אֲשֶׁר in all periods of the language (otherwise, the use of –שֶׁ was a rather foolish blunder for an otherwise very effective archaizer).[52] The contention that various words were influenced by or dependent upon late Aramaic is equally questionable.[53] The word עֲמָמִים, for instance, occurs not only in late Aramaic but also in the much earlier Aramaic Sefire Treaty,[54] and the possibility that the dialect of the Northern Kingdom was influenced by the nearby Arameans seems quite likely.[55] Vernes did not ex-

---

51. M. Vernes, "Le Cantique de Débora," *REJ* 24 (1892) 52–67, 225–55.

52. G. F. Moore, *A Critical and Exegetical Commentary on Judges* (ICC: Edinburgh: T. & T. Clark, 1895) 131, 144–45; J. A. Soggin, *Judges* (OTL; Philadelphia: Westminster, 1981) 87. It is often commented that –שֶׁ is probably archaic and closely related to the Akkadian *ša* and the Phoenician אֲשׁ. See especially the very useful study of G. Bergsträsser, "Das hebräische Präfix שׁ," *ZAW* 29 (1909) 40–56.

53. See the summary by B. Lindars, *Judges 1–5* (Edinburgh: T. & T. Clark, 1975) 214–15.

54. See the comments of J. C. L. Gibson, *Textbook of Syrian Semitic Inscriptions* (3 vols.; Oxford: Clarendon, 1971–82) 2.54.

55. See the antiquated but still useful observations of C. F. Burney, *The Book of Judges* (ICC; London: Rivingtons, 1918) 171–76.

plain why his late author would list only ten tribes, why Judah was excepted from the list, why Yahweh came from Seir rather than from Sinai or Jerusalem,[56] or why the text is so cryptic that parts of it are almost unreadable,[57] so there are many problems with a thesis like his. But the rejection of Vernes's very late dating of the song should not distract us from the equally problematic tendency to assume that the song is very early. For instance, B. Halpern suggests that the song "can be located with relative confidence in the pre-monarchic period," that is, near the time of Merneptah.[58] These sympathies are often expressed by scholars, frequently with a rather thin supporting argument.[59] There have been some serious efforts to demonstrate the antiquity of the song, particularly the work of D. Robertson, who seems to have identified some correspondences between Ugaritic poetry and several traditionally early Hebrew pieces, including SDeb.[60] But our enthusiasm for such a conclusion must be somewhat bridled by the well-known complexity associated with Ugaritic studies[61] and by the fact that Robertson's view only supports the conclusion that SDeb is earlier than most of our other Hebrew sources—not that it dates to a period near the Ugaritic period.[62] As a result it is only natural that a number of

56. Cf. É. Lipiński, "Judges 5, 4–5 et Psaume 68, 1–11," *Bib* 48 (1967) 185–206.

57. As Soggin has noted, both the A and B recensions of the LXX seem thoroughly confused by the song (*Judges*, 92).

58. Halpern, *The Emergence of Israel in Canaan*, 32, 117. The early date has a longstanding tradition. See Y. Aharoni, "New Aspects of the Israelite Occupation in the North," in *Near Eastern Archaeology in the Twentieth Century: Essays in Honor of Nelson Glueck* (ed. J. A. Sanders; Garden City, N.Y.: Doubleday, 1970) 260; W. F. Albright, *Yahweh and the Gods of Canaan*, 13; R. G. Boling, *Judges* (AB 6A; Garden City: Doubleday, 1975) 98–100; F. M. Cross and D. N. Freedman, *Studies in Ancient Yahwistic Poetry* (SBLDS 21; Missoula, Mont.: Scholars Press, 1975) 5; R. de Vaux, *Histoire ancienne d'Israël* (Paris: Gabalda, 1973) 105. A. W. Hertzberg, *Die Bücher Josua, Richter, Ruth* (ATD; 2d ed.; Göttingen: Vandenhoeck & Ruprecht, 1959) 173; R. Albertz's recent history of Israelite religion utilizes the song as a source for reconstructing prestate Israel: *A History of Israelite Religion in the Old Testament Period* (2 vols.; OTL; Louisville: Westminster/John Knox, 1994) 1.80–82.

59. See, for instance, the work of D. K. Stuart, *Studies in Early Hebrew Meter* (HSM 13; Missoula, Mont.: Scholars Press, 1976).

60. D. A. Robertson, *Linguistic Evidence in Dating Early Hebrew Poetry* (SBLDS 3; Missoula, Mont.: Scholars Press, 1972) 31–34.

61. T. J. Lewis, "The Disappearance of the Goddess Anat: The 1995 West Semitic Research Project on Ugaritic Epigraphy," *BA* 59 (1996) 115–21.

62. To complicate matters further, we really understand very little about Hebrew poetry, as Soggin has noted: J. A. Soggin, *Introduction to the Old Testament* (OTL; Louisville: Westminster, John Knox, 1989) x, 71–77.

scholars have recently questioned the hoary antiquity of the song,[63] frequently explaining that the song's archaic features are a consequence of its poetic genre—that is, poetry tends to preserve earlier morphological forms. G. Garbini has lent his support to this view by pointing out that the language of the song is, after all, not so archaic and includes features that postdate the tenth-century Gezer calendar, such as the definite article and the common plural construct.[64] Although one might attempt to explain this via modernization of the text, it does not seem necessary to do so when we take account of one additional point.[65] It must also be borne in mind that another important reason the song has been dated early—normally to the twelfth century B.C.E.—is the presumed antiquity of the pentateuchal sources, and this is now a part of the debate. As long as a person dates the Yahwist to the early monarchic period, it is necessary to date SDeb even earlier, since it looks, linguistically speaking, much older than the pentateuchal narratives. But since we are setting aside those narratives for the time being, a sound conclusion is that the song dates sometime between the twelfth and ninth centuries B.C.E., with a date near our terminus ad quem being quite likely.[66]

Even if a person tends toward the ninth-century date, an important problem remains unresolved. As Gray has suggested, the tradition

63. G. W. Ahlström, *Who Were the Israelites?* (Winona Lake, Ind.: Eisenbrauns, 1986) 80–81; L. E. Axelsson, *The Lord Rose Up from Seir: Studies in the History and Traditions of the Negev and Southern Judah* (ConBOT 25; Stockholm: Almqvist & Wiksell, 1987) 52; U. Bechmann, *Das Deboralied zwischen Geschichte und Fiktion: Eine exegetische Untersuchung zu Richter 5* (St. Ottilien: EOS, 1989); Lemche, *The Canaanites and Their Land*, 92–93; J. A. Soggin, "Bemerkungen zum Debora lied, Richter Kap. 5," *ThLZ* 106 (1981) 625–39; van der Toorn, *Family Religion*, 236. For a very late Hasmonean dating of the song, see B.-J. Diebner, "Wann sang Deborah ihr Lied? Überlegungen zu zwei der ältesten Texte des TNK (Ri 4 und 5)," *ACEBT* 14 (1995) 106–30.

64. G. Garbini, "Il Cantico di Debora," *La Parola del Passato* 33 (1978) 5–31; idem, *History and Ideology in Ancient Israel* (New York: Crossroad, 1988) 32. Soggin and Lindars generally follow Garbini's conclusion (Soggin, *Judges,* 80–1; Lindars, *Judges 1–5*, 214–15). Soggin also finds in the text rather advanced theological notions that point us toward a later rather than earlier date.

65. On the tendency to update grammatical and morphological archaisms, see B. K. Waltke and M. O'Connor, *An Introduction to Biblical Hebrew Syntax* (Winona Lake, Ind.: Eisenbrauns, 1990) 17.

66. Lending additional support to this view is the recent observation of Lemaire that the geographical regions listed in the song best fit a ninth-century B.C.E. context (A. Lemaire, "Galaad et Makir," *VT* 31 [1981] 39–61).

behind the song might be older than the song itself,[67] and this seems all the more likely when we realize the reason for the fact that even scholars open to the later dating tend to treat the song as a source of premonarchic history.[68] The problem is that we are hard-pressed to explain why a ninth-century poet felt it necessary to point out that four of the tribes failed to enter the conflict against Canaan. As far as I know, a suitable ninth-century *Sitz im Leben* for the polemic against these tribes has not been suggested. The strength of the Omride dynasty during this period appears to preclude the unstable political context reflected in the song, and the tribe of Gad, which in the ninth-century Mesha Stele figures so prominently, is curiously missing, as is the tribe of Manasseh.[69] In lieu of such a context, we are pushed to the conclusion that the song, even if it is from a later date, probably reflects an earlier and perhaps premonarchical tradition. This problem is of course related to the much-debated composition history of the piece. Although most agree that we are dealing with a *Siegeslieder* or something similar in terms of final form,[70] Weiser has emphasized that a number of separate form-critical units lie behind the poem, and Müller has argued that one can discern both epic and nonepic contributions to it.[71] H.-D. Neef has recently defended the compositional unity of the poem on the basis of its consistent style

---

67. J. Gray, *Joshua, Judges, Ruth* (NCBC; Grand Rapids, Mich.: Eerdmans, 1986) 261.

68. See the following discussions: Lindars, *Judges 1–5*, 265–67; Soggin, *Judges*, 97–99.

69. Gibson, *Syrian Semitic Inscriptions*, 1.75–6. In fact the text tells us that the Gadites had lived in the region since ancient times (ואש גד ישב בערץ עטרת מעלם). Regarding the absence of Manasseh, Finkelstein believes that the Iron Age archaeological data allows us to distinguish a Canaanite population in the region that is distinct from an Israelite population in nearby Ephraim and in the marginal areas of Manasseh. This is at least interesting (Finkelstein, *The Archaeology of the Israelite Settlement*, 352–56).

70. However, as R. de Vaux noted (*Histoire ancienne d'Israël*, 100), the Sitz im Leben in which the text was used is difficult. Of course the most common approach is to view the text as a victory song used in the context of the amphictyonic festivals, but this is very much in question.

71. According to Müller, we are dealing primarily with an old battle report in vv. 2–5, 9–11, and 31a. Weiser has especially emphasized that vv. 13–18 constitute a "roll-call" used in the amphictyonic festival (Hans-Peter Müller, "Der Aufbau des Deboraliedes," *VT* 16 [1966] 447). See also D. A. Weiser, "Das Deboralied: Eine gattungs- und traditionsgeschichtliche Studien," *ZAW* 71 (1959) 67–69.

and morphology, and I think that his observations have merit.[72] In my view the chief problem is that the song's complexity, which causes some to view it as a composite text, also makes it difficult to provide a convincing explanation of its supposed compositeness. In light of this, it seems wise to begin with the final form of the text, which few would date any later than the ninth century.

Although the heroic genre of the poem is of the sort that is a poor substitute for history,[73] we must nonetheless ask what it can tell us about Israelite identity. As it is usually translated, the poem recounts a battle in which ten entities, collectively known as "Israel" (5:5, 13–18), participated (or should have participated) in a battle against the "kings of Canaan" (5:19).[74] Of primary importance with respect to the question of Israelite ethnicity is this: what is the nature of these ten modalities and in what sense do they share a common identity as Israel? Geographic explanations of the text seem to be in vogue recently: de Geus argues that the ten-name list enumerates geographical regions and Ahlström contends that Israel should be understood in this period primarily as a territory rather than a people.[75] But as B. Lindars has pointed out, this does not explain the reference in 5:15–16 to Reuben's 'clans' (פלגות, twice), and even less does it explain the reference to Benjamin's 'kinsmen' (עממיך) in 5:14.[76] Furthermore, one must reckon with the fact that these so-called geographical units are behaving throughout very much like social modalities that make and follow corporate decisions concerning participation in the conflict. Whether

72. Neef, "Der Stil des Deboraliedes (Ri 5)," *ZAH* 8 (1995) 275–93. Lending support to this view is G. Gerleman, "The Song of Deborah in the Light of Stylistics," *VT* 1 (1951) 168–80. We should note that the quite uniform obscurity of the text's Hebrew also argues, paradoxically, for its unity.

73. C. M. Bowra, *Heroic Poetry* (London: Macmillan, 1961) 535.

74. Although unlikely in my view, it has been argued that the text, rightly understood, actually indicates that all of the tribes participated. See B. Halpern, "The Resourceful Israelite Historian: The Song of Deborah and Israelite Historiography," *HTR* 76 (1983) 379–401; See also Halpern's reworked version of the same article in *The First Historians: The Hebrew Bible and History* (University Park, Penn.: Penn State University Press, 1996) 76–103.

75. Ahlström, *Who Were the Israelites?* 57–83; C. H. J. de Geus, *The Tribes of Israel: An Investigation into Some of the Presuppositions of Martin Noth's Amphictyony Hypothesis* (Studia Semitica Neerlandica 18; Assen: Van Gorcum, 1976) 111.

76. On the possible ethnic significance of פלגה, see the rather late text of 2 Chr 35:5: לפלגות בית האבות. See also the use of פלג on a weight published by Moscati in 1951 (Gibson, *Syrian Semitic Inscriptions*, 1.68).

these social modalities were envisioned along ethnic lines is somewhat obscure to us, and even in the case of Benjamin and Reuben one must be careful not to draw hasty conclusions from slippery Hebrew terminology. However, we should probably not be satisfied with the conclusion that we have here nothing more than a list of geographical regions. Rather, we have social modalities associated with geographical regions—and this is something quite different. This explanation also implies the whole notion of *homeland*, a notion frequently associated with ethnicity.

But setting aside the question of ethnicity *within* the supposedly "tribal" modalities of our text, we should ask ourselves what essential ties connected these groups with each other and so, for the poet, created the entity called Israel. Of course, a common answer has been Noth's amphictyonic proposal—that they shared a cultic shrine and therefore fought to protect it—but this thesis has been questioned so much of late that most everyone is leery of it. It is no doubt true that the text presumes a certain mutual responsibility on the part of the ten groups listed here, and this is as one would expect from Noth's thesis. But there is no sense that the responsibility hinged on a particular sanctuary. Rather, the text explicitly tells us only that the groups shared a common responsibility as the people of the god Yahweh to fight in battle against the non-Israelite "kings of Canaan," as Smend told us some time ago.[77] It was this common Yahwistic religious identity that seems to have connected the tribes together and made Israel what it was for the composer of SDeb. Strictly speaking, then, one should be careful to avoid speaking of these ten groups as "tribes" in the sense of ethnic groups, for if ethnic identity is reflected in the text (and I will argue it may well be), its prominence is secondary to the religious ties that linked the tribes together. Our song speaks primarily of a common religious identity that united various groups of Yahwists rather than an ethnic identity that united various groups of Israelites. But we should remind ourselves again that perhaps we are dealing with a viewpoint that postdates the supposed events by some time, and if this is the case, the song could well contain historical or sociological anachronisms that are not evident to us.

77. R. Smend, *Yahweh War and Tribal Confederation: Reflections upon Israel's Earliest History* (Nashville: Abingdon, 1970) 1–42. As Hertzberg has noted, the sense of expectation for participation in the battle precluded military neutrality (Hertzberg, *Die Bücher Josua, Richter, Ruth*, 180).

There is perhaps something more that we can say about the religious identity reflected in the song. Facing an admittedly difficult and cryptic section of the text, the RSV translates the beginning of Judg 5:8: 'When new gods were chosen, then war was in the gates'. The first few words, יבחר אלהים אחרים, read rather clearly if one assumes with most commentators that יבחר is singular with an indefinite subject.[78] On the other hand, Soggin and Lindars read the verb as written (third-person singular), and this results in a translation 'God chose others', that is, 'God chose new men'.[79] The next phrase, אז לחם שערים, is more difficult, and a number of emendations and diverse readings have been proposed.[80] But if we follow the most common tack on this text, as the RSV has done, then the text is very close to the ideology (but not the language) of the Deuteronomic and Deuteronomistic sources, namely, that Yahweh was the sole God of Israel and that, despite this, Israel nonetheless had a propensity to follow after other gods—with unpleasant results. If one dates the song to the ninth century, then this should come as no real surprise, since the roughly contemporary Mesha Stele confirms Yahweh as Israel's national deity (and also the theology of divine retribution). But if one either dates the song earlier or finds in it traditions from the prestate period, then this kind of theology is somewhat unexpected. Lest we build a "house of cards," however, the unfortunate state of the text dictates that we end our speculations here. Let it suffice that, for the writer of SDeb, the entity Israel was composed of ten groups that were united by a common devotion to Yahweh and by a common obligation to fight on his side. Israel was the 'people of Yahweh' (עם יהוה), and Yahweh was the god of Israel (אלהי ישראל).

Setting aside the preliminary question of Israel's religious identity in the song, we turn our attention more directly to the question of ethnic identity. Ethnicity requires a contextual contrast between various

78. Following Gray, *Joshua, Judges, Ruth*, 267. This is contra Moore, who does not view this reading as very likely (Moore, *A Critical and Exegetical Commentary on Judges*, 145).

79. Lindars, *Judges 1–5*, 207; Soggin, *Judges*, 82.

80. For instance, Weiser translated the text as the '[Gods] whom they formerly had not known', while Budde suggested '[the] barley bread was spent'. For their discussion as well as for other possible solutions, see C. F. Burney, *The Book of Judges*, 117–19; K. Budde *Das Buch der Richter* (KHAT 7; Freiburg: Mohr, 1897) 43; Hertzberg, *Die Bücher Josua, Richter, Ruth*, 171; A. Weiser, *The Old Testament: Its Formation and Development* (New York: Association Press, 1961) 75–76.

social modalities, and in the song we have this contrast on two levels. First, we have a sense of contrast between the Israelite groups. Despite their religious unity as Israel, the song reflects the notion that Ephraimites were not Reubenites, that Reubenites were not Benjaminites, and so forth. And so we must imagine how these Israelites construed the tension between their common religious identity and their obvious sociological distinctiveness. As I have pointed out concerning the "Table of Nations" in Genesis 10, and as ethnicity studies have frequently observed, a common way to handle this tension is through the creation of segmented genealogies that explain both the perceived similarities (we share a common ancestry) and the perceived differences (but, after all, we are not entirely of the same stock).[81] Even more significant from an ethnic point of view is the second sociological contrast in our text, the intense atmosphere of competition between Israel and Canaan. Without necessarily assenting to the solutions suggested by Mendenhall and Gottwald or their early dating of the song,[82] we can nevertheless see here a tension between Canaanite city-states around Jezreel and the Israelite groups nearby.[83] We are forced to pause here, because Lemche has suggested that the phrase "kings of Canaan" might be a Deuteronomistic gloss inspired by the prose account of Judges 4, wherein Jabin of Hazor is a "king of Canaan."[84] This conclusion ought to be rejected for several reasons. First, since Merneptah's text has already suggested a possible contrast between Canaan and Israel, there is no compelling reason to view a similar contrast in the later SDeb as problematic.[85] Second, we must see in the song an Israelite military opponent, and even if we follow Lemche's suggestion to exclude Canaan,

81. The genealogy constructed in Genesis 10 attempts to account, in part, for Semitic linguistic similarities, as in the case of Aram and Israel, by making them fellow Semites. See K. L. Sparks, "Semites," *EDB* (forthcoming).

82. Mendenhall, *The Tenth Generation*; Gottwald, *The Tribes of Yahweh*.

83. And if one follows Stager, as Lindars does, then we can go as far as seeing a sociological struggle between village highlanders and city-state lowlanders, although not for the same reasons that Mendenhall and Gottwald suggest. See L. E. Stager, "Archeology, Ecology, and Social History: Background Themes to the Song of Deborah," *Congress Volume: Jerusalem, 1986* (VTSup 40; Leiden: Brill, 1988) 221–34; Lindars, *Judges 1–5*, 237–38.

84. Lemche, *The Canaanites and Their Land*, 95.

85. In fact, in a later study even Lemche has noted that "it may still be possible to refer the antagonism between the Israelites and the Canaanites back to premonarchical and early monarchical times." For his theory on this, see N. P. Lemche, "City-Dwellers or Administrators: Further Light on the Canaanites," *History and Tradition of*

we must still identify a suitable candidate—and who would be a better candidate for a ninth-century poet than Canaan? Probably the most important reason to question Lemche's conclusion, however, is that the "king of Canaan" references in the prose account of 4:2, 23–24 are, as Richter pointed out long ago, a part of the Deuteronomistic editor's work in Judges 4.[86] Because this is the only time that Dtr uses the phrase "king(s) of Canaan," it seems to me very likely that the editor has borrowed the terminology from one of his sources, namely SDeb, and this seems to be confirmed by Halpern's thesis that the prose account of Judges 4 stems rather directly from the poetic account of Judges 5.[87]

For Lemche, the Canaanites were primarily a *literary* antagonist of the Israelites rather than their ancient, historical opponent.[88] His thesis needs מלכי כנען to be redactional, despite the fact that even he seems to realize that there is thin evidence for making it so.[89] For the most part, I have some sympathy with Lemche's thesis. But the literary Canaanites did not appear from thin air; they were derived from previous traditions, and their presence in a ninth-century source presents us with no real problem. What we should conclude, then, is that according to our poet the entity Israel was a religiously united group of separate—but perhaps similar—social modalities that took up arms against Canaanite city-state populations in the lowlands around Taanach and Megiddo.

If we continue to assume a ninth-century terminus ad quem for the Song of Deborah, how can we summarize Israelite identity and its

---

Early Israel: Studies Presented to Eduard Nielsen (ed. A. Lemaire and B. Otzen; Leiden: Brill, 1993) 86.

86. W. Richter, *Die Bearbeitungen des 'Retterbuches' in der deuteronomischen Epoche* (BBB 21; Bonn: Hanstein, 1964) 6–9. Cf. Becker's view that Judges 4 is basically a composition of Dtr (based on the Song of Deborah and the Jabin tradition in Josh 11:1–15) that was subsequently subjected to minor additions by a post-Dtr redactor: U. Becker, *Richterzeit und Königtum: Redaktionsgeschichtliche Studien zum Richterbuch* (BZAW 192; Berlin: de Gruyter, 1990) 126–28, 138.

87. B. Halpern, *The First Historians: The Hebrew Bible and History* (University Park, Penn.: Penn State University Press, 1996) 76–97.

88. This is certainly true of Lemche's work in *The Canaanites and Their Land* (152–55). However, his previously cited and more recent study, "City-Dwellers or Administrators: Further Light on the Canaanites," does postulate a Late Bronze conflict between the Israelites and the functionaries of the Egyptian provincial system, who were dubbed "Canaanites."

89. As evidenced in his own phrase "should this be the case" (ibid., 95).

relationship to Canaanite identity at that point? First, we can say, at least from a polemical standpoint, that the supposed religious contrast between Canaanites and Yahwists was firmly established by the ninth century B.C.E., and if the composition histories of Müller and Mathys are correct, then this contrast was known from an even older epic battle report (see v. 31a).[90] This is somewhat counter to present trends in biblical scholarship, which are wont to push the Israelite/Canaanite religious contrast very late in Israel's history and to combine ancient Israelite and Canaanite religion under the rubric of "West Semitic Religion."[91] But in our text the entity called Canaan stands in opposition to the people of Yahweh, and it makes precious little sense constantly to emphasize that Israelite and Canaanite religion are of one cloth when even our earliest biblical sources stress the distinctions between them.[92] Second, from a historical perspective, the poet understood Israel's early history as one of conflict between Canaan and Israel, in this case a conflict that was probably spurred by both ecological competition for the fertile areas of the Jezreel valley and by economic competition to control trade routes through the region.[93] Theoretically speaking, this is precisely the kind of conflict that gives rise to and/or intensifies ethnic sentiments. Third, from a geographical perspective, it has long been noted that an important aspect of tribal identity in the song is geographic.[94] We should suppose from this not only that geography distinguished the tribes from each other but also that it necessarily distinguished them from non-Israelites, that is,

90. Müller, "Der Aufbau des Deboraliedes," 447; H.-P. Mathys, *Dichter und Beter: Theologen aus spätalttestamentlicher Zeit* (OBO 132; Göttingen: Vandenhoeck & Ruprecht / Freiburg: Universitätsverlag, 1994) 174–75.

91. Lemche, *The Canaanites and Their Land,* 170.

92. On the question of Israelite religious distinctiveness, see especially P. Machinist, "The Question of Distinctiveness in Ancient Israel," *Essential Papers on Israel and the Ancient Near East* (ed. F. E. Greenspahn; New York: New York University Press, 1991) 420–42.

93. As N. Na'aman has pointed out, the Jezreel Valley was regarded as "crown property" from very ancient times to the Second Temple Period, and even later. See his "Pharaonic Lands in the Jezreel Valley in the Late Bronze Age," in *Society and Economy in the Eastern Mediterranean (c. 1500–1000 B.C.): Proceedings of the International Symposium Held at the University of Haifa from the 28th of April to the 2nd of May 1985* (ed. M. Heltzer and E. Lipiński; Orientalia Lovaniensia Analecta 23; Leuven: Peeters, 1988) 177–85.

94. Lindars, "The Israelite Tribes in Judges," 103–4; M. Noth, *Das System der Zwölf Stämme Israels* (Stuttgart: Kohlhammer, 1930) 5–36.

Canaan and the like. Fourth, from a political perspective, the two entities could not be more different. Canaan's city-states were ruled by
"kings," while Israel followed Deborah and Barak (and its 'commanders?' חוקקי ישראל), who, whatever they were, were not kings. Rather, it
is perhaps best to think of Deborah and Barak as "military saviors" in
the sense suggested by W. Richter some time ago.[95] Finally, from a sociological and cultural perspective the poet viewed Canaan as distinct
from Israel. This is not only because of their religious, political, and
geographical differences. It is also because of a kinship distinction between Israel and Canaan, reflected in the poet's references to Benjamin's kinsmen (עממיך) and Reuben's clans (פלגות), a distinction that
is valid even if we are not sure how the poet thought that these sub-
tribal modalities worked and operated. So, in the song we have kinship; we have contrasting sociopolitical modalities; we have intense
economic and ecological competition; and we have religiously charged
rhetoric. In sum, we have all of the ingredients necessary to suggest
that Israel, as depicted in the Song of Deborah, was probably an ethnic
modality, or to be more precise, was at least composed of ethnic modalities. Because of this, it is my view that our social histories of Israel
can no longer postpone the development of Israelite ethnicity to a period later than the ninth century B.C.E. And the fact that the tradition
behind our song is probably older than the song itself suggests an even
earlier date for the emergence of Israelite ethnic sentiments.

Before summarizing our work in this chapter, we should ask if it is
appropriate to speak of *amphictyony* in association with Israel's tribes in
the Song of Deborah. In one sense, it certainly is not, for if by *amphictyony* we mean that Israel was organized like and functioned analogous
to the Greek amphictyonies, then the idea of an amphictyony has always been wrong-headed. As soon as one examines the two quite different cultural and historical contexts, one is bound to find that they
were not the same thing. On the other hand, if one is looking for comparative data that is similar to ancient Israel, then it is useful to exam-

---

95. W. Richter, *Traditionsgeschictliche Untersuchungen zum Richterbuch* (BBB 18;
Bonn: Hanstein, 1963); as well as the previously cited *Die Bearbeitungen des 'Retterbuches' in der deuteronomischen Epoche.* This conclusion of course assumes Richter's
view of a predeuteronomistic *Retterbuch,* which has been challenged recently by
Becker. Nevertheless, in the case of Deborah, Becker concedes that we are dealing with
a *Rettererzählung* (Becker, *Richterzeit und Königtum,* 123).

ine the concept of *amphictyony* more closely.[96] As Lemche has noted, there were three primary types of leagues described in classical materials, the ἀμφικτυονία ('sacral league'), the συμπολιτεία ('political league') and the συμμαχία ('military league').[97] These structures are much more complex than biblical scholars sometimes realize, and it is difficult to make generalizations about them, especially when the classical sources often postdate the structures themselves by many years. Although it is common to think of the amphictyony as a twelve-, ten-, or six-tribe league, this was not always the case. Further, the use of ἔθνη cannot be taken as evidence that the groups were always ethnic tribal federations, for it appears that the term was also used when federal states were joined together. Nevertheless, there are generalities that we can highlight. With respect to its religious nature, the obligations and the ten-tribe list reflected in the Song of Deborah are most similar to those of the Greek "sacral leagues." Unlike the Greek amphictyonies, however, the Israelite obligation does not reflect a common religious shrine or cultic assembly. Such a pre-state institution may have existed, but to say that it did on the basis of Deborah's song would be guessing. Therefore, although the Israelite obligation appears to be religiously motivated, in terms of expectation it stands closer to the Greek military leagues (*symmachies*). This is because the Israelite action does not appear to have been motivated by threatening sacral encroachments but rather by a desire to control ecologically productive territory. So if by *amphictyony* we mean only that a group of independent sociopolitical modalities shared a common religious identity that linked them together in an effective and functional way, especially with regard to warfare, then it seems quite appropriate to say that the Israel of our song was not only amphictyonic but also symmachic; it is not proper to speak of it as an amphictyony or as a symmachy.

---

96. For a somewhat speculative discussion of parallels between the Israelite "amphictyony" and comparative materials from Philistia and the Sumerians, see H. E. Chambers, "Ancient Amphictyonies, Sic et Non," in *Scripture in Context II: More Essays on the Comparative Method* (ed. W. W. Hallo; Winona Lake, Ind.: Eisenbrauns, 1983) 39–59.

97. Lemche's short study is very valuable (N. P. Lemche, "The Greek Amphictyony: Could It Be a Prototype for the Israelite Society in the Period of the Judges?" *JSOT* 4 [1977] 48–59).

Summary and Conclusions

To draw the proper conclusions, we must steer a middle way between the tendency, on the one hand, to make probabilities out of possibilities and, on the other, to make possibilities into irrelevancies. The
Merneptah Stele seems to provide slim but reasonable evidence of an
early context where an entity called Israel stood in geographical and sociological juxtaposition to the city-states of Canaan, in this case Ashkelon, Gezer, and Yano'am. However, this proposition is somewhat
misleading unless we rephrase it. We might equally well say that the
text of the stele distinguishes between a Canaanite people called Israel
and the Canaanite peoples of the nearby city-states, for I doubt seriously that it allows us to determine with confidence whether the scribe
intended us to locate Israel within Canaan or alongside it. Our confusion along these lines is somewhat obviated (1) by the scribe's use of
the "people" determinative in conjunction with "Israel," (2) by the fact
that Israel is probably an endonym rather than an exonym, and (3) by
the fact that the name Israel contains the theophoric element *El*. These
are three different but related pieces of evidence that suggest we are
dealing with a sociocultural entity that called itself Israel and that worshiped (among other deities?) the high god El. Apart from a good deal
of speculation, this is about all that can be said regarding Merneptah's
Israel. But the text provides us with the first evidence of a possible
situation in which Israelite ethnicity might have either emerged or
intensified.[98]

The Song of Deborah probably dates several centuries later and
was composed by a Northern poet for reasons that are not entirely
clear.[99] It reflects a context that was very suitable for the emergence or

---

98. I am obviously more guarded than H. N. Rösel, who asserts that Merneptah's
Israel was already an ethnic entity during the thirteenth century B.C.E. See chap. 6 of
his *Israel in Kanaan: Zum Problem der Entstehung Israels* (Beiträge zur Erforschung des
Alten Testaments und des Antiken Judentums 11; Frankfurt am Main: Peter Lang,
1992).

99. To determine the reason for the song's composition we would have to know
the extent to which the poet followed earlier traditions to inform his work (a very difficult problem that I will not attempt to work out here!) and also the particular Sitz im
Leben in which the song might have been used. On the basis of Judges 5:10–11, we
might suppose that the poem was recited in "Homeric style" at local "watering places"
to fulfill a natural curiosity about the ancient traditions of Israel and also for entertain-
ment (cf. Lindars, *Judges 1–5*, 245). On the other hand the song may have been composed for the royal courts to mimic this musical experience of the peasantry. It might

intensification of ethnic sentiments among the Israelites. The descriptions of Benjamin and Ephraim appear to reflect ethnic modes of identity, and it seems plausible that this was true of other groups as well. But for our poet the most powerful integrating force in Israelite identity was a common devotion to the god Yahweh, and this religious distinctiveness, joined with other sociological, political, and geographical distinctives, served to divide the Israelites from the nearby peoples—in this case from the Canaanites. We cannot prove from the song that the Israelites had taken the step of connecting themselves to each other via segmented genealogy and the like, but in my view, the poem's context, coupled with the ecological and economic competition that originally lay behind it, makes the presence of Israelite ethnicity likely in the ninth century, probably even earlier.[100]

It is tempting at this point, despite the chronological disparity, to draw a straight line from the Israelite/Canaanite polarity of the Merneptah Stele to the same sociological polarity in the Song of Deborah. This is possible, but only possible. Soggin and others have pointed out that the original antagonist in Deborah's Song was probably Sisera, and his name is not what we would expect of a West Semitic king.[101] Although this does not preclude the fact that early traditions identified Sisera as a Canaanite, it does mean that we must be careful to avoid hasty conclusions about the antiquity of a supposed Canaanite/Israelite rivalry. It is possible that the Sisera tradition originated during the Philistine conflicts (as reflected in the Samuel narratives) and that it was only subsequently connected with "Canaanite" terminology. Given these parameters, we may guardedly say that, by the ninth century B.C.E., the Canaanite opposition to Israel was already rooted in the collective memory of Israel as an important element within its national

---

also have been used in ritual or cultic contexts to celebrate the power of Yahweh. The song might have been excerpted from a longer epic tradition, or it may have been composed as an independent poem. In other words, outside of the observation that it is a song of victory (and even some would debate this), its contextual character remains unclear to us if we date it to the ninth century.

100. R. Neu finds that early Israel was comprised of several kinship groups that conceptualized their identity with segmented genealogies. The groups were subsequently united as ecological pressures in the region grew (Neu, *Von der Anarchie zum Staat: Entwicklungsgeschichte Israels von Nomadentum zur Monarchie im Spiegel der Ethnosoziologie* (Neukirchen-Vluyn: Neukirchener Verlag, 1992) 19–138.

101. Boling, *Judges*, 94; Burney, *The Book of Judges*, 84; Gray, *Joshua, Judges, Ruth*, 254; Soggin, *Judges*, 63.

history; we may also say that the tradition behind SDeb shows evidence of a healthy context in which Israelite ethnicity could either emerge or intensify, in spite of the fact that it is difficult to connect SDeb with one specific context.

Despite the fact that I have already cautioned against positing a relationship between Merneptah's Israel and Deborah's Israel, it is nevertheless interesting that the two sources appear to share several common features. First, both portray a sociocultural modality called Israel and distinguish it from the Canaanite city-states nearby. Second, both sources focus our attention on the religious identity of Israel as an important factor in its sociological integration, in one case a common devotion to El and in the other to Yahweh. Third, depending on how we interpret the name "Israel" in the Merneptah text (for example, 'El fights'), we can see the slender possibility that both texts reflect certain "martial tendencies" among the people called "Israel." In light of this evidence, although it seems to me that we cannot prove the legitimacy of closely linking the two texts, we are on equally tenuous footing if we insist that they describe two different "Israels."

Chapter Four

Ethnicity and Identity in the Assyrian Period

In comparison with the Merneptah text and the Song of Deborah, the texts to be examined here, namely the eighth-century Hebrew literary prophets, provide us with a much more stable collection of evidence for our inquiry into ethnicity. It may seem unfortunate to some that a point so late in Israel's history is given this much weight, but my own view of the materials suggests that we have few substantial sources in the biblical or extrabiblical materials that may be unambiguously dated before the eighth century (although these sources may frequently be informed by traditions of greater antiquity).[1] It is, then, not as though we must set aside a vast cornucopia of materials from the Late Bronze Age until the fall of Samaria. As we have already seen, a source like the "Israel Stele" is somewhat obscure and leaves us with the obvious problem that we have trouble linking it directly with biblical Israel. So we must give special attention to Hosea, Amos, and Isaiah. It is very unfortunate that our sources for the origins and early history of the Israelite state are so late, since anyone examining Israelite identity hopes to deal with the issue of state and ethnicity. But my focus on the more "stable" sources precludes this; consequently, we must (regrettably) proceed directly from SDeb to the ministry of Hosea.[2] Throughout this discussion, I will weigh the data provided by these texts with data

---

1. As a reminder, I must again stress that this approach to the sources means that when we begin with Hosea and Amos, we are basically starting "from scratch." We cannot assume that these prophets were familiar with any of the portions of the biblical corpus that are commonly viewed as early, and I am referring here especially to the J and E documents of the Pentateuch.

2. For a recent and useful (but necessarily speculative) discussion of identity and the state, see S. Grosby, "Kinship, Territory, and the Nation in the Historiography of Ancient Israel," *ZAW* 105 (1993) 3–18.

provided by the Assyrian, Greek, and Egyptian sources examined in chap. 2. When the biblical materials are examined in light of these comparative sources, the resulting picture of Israelite ethnic identity and its historical development is somewhat different from that generally presupposed in biblical scholarship.

The Neo-Assyrian period must play a pivotal role in any inquiry into ancient Israelite identity. It is generally agreed that, despite their cultural ties, the Northern and Southern traditions had a certain degree of independence from each other and that, after the fall of the North, the Northern traditions migrated South, where they were transmitted via the Judean scribal community. Because of this it is essential that we give proper attention to the various concepts of identity (ethnic, political, cultural, etc.) that existed before these two bodies of tradition merged during the late eighth century. The major limiting factor in this endeavor is that we are dealing with three relatively short collections, one from the North (Hosea) and two from the South (Amos, Isaiah), and this kind of evidence is naturally suspect if we hope to draw far-reaching and detailed conclusions about the social landscape of ancient Israel and Judah. I do not say this pessimistically. We can reach very useful and accurate conclusions about the work of these prophets and, from it, attempt to isolate and characterize their opponents and the like. It is much more difficult, however, to extrapolate from their work information such as the number of people involved in a given ideological party or even something as broad as the general trajectory of thoughts and ideas in Israel and Judah. What we must be content with, instead, is evidence about some of these trajectories. To put our dilemma in mathematical terms, we face the problem that our sources may not always be as "statistically significant" as we would like. But they are all that we have.

Ethnicity and Identity in Hosea

While I hope to avoid encumbering the present study with excessive literary analysis, I must stake out my own position. In the case of Hosea there seem to be two general schools of thought about its redactional character. The major problem that Hosea presents as an eighth-century source is this: in the decades after the fall of Israel, its text was transmitted in a Judean context and therefore reflects certain ideas that may have originated in the North. For many commentators this does not present a serious problem because they see "little evidence of any tampering with the text in the interest of updating its material."[3] On the other hand a number of scholars, because of the relative prominence given to Judah in Hosea, suggest that a fair number of later additions have been made to the text.[4] The differences between these two perspectives are, in many instances, more a matter of tone than substance. Mays and Wolff struggle with the authenticity of the same texts that "skeptics" like Jeremias and Rudolph question. The recent commentary of G. I. Davies provides a very balanced and useful summary of the redactional character of Hosea, which he divides into five basic literary components. First, the bulk of the materials stems from Hosea's own day and underwent very little change before the collections were brought to Judah. Second, a Judean phase of redaction followed, which stressed the distinction between Israel's fate and Judah's preservation. A third stage, which dates near or after the fall of the South to Babylon, includes accusations and threats against Judah as well as Israel. Finally, during the Babylonian and Persian periods, a fourth layer of tradition, designed to provide hope for Jews, was added; this layer predicted that the exiles would return, the two kingdoms would reunite, and a new David would arise. This analysis makes good sense of the materials in Hosea and contextualizes them within appropriate, concrete circumstances. It also provides a useful baseline for my work, since by focusing primarily on the first and supposedly original layer of tradition I hope to preempt excessive debate about the dating of my sources and, therefore, about the validity of my study with respect to eighth-century Israel.

In addition to outlining this general approach, I should state a few theoretical and methodological prejudices clearly from the outset. I tend to regard a given text as original with Hosea unless there are suitable reasons to exclude it, and this is at variance with the tendency of

3. Francis I. Andersen and David Noel Freedman, *Hosea* (AB 24; Garden City, N.Y.: Doubleday, 1980) 57. Concurring with this sentiment are G. I. Davies, *Hosea* (NCBC; Grand Rapids: Eerdmans, 1992) 34–38; J. L. Mays, *Hosea: A Commentary* (OTL; Philadelphia: Westminster, 1969) 16; D. Stuart, *Hosea–Jonah* (WBC; Waco, Tex.: Word, 1987) 14–15; H. W. Wolff, *Hosea* (Hermeneia; Philadelphia: Fortress, 1974) xxix–xxxii.

4. J. Jeremias, *Der Prophet Hosea* (ATD; Göttingen: Vandenhoeck & Ruprecht, 1983) 18–19; W. Rudolph, *Hosea* (KAT; Gütersloh: Gütersloh Verlagshaus, 1966) 25–27; N. H. Snaith, *Mercy and Sacrifice: A Study of the Book of Hosea* (London: Epworth, 1953) 50.

some to deny a text's authenticity unless a strong case can be made for it. One reason for my position is that the present trend in scholarship is to view the Hosean corpus as a generally authentic corpus that contains only scattered redactional elements. A second and more important reason is that there are problems with the tendency of some scholars to view the literary history of Hosea along the lines of the history of Jeremiah—to say that the work reflects Deuteronomistic ideology and is, therefore, largely the product of Deuteronomistic redaction.[5] This is a problem because Deuteronomic ideology as represented in the older "core" of Deuteronomy betrays its Northern provenience and is, therefore, quite at home in a Northern, eighth-century prophetic work like Hosea.[6] Furthermore, even if we set aside the so-called "Deuteronomistic" materials, what remains of Hosea must certainly be viewed as proto-Deuteronomic; how can one differentiate between the older and newer elements if they share such fundamental theological tendencies? Not very easily, I think. The mere presence of Deuteronomic ideology in passages in Hosea does not justify viewing them as redactional, unless there are other criteria, such as are suggested above by Davies. This is not to say that I deny Judean additions to Hosea's text, for it is no doubt true that some texts betray the influence of later Southern editorial activity. I am only making the point that it is more appropriate to think of Hosea as a proto-Deuteronomic work than as a book that has been subjected to a full-scale Deuteronomistic redaction. Therefore, any supposed additions to the text must be identified with more care than is sometimes exercised.

The texts to be examined from Hosea include 2:4–25, 4:1–19, 7:8–13, 9:1–3, and 12:1–14.[7] These are generally accepted as a part of

5. The "Deutero-" terminology can be slippery. Here I use *proto-Deuteronomic* to refer to the ideas that eventually took shape in the book of Deuteronomy, whose ideas I classify as *Deuteronomic*. But the book of Deuteronomy itself contains an older base of materials that preceded the Josianic edition itself, and these portions are usually referred to as the "Kern" or "core" of that book. The adjective "Deuteronomistic" refers to those later writers and editors who took their cues from Deuteronomy in producing the Deuteronomistic History and also in editing the prophetic materials, especially Jeremiah.

6. For a summary comparison of the similarities between Deuteronomy and Hosea, see M. Weinfeld, *Deuteronomy and the Deuteronomic School* (Oxford: Oxford University Press, 1972; reprinted, Winona Lake, Ind.: Eisenbrauns, 1992) 366–70.

7. All references are to the Hebrew text. English equivalents are 2:2–23, 4:1–19, 7:8–13, 9:1–3, and 11:12–12:14.

the original corpus, and the few exceptions can be handled on an ad hoc basis. Why these texts? I think that they have a direct bearing on four primary questions that we should ask of Hosea if we hope to lay bare his perspectives on Israelite identity and ethnicity. First, it is abundantly clear that Hosea criticized the non-Yahwistic cults because they represented religious competition for Yahweh. But this circumstance raises an important question for anyone interested in Israel's ethnic identity. Was this polemic grounded only in the non-Yahwistic nature of the other cults, or was part of the problem also that these deities were foreign deities? Related to this question is a second. Were the various cultic features that Hosea rejected—idols, multiplication of altars, and so on—viewed as foreign or simply as non-Yahwistic? Third, how important for Hosea were the traditions that linked Israel with Judah and what does this tell us about eighth-century Northern identity? And finally, what role did the historical tradition play in the Israelite sense of identity, especially as regards its forefather and ancestor traditions? It is with this last question that our inquiry begins.

The Jacob Traditions: Hosea 12:1–14

In the previous chapter, the Merneptah and Deborah sources yielded pertinent insights only after we pressed them rather hard, and the resulting details are admittedly speculative at points. Here it requires no detailed analysis whatsoever to show that ethnicity played a role in eighth-century Israelite identity, as the Jacob ancestral tradition demonstrates. I think it is fair to characterize this tradition as a "popular" one because the references to it are more properly understood as allusions, and these are only effective if an author can assume his audience's familiarity with them—that is, these traditions must have belonged to the people. Beyond these truisms, the real question is how intense this ethnic sentiment was and also how this ethnicity was related to other modes of identity, particularly religious and political identity. As I attempt to address these issues, I will bring into the discussion a number of complexities found in the text, and my attempts to address these are admittedly tedious at points. But if the problems can be worked out carefully and patiently, then I believe that we will see valuable results.

Following Yahweh's indictment of Israel[8] in 12:3, we meet Israel's
ethnic forefather in vv. 4–7, in which most commentators see Jacob as
either a character with both positive and negative traits or as an entirely
positive role model for Israel.[9] The text of vv. 4–7 has its difficulties, especially in v. 5.[10] The subject of the first clause is unclear, in part because of a text-critical question and also because the subject of the
received text seems to be at odds with the surrounding context. The
verb of the clause is also unclear, for both morphological and lexical
reasons. Taking the last problem first, some have viewed וישׂר as a dou-
blet of 4b and have translated the verb as שׂרה/שׂרי 'to struggle'.[11] Others (Davies, Jeremias, Wolff, and Whitt, for instance) view the verb as a
form of שׂרר ('to reign', 'to play the prince'[12]), with the form in this
case being identical to the form in Judg 9:22.[13] I tend to side with the
latter view, but the problem of the verb's subject is more crucial to our
understanding of the text. As Whitt has noted, how one solves the ambiguity of the subject (is it Jacob or the deity?) is dependent upon how
one handles מלאך in v. 5a. Several scholars view מלאך as a gloss and
thus emend וישׂר אל-מלאך to וישׂר אל, the change allowing El to serve
as the verb's subject (i.e., El was the victor!).[14] This is contrary to most
commentators, who retain מלאך and so have Jacob struggle against the

8. The text reads "Judah," but this is almost universally understood as a part of
the Judean redaction since, for Hosea, Jacob (vv. 3ff.) is everywhere else associated with
the Northern Kingdom. Furthermore, the parallelism of the text (ישׂראל with שׂרה) requires that we read "Israel" rather than "Judah." Andersen and Freedman characterize
the substitution of "Israel" for "Judah" as "desperate" but then proceed to do acrobatic
maneuvers with the word רד in 12:1 to make their scheme work (*Hosea*, 601–2).

9. On the dual role model, see R. B. Coote, "Hosea XII," *VT* 21 (1971) 389–
402; Mays, *Hosea*, 169. On the positive role model, see H.-D. Neef, *Die Heilstraditionen Israels in der Verkündigung des Propheten Hosea* (BZAW 169; Berlin: de Gruyter,
1987) 15–49, 231–35; Stuart, *Hosea–Jonah*, 190.

10. Our discussion of the text is facilitated by the RSV translation and the BHS
text of 12:5, which read, respectively: 'He strove with the angel and prevailed; he wept
and sought his favor. He met God at Bethel, and there God spoke with him' (וַיָּשַׂר
אֶל-מַלְאָךְ וַיֻּכָל בָּכָה וַיִּתְחַנֶּן-לוֹ בֵּית-אֵל יִמְצָאֶנּוּ וְשָׁם יְדַבֵּר עִמָּנוּ).

11. Thus emending the text from וַיָּשַׂר to וַיָּרֶב, as done by Andersen and Freedman, *Hosea*, 593, 607–8; Mays, *Hosea*, 161; S. L. McKenzie, "The Jacob Tradition in
Hosea XII 4–5," *VT* 36 (1986) 313–14; Stuart, *Hosea–Jonah*, 185, 191.

12. BDB 979.

13. Davies, *Hosea*, 274; Jeremias, *Der Prophet Hosea*, 153; Wolff, *Hosea*, 212,
W. D. Whitt, "The Jacob Traditions in Hosea and Their Relation to Genesis," *ZAW*
103 (1991) 32.

14. Jeremias, *Der Prophet Hosea*, 153; Wolff, *Hosea*, 212; H. S. Nyberg emends
the text to אֵל but retains מלאך, in *Studien zum Hoseabuche* (UUA 6; Uppsala: Lunde-
quistska, 1935) 94–95.

angel of God. As J. Vollmer has pointed out, the phrase וישׂר אל־מלאך is *verdächtig* and appears to reflect a redactional effort to soften v. 4b's claim that Jacob wrestled with God himself. But this does not require, as Rudolph and Vollmer suggest, that we delete the entire text.[15] Deleting מלאך alone solves a number of problems and is preferable for several reasons. First, it preserves continuity with ובאונו שׂרה את־ אלהים in 4b, where the struggle is between Jacob and the deity, not Jacob and an angel. Second, as Wolff points out, Hosea uses the divine name אֵל on several occasions (2:1, 11:9, 12:1) but never uses מלאך. Third, it fits well with what follows in v. 5, since Jacob's plea for favor is now prompted by El's victory (יכל) over him.[16] If one is willing to adopt my reasoning here, then the resulting text reads like that of Wolff:

> But God proved himself Lord and prevailed. He [Jacob] wept and made supplication to him [El]. In Bethel[17] he [El] finds him [Jacob] and there speaks with him [Jacob].[18]

The doxology that follows in v. 6 is sometimes viewed as a later addition, but the question of its authenticity is less relevant than the interpretive issues of v. 7, which I read as follows: 'Likewise you (Israel), with your god's help, turn back. Preserve loyalty and justice, and wait continually for your god'. Most important in this rendition of the verse is my translation of ואתה as 'likewise you', which more loosely paraphrased reads in vv. 6–7: "Just as Jacob sought god's favor after his rebellions and found it at Bethel, so *likewise you* should repent of your

15. Vollmer takes all of vv. 5–7 as a gloss, for the reasons cited above and also because he considers שׁמר with the objects משׁפט and חסד in v. 7 to be characteristic of Deuteronomic thinking. I have already argued that Deuteronomic ideology alone is insufficient ground for questioning a text's authenticity. See J. Vollmer, *Geschictliche Rückblicke und Motive* (BZAW 119; Berlin: de Gruyter, 1971); and also Rudolph, *Hosea*, 222.

16. In a unique approach, M. Gertner views Jacob as the victor and the divinity as the one seeking favor. This would seem to be unlikely, but it is nonetheless a possibility. See the appendix of "The Masorah and the Levites: An Essay in the History of a Concept," *VT* 10 (1960) 272ff.

17. Whitt et al. read בית אל as a divine name (see Whitt, "The Jacob Traditions in Hosea," 35–37), which is plausible but speculative. Even if one agrees with him, as I do, that the J/E pentateuchal sources may postdate Hosea, this does not make Hosea's testimony irrelevant. The tradition as known in Genesis would cause us to expect Bethel to be a geographical name (GN), and since Beth El as a divine name is poorly attested in the Hebrew Bible (if at all) the GN makes more sense, especially with the resumptive ושׁם that follows in 5b.

18. Ibid., 206, reading עמו with 𝔊 contra עמנו in 𝔐 (brackets mine).

rebellions and return to god."[19] This approach to the text explains why the negative forefather tradition is juxtaposed with a call to repentance, since now the ancestor has become an example of one who rebelled and then subsequently repented.[20] But with the exception of Jacob's repentance, the prophet's portrait of the patriarch is not a very flattering one.

I suppose that we would be remiss to neglect the other side of this debate, which would include some number of Hosean opponents who thought a great deal of the Jacob traditions and, we would suspect, of the Jacob forefather as well. Even in the cryptic story that we can glean from Hosea, it is clear that Jacob was something of a heroic figure, the kind of fellow who can struggle with God and live to seek his favor. The human that can last even a few moments in the ring with God is still a very special kind of figure, more like Gilgamesh or Prometheus than like other men.[21] So it would appear that many Israelites viewed their Jacobite origins as a noble kind of pedigree.

But this was not the pedigree of choice for Hosea, who continued his negative portrayal of the forefather in 12:13. The verse, which should obviously be treated as a unit with 12:14, has two major problems: its poor integration into the surrounding text and the absence of direct objects for either עבד or שׁמר. With regard to the first problem, one of two answers is usually suggested. First, 12:13–14 is sometimes viewed as a continuation of 12:4–7. Since this suggests that the texts are both intrusive, the minority of scholars who adopt this approach usually view both texts as late additions, although not always.[22] However, most scholars view vv. 13–14 as authentic and try to integrate them into the text on the basis of the common religious theme that runs through the text. Wolff does so by suggesting that the religious concerns expressed in vv. 11–12 are also reflected in v. 13, particularly in the repetition of באשׁה, which indicates that "the patriarch of Israel

19. A similar idea is expressed by S. Romerowski, "Le prophéte Osée prêche sur l'histoire de Jacob," *Hokhma* 52 (1993) 33–66.

20. As Davies has pointed out, this polemic can only be meaningful if Hosea believed that some hope for the future of Israel remained (*Hosea*, 37).

21. For a discussion of the Jacob tradition and its similarity to the epic heroes, see R. S. Hendel, *The Epic of the Patriarch: The Jacob Cycle and the Narrative Traditions of Canaan and Israel* (HSM 42; Atlanta: Scholars Press, 1987).

22. J. Mauchline, "Hosea," *IB* 6.703; Mays, *Hosea*, 169; Rudolph, *Hosea*, 227; Vollmer, *Geschictliche Rückblicke und Motive*, 110. Neither Mays nor Rudolph views the text as redactional.

had begun his disgraceful association with the foreign women of Aram
. . ." (i.e., Jacob involved himself in unacceptable sexual rituals).[23]
W. D. Whitt similarly understands the text in a religious sense but sees
in the objectless verbs עבד and שׁמר evidence that Jacob participated in
illicit cultic activity. The ancestor's transgression was his service (עבד/
שׁמר) to a foreign priest and god in exchange for the priest's daughter.[24]
While the detailed suggestions of both Whitt and Wolff are somewhat
speculative, they, along with Davies, Jeremias, and Rudolph, are most
likely correct that the problem envisioned here is a religious one, since
the previous text is concerned with cultic activity, and the contrast between vv. 13 and 14 centers on the distinction between Jacob and a religious leader, "the prophet."[25] This would seem to indicate that one
component of Hosea's criticism of Jacob was prompted by his religious
affiliation, and this affiliation was understood in connection with a foreign land and a foreign spouse (or possibly spouses). This tradition
seems to be at odds with the Jacob tradition of J (which is at pains to
explain that Jacob married among Israelite relatives in Aram)[26] and
thus probably reflects an eighth-century Yahwistic perspective that rejected cultic activities with foreign connections.

Hosea's Jacob will perhaps become a more transparent figure if we
can clarify our perspective of "the prophet" mentioned in 12:14, who
is obviously to be understood in terms of his relationship to the patriarch Jacob and also in relation to Israel as a whole.[27] In a recent article,
de Pury has argued that the text of 12:13–14 deliberately contrasts the
Patriarchal and Exodus origin traditions, calling upon Israel to make a
choice between two alternatives represented by Jacob and by the

23. J. Jeremias, *Der Prophet Hosea,* 157; Rudolph, *Hosea,* 231; Wolff, *Hosea,* 216.

24. Whitt, "The Jacob Traditions in Hosea," 38–41.

25. I have some sympathy with Davies' claim (see *Hosea,* 282) that this text
"serves to underline that Jacob's humiliation was 'only' for the sake of a woman, just as
Israel of Hosea's day humiliated itself in the rituals of Baal worship which were designed to create fertility."

26. Gen 28:1–2, 6–9; 29:11.

27. Neef argues that Jacob serves as a positive role model. Jacob, unlike the
people of Israel, pursued God to the point of struggling with him. Likewise, Jacob
served tirelessly for his wives, much as Moses served Yahweh as a prophet. The problem
with Neef's proposal is that he assumes that the Genesis traditions served as the
Hintergrund for Hosea's work, which is, in my view, a questionable assumption (Neef,
Die Heilstraditionen Israels in der Verkündigung des Propheten Hosea, 15–49, and especially pp. 231–35).

prophet (נביא). Both Mays and Römer have made similar suggestions.[28] The essential contrasts between Jacob and the prophet can be
summarized like this: while Jacob fled the land to live on foreign soil
and, in so doing, turned to foreign deities, the prophet led Israel into
its land and was a faithful servant of Yahweh. So it would appear that
Jacob served as the poor role model and the Exodus tradition as the
ideal mono-Yahwistic origin tradition. The contrast between the views
of Hosea and popular thinking in the North is clear enough. Northerners embraced an origin tradition that featured a patriarchal figure
who, even in the womb, made trouble for his brother. As an adult, he
contended with the deity, took up residence on foreign soil, married a
foreign woman and worshiped foreign deities. His only redemptive act
was his pursuit of the deity's favor, and even this was prompted by his
defeat at the hands of God. Obviously, if one accepts this reading of
the material (as I do), then Hosea's Jacob was of very poor religious
character and a particularly objectionable example of normative behavior. Yet in this view, contemporary Israel was emulating the forefather's
vices rather scrupulously, and it was precisely this that would prompt
Yahweh's punishment of Israel (cf. 12:2–3). The only appropriate origin tradition had Yahweh at its center, as he led Israel out of Egypt by
the hand of a prophet.

How does the Jacob tradition compare with the other ancient
Near Eastern materials? The whole debate of Hosea 12 presupposes
two competing origin traditions, both ethnic, that were founded on
the idea of either a communal migration or a common forefather. Although we did find evidence of ethnic traditions like these in the Old
Babylonian sources, from a comparative perspective these two types of
origin traditions were not very prominent in the national traditions of
either Neo-Assyria or Egypt. Both kinds of origin traditions are very
prominent, however, in the Greek sources, and the affinities of Hosea's
origin traditions with Herodotus's are not limited to these general
kinds of observations but include some specific features as well. This is
particularly true in the traditions' emphasis on a "heroic" figure, in
their common effort to choose one origin tradition over another, and

28. A. de Pury, "Osée 12 et ses implications pour le débat actuel sur le Pentateuque," in *Le Pentateuque: Débats et Recherches* (ed. Pierre Haudebert; Lectio Divina
151; Paris: du Cerf, 1992) 175–202; Mays, *Hosea*, 169; T. Römer, *Israels Väter: Untersuchungen zur Väterthematik im Deuteronomium und in der deuteronomistischen Tradition* (OBO 99; Göttingen: Vandenhoeck & Ruprecht, 1990) 532.

in their preference for higher culture (Egypt) as an appropriate point of cultural origin. Whether these similarities can be traced to some common point of origin is a good question, but one that I will postpone discussing until we have examined the Jacob figure in the Southern prophetic tradition.

So far, our discussion of Hos 12:1–14 has lingered on the theme of the Jacob ancestor, but in doing so we have passed over a relatively important issue that is raised in our text by the RSV's reading of Hos 12:8, which chastises Ephraim as "a trader (כנען) in whose hands are false balances." As has been done here, translators have in some cases chosen to render the term כנען 'trader, merchant' rather than 'Canaan'. There are no doubt two reasons for this. The first is a precedent discerned from Ezekiel, where the term can (or seems to) function as a sociological designation (merchant) rather than as an ethnic identifier (Canaan).[29] The second reason is that Ephraim's arrogant remark in the following verse (Hos 12:9) alludes to riches gained in the trade industry, so that in Hosea we may be dealing with the same semantic value for כנען as in Ezekiel. While I do not wish to haggle over the texts from Ezekiel, I do have several objections to thinking that Hos 12:8 refers only to a 'trader' and not to 'Canaan'.

It seems clear to me from the previous chapter that the terms "Canaan" and "Canaanite" were employed for a long time, both before and after Hosea's ministry, as designations for a land and its people. This being the case, it is difficult for me to believe that the word כנען actually took on an entirely different semantic value and at the same time lost its implied connection with Canaan and with the Canaanites. It is much more likely that the word "Canaan" denoted the land and its people but connoted, in a pejorative way, the dishonest merchants so closely associated with the land during the first millennium. The appropriate context for this connotative shift would have been the period of Phoenician expansion in the eighth century and afterward—in other words, beginning with the time of Hosea and increasing rapidly as we approach the time of Ezekiel's ministry.[30] A second reason for rejecting the RSV's reading is that comparing "Ephraim" and a "trader" does not strike me as being as rhetorically effective as likening Ephraim to

29. Cf. Ezek 16:29, 17:2; Zeph 1:11.
30. Lemche, *The Canaanites and Their Land*, 135–38, 156; B. Mazar, "Canaan and the Canaanites," *BASOR* 102 (1946) 7–12; A. F. Rainey, "Who is a Canaanite?" 6; cf. Isa 23:8–11.

Canaan. The latter pair are much better analogues, and we know from the last chapter that Israel had rather negative feelings about Canaan and the Canaanites in any case. This is not an effort to deny the obvious mercantile connotations of the term "Canaan" but is, rather, an effort to say that the following translation is a better one (Hos 12:8–9):

> Canaan, in his hands are false balances, he loves to oppress. Ephraim has said, "Ah, but I am rich, I have gained wealth for myself": but all his riches can never offset the guilt he has incurred.

As a result of this reading, we find that Hosea's rhetoric is decidedly ethnic, in that he hopes to stimulate change by comparing ethnic Israel with an out-group about which Israel feels particularly negative (the Canaanites).[31] If one is comfortable with this reading, then our text can be profitably compared with the texts about Canaan that we examined in the previous chapter.

In the case of both Merneptah and SDeb, the Canaanites were city-state populations within Palestine and, at least in the case of SDeb, military opponents of Israel. Hosea's eighth-century text probably preserves some memory of this competitive relationship in that it obviously depicts Canaan (and its people) as dishonest and oppressive. But here the similarity ends, because in Hosea the Canaanites are almost certainly the Phoenicians (and therefore not in Palestine) and the problem (at least in this text) is not competition with them, but rather, Israel's propensity to be like them. So whatever the Canaanites may have been in the second millennium and in SDeb, it is clear that we have identified something different in Hosea, and in so doing we have isolated a step in the development of Israel's ideas about Canaan and the Canaanites.

The Harlot and Her Children: Hosea 2:4–17

We have already confirmed the importance of ethnicity in eighth-century Israel and have demonstrated that, at least for Hosea's party, it is was rather closely tied to religious identity. Perhaps we can construct a more lucid picture of the prophet's sense of religious identity by examining one of the more important religious images employed by him,

---

31. Most commentators follow my reading of this. See Andersen and Freedman, *Hosea*, 615–16; Davies, *Hosea*, 278; W. R. Harper, *A Critical and Exegetical Commentary on Amos and Hosea* (ICC; Edinburgh: T. & T. Clark, 1905) 384; Mays, *Hosea*, 165–67; Stuart, *Hosea–Jonah*, 192; Wolff, *Hosea*, 214.

namely, the image of the unfaithful harlot. In doing so I hope to elucidate not only Hosea's sense of religious identity but also to show more
clearly how ethnicity and religious identity were related to each other
in his theology. When this is done it will become clear that Hosea and
his party were the forerunners of the seventh-century Deuteronomic
reforms, especially with regard to their emphasis on ethnicity.[32]

Although most scholars follow Wolff's conclusion that vv. 4–17
represent a "completely indivisible kerygmatic unit,"[33] Rudolph and
Whitt have concluded that the unit should end at v. 15.[34] The text's
unity has also been questioned, particularly by Harper (who views
2:4a, 5, 7, 10–11, 13–15 as authentic), and also by Whitt (who accepts
2:4–7, 12–14 as authentic).[35] Harper employs a number of criteria to
reach this conclusion, beginning with the assertion that 2:8–9 cannot
be authentic because: (1) they break the otherwise close connection between vv. 7 and 10; (2) 2:8–9 does not harmonize with 3:3, since in
3:3 a voluntary return of the woman is described, while in 2:8–9 she is
held in forcible restraint; (3) 2:8–9 is rendered superfluous by 3:3;
(4) 2:8–9 prematurely introduces the element of chastisement, which
fits in naturally in v. 11; and (5) the rhythm and strophic structure of
2:8–9 differ from the structure of the context. The third and fourth arguments are immaterial, since they admit that the ideology is consistent with Hosea's thought anyway, and arguments based on poetic
features (see #5) are always problematic, given our limited mastery of
Hebrew verse. The first argument is weak because it fails to apprehend
the distinction between redaction criticism of narratives (as in the Pentateuch) and redactional analysis of prophetic collections. Interrup-
tions in prophetic texts are to be expected since they are, by nature, a
collection of various speeches and oracles that have come from a broad

---

32. For a discussion of this, see E. Theodore Mullen, Jr., *Narrative History and
Ethnic Boundaries: The Deuteronomistic History and the Creation of Israelite National
Identity* (Semeia Studies; Atlanta: Scholars Press, 1993).

33. Andersen and Freedman, *Hosea*, 57–58 ; Davies, *Hosea*, 64–67; Jeremias, *Der
Prophet Hosea*, 36–44; Mays, *Hosea*, 34–37; Stuart, *Hosea–Jonah*, 45–46; Wolff, *Hosea*,
33. Jeremias, although he accepts most of the text, views vv. 6 and 10c as redactional.

34. Rudolph, *Hosea*, 61–72; W. D. Whitt, "The Divorce of Yahweh and Asherah
in Hos 2, 4–7.12ff.," *SJOT* 6 (1992) 33–34. Rudolph and Whitt fail to appreciate the
connective force of לכן הנה אנכי in v. 16, which serves to explain the contrast they perceive between vv. 15 and 16ff.

35. Harper, *Amos and Hosea*, clx, 236–38; Whitt, "The Divorce of Yahweh and
Asherah," 31–67.

range of contexts and have been knitted into a single piece. Harper's other argument (#2), that an ideological inconsistency exists between 2:8–9 and 3:3, is simply untrue, because Yahweh prohibits the pursuit of lovers in both cases. Harper's remaining arguments have similar weaknesses. Whitt's argument that the authentic materials include only 2:4–7, 12–14 is based on the form-critical ground that these texts refer to the specific proceedings of a divorce suit, while the remaining texts are rejected both because they do not contribute to this formal structure and because of "late" vocabulary. But given the similar thematic ties within the material of 2:4–17, it seems quite natural for the features of a formal divorce proceeding to be interspersed within a larger discussion of related issues. Regarding the "late" vocabulary, Whitt eliminates vv. 10–11 because they contain Deuteronomistic features (הדגן והתירוש והיצהר; cf. 2:11, 2:24) instead of the earlier Hosean features (והתירוש הדגן; cf. 7:14, 9:1–2). But this is very slender evidence. As I have pointed out, one cannot discount a text in Hosea simply because it looks "Deuteronomistic." When I examine the central thesis of Whitt's article, I will assess his arguments in greater detail. Despite these objections from Whitt and Harper, most scholars find Hos 2:4–17 relatively free of problems. As Mays has noted, "Any division of the sequence into smaller units creates fragments which presuppose the very context from which they are separated."[36]

The most pressing problem raised by this text is the interpretation of the "wife/harlot" imagery and its relationship to the 'children' (בנים) mentioned in the text. Taken independently, either of the images makes sense, the former portraying Israel as the wife of Yahweh and the latter depicting Israel as the children of Yahweh. But taken together, the two features create a mixed metaphor, which commentators have tended to live with, despite its awkwardness. The most common solution, with a few permutations, is to understand the wife as corporate Israel and the children as Israel's citizens.[37] In a recent article, W. D. Whitt has taken issue with this general approach to Hosea 2 and has argued that Hosea never used the metaphor of Israel as Yahweh's wife. According to him, the symbolism represents a secondary layer of tradi-

36. Mays, *Hosea*, 36.
37. In a minor twist, Andersen and Freedman view the unfaithful harlot as Hosea's wife (symbolizing corporate Israel) and the children as his children, in which case the demand to renounce adulterous behavior applies literally to Hosea's wife and figuratively to Israel (Andersen and Freedman, *Hosea*, 217–20).

tion which corresponds to the time of Jeremiah, who freely utilized such imagery. Whitt's conclusions are based on four basic premises: (1) the mixed metaphor of Israel as both wife and children is a problem that must be solved;[38] (2) a formal divorce proceeding exists in Hosea 2, and all texts that do not contribute to it are non-Hosean; (3) the wife described in Hosea 2, on the basis of the historical and literary context, is best understood as Asherah; (4) all of the texts that portray the wife as Yahweh's wife (vv. 16–17) are exilic or postexilic additions, and texts with features that would contradict the Asherah theory are also late (vv. 10, 15).

Whitt's arguments are problematic for several reasons. First, even if Whitt has demonstrated that a formal divorce proceeding exists here, this conclusion does not preclude intrusive (vv. 10–11) texts' belonging to the Hosean corpus. Second, if one excludes the "hedge of protection" text in vv. 8–9, which seems to intrude between vv. 7 and 10, the remaining text of 2:4–11 reads quite smoothly with vv. 10–11 and without v. 12, a verse that is a crucial portion of Whitt's form-critical structure:[39]

> Say to your brother, "My people," and to your sister, "She has obtained pity." Plead with your mother, plead—for she is not my wife, and I am not her husband—that she put away her harlotry from her face, and her adultery from between her breasts; lest I strip her naked and make her as in the day she was born, and make her like a wilderness, and set her like a parched land, and slay her with thirst. Upon her children also I will have no pity, because they are children of harlotry. For their mother has played the harlot; she that conceived them has acted shamefully. For she said, "I will go after my lovers, who give me my bread and my water, my wool and my flax, my oil and my drink." She did not know that it was I who gave her the grain, the wine, and the oil, and who lavished upon her silver and gold which they used for Baal. Therefore I will take back my grain in its time, and my wine in its season; and I will take away my wool and my flax, which were to cover her nakedness. (Hos 2:4–7, 10–11)

Whitt's form-critical argument is also weak because the introductory verses (vv. 4–7) are a plea for the wife to remain faithful to her marriage relationship. It does not seem likely that they are part of a divorce proceeding. In other words, what Whitt has found are features of a divorce

---

38. In fact, this problem will be solved—but by Ezekiel, not Hosea.
39. He sees this form-critical unit in 2:4–7, 12–14.

proceeding; he has not found an independent, form-critical unit that can be extracted from its context in Hosea.[40] Finally, Whitt argues that vv. 16–22, which portray Israel as Yahweh's wife, must be late because this ideology appears in the time of Jeremiah and can only be comprehensible when "henotheism had made a strong impact," that is, after the Deuteronomic reform of the late seventh century. But these arguments will not do. For Whitt, like myself, much of the material in the Hebrew Bible, particularly the pentateuchal material, is of questionable antiquity. This means that eighth-century prophetic works like Hosea become the most substantive early sources at our disposal. And when this is the case, Hosea no longer lies in the middle of a broad literary context against which it can be evaluated, but rather, it lies at the beginning (or close to it). To argue that portions of Hosea are Deuteronomistic or that they reflect the thinking of Jeremiah is problematic, because almost all agree that both the Deuteronomists and Jeremiah are to a degree dependent on the proto-Deuteronomistic thought reflected in Hosea.[41] Furthermore , I cannot agree with Whitt's conclusion that henotheism only made a strong impact in the seventh century and therefore could not have existed in the eighth. The Deuteronomistic movement did not appear out of thin air; at some point it must have existed in its infancy, and it is possible that with Hosea we have found its headwaters.[42]

By now it is obvious that I do not concur with Whitt's conclusion that Hosea 2 refers to Asherah and her divorce from Yahweh, not only for the reasons that I have already cited but also for this reason: in almost all of its 18 uses in the Hebrew Bible, אשרה is best understood as a stylized tree; it is something 'made' (עשה), 'cut down' (כרת), 'carved' (פסל), 'burned' (שרף), 'planted' (נטע), and 'set up' (שים), and is often

---

40. See also Paul A. Kruger's article, "The Marriage Metaphor in Hosea 2:4–17 against Its Ancient Near Eastern Background," *Old Testament Essays* 5 (1992) 7–25. Kruger argues that there is a logical progression from beginning to end in the divorce ritual. But this evidence does not show that there is an independent form-critical unit that one can identify as a divorce proceeding and that is separated from the context of chap. 2, especially when it is recognized that elements are not listed in a consistent order and sometimes create illogical sequences. For example, part of the proposed ritual includes the following: exposure of wife, provision for her, bridal gifts, termination of the marriage, bridal gifts again, etc.

41. For a discussion of Jeremiah's dependence on Hosea, see K. Goss, *Die literarische Verwandschaft Jeremias mit Hosea* (Ph.D. diss., Berlin, 1930); J. A. Thompson, *Jeremiah* (NICOT; Grand Rapids: Eerdmans, 1980) 81–85.

42. Whitt admits that Hosea himself was henotheistic ("The Divorce of Yahweh and Asherah," 67).

depicted as an עֵץ ('tree'/'wood'). Consequently, the term appears to be a common noun referring to some kind of wooden cult object, a conclusion that is borne out by the eighth-century evidence from Kuntillet Ajrud and Khirbet el-Qôm. In both cases, most scholars read the text 'by Yahweh and by his asherah' (ליהוה ולאאשרתה), with the possessive third-person suffix showing that *asherah* should not be understood as a proper name.[43] This reading is supported by the iconographic evidence on pithos A from Kuntillet Ajrud, which depicts the asherah as a stylized tree flanked with ibexes. That this tree was a symbol of Asherah is confirmed first by the fact that the handwritten text ('by Yahweh and his asherah') is from the same hand as the tree figure[44] and second by the iconographic evidence, which clearly reflects a connection between Asherah and the stylized tree from the thirteenth-century "Lachish Ewer" onward.[45] Taken together, this evidence seems to indicate that in eighth-century Israel the goddess Asherah, though a consort of Yahweh, had become more of a cult fetish than a functioning consort and "mother of the people." While one cannot state this thesis in a categorical way, its may suggest why the goddess herself has left so little impact in the Hebrew Bible and the extrabiblical Israelite evidence. S. A. Wiggins has independently arrived at a similar conclusion:

43. In fact, pithos A from Kuntillet Ajrud mentions "Yahweh of Samaria." For more on the Asherah question, see W. G. Dever, "Asherah, Consort of Yahweh? New Evidence from Kuntillet Ajrud," *BASOR* 255 (1984) 21–37; J. Emerton, "New Light on Israelite Religion: The Implications of the Inscriptions from Kuntillet Ajrud," *ZAW* 94 (1992) 14ff.; W. A. Maier III, *Asherah: Extrabiblical Evidence* (HSM 37; Atlanta: Scholars Press, 1986); B. Margalit, "The Meaning and Significance of Asherah," *VT* 40 (1990) 264–97; Z. Meshel, "Did Yahweh Have a Consort?" *BARev* 5/2 (1979) 24–35; S. Olyan, *Asherah and the Cult of Yahweh in Israel* (SBLMS 3; Atlanta: Scholars Press, 1988); M. S. Smith, *The Early History of God* (San Francisco: Harper, 1990) 89–114; Z. Zevit, "The Khirbet el-Qôm Inscription Mentioning a Goddess," *BASOR* 225 (1984) 39–47.

44. Whitt follows Margalit's conclusion that the two standing figures are Yahweh and Asherah. Clearly, however, the head of one of these figures crosses over so obviously into the written text that it cannot be from the same hand, not to mention the fact that the tree and inscription are carefully inscribed, while the two standing figures and the seated lyre-player are more sloppy. The standing figures should instead be viewed as Bes figures, as a comparison with the Bes iconography shows. For a description of Bes iconography with illustrations, see V. Wilson, "The Iconography of Bes with Particular Reference to the Cypriot Evidence," *Journal of the British School of Archaeology in Jerusalem* 7 (1975) 77–103. For a concurring argument, see P. Beck, "The Drawings from Horvat Teiman (Kuntillet Ajrûd)," *Tel Aviv* 9 (1982) 3–86.

45. For an extended discussion of this, see Ruth Hestrin, "Understanding Asherah: Exploring Semitic Iconography," *BARev* 17/5 (1991) 50–59.

> The Old Testament material also raises the question of the relation-
> ship of the goddess Asherah to the cultic object asherah. . . . The
> texts are not explicit about the connection between the cultic objects
> and the deities. To me it seems unlikely that no connection existed
> between Asherah and asherah. It may be that the cultic object out-
> lived the memory of the goddess in ancient Israel.[46]

With this *Hausputz* out of the way, we can proceed with our examination of Hos 2:4–17.

Although some portions of the text may come from other periods
in Hosea's ministry, the text generally assumes a high degree of economic prosperity and consequently best fits the period of Jeroboam II's
reign, in other words, some time before 750 B.C.E. As commentators
frequently point out, it is the use of an apparently mixed metaphor
that gives the text its unique character. I would suggest that the ambiguities of this metaphor need not be resolved but instead be read as
several portraits of Israel: first as the land, then as the estranged wife of
Yahweh, then as children of Yahweh's estranged spouse, and finally as
the children of Yahweh himself.[47] We should steer clear of resolving
these ambiguities, because it seems to me very unlikely that such a
combination of metaphors would arise accidentally. Furthermore, the
metaphors are interrelated in a way that prevents a neat dissection of
them. For instance, the first two images—the land and estranged wife
of Yahweh—often blend together so that the land *is* the estranged wife:
"lest I strip her naked . . . and make her like a wilderness, and set her
like a parched land . . . and I will lay waste her vines and her fig trees."
Additionally, the image of the wife's children is a natural extension of
the estranged spouse imagery and can hardly be labeled an inconsistency. Although I will refer to this problem briefly during our discussion, we should dispense with our attempts to solve the imaginary
riddle and instead focus on the way each metaphor contributes to our
understanding of the prophet's message.

I will begin with Hosea's "land imagery." Here as in chap. 1 the
land corresponds to Yahweh's unfaithful wife and is an image that
stems from the religious competition Hosea perceives between Yahweh
and Baal, primarily because the land (i.e., Israel, Yahweh's wife) sees in

---

46. S. A. Wiggins, *A Reassessment of 'Asherah': A Study according to the Textual Sources of the First Two Millennia B.C.E.* (AOAT 235; Neukirchen-Vluyn: Neukirch-ener Verlag, 1993) 190.

47. This conclusion is more or less supported by Harper, *Amos and Hosea*, 226–27; Mays, *Hosea*, 35–37; Wolff, *Hosea*, 33–34.

Baal rather than Yahweh its source of fecundity. Although this comes as no surprise to us, since Baal in the Levant and elsewhere was a god of fertility, I think that for Hosea this lack of dependence on Yahweh constituted a theological heresy that prompted Yahweh to prove his lordship by withdrawing support for the agricultural yield. Interspersed within this agricultural threat are images of the divorce proceeding occasioned by acts of infidelity with Baal, as Whitt has shown (see above). The competitive threat raised against Yahweh should perhaps not be understood as *Baal* alone, but more likely as the *baalim*, the various local manifestations of Baal.[48] Whether the plural *baalim* might also be taken as a generic reference to other deities is difficult to say, but certainly Baal is the chief culprit here.[49]

Perhaps more telling than Hosea's land imagery is his image of the children (בנים) in chap. 2, which reflects his deep ambivalence toward his ethnic brothers. On the one hand, the בנים are Yahweh's children who appeal to their mother and,[50] on the other hand, they are 'children of harlotry' (בני זנונים, v. 6) who were begotten of the illicit relationship between Israel and Baal.[51] Although we cannot

---

48. Wolff argues against this view and sees the *Baalim* of 2:15 as deriving from the imagery of Israel's various adulterous relationships, mainly because the second-millennium Ugaritic evidence does not support a belief in widespread local *Baal* divinities. But the second-millennium evidence that Wolff cites is several centuries previous to Hosea's day and the texts are mythic texts, a genre notoriously poor as sources for elucidating actual historical situations. Against Wolff, the Hebrew Bible refers to local manifestatons of Baal (e.g., Baal of Peor in Hos 9:10; Baal-Zebub of Ekron in 2 Kgs 1:2), and the eighth-century inscriptional evidence reflects similar local manifestations of Yahweh (Yahweh of Samaria and Yahweh of Teman, mentioned on Pithoi A and B, respectively, from Kuntillet Ajrud).

49. The problem of clarity in understanding בעל and בעלים is well known. According to M. S. Smith, Hosea uses the terms in three different senses: (1) Baal the deity, (2) local manifestations of Baal, and (3) as more general terminology referring to deities. While I tend to follow Smith's conclusions, I cannot be sure that Hosea is taking issue with other deities in addition to Baal in Hosea 2, especially when the issue here seems limited to fertility. See Smith, *The Early History of God*, 48–49.

50. According to Davies, these were "lay members of the community [called] to join him in denouncing the rampant paganism of his day," a reading that is plausible but difficult to substantiate (Davies, *Hosea*, 69–70).

51. Cf. M. Smith, *Palestinian Parties and Politics That Shaped the Old Testament* (New York: Columbia University Press, 1971) 31–32. Whitt has argued, contrary to the grammar of the text, that ריב ב־ and the accompanying text of 2:4 should be interpreted as 'take your mother's side in my lawsuit', rather than the more common rendering 'Accuse your mother . . .'. Even if he is right, the text still implies two different categories of children, those who are of harlotry and the ideal children that Israel ought to be (Whitt, "The Divorce of Yahweh and Asherah," 52).

hastily identify these 'children of harlotry' as ethnic foreigners, the imagery brings to mind another text in Hosea, where the prophet reprimands Israel for begetting 'strange children' (בנים זרים in 5:7). Wolff tells us that these בנים זרים were children born of foreign cultic activities,[52] and this is a reasonable conclusion given that elsewhere in Hosea the זרים are clearly foreigners. This should direct our attention again to the question of whether or not Hosea viewed the cult of Baal as foreign activity or merely as non-Yahwistic activity, a distinction that may at first seem superficially minor but that is actually rhetorically important. I think that these texts make it a virtual certainty that Hosea viewed Baal not only as a competitor of Yahweh but also as a foreign competitor, so that already in the eighth century we have a close connection between Israel's ethnic identity and its religious sentiments.[53] So it appears that in spite of the fact that no one seems to have adequately explained all of the confusing metaphors used by Hosea, we have nevertheless been able to draw some reasonable conclusions about Israelite identity from the materials.

As I did in the case of the Jacob story, here I have argued for Hosea's antipathy toward foreign influence in general and toward foreign religious institutions in particular (an argument to be reinforced by my discussion of Hos 7:8–13). The eighth-century historical context was quite favorable for the development of these ideas, primarily because Yahweh was the national deity of Israel and therefore already possessed a unique and exclusive claim to Israelite affections. The reasonableness of this conclusion is threefold. First, we know that national deities played important roles in the nations surrounding Israel, particularly in Judah (Yahweh), Moab (Chemosh), and Ammon (Milkom).[54] Second, the onomastic evidence from the epigraphic sources, regionally limited as it is, reflects a strongly Yahwistic flavor.[55] Third, Holladay's

52. Wolff, *Hosea*, 101.

53. See especially Mullen, *Narrative History and Ethnic Boundaries*, which argues that Dtr viewed the political and religious identities of Israel as important components in its ethnic sense of identity.

54. As reflected by the Mesha Stele (Chemosh in Moab) and the Rabbath-ammon Inscription (Milkom in Ammon).

55. See J. H. Tigay, *You Shall Have No Other Gods: Israelite Religion in the Light of Hebrew Inscriptions* (HSS 31; Atlanta: Scholars Press, 1986), especially pp. 47–89. Some argue that Tigay's data is skewed by his assumption that El names are congruent with Yahweh's, especially since the eighth-century Kuntillet Ajrud inscriptions mention El as parallel with Baal. However, this argument is only partially valid, if at all, because

archaeological study of religious activity during the monarchic period suggests a dichotomy between "official" religious activities at national temple shrines and "popular religion" distributed away from major centers.[56] If, as this evidence seems to indicate, Hosea prohibited the worship of all deities except for the national God Yahweh, it would seem that the prophet had for some reason "radicalized" devotion to the national deity in a way that most others had not. This makes it very clear that Hosea rejected other cults not only because they were non-Yahwistic but also because they were non-Israelite; in other words, they were foreign cults.

Both the text and the historical context suggest, therefore, that Hosea's views were not only Yahwistic but also ethnic in character. The problem that remains, then, is not whether this was the case but, rather, how many Israelites agreed with the prophet and, even if they did not, how much their views overlapped with his. I do not know if we can answer these questions in any definitive way, but it does seem that Hosea's religious perspective represented a minority position within Israel's eighth-century social matrix, because his polemic is leveled against every sector of his society: its religious leaders, political leaders, and the people in general.[57] But minority view or not, his was the view that eventually found its way into Deuteronomy and into many of the later biblical sources, giving shape, if one is willing to admit the idea, to biblical theology as a whole.

To summarize, although we are missing concrete terminology like נכרי ('foreigner'), the language and polemic of Hosea strongly suggests that the non-Yahwist cults were perceived to be foreign in origin and therefore a threat to the national cult. The categories of 'children of

---

El also functions generically as the title for god. As I argued above, Asherah had been the consort of Yahweh for some time by the eighth century, and this makes it very likely that El, Asherah's consort, had long since merged with Yahweh in Israelite thinking.

56. See J. S. Holladay, Jr., "Religion in Israel and Judah under the Monarchy: An Explicitly Archaeological Approach," *Ancient Isrealite Religion* (ed. P. D. Miller, Jr.; Philadelphia: Fortress, 1987) 249–83. Notice also the call narrative of Amos (7:12), which demonstrates an awareness of Bethel as the "king's sanctuary" and as the "temple of the kingdom."

57. As suggested by N. P. Lemche, "The God of Hosea," in *Priests, Prophets and Scribes: Essays on the Formation and Heritage of the Second Temple Judaism in Honour of Joseph Blenkinsopp* (ed. E. Ulrich; JSOTSup 149; Sheffield: JSOT Press, 1992) 241–57; Smith, *Palestinian Parties and Politics*, 31–34.

harlotry' (בני זנונים) and 'strange children' (בנים זרים) reflect an environment of religious competition and a growing sense of differentiation, within the population of Israel, between those who followed
"Israelite" religious practices and those who participated in "foreign"
cultic activities.[58] This seems to be confirmed by Psalm 81, which according to Davies dates to the time of Hosea and offers conclusive evidence for this ethnoreligious ideology: לא־יהיה בך אל זר ולא תשתחוה
לאל נכר (Ps 81:10).[59] In my view, one of two developments will account for this trend. Either Hosea's mono-Yahwist party was responsible for merging two previously separate modes of identity (religious
and ethnic) into one vision of community or it successfully augmented
an older and neglected ethnoreligious theme such as may be represented in the Song of Deborah. The choice between these two options
hinges on how much confidence we have in our reading of SDeb and
how detailed we are willing to be in laying out its implications about
Israelite ethnicity, its religious identity, and the relationship between
the two. If I must lean in one direction (and *lean* is the proper word
here), then I believe that Israel's ethnoreligious ideas antedated Hosea's
party and were taken up by them in support of their pro-Yahwist
agenda. But one should view this conclusion in the noncategorical
spirit in which I intend it.

The Ethnoreligious Party and Its Criticism of the Priests: Hosea 4:1–14

Even if we cannot know precisely when and how the ethnoreligious party originated, we can deduce from Hosea something about
its essential doctrines and ideas during the eighth century. Our examination of this text will lay bare some of the features that characterized
the mono-Yahwist party that we have been examining, including its essential foundations in law, the place of covenant in its theology, and
also the indicia it used to distinguish "Israelite" worship from "non-
Israelite" activities. The charge that Israel and its leaders no longer
knew Yahweh is one of Hosea's most important themes, and it is the
leitmotif that ties vv. 1–3 to vv. 4–14, with the former charging that
the people had no knowledge of God and the latter that the priests

58. L. A. Snijders has argued that the prophetic use of זר generally refers to either
foreign peoples or deities ("The Meaning of *zar*," *OTS* 10 [1954] 22–59).
59. Davies dates the text to ca. 733–722 B.C.E. (*Hosea*, 32–34).

were the cause of it. [60] Scholarly consensus is that the chapter wholly reflects authentic Hosean materials,[61] with the minor exceptions of 4:1a, 4:3, and 4:10.[62] These exceptions have no great bearing on my thesis, and so I have no interest in defending their authenticity here.

The text of 4:1–14 breaks up fairly easily into three units: vv. 1–3, 4–10, and 11–14. Yahweh's "controversy" with the inhabitants of Israel is introduced by the initial unit (4:1b) in what would appear to be Hosea's first use of ריב in a potentially "covenantal" context.[63] But viewing the term in this way is premature, since a lively debate surrounds the question of whether or not covenantal theology informed Hosea's work. I will take up this question a bit later, but to foreshadow my discussion, I must mention that a similar use of the root ריב in the roughly contemporary Sefîre treaties may support a covenantal reading.[64] Yahweh's controversy with Israel stems from the fact that Israel lacks certain necessities—particularly faithfulness (אמת), kindness (חסד), and knowledge of God (דעת־אלהים)—and that these inadequacies have resulted in various ethical lapses, such as swearing (אלה),[65] lying (כחש), killing (רצח), stealing (גנב), and adultery (נאף). The presence of אלה in the list is unexpected, because taking an oath would not seem to constitute a moral blunder. But if one follows Harper's suggestion, that אלה and כחש are a hendiadys roughly equivalent to 'bearing false witness', then we have here a brief list of breaches of the sixth, seventh, eighth, and ninth commandments.[66] Even if one rejects Harper's solution to

60. This criticism is phrased in a number of ways but normally uses either the verb ידע (as in Israel 'does not know Yahwh' ואת־יהוה לא ידעו) or the noun דעת (as in Israel lacks 'knowledge of Yahweh' אין־דעת יהוה/אלהים בארץ). Cf. Hos 2:22; 4:1, 6; 5:4; 6:3, 6; 8:2; 11:3.

61. This is true even for Harper, who is quite prone to isolating later additions even when others do not (*Amos and Hosea*, clx).

62. Jeremias, *Hosea*, 62, 68.

63. The use of ריב in Hosea 2 is often viewed as idiosyncratic. For a discussion of the term's use in covenantal contexts in the Hebrew Bible, see H. B. Huffmon, "The Covenant Lawsuit in the Prophets," *JBL* 78 (1959) 285–95.

64. Interestingly, Hebrew uses the verbal form of ריב in a manner similar to its use in the Sefîre Treaty III 26: "If my son contends (ירב) and if my grandson contends and if my offspring contends with your offspring about Tal'ayim and its villages, its lords. . . ."

65. The precise meaning of the term is not clear here. Normally אלה means 'to take an oath, to swear', but it can occasionally suggest the invocation of a curse, i.e., an imprecation. The former is adopted by Andersen and Freedman, *Hosea*, 331–37; the latter by Mays, *Hosea*, 64.

66. Harper, *Amos and Hosea*, 250.

the problem, the list is formally similar to the Decalogue's moral code, suggesting that we have here, not just moral lapses, but the transgression of legal statutes. That Hosea perceived a conceptual link between these statutory failures and Israel's religious infidelity is suggested by the fact that in two cases the resulting punishment was an ebbing of the land's productivity (cf. Hos 2:11 and 4:3).

Although Hosea was vexed by the impotent religion of Israel (4:1–3), his stance toward the priests was even more caustic because, in his view, they had caused the spiritual crisis (4:4–10). The failure that sealed their doom (as well as their mothers' and children's) was neglect of their role as the arbiters of דעת to the people: "My people are destroyed for lack of knowledge, because you have rejected knowledge" (v. 6). The explanation for this priestly impiety apparently stemmed from their disregard for God's law, as indicated by v. 6c: ותשכח תורת אלהים. To summarize our progress more clearly, the priests served as the arbiters of the דעת־אלהים that was embodied in the תורת אלהים, and this law of God contained moral prescriptions similar to those in the Decalogue. When this information is joined to Hos 8:12, which speaks of the written תורה, it seems that Hosea's תורה is best understood as a formal collection of written religious statutes that were concerned primarily with ethical standards of behavior. These ethical standards were not merely prescripts for moral living but were related both to an intimate relationship with the deity ("to know Yahweh") and, as I will argue below, to the concept of covenant.

Although Hosea's oracle against the priests also included a brief criticism of Israel's prophets (v. 5), I find this noteworthy not so much because of his posture toward the prophets but because, having taken up Yahweh's ריב with both the religious leaders (priests and prophets) and the people of Israel, Hosea did not single out the political figures of the Northern Kingdom. The fact that his jabs at the political elite were curt and thematically secondary (cf. 1:4; 5:1; 7:3–7; 10:3, 7, 15) requires an explanation. The best explanation is that Hosea embraced a rather negative view of the monarchic institution, as suggested by Hos 8:4 and 13:10–11:

> They made kings, but not through me. They set up princes, but without my knowledge. With their silver and gold they made idols for their own destruction.

Where now is your king, to save you; where are all your princes, to
defend you—those of whom you said, "Give me a king and princes"?
I have given you kings in my anger, and I have taken them away in
my wrath.

Whether Hosea's negative view of the Northern monarchy was
prompted by an endorsement of Yahweh's kingship, as Wolff has suggested, is debatable.[67] But it seems that he did reject the institution of
kingship and that his concept of identity embraced political structures
grounded in Israel's religious life, namely, in its priests and prophets.
Thus Hosea envisioned a more theocratic kind of arrangement than
kingship could provide, and in this he reveals his proto-Deuteronomic
colors because, like Deuteronomy, he shows very little interest in the
monarchy.

The next unit of our text (vv. 11–14) continues the discussion of
religious themes but moves beyond the criticism of Israel to explore
the religious behaviors and practices that Hosea deemed inappropriate.
The brief catalog of rejected cultic activities includes certain oracular
activities (v. 12),[68] sacrificial rituals on mountaintops and under trees
(v. 13), cult prostitution (קדשות, v. 14),[69] and the use of idols (עצבים).
On six occasions we find that these kinds of practices were condemned
as "harlotry," which in Hosea is a rhetorical way of saying that someone is worshiping other deities (cf. our discussion of Hosea 2). While
this leaves us with the distinct impression that the mono-Yahwists
associated these practices with foreign cults and rejected them for that
reason, it raises a more subtle question. Did Hosea reject practices associated with other deities *only* in foreign cultic contexts or also in

67. Wolff, *Hosea*, 227. Most agree that we have here a rejection of the kingship
institution: Harper, *Amos and Hosea*, 400; Mays, *Hosea*, 178.
68. Drinkard argues that the terms עם and מקל are references to Asherah. This is
possible but quite difficult to prove (J. F. Drinkard, Jr., "Religious Practices Reflected
in the Book of Hosea," *RevExp* 90 [1993] 205–18).
69. I have stayed with the traditional understanding of קדשה as 'cult prostitute',
despite Westenholz's recent argument, on the basis of Ugaritic and Mesopotamian evidence, that this is erroneous. The translation 'cult prostitute' fits the context well here
(including the unambiguous term, זנה), and Westenholz's argument against this understanding of קדשה in Genesis 38 is not entirely convincing. For a discussion of this
issue, see D. Arnaud, "La prostitution sacrée en Mésopotamie: Le mythe historique?"
RHR 183 (1973) 111–15; M. Astour, "Tamar the Hierodule: An Essay on the Method
of Vestigial Motifs," *JBL* 85 (1966) 185–96; J. G. Westenholz, "Tamar, Qedeša, Qa-
dištu, and Sacred Prostitution in Mesopotamia," *HTR* 82 (1989) 246–65.

Yahwistic contexts? The answer to this question is an important one, because if Hosea rejected these practices in both Yahwistic and non-Yahwistic contexts, then we might conclude that religious practices served his community to distinguish proper Israelite worship from foreign worship. In other words, religious practices differentiated the orthodox ethnoreligious community from heretical outsiders.

The first clue is Hosea's use of the semantically related concepts of זנה ('adulterer') and נאף ('to commit adultery'). His polemic in 2:4–14 rejected Israel's pursuit of other gods on the grounds that it was equivalent to spiritual "harlotry" and "adultery" (2:4). The illegitimacy of these two social practices themselves, as I have pointed out earlier in this section, was based on the ethical ideals outlined in the תורה of God, which explicitly condemned נאף and probably by implication the sexual practices of the זנה. When one turns then to the use of זנה and נאף in the present text (4:14), it would seem that Hosea rejected the acts of adultery, harlotry, and cult prostitution not merely because they were being done in non-Yahwistic contexts but because of religious principle. If so, then by analogy the other practices mentioned in this text, such as oracular activities with wooden objects, peripheral cultic activities, and the idolatry involving עצבים, were equally odious to the prophet and so were not to be associated with authentic Yahwism. As Yahweh said: אפרים מה־לי עוד לעצבים אני עניתי ואשורנו (14:9). So these practices were, from Hosea's point of view, "negative indicia" that distinguished foreign religious practices from Israelite practice.

The Problem of Foreign Alliances: Hosea 7:8–13

Let us go further with this issue of Hosea's foreign polemic. If he tended to reject even "minor" foreign religious elements, then it seems reasonable to ask if we can discern in him a more general tendency to reject everything of foreign origin, including political relationships. As in any historical context, it was standard practice in the ancient Near East to forge political relationships that would promote national security and foster, at least from the participants' perspective, international stability. As one would expect, our text reflects Israel's participation in these diplomatic maneuvers but adds the additional twist that Hosea objected to this standard practice. Such a break with traditional expectation is noteworthy and invites an investigation. Our passage most likely describes Israel's helter-skelter foreign policy in the face of Tiglath-pileser III's threat to the nation, around 733 B.C.E. This time-frame suits the context best because it juxtaposes Hoshea's payment of Assyrian tribute and the Syro-Ephraimite coalition backed by Egypt.[70] The prophet describes Israel as a "silly dove" that flutters from one alliance to another, and this bids us first to see the prophet's concern that the nation lacked political vision. But this is only one aspect of his criticism. For Hosea, the result of these diplomatic activities, which would from a pragmatic perspective seem to benefit Israel, is actually a "mixing among the peoples" that is detrimental to the nation's health: "Aliens devour his strength, and he knows it not; gray hairs are sprinkled upon him, and he knows it not" (7:9). Although the Assyrians represented the most tangible threat to Israel in those days, as Mays has pointed, the threat in this case was subtle, insidious, and on-going—not a threat to the future but a disease of the present.[71] Israel's pursuit of new military alliances was for Hosea a continuing process of religious contamination that was bringing the nation ever closer to destruction, and we should ask why he felt this way about it.

At one level, we can answer this question on the basis of what follows in 7:13, that Israel's destruction was imminent because its endorsement of foreign alliances constituted rebellion (פשע) against Yahweh. But this holds us at arm's length from the more important observation that these alliances were considered rebellion because they threatened Israel's exclusive covenantal relationship with Yahweh.[72] I suggest this on the basis of two lines of evidence; first, Hosea explicitly identifies the foreign political relationships that he rejects as 'covenants' (וברית עם־אשור יכרתו in 12:2); second, there is substantial evidence—both internal and external—that Hosea's religious ideology included a covenantal relationship between Israel and Yahweh.

---

70. Cf. 2 Kgs 16:7ff.; *ANET* 283–84. That Egypt was behind these coalitions against Assyria is a natural assumption and is also suggested by Hanun of Gaza's flight to Egypt.

71. Mays, *Hosea*, 108–9. See also Andersen and Freedman, *Hosea*, 466–67; Harper, *Amos and Hosea*, 302. I strongly disagree with Wolff's suggestion that the problem here is a military threat (*Hosea*, 126).

72. As I will show later, Isaiah was equally critical of foreign political relationships. Although he, like Hosea, viewed such relationships as "rebellion" against Yahweh, he did not utilize covenant imagery to express this relationship, as I am arguing that Hosea has done.

This second claim is a matter of contention, since L. Perlitt has argued that the concept of Israel's covenant with Yahweh did not date to hoary antiquity but instead originated with Josiah's seventh-century Deuteronomic reforms.[73] Although this perspective has gained a substantial following in contemporary scholarship, E. W. Nicholson has raised some important objections to Perlitt's thesis. At the center of the covenant controversy is the book of Hosea, a situation that is the result of two simple facts. First, the continuing debate about the date of the pentateuchal sources has made their witness suspect, so that their witness to Israel's covenant tradition cannot provide a concrete dating of the tradition. Second, Hosea dates prior to the seventh-century watershed date suggested by Perlitt and, contrary to Perlitt's view, appears on the surface to embrace covenant ideology. As one might expect, Perlitt claims that Hosea's apparent references to covenant are redactional, and Nicholson claims that they are not. So we should properly begin by outlining Perlitt's reasons for rejecting them. The texts in question, Hos 6:7 and 8:1, read as follows:

> But at Adam they transgressed (עברו) the covenant (ברית); there they dealt faithlessly with me (6:7).
> Set the trumpet to your lips, for a vulture is over the house of the Lord, because they have broken (עברו) my covenant (בריתי), and transgressed (פשעו) my law (תורתי) (8.1).

Perlitt argues that 6:7 does not refer to a broken covenant with Yahweh but with some other nation or group, a ברית like the one with Assyria mentioned in Hos 12:2. For Perlitt, the sense of 6:7 is like the sense of Hos 10:4: "They utter mere words; with empty oaths they make covenants (ברית); so judgment springs up like poisonous weeds in the furrows of the field."[74] Perlitt views 8:1 as a Deuteronomistic addition because בריתי 'my covenant' is characteristic of the Deuteronomistic sources. But such an argument is somewhat circular and runs the risk of saying "*bᵉrîtî* is Deuteronomistic because *bᵉrîtî* is Deuteronomistic."[75]

73. L. Perlitt, *Bundestheologie im Alten Testament* (WMANT 36; Neukirchen-Vluyn: Neukirchener Verlag, 1969). For his discussion of ברית in Hosea, see pp. 139–52.

74. Ibid., 143.

75. D. J. McCarthy, "*Berît* in Old Testament History and Theology," *Bib* 53 (1972) 114.

E. W. Nicholson's response to Perlitt's analysis of the evidence
from Hosea is persuasive, especially in light of my contextual analysis
above.[76] First, Nicholson points out that ברית in Hos 6:7 cannot be a
reference to transgressions against foreigners because the surrounding
context is concerned only with Israel's internal ethical failures (6:8),
which stand in contrast to the חסד and דעת אלהים that Israel ought to
possess (6:9). Second, Nicholson points out that the grammar of 6:7
clearly shows that the transgression was against Yahweh rather than a
breaching of a political agreement. Perlitt would counter, with apparent support from Ezek 17:11–21, that the breach of a foreign treaty
was equivalent to treachery against Yahweh (Ezek 17:20).[77] However,
as I have already shown and as Nicholson points out, Hosea does not
accept the validity of foreign covenants in the first place, and so the
evidence from Ezekiel does not apply here. All of this makes it difficult
to view Hos 6:7 as other than Israel's transgression (עבר) of its covenant with Yahweh, and the context implies that this transgression was
closely related to Israel's failure to adhere to 'law' (תורה).

This implicit connection between law and covenant in 6:7 is made
explicit in 8:1: "they have broken my covenant (עברו בריתי), and
transgressed my law (פשעו תורתי)'. Perlitt argues that this is not
evidence of an eighth-century covenant tradition but rather a Deuteronomistic addition, as suggested by the use of בריתי, supposedly a
Deuteronomistic feature. But the בריתי terminology occurs only six
times in Deuteronomy and Dtr combined.[78] And the parallel phrase
ועל תורתי פשעו is peculiar to Hosea and is never used in the Deuteronomistic corpus, even though there are many occasions when it
would have been appropriate. The only possible argument left against
8:1 is its reference to the בית יהוה 'the house of Yahweh', which might
indicate a later Judean context associated with cult centralization (i.e.,
Josianic redaction). But this is slender evidence upon which to build a
case, first because the singular noun would fit Hosea's context in either
a collective sense or with reference to a particular cultic site (like Amos,
who describes Bethel as the "king's sanctuary" and as the "temple of
the kingdom" in 7:13); second, Hos 9:4, which is normally accepted as

---

76. I am referring to the evidence that Hosea rejected foreign covenants for religious reasons. My discussion of Nicholson's argument is based on his *God and His
People: Covenant Theology in the Old Testament* (Oxford: Clarendon, 1986) 179–88.

77. Perlitt, *Bundestheologie im Alten Testament*, 143–44.

78. See Deut 31:16, 20; Josh 7:11; Judg 2:11, 20; 1 Kgs 11:11.

an authentic Hosean text,[79] uses בית יהוה as well. So far, then, the thesis that Hosea embraced a Yahwistic covenantal ideology has faired
rather well. Furthermore, this argument can be strengthened by an examination of the comparative materials, the closest example being the
eighth-century Aramaic inscriptions unearthed at Sefîre.

The Aramaic inscriptions of Sefîre (AIS), first published in 1931,
preserve the texts of three treaties made by a north Syrian ruler of Ar-
pad at approximately the time of Hosea's ministry in Israel.[80] The text's
geographical, chronological, and linguistic affinities to Hosea's historical context make it an ideal source of comparative data. Here I will assume as a working hypothesis that Hosea's perspective did include
covenantal ideology. Whether the data will support this assumption
should be evaluated on the basis of the relative strengths and weaknesses of the perceived similarities, but in my view the evidence shows
that the two documents share both form-critical and lexical similarities, and that they also employ similar imagery.

Form-critically, several similarities should be noted. First, both
Hosea and AIS use a technical term in reference to international treaties: in Hosea ברית (in 12:2) and in AIS עדי (I 1ff.). (1) In each case,
the concluding of a treaty is characterized as 'cutting' a treaty: ברית
כרת in Hosea and גזר עדי in AIS (see Hos 10:4, 12:2; AIS I 7). (2) In
both texts ריב serves as a technical term for controversies that arise between the treaty's parties (Hos 2:4, 4:1; AIS III 26): in AIS as a verbal
form and in Hosea as both a verb and a noun. (3) Both texts refer to
the function of a written text within the covenant/treaty context (Hos
8:12; AIS II c 1ff.). And (4) in each case the terms of the treaty are
enforced by the witnessing deities (Hos 8:15: ופקדתי עליה את־ימי
הבעלים; Hos 7:2: מעלליהם נגד פני היו; AIS I a 25–6: מה כל הדד יסך
קדם נרגל). לחיה בארק ובשמין ולשׁ מה עמל; AIS I a 7–8: ועדיא אלן זי גזר קדם מרדך).

In terms of imagery and vocabulary, the following similarities between Hosea and AIS should be noted. In both Hosea and AIS, the imagery of a wife stripped naked as a harlot (Hosea זנה; AIS, זניה) is used
to describe the consequences of covenant infidelity (Hos 2:1ff.; AIS I

---

79. Harper, *Amos and Hosea*, clx; Mays, *Hosea*, 125–27. Wolff views בית יהוה as
an addition to 9:4 precisely because he thinks it does not fit Hosea's context. However,
for some reason he accepts the phrase in 8:1.

80. I will be referring to Fitzmyer's text, *The Aramaic Inscriptions of Sefîre* (BibOr
19/A; rev. ed.; Rome: Biblical Institute Press, 1995).

40–42).[81] Added to this punishment could be attacks from wild beasts and various agricultural disasters (Hos 2:8–9; AIS I 27–32). Correction by the sword (חרב) was also a possible measure of discipline (Hos 7:16, 11:6; AIS III 13–14), including the avenging of blood for those killed outside of the treaty's terms (cf. Hos 1:4: ופקדתי את־דמי יזרעאל על־בית יהוא; AIS III 11: ותקם דמי מן יד שנאי). In both cases, the military power of those unfaithful to the treaty's terms would be eliminated when the witnessing deity or deities would 'break the bow' (שבר קשת and שבר קשתא) of the offender (Hos 1:5; AIS I 38). The infidelities that could prompt such retributions varied, but included deception (Hos 7:13; AIS III 4–6) as well as actions, expressions, or even thoughts of rebellion (Hos 4:7, 7:13–15; AIS I 26–7, III 1–2), particularly focusing attention on the heart (לבב/לב) of those involved in the treaty arrangement (Hos 10:2; AIS II b 5–6). Like AIS, Hosea used the natural pairing of "heaven and earth," which served as treaty witnesses in AIS (II 11–12) but were adapted to Hosea's mono-Yahwism in Hos 2:21: "And in that day, says the Lord, I will answer the heavens and they shall answer the earth."[82] The many similar features shared by Hosea and AIS are too numerous to attribute to coincidence, especially when one considers that with both Hosea and AIS we are dealing with a relatively small textual corpus. These similarities, coupled with the close geographical and chronological relationship between the texts, make it all but certain that Hosea freely utilized covenant imagery to express his understanding of Israel's relationship with Yahweh.

If one supposes, as I think the evidence shows, that Hosea utilized covenant imagery in his work, then this raises another question: was this purely a matter of the prophet's creative discourse or was Hosea's theology influenced by a formal covenant arrangement? Our answer to this question will largely determine whether we should see the prophet's work as the "headwater" of covenantal Yahwism or rather as standing in an older covenantal tradition that preceded him. Let us begin this part of our discussion with my previous observation, that Hosea appears to have used this covenant imagery in close conjunction

---

81. The imagery in Hosea is more properly associated with a divorce proceeding. The natural similarities between marriage agreements and treaties probably accounts for the use of common imagery.

82. This similarity suggests the possibility that ענה, usually translated here as 'answer', should instead be rendered in terms of its common secondary meaning, 'to witness'.

with the concept of תורה, a religious code that enumerated proper ethical behavior for those who desired to "know Yahweh." As Davies has recognized, this association of covenant with the concrete law of Yahweh certainly does suggest that one ought to think seriously about the thesis that Hosea's religious perspective was informed by some kind of formal covenant arrangement between Yahweh and Israel.[83] And I think that we should also agree with Nicholson that Hosea's covenant references "have the character of allusions to something familiar both to Hosea and to his audience," and this again suggests that we are dealing with something that is referentially concrete rather than with a discursive creation of the prophet. Still, it can be averred that those who would argue for a formal eighth-century Yahwistic covenant must propose and defend a suitable Sitz im Leben for the covenant's operation within the community.[84] While I am not entirely in sympathy with this rationale, since there can be evidence of covenant even in the absence of evidence about how it functioned, it does make sense to explore how this covenant might have been worked out, especially in relation to its cultic features.

While neither Davies nor Nicholson actually explains how such a covenant might have worked, D. R. Daniels's recent study does suggest a context for the expected covenant renewal ceremony. He argues that renewal of the covenant occurred within the context of the cultic rituals performed on the occasion of both national and local catastrophes.[85] Such a ceremony would therefore be characterized by its irregularity, since it would occur only when disaster highlighted the broken state of Israel's covenant relationship with Yahweh. Daniels's example of such a renewal context is Hos 2:16–25, which is problematic because it is of questionable provenience and, furthermore, its contents do not firmly locate it in a covenant renewal context.[86] While Daniels's suggestion is plausible, therefore, it is only plausible.

Another, perhaps more promising, possibility is presented by the book of Deuteronomy. Although its limits are debated, it is generally agreed that an older core of legislation is imbedded within the final

83. Davies, *Hosea,* 171–72.
84. Nicholson, *God and His People,* 188.
85. D. R. Daniels, *Hosea and Salvation History* (BZAW 191; Berlin: de Gruyter, 1990) 91–92.
86. Harper, *Amos and Hosea* clx, 239–46; Jeremias, *Der Prophet Hosea,* 36–39, 46–52; Rudolph, *Hosea,* 72–83.

form of Deuteronomy. This core is, furthermore, thought to reflect Northern provenience, which is in keeping with both Hosea's proto-Deuteronomistc outlook and the "decalogue-like" legislation reflected in Hosea. This raises an important question: is it a coincidence that Hosea associates law with covenant and that Deuteronomy, in its present form, does the same? The texts in Deuteronomy that are at once most "Northern" are Deut 11:29–30 and 27:12, which speak of a covenant renewal ceremony at Mounts Gerizim and Ebal. These texts, however, are often viewed as secondary to the original Deuteronomic core,[87] and J. Van Seters has argued, on the basis of their association with Exod 20:25 and Gen 12:6, that both are additions by the exilic Yahwist.[88] But even if this is so, it is profitable to ask why the Yahwist or Deuteronomistic editor, whichever the case may be, would locate this cultic ritual in a Northern milieu unless the environs of Shechem were known already for their association with covenant renewal ceremonies. Since no clear consensus about the extent of the original Deuteronomy has been reached, it is difficult to answer these questions. Nevertheless, I tend to agree with Mayes that the "existence in pre-Deuteronomic time of a covenant tradition is suggested . . . by the strong association of covenant ideas with Shechem."[89] I think that one can find evidence of a Northern context in which covenant renewal ceremonies took place prior to the fall of Samaria, even if we do not know exactly how it worked or how much time had elapsed between the last formal ceremony and Hosea's references to it. After all, one does not need a working covenant renewal ceremony to have a covenant idea. One needs only a tradition about covenant, and it seems quite clear to me that eighth-century Israel knew such a tradition.

However, none of this addresses the question of which eighth-century community we should associate with this covenant tradition. After all, here we are dealing with Hosea, with law, and with covenant ideas that are the precursors to Deuteronomy,[90] and we must consider

---

87. A. D. H. Mayes, *Deuteronomy* (NCBC; Grand Rapids, Mich.: Eerdmans, 1979) 218, 343–44.

88. J. Van Seters, *In Search of History: Historiography in the Ancient World and the Origins of Biblical History* (New Haven: Yale University Press, 1983; repr., Winona Lake, Ind.: Eisenbrauns, 1997) 328.

89. Mayes, *Deuteronomy*, 68.

90. Although an early edition of the Deuteronomic Code may have existed prior to the time of Hosea.

the very real possibility that only a small community within ancient Israel actually adhered strongly to these ideas. In my mind it would seem that we are dealing with a rather old but familiar covenant tradition, perhaps associated with Shechem, that Hosea and his associates resurrected and amplified in support of their mono-Yahwist agenda. As the prophet's polemical stance shows, most Israelites would not have shared his excitement about the notion of covenant, at least the notion of covenant as Hosea's party conceived it. Although I am confident that Hosea adhered to a preexisting covenant tradition of some sort, it is difficult to offer very much detail about this eighth-century phenomenon. In spite of this limitation, there remain some related issues that need to be explored more fully, and one of them is the prophet's theology of Israel's homeland.

Land Theology in Hosea 9:1–3

Because of the ideological stance of Deuteronomy, there has been a long-standing interest in the concept of land and its theological nexus with covenant in ancient Israel. Thus our interest in this text stems first from the fact that this early source discloses to us one of the earliest (if not the earliest) portraits of Israel's land theology. Perhaps even more significant for a study of ethnicity, however, is the fact that the concept of *homeland* has often been emphasized as an important component of group identity, and we ought to see what role it played in the Israelite sense of identity.[91] Hos 9:1–3, which is brief and relatively free of problems, levels against the Israelites the now familiar charge that they have played the harlot and adds the familiar warning that, as a result, the fecundity of the land will fail. In this respect its theology is like the theology of Hosea 2, although it adds to our growing list of unacceptable religious practices its condemnation of cultic activity at the 'threshing floors' (גרם), which we should apparently tie to the Baal cult.[92]

91. H. Isaacs, "Basic Group Identity," in *Ethnicity: Theory and Experience* (ed. N. Glazer and D. P. Moynihan; Cambridge: Harvard University Press, 1975) 29–52; F. W. Riggs (ed.), *Ethnicity: Concepts and Terms Used in Ethnicity Research* (International Conceptual Encyclopedia for the Social Sciences 1; Honolulu: COCTA, 1985) 30–37. For a helpful but general discussion of land theology in the Hebrew Bible, see Walter Brueggemann, *The Land: Place as Gift, Promise, and Challenge in Biblical Faith* (OBT 1; Philadelphia: Fortress, 1977).
92. Wolff, *Hosea*, 154. Here, as elsewhere, Wolff sees these activites in light of an ancient sex-cult associated with fertility religion.

The rationale behind Hosea's condemnation of Israel's Baal worship is clarified by his comment in 9:3, that Israel "will not remain long in the land of the Lord (ארץ יהוה)." For Hosea, the land that Israel inhabited belonged to Yahweh, and this necessarily precluded the worship of Baal and other deities because the land was not Baal's land. Just as Baal was not welcome in Yahweh's land, likewise those who polluted the land with Baal worship were to be exiled. Exile from the land was a serious consequence, since it not only made Israel a refugee but also sentenced it to life in an unclean and foreign environment (באשׁור טמא יאכל, 9:3). Care should be taken to distinguish this theology from later Deuteronomic theologies of land. As M. Köckert's brief study shows, Hosea did not view the land as a gift from Yahweh. Rather, the land was Yahweh's own possession and Israel his tenant.[93] The theological overlap in Hosea and the Deuteronomic traditions is that Israel could remain in the land as long as it was faithful to Yahweh.

It is important to tie together some of the features that we have noted in Hosea and their relationship to the prophet's land theology. For Hosea, failure of the land's fecundity could be equally attributed to both non-Yahwistic cultic activities (Hos 2:4ff.) and transgressions of the ethical principles enumerated in the תורה of Yahweh (Hos 4:1ff.).[94] Both kinds of rebellion were understood as transgressions of the basic covenant notions that Hosea embraced, an ideology that demanded, on the one hand, faithfulness to the ethical principles of law and, on the other, exclusive devotion to Yahweh against all competing deities. Moreover, this exclusive ideology extended beyond the religious realm to the political sphere, where Hosea and his party also objected to Israel's relationships with foreign nations.

Hosea and Israel's Ancient Traditions

Before summarizing my work in Hosea, I must remark on Hosea's many allusions to the ancient Israelite traditions. As H. R. Isaacs has pointed out, a group's perception of its past and origins is a powerful component of identity, particularly any supposed ethnic identity,[95]

93. M. Köckert, "Jahwe, Israel und das Land bei den Propheten Amos und Hosea," *Gottesvolk: Beiträge zu einen Thema biblischer Theologie: Festschrift S. Wagner* (ed. Arndt Meinhold and Rudiger Lux; Berlin: Evangelische Verlagsanstalt, 1991) 43–74.

94. A similar conclusion is argued by J. Van Seters, *Prologue to History* (Louisville: Westminster/John Knox, 1992) 231.

95. Isaacs, "Basic Group Identity."

and we are fortunate that Hosea offers us a number of details in his recollections of Israelite tradition.[96] Specifically, I think that we need to discuss Hosea's perspective on Israelite origins, on the progress of Israelite history, and on the place of Judah and tribal traditions within this history.

The Origin Traditions.   The prophet mentions two different origin traditions: (1) Israel as the progeny of a forefather and (2) Israel as a people brought up from Egypt by Yahweh's prophet. Although both traditions were well known in Hosea's day, Hosea embraced the Exodus tradition rather than the Jacob tradition and challenged Israel to do the same. The prophet's rejection of the Jacob tradition raises the question of its historical[97] status for Hosea: did he doubt the tradition's veracity or did he simply dismiss it as a normative example of proper behavior? And if he did reject the tradition, what then becomes of ethnic sentiment within the prophet's concept of identity? First, it seems doubtful that Hosea rejected the Jacob tradition outright, since he used the patriarch's repentance as an example for Israel to emulate. Second, even if he did reject the tradition, it is very unlikely that this would completely undermine his perception that Israel constituted a people who shared a common ancestry, even if that ancestry could no longer be conceptualized as a "forefather" but rather as a group of "forefathers," as seems to be the case in Hos 9:10:

> Like grapes in the wilderness, I found Israel
> Like the first fruit on the fig tree, in its first season, I saw your fathers
> (אבותיכם).

This parallelism equates Israel with the ancient fathers from the days of the wilderness. The fact that Hosea situates these "fathers" within the Exodus/Wilderness tradition, which he presents as a competing tradi-

---

96. The most complete study of the historical traditions in Hosea, as well as in Amos and Isaiah, is J. Vollmer's *Geschichtliche Rückblicke und Motive.* In addition to the works I cite during my discussion, see also the following: P. Arnold, "Hosea and the Sin of Gibeah," *CBQ* 51 (1989) 447–60; and for Dutch readers, A. Breytenbach, "Pentateuchtradisies in die boek Hosea," *HTS* 48 (1992) 645–62.

97. Throughout this discussion, it is important to keep in mind the sense in which I use the term *history.* I do not mean history in the modern sense, in which one evaluates critically events of the past on the basis of evidence and probability. I am instead referring to the common distinctions made apart from critical inquiry—"then . . . now," "once upon a time . . . today"—distinctions that are as valid in myth as in history.

tion to the patriarchal tradition, shows that these fathers should probably not be equated with the patriarchal figures mentioned in the pentateuchal sources.[98]

Wolff has suggested that this text actually refers to a "finding" origin tradition that was independent from the Exodus tradition.[99] Although this is possible, I find it unlikely for several reasons. Davies has pointed out that "like finding grapes" is a part of the imagery and not necessarily a reference to an additional origin tradition.[100] One could argue that if I am willing to admit two origin traditions—the Jacob tradition and the Exodus tradition—why not go the whole way and add a third? The reason is that the Jacob and Exodus traditions are quite different: one begins with a single forefather and the other with the people as a whole. In other words, although I can see Hosea embracing two quite different origin traditions, such as the Exodus and Jacob traditions, it does not seem very natural for him to embrace two different origin traditions of the corporate type, one associated with Egypt and the other with the Wilderness. If ever these traditions existed independently, they would have quickly been assimilated to each other, as appears to be the case already in Hosea. The geographical proximity of the wilderness region and Egypt creates a certain ambiguity, so that one can refer to the entire corporate origin tradition by referring to one place or the other, as in the case of Deut 32:10, where God finds Jacob in the desert."[101]

Hosea's Philosophy of History.   As Vollmer has suggested, Hosea puts the whole of Israel's history from the earliest times up to the present before his hearers.[102] Further, it is my contention that Hosea's view of Israelite tradition, from its beginnings until his own time, reflects a rather clear theology of progressive degeneration, a degeneration

98. If one views Hosea as proto-Deuteronomic, as most do, then this observation seems to support the conclusion of T. Römer that "the fathers" of Deuteronomy originally had no connection with the three patriarchs of Genesis. For his specific comments on this text, which agree with my analysis, see *Israels Väter*, 531–32. For general arguments contra Römer, see N. Lohfink, *Die Väter Israels in Deuteronomium, mit einer Stellungnahme von Thomas Römer* (OBO 111; Göttingen: Vandenhoeck & Ruprecht, 1991).

99. Wolff, *Hosea*, 163–64.

100. Davies, *Hosea*, 226.

101. Mayes, *Deuteronomy*, 380–85.

102. Vollmer, *Geschichtliche Rückblicke und Motive*, 55.

that could be reversed only by a return to the day of Israel's origins in Egypt and the wilderness, to the days before kingship. This theology of degeneration necessarily implies that such a deterioration can be detected within Hosea's treatment of Israel's religious, political, and economic life, and I will attempt to demonstrate this.

We should begin our historical survey with the time before Israel's entry into the *Kulturland*, when, according to Vollmer, we have the golden age of Yahweh's relationship with Israel.[103] This was the harmonious day of Israel's youth in Egypt and the wilderness, when the people were responsive to Yahweh's call (2:17) and when he provided every need for them (13:6). However, the religious degeneration of the people followed closely on the heels of this idyllic venue, as 13:5–6 indicates:

> It was I (Yahweh) who knew you in the wilderness, and in the land of drought; but when they had fed to the full, they were filled, and their heart was lifted up; therefore they forgot me.[104]

When Hosea claimed that Israel "forgot Yahweh," he had a particular event in mind, namely, the wilderness apostasy at Baal-peor that he already mentioned in Hos 9:10. Although this tradition was also known to other sources in the Hebrew Bible, Hosea's version of it reads like this:

> Like grapes in the wilderness I found Israel. Like the first fruit on the fig tree, in its first season, I saw your fathers. But they came to Baal-peor and consecrated themselves to Baal,[105] and became detestable like the thing they loved.

This text historically juxtaposes the golden age in the wilderness with its more sinister element, the ancestral apostasy after Baal.[106] This is important for two reasons. First, it helps to explain the origins of Baal-

---

103. Ibid.

104. Contra most commentators, Vollmer takes על־כן שכחוני 'therefore they forgot me' as a gloss because it does not conform to the poetic meter he finds in the text. Even if this is the case, the context of 13:6 demands that the clause correctly reflects the meaning of וירם לבם 'and their heart became proud' (ibid., 66–67).

105. The Hebrew reads בשת, but some view this as a copyist revision from an original בעל (e.g., Harper, *Amos and Hosea*, 336–37). I follow Mays, Vollmer, and Wolff in retaining בשת, but it remains obvious that Baal is the deity in question.

106. Even if one is inclined to view the "wilderness discovery" tradition, along with Wolff, as separate from the Exodus origin tradition, this does not substantively affect my argument here.

ism, for if Israel is living in the land of Yahweh, as Hosea has already suggested, then we need to know how this foreign god has gained a foothold within the ethnic community. According to the prophet's history, this foothold was gained among the Israelites prior to their entry into Yahweh's land at the foreign cult-center of Baal-peor. The second reason that this text is important is that it reveals a pattern that is a common one in Hosea and from which we can derive his typological paradigm of Israel's history: Yahweh's gift of prosperity tends to be followed by Israel's religious apostasy and subsequent degeneration.[107] A similar idea is expressed in Hos 10:1, which tells us that the more Israel prospered economically, "the more altars it built" and the more it "improved" its cult pillars. This pattern of degeneration was extended to Israel's religious leaders as well, whose increasing numbers (like the growing count of pillars and altars) represented not only economic prosperity but also an increase in the proliferation of evil (cf. Hos 4:7). Although in Hosea this degenerative paradigm is somewhat fragmented and unsystematic, and although it is unencumbered by Deuteronomic phraseology, when we compare these theological features to a text like Deut 8:12–14, the proto-Deuteronomic character of Hosea's theology of history becomes clear:

> When you have eaten and are satisfied, praise the Lord your God for the good land he has given you. Be careful not to forget the Lord your God, failing to observe his commands, his laws and his decrees that I am giving you this day. Otherwise, when you eat and are satisfied, when you build fine houses and settle down, and when your herds and flocks grow large and your silver and gold increase and all you have is multiplied, then your heart will become proud and you will forget the Lord your God, who brought you out of the land of slavery.

From this we might deduce that although Hosea did not write a history, his view of history (or at least the views of his community) may have played a pivotal role in the development of Hebrew historiography. This is not to say that one should view the Deuteronomistic History as nothing more than an extended application of Hosea's philosophy to the events of Israel's past, for the Deuteronomist's work was certainly of a more complex nature than what we see in Hosea. But it

---

107. As I will point out, Amos was even more preoccupied with the connection between material prosperity and the appearance of social evils.

does mean that one does not begin looking for nascent conceptions of Hebrew historiography in the historiographical sources. We must begin with the earliest sources that reflect a historical perspective, and our analysis of Hosea shows that the early concepts of Israelite history were formed, at least in part, within the decidedly ethnic paradigm of Hosea's community.

As I have implied already, not only did the religious life of Israel follow this degenerative historical paradigm but its political life as well. I think that there is a natural tendency among scholars to view my distinction between the "religious" and "political" with skepticism since, after all, in ancient Israel we are not dealing with a "secular" society. But it was Hosea himself who implied that the priests and prophets were Israel's legitimate leaders and, in doing so, he rhetorically classified the monarchy as a secular institution. Thus the distinction between political and religious authorities was his. But it is too simple to notice only that Hosea viewed the monarchy with suspicion, for there is a decidedly diachronic element in his perspective. He knows of a time in Israel's early history when there was no king, and when this is viewed in conjunction with his negative feelings about kingship we may infer that he viewed the emergence of kingship as a degenerative affair. Hosea's political views were in keeping with his more general theory of history, that Israel had degenerated appreciably since its origins in the wilderness, in large part due to its continuing economic and political prosperity.

If prosperity had contributed to the continuing decline of Israel, then we should expect at some point that the prophet would hope to undo this prosperous trajectory, and he did so in 12:10: "I am the Lord your God from the land of Egypt; I will again make you dwell in tents, as in the days of the appointed feast (מוֹעֵד)." Regardless of how one takes מוֹעֵד here, whether as a reference to the tabernacle or as a reference to a religious festival, our text shows that Israel's early history was a nomadic one and that chastisement from Yahweh might include a return to that nomadic lifestyle. Or to put it another way, if material prosperity had caused Israel's religious infidelity, then a return to economic simplicity might secure anew its religious affections. It is interesting to speculate about how this nomadic "tent-dwelling" tradition might have originated. We could see in it (and I think that we should) a model of social progress such as in Greece, whereby societies naturally progress from a primitive nomadism to more advanced sedentary living. We could equally attribute it to the "collective memory" of Israel and see in it a dim reflection of Israel's early history. Above all, we should certainly consider the relationship between this tradition in Hosea and the contemporary Neo-Assyrian tradition that the early kings lived in tents. As I pointed out in the discussion of AKL, the Neo-Assyrian tradition was only accurate to a point. It did preserve a memory of Old Babylonian nomadic tribal groups, but this was a somewhat distorted memory because, by the Neo-Assyrian period, these Amorite tribes had become the early nomadic kings of the Assyrian tradition. What this tells us, I think, is that we cannot confidently make use of Hosea's "tent tradition" in our quest to discover early Israel. However, we can draw the valuable inference that by the eighth-century B.C.E. the Israelites, like the Assyrians, already viewed their past as a period of historical progress from a nomadic to a sedentary lifestyle. Whether the Israelites borrowed this convention from the Assyrians or developed the tradition independently is difficult to say. But whatever the case, it seems clear that Hosea did not view this socioeconomic progress as evidence of religious progress, and in this respect his ideas remind us of a Mari text that extols the benefit of the nomadic life and of its simplicity.[108] For Hosea the loss of the nomadic life was just one in a number of degenerative shifts that could be associated with the fundamental decline of Israel:

1. From Yahweh	1. To Baal
2. From wilderness	2. To arable land
3. From divine provisions	3. To haughty prosperity
4. From few people	4. To many
5. From few priests	5. To many
6. From no king	6. To kingship
7. From few cultic altars	7. To many
8. From nomadism	8. To sendentary living

This series of changes reflected Hosea's basic understanding of Israel's history. Beginning with the entry into the arable land, Israel had turned away from Yahweh and had regressively moved away from him over the course of its corporate life. The solution to this problem was

---

108. P. Marello, "Vie nomade," in *Florilegium marianum: Recueil d'études en l'honneur de Michel Fleury* (ed. J.-M. Durand; Memoires de N.A.B.U. 1; Paris: SEPOA, 1992) 115–25.

none other than a radical reversal of the tradition process, whereby Israel could return to the "golden age" of its origins in Egypt:[109]

> Therefore, behold, I will allure her, and bring her back into the wilderness, and speak tenderly to her. And there I will give her her vineyards, and make the Valley of Achor a door of hope. And there she shall answer as in the days of her youth, as at the time when she came out of the land of Egypt. (Hos 2:16–17)

Hosea believed that this dramatic reversal of direction would require a substantial change in the religious, political, and social fabric of ancient Israel, and we can surmise that many in Israel did not share his sympathies or agenda. But he remained dedicated to the vision that Israel might turn away from its historical degeneration and recoup the glory of its past, when the people of Israel knew Yahweh and adhered to his law. The prophet called upon Israel to reestablish the ethnic boundaries that had long ago protected them from foreign religious and political influences and to emulate, not the stubborn disobedient forefather Jacob, but the faithful prophet who led Israel out of Egypt.

One issue that has eluded my brief discussion of Hosea and his historical allusions up to this point is the problem of Judah and its connection to the Northern Kingdom. After all, the tradition that Judah and Israel together originally composed a single political entity is an important one in the Hebrew Bible. However, once the supposedly post-Hosean redactional materials have been excluded, there is very little said about Judah in Hosea. With the exception of 5:16, which is a reprimand of Judah for its border encroachments into Northern territory, our understanding of the historical relationship between Israel and Judah is scarcely elucidated by this prophetic collection. For that we will have to turn to Amos and Isaiah. There is a brief reference to the 'tribes of Israel' (שבטי־ישראל) in 5:9, and although I suppose someone might argue that this collectivity implies Judah, such a conclusion seems altogether reckless and careless in the absence of other references to Judah in the book. Nevertheless this phrase does tell us that Hosea's model of Israelite society included the concept of tribal composition, as we also saw in our examination of Deborah's Song. If we are curious about the details of this eighth-century tribal composition, however, we cannot depend on SDeb, because a rather long chro-

---

109. As argued by Y. Hoffman, "A North Israelite Typological Myth and a Judean Historical Tradition: The Exodus in Hosea and Amos," *VT* 39 (1989) 169–82.

nological span probably separates Hosea from the song. But we are fortunate to have the collection of Deuteronomy 33 (along with the associated tribal list), and the early edition of that collection should be dated no later, I think, than to the eighth century.[110] We will examine these texts in the next chapter.

Summary

This examination of Hosea has yielded the following results. It is clear that ethnic sentiments were an important component of identity in the Northern Kingdom, as demonstrated by the fact that the people shared a common ancestor, Jacob, and a common historical origin in Egypt. These traditions are similar to the Greek traditions, both in the general sense and in the particular, and they are quite different from both Assyrian and Egyptian literary traditions. Although we might speculate about the origins of these ethnic traditions, and I will do so at the conclusion of this chapter, we can safely conclude at this juncture that Israel's ethnic traditions already existed prior to Hosea's ministry. This conclusion squares well with my contention that ethnicity was probably a factor in the ninth-century (or earlier) composition of SDeb.

But the fact that ethnicity was one aspect of Israel's social identity does not necessarily mean that the boundaries associated with these ethnic sentiments were particularly intense among most Israelites. It was perhaps only in the case of Hosea and his (small?) party that antipathies for foreign influence were strong, as we see in his rejection of gods, religious practices, and ethical mores that failed to pass his tests for being Yahwistic and Israelite. His distaste for foreign influence extended beyond what we might call the religious realm into the political, so that he also objected to treaty relationships with foreign nations on the grounds that they somehow threatened the covenant relationship he envisioned between Yahweh and Israel. While these features share many traits with later Hebrew texts, particularly with popular notions assumed by Jeremiah and Deuteronomy, in Hosea we seem to have a peripheral, minority position shared by a small community of mono-Yahwists who had radicalized devotion to Israel's national deity. This ethnoreligious movement was responsible for combining preexisting

110. For a discussion of the "tribal list" tradition in the Hebrew Bible, see pp. 267–272, 297–299.

ethnic traditions with a new (or resurrected?) brand of mono-Yahwism, the goal being to utilize and intensify those ethnic sentiments in support of their religious program. We should therefore conclude that the primary concerns of the proto-Deuteronomic movement were more religious than ethnic in character. And although the Northern state of Israel ultimately disappeared from the historical scene, these mono-Yahwists did not. At least in certain ways, therefore, the effort to secure and preserve the identity of this religious party succeeded.

Ethnicity and Identity in Amos

Our study of Hosea provided a glimpse, albeit a Northern one, into the contextual situation that faced the prophet Amos during his ministry. Although Amos's roots were in the South, he provides us not only with a partial window into eighth-century Judean identity but also with a Judean perception of the surrounding nations, including Israel. This affords us the opportunity to clarify the various concepts of identity represented in the eighth-century social matrix of Palestine and to evaluate the role that ethnicity played within them. One of our working assumptions will be that Amos was already familiar with the popular ethnic traditions of the Northern Kingdom (an assumption that the evidence will bear out). This means that our focus should be duly placed on the way that he tends to characterize the non-Israelite and non-Judean populations.[111] If we wanted to put our primary concerns in the form of three questions, I would suggest these. First, we have established the presence of ethnic sentiments within the eighth-century Northern context, but now we must ask, to what extent did Israel's neighbors share in this mode of identity? Second, what contribution does the prophet make toward our understanding of Northern identity, particularly with regard to the various ancestral figures known to us from the biblical corpus? And third, as we come to understand Judean identity from the prophecies of Amos, we should ask: what role does Israel play in this sense of identity and what function, if any, does ethnicity serve within Judean thought?

---

111. Hosea's prophetic work presumed the ethnic sentiments of his audience, especially their familiarity with the Jacob tradition. Amos refers to the Northern Kingdom as "Jacob" on six occasions (3:13, 6:8, 7:2, 7:5, 8:7, 9:8) and also refers to "Isaac" (7:9, 16), which makes his acquaintance with the Israelite forefather traditions a virtual certainty. The degree of his familiarity with these traditions is more difficult to assess and will be discussed below.

Our discussion of these questions is necessarily, but temporarily, preempted by a few comments about the redactional history of Amos. More than any other study, H. W. Wolff's commentary has been responsible for defining and clarifying the lines of critical research in Amos studies.[112] In general terms, although there is a strong tendency to exclude the oracles against Tyre, Edom, and Judah, we can say that only in the case of the superscription and Amos 9:11–15 is there unqualified agreement that Amos is the work of later Judean editors.[113] In addition to these texts, Wolff has identified a number of minor additions and editorial changes that have been made in Amos, but none of these substantially alters the texts of my selected readings.[114] Our inquiry can therefore move ahead with minimal obstruction. My primary focus in Amos will be the "nations oracles" in chaps. 1–2, and I will be giving particular attention to the place of ethnicity in Amos's representation of those nations. We will also examine three texts in chaps. 6, 7, and 9 that describe, respectively, the social stratification present in Northern society, the ancestral figures known to Amos, and the prophet's evaluation of Israel's supposedly unique Exodus origin tradition. Although I investigated Hosea's view of history extensively, I will not do so with the book of Amos, primarily because there is very little in Amos from which to build a case. I agree with Vollmer that Amos's historical picture is incomplete.[115]

Oracles against the Nations: Amos 1:3–2:16

The most pressing introductory issue presented by the oracles is that three of the eight (the oracles against Tyre, Edom, and Judah) are often viewed as later additions for form-critical, literary, historical, and ideological reasons.[116] Form-critically, three characteristics of these

112. H. W. Wolff, *Joel and Amos* (Hermeneia; Philadelphia: Fortress, 1977) 106–13. Wolff's position in the English edition has changed somewhat from the earlier German edition, which listed the following as later additions to the text: 1:1–2; 1:9–11; 2:4–5; 3:1–2; 3:7; 4:13; 5:8–9; 5:25–27; 9:5–6, 11–15.

113. But see S. Paul's recent commentary, *Amos* (Hermeneia; Philadelphia: Fortress, 1991) 288–89.

114. Wolff, *Joel and Amos*, 106–13.

115. Vollmer, *Geschichtliche Rückbliche und Motive*, 43–46.

116. Contrary to this near consensus, V. Fritz has asserted that the entire collection, all eight oracles, is late *vaticinia ex eventu*. This view has little to commend it and has been refuted in G. Pfeifer's recent article. See V. Fritz, "Die Fremdvölkersprüche des Amos," *VT* 37 (1987) 26–38; and G. Pfeifer, "Die Fremdvölkersprüche des Amos—später vaticinia ex eventu?" *VT* 38 (1988) 230–33.

oracles distinguish them from the other oracles to which they are superficially similar: (1) the infinitival clause following עַל־ is expanded
with one or more finite verbs, (2) the threat of punishment is brief and
lacks detail, and (3) the concluding אמר יהוה is missing.[117] From a literary point of view, Harper argues that the strophic arrangements of
these oracles differ from the other five oracles.[118] Historically, it is usually argued that Edom's mistreatment of Judah in 1:11 is more properly associated with the exilic period[119] and that Tyre's ascendancy as
an opponent of Israel in 1:9 dates to the late seventh century.[120] And as
has often been argued (by B. Gosse most recently), the ideology of
these oracles, particularly the oracle against Judah, supposedly betrays
their Deuteronomistic origin. Thus the Judah oracle is thought to contain a cluster of features similar to those of 2 Kgs 17:13–15 (תורה,
אבות, הלך, חק, מאס, and שמר) and the oracle against Tyre likewise to
be Deuteronomistic in its use of זכר ברית.[121]

S. Paul has argued for the authenticity of all eight oracles.[122] He
points out, for instance, that because Philistia and Tyre are often cited
together in the Hebrew Bible, the Tyrian oracle must be an integral
part of the original prophecy. Likewise, the omission of the Judah
oracle effectively removes the Southern Kingdom from Amos's purview
and because, as Paul says, this is unlikely, the oracle must also be an authentic one. As for the Edomites, their struggle with Judah does not

---

117. J. Barton, *Amos's Oracles against the Nations* (Cambridge: Cambridge University Press, 1980) 22; Wolff, *Joel and Amos*, 135–44. H. Reventlow attempts unsuc-
cessfully, via literary gymnastics, to restore a common form to all of the oracles in 1:3ff.
(*Das Amt des Propheten bei Amos* [FRLANT 8; Göttingen: Vandenhoeck & Ruprecht,
1962] 62). Agreeing with the conclusions of Barton and Wolff are J. L. Mays, *Amos*
(OTL; Philadelphia: Westminster, 1969) 22–26; H. Reimer, *Richtet auf das Recht!
Studien zur Botschaft des Amos* (Stuttgarter Bibelstudien 149; Stuttgart: Katholisches
Bibelwerk, 1992) 28–29; W. Rudolph, *Joel, Amos, Obadija, Jona* (KAT 13/2; Güters-
loh: Gütersloh Verlagshaus / Gerd Mohn, 1971) 102, 133–37.

118. The oracles against Tyre, Edom, and Judah contain strophes of five and two
lines, while the other oracles contain five, three, and four lines (see Harper, *Amos and
Hosea*, 12–13).

119. Edom is reprimanded for its aggressive attitude toward Judah only after
Jerusalem's fall. See Ezekiel 25 and 35 as well as Obadiah 10–14 and Lam 4:21–22.

120. Cf. Isa 23:1–18, Ezekiel 26–29, Joel 4:4ff.

121. See B. Gosse, "Le Recueil d'oracles contre les nations du livre d'Amos et
l'histoire deutéronomique," *VT* 38 (1988) 29–30, 32–33. For several relatively late
uses of זכר ברית, see Lev 26:42–45; Deut 8:18; Josh 4:7; Jer 3:16, 14:21; Ezek 16:60–
61; 1 Chr 16:15; 2 Chr 23:1; Neh 13:29.

122. Paul, *Amos*, 7–30.

need to be dated to the sixth century, since "skirmishes between Israel and Edom must have occurred for hundreds of years before Amos."[123] Paul's many arguments have merit, and I could add to them that the distinctive form-critical pattern of the questionable oracles might be explained by their thematic relationship to each other. In each case, the concept of *brotherhood* plays a part in the oracle (Tyre/Edom explicitly, Judah implicitly), making it possible that the three oracles previously existed as a collection independent of the other five oracles. But this does not address the real problem with these texts: their Deuteronomistic features. Unlike Hosea, Amos is not a proto-Deuteronomistic work, and therefore these features must necessarily be viewed with suspicion. The Deuteronomistic color, coupled with the other problems that I have cited above, put some momentum behind the cumulative argument that these three oracles are not authentic. It is therefore difficult to agree in an unqualified way with S. Paul or with those who share his sympathies about these oracles.[124] My methodological desire to ground this study in unimpeachable sources therefore dictates that I examine only the five oracles that are, by consensus, authentic: the oracles against Syria, Philistia, Ammon, Moab, and Israel.

Two other problems require attention before these judgment oracles can be properly evaluated. First, on what theoretical basis did Amos condemn the 'rebellions' (פשעים) of the foreign nations? And second, why are the oracles arranged in their present order? As J. Barton has pointed out, the range of possible answers to the first question is limited to four:[125]

1. *Nationalism and Covenant*: the nations are denounced for opposing Yahweh's people, Israel.

---

123. Ibid., 20. This is possible, but the archaeological record does not lend much support for the view that Edom existed during the second millennium B.C.E.

124. See Andersen and Freedman, *Amos* (AB 24A; New York: Doubleday, 1987) 199–218; E. Hammershaimb, *Amos: A Commentary* (New York: Schocken, 1970) 35–46; J. H. Hayes, *Amos the Eighth-Century Prophet* (Nashville: Abingdon, 1988) 52–55; G. Smith, *Amos* (Grand Rapids: Zondervan, 1989) 40–42; Stuart, *Hosea–Jonah*, 308–9. A. E. Steinmann has recently argued for the authenticity of all eight oracles because the two oracle forms reflected in the text follow a discernible pattern. The problem with this is that the Israel oracle does not actually conform to the pattern, thus negating his argument (Steinmann, "The Order of Amos's Oracles against the Nations: 1:3–2:16," *JBL* 111 [1992] 683–89). I will review this in detail during my discussion of the order of these oracles.

125. See Barton, *Amos's Oracles against the Nations*, 39–45.

2. *Logical Extension*: the moral obligations that Israel owes to Yahweh apply, by extension, to the surrounding nations, despite the fact that they have no covenant relationship with Yahweh.
3. *Universal Law*: all nations are subject to a divine, universal law because Yahweh's dominion is over all mankind.
4. *International Customary Law*: the nations are condemned for infringing on customs of war accepted or believed to be accepted by all civilized nations.

Contrary to E. Würthwein, who argues for case #1, the oracles against Moab and Philistia cannot have been prompted by aggressions against Israel.[126] Option #2 does no justice to texts like Amos 4:10, 6:2, and 9:7, which highlight the prophet's universalistic perspective that all nations are subject to Yahweh on the same grounds. Rather, this notion of "logical extension" can only help us if it is viewed as a path to the third option, universal law. About this Mays writes:

> Amos sees Yahweh as the sovereign of history who moves nations in their national careers and can remove them to their earlier spheres (1:5). By analogy with Yahweh's relation to Israel, that sovereignty in the nations' history furnishes the foundation for their responsibility to him. It seems clear that for Amos the ethos over which Yahweh watched was not exhausted in or confined to a particular covenant legal tradition which was Israel's possession by special revelation.[127]

The conclusion that universal ethical standards are applied by Amos in these oracles is followed not only by Mays but also, albeit idiosyncratically, by Paul, Reimer, Reventlow, and Wolff,[128] and it is by far the most common approach to our problem.

But Barton's short monograph challenges this conclusion and embraces option #4, that the פשעים which Amos denounces are transgressions of "accepted norms of international conduct." This can only be the case if at least two things are true: (1) that the most obvious possibility, the universalistic argument, is invalid; and (2) that Barton can demonstrate the existence of the internationally recognized norms that correspond to the crimes Amos denounces. First, Barton's argument against the universalistic position is very weak. He writes:

126. E. Würthwein, "Amos-Studien," *ZAW* 62 (1950) 10–52.
127. Mays, *Amos*, 27–28.
128. Paul, *Amos*, 45; Reimer, *Richtet auf des Recht*, 31; Reventlow, *Das Amt des Propheten bei Amos*, 70; Wolff, *Joel and Amos*, 152.

> If we say that the humanitarian principles the nations are con-
> demned for flouting are part of a divine law, we still run the risk of
> suggesting that they are condemned for breaking an edict they were
> unaware of: for what reason was there to think that God's will had
> been revealed to them? In other words, we shall seem to accuse Amos
> of irrationality if we hold that he appealed to a supposed divine
> law. . . . [129]

If we must so "accuse" Amos, we must necessarily accuse the entire
Deuteronomic movement for its similar condemnation of foreigners
and their idolatry. The fact is that there is nothing surprising about
such a rigid, particularistic view. Barton is right that the foreign nations
have contravened "moral principles which even they should have recognized," but there is no compelling reason why universal moral principles cannot be the underlying basis of the prophet's criticism.

Second, Barton has not adequately demonstrated the existence of
international norms that correspond to the crimes Amos has denounced. He realizes that the evidence itself preempts the view that
these norms correspond to formal international laws. But in examining
several parallels from the Amarna Letters, Mari, Hittite texts, and the
Iliad, Barton finds a few connections between Amos's rationale and the
ethical codes expected between international parties, particularly with
respect to the problems of boundary rights and extreme cruelty. [130]
However, these similarities amount to nothing more than the kinds of
universal principles that Amos routinely applies within Israel itself and
that he views as transgressions against Yahweh. And with respect to
boundary rights, Amos clearly views these as established by Yahweh
(Amos 9:7). Or to put it another way, there may well be a similarity
between international norms and Amos's ethical code, but this does
not mean that Amos embraced his code on the basis of international
practice. Amos envisioned a moral code that applied equally to Israel
and the surrounding nations because all of them lived under the sovereignty of his God. The term פשע refers to rebellions against authority, [131] and for the prophet this authority was Yahweh.

The last important problem, the order of these oracles, is of concern because a discernible pattern might provide a glimpse into the
prophet's conceptual model of the world. The difficulties of finding a

---

129. Barton, *Amos's Oracles against the Nations*, 43.
130. Ibid., 51–61.
131. Harper, *Amos and Hosea*, 14.

modus operandi are magnified by the fact that three of them are later additions. As Harper points out, these late additions may well have displaced original oracles, meaning that it is hard to know whether they would contribute to any assumed pattern, and this must be kept in mind as we proceed.[132] First, A. Bentzen, among others, has argued that the five original oracles follow the geographical organization of Egyptian execration texts and therefore reflect a cultic setting for the collection. But this view is wanting, because most now recognize that the order in Amos is quite different from the order in the execration texts.[133] K. Marti attempted to find a circular geographical pattern in the oracles, but he did so by selectively eliminating the oracles against Philistia, Tyre, and Edom, which is methodologically questionable and not convincing.[134] Wolff's analysis identifies several loose connections between the various oracles but finds no overarching order.[135] More recently, A. E. Steinmann has attempted to explain the oracles by systematically tying together the ideas of several scholars with his own. Following Paul (who finds connections between the oracles via catchwords and phrases) and Hayes (who sees a form-critical pattern that joins all eight oracles together),[136] Steinmann argues that all eight of these oracles were the contribution of Amos because they conform to the formal arrangement below.[137] The problem with this

132. Ibid., cxxx–cxxxii.
133. A. Bentzen, "The Ritual Background of Amos i.2–ii.16," *OTS* 8 (1950) 85–99. For the problems with this view, see J. Barton, *Amos's Oracles against the Nations* 12–3; Steinmann, "The Order of Amos's Oracles against the Nations," 683–84; Wolff, *Joel and Amos*, 145–47.
134. K. Marti, "Zur Komposition von Amos 1:3–2:3," *Abhandlungen zur Semitischen Religionskunde und Sprachwissenschaft* (ed. W. Frankenberg and F. Küchler; BZAW 33; Giessen: Alfred Töpelman, 1918) 323–30.
135. Wolff, *Joel and Amos*, 144–50.
136. S. Paul, "Amos 1:3–2:3: A Concatenous Literary Pattern," *JBL* 90 (1971) 397–403; Hayes, *Amos the Eighth-Century Prophet*, 52.
137. In this table, "group" refers to the two form-critical patterns of the oracles involved. I have already discussed these above.

Text	Nation	Presented as	Neighbor of	Group
1:3–5	Damascus	City-State	Israel	1
1:6–8	Gaza	City-State	Judah	1
1:9–10	Tyre	City-State	Israel	2
1:11–12	Edom	Nation	Judah	2
1:13–15	Ammon	Nation	Israel	1
2:1–3	Moab	Nation	Judah	1
2:4–5	Judah	Special Nation	Israel	2
2:6–16	Israel	Special Nation	Judah	2

is that, as Steinmann recognizes, the Israel oracle is missing several elements of the form and does not actually fit the pattern.[138] Furthermore, Hayes's "group" structure actually works even if we eliminate all three of the questionable oracles.[139] In the end I can only say that no convincing resolutions to the question of the oracles' order have been suggested up to this point. Nevertheless, I think that my discussion will shed some light on the problem. My examination of the oracles is organized into three parts, beginning with Aram and Philistia, moving on to Ammon and Moab, and then completing the discussion with Israel. The rationale behind this threefold scheme will become clear as we proceed.

Although from a political perspective Aram (עם־ארם) and Philistia (פלשתים) were different kinds of modalities, one being a monarchic kingdom and the other a confederation of city-states, this fact did not preclude Amos from recognizing that they shared something in common.[140] Both peoples originated as the progeny of ancestral migrations, the Arameans from Kir and the Philistines from Caphtor (cf. 1:5, 9:7). Although we know that the Philistine homeland should be identified with either Crete or Cyprus,[141] the location of Kir, sometimes thought to be in the environs of Elam, is more difficult.[142] But this Aramean migration tradition should no doubt be associated with the rapid Aramean population expansions between 1200 and 1000 B.C.E., an expansion that, as G. Roux has pointed out, can be traced to the ancient textual evidence.[143] There is also some truth behind the Philistine tradition. Although it is doubtful that the Philistine ancestors stemmed entirely from either Cretan or Cypriot stock, there is substantial evidence that they migrated across the Mediterranean to

138. Steinmann, "The Order of Amos's Oracles against the Nations," 684–85. As Wolff notes, "Israel falls into neither group" (*Joel and Amos*, 144).

139. Steinmann also fails to address the problem of the Deuteronomistic features in the later texts.

140. Because Sargon II destroyed Gath in 711 B.C.E. (see *ANET* 286), it is sometimes suggested that the Philistine oracle is a later addition to the series. However, there are a host of other possibilities (the most likely being that Gath had been subsumed by Ashdod at this point) and, generally speaking, scholars take the oracle as authentic. See Mays, *Amos*, 32–33; Paul, *Amos*, 17, 56; Reimer, *Richtet auf das Recht*, 58–66; Wolff, *Joel and Amos*, 158.

141. R. S. Hess, "Caphtor," *ABD* 1.869–70.

142. H. O. Thompson, "Kir," *ABD* 4.83–84.

143. G. Roux, *Ancient Iraq* (2d ed.; New York: Penguin, 1980) 253–61.

their levantine settlements.[144] Thus both the Philistine and the Aramean traditions reflect a generally accurate (though undoubtedly distorted) collective memory of their ancestral ethnic origins. This is to say that they knew that they were different because their forefathers had come from somewhere else. The passages in Amos, therefore, are not Israelite models of foreign origins but are Philistine and Aramean traditions, with which Israel was familiar. Nevertheless, as Amos himself recognized in 9:7, these traditions were quite similar to the Israelite tradition that an ancestral migration from Egypt accounted for the distinctive identity of the Northern Kingdom. As one can plainly see, Hosea and Amos have exploited their familiarity with this tradition in quite different ways. At about the same time that Hosea was trying to reestablish a sense of ethnic distinctiveness by emphasizing the uniqueness of Yahweh's divine election in the Exodus event, Amos was busy pointing out that Yahweh had done similar things for the Philistines and Arameans: "Did I not bring . . . the Philistines from Caphtor and the Syrians from Kir?" While the ideological differences between these two prophets is not as great as it might seem, since both of them pronounced doom upon the North and embraced a hope (of sorts) for the future of Israel, their rhetorical strategies are entirely different from an ethnic perspective, with one hoping to intensify ethnic sentiments and the other hoping to subvert them. The reason for this rhetorical difference stems in part from the different theologies that inform their work, since for Hosea Yahweh was the God of Israel's land and for Amos he was the God of every land. This explains not only why Amos has attributed the ancestral migrations of several groups to Yahweh's divine initiative but also why the groups were equally culpable before him and would be punished for their rebellions.

There is more that can be culled from Amos on the subject of punishment, if we tarry a bit on this subject. If we are willing to believe that there was such a thing as a prophetic tradition that was Yahwistic (as opposed to Northern or Southern), then in spite of their differences there appears to have been a common notion of punishment among Yahweh's prophets. We have already noticed that Hosea had pronounced upon Israel a "punishment of return," wherein the people

144. T. Dothan and M. Dothan, *People of the Sea: The Search for the Philistines* (New York: Macmillan, 1992). As Redford has pointed out, the Philistines managed to preserve a distinct sense of identity as late as the first century B.C.E. (Redford, *Egypt, Canaan and Israel in Ancient Times*, 294–95; cf. Strabo 16.2.2).

would be returned to their place of Egyptian origins. A similar fate was also predicted by Amos for the Arameans in 1:5, so that punishment was in some sense a reversal of national fortunes that returned the people to their beginnings. This ideology probably stemmed, at least in part, from the then-current threat of Assyria, an aggressor that had a long-standing reputation for exiling population groups. That Assyria should be viewed as the primary means of punishment here is all too clear from 1:5, which predicted a military siege that would end with the city's gate broken, with its buildings burned, and with the people in exile. Because this description corresponds rather precisely with Assyrian imperial policy, it suggests that the theology of Amos both permitted Assyria to be and envisioned it as the instrument of Yahweh's wrath.

We need to look at the issue of Yahweh's wrath in a little more detail because Amos predicted that it would consume "the remnant of the Philistines." The prediction prompts H. Reimer to raise the question of whether Amos offered any hope to the non-Israelite peoples mentioned in his oracles. He has argued that the oracles never envisioned a complete destruction of the people but only predicted the destruction of their core power structures, as represented by Damascus in the case of Aram or by Gaza in the case of Philistia.[145] Although we might infer hope for Israel from other texts in Amos, we cannot arrive at this position via the oracles to the other nations because there is no explicit (or implicit) expression of hope for the foreigners. We need to be careful on this point, however, because we are assuming that Amos was interested in the question we have raised. After all, he was a man of compassion toward the oppressed, and if we could have put to him the question "will the poor of Philistia be destroyed?" he might well have answered "no," in spite of the fact that the corpus fails to include a message of hope for them.

The first two oracles that we have examined, the oracles against Aram and Philistia, share with the next two, against Ammon and Moab, the judgment that their punishment was prompted by the transgression of international boundaries established by Yahweh. In the case of Ammon this was because they trespassed their northern border to oppress the Gileadites, and in the case of Moab it was because of their southern forays into Edom. In spite of this general similarity to

145. Reimer, *Richtet auf das Recht,* 63.

the other oracles, however, the Ammonite and Moabite oracles display a number of features that link them together. The oracles are structurally identical. Both refer to the 'shout' (תרועה) that will accompany destruction and envision this imminent destruction in a context of confusion, in the Ammon oracle as "a tempest (סער) in the day of the whirlwind" and in the Moab oracle an 'uproar' (שאון) accompanied by "the sound of the trumpet." In each oracle both the political and military leaders are chastised: in the case of Ammon its king (מלך)[146] and princes (שרים) and in the case of Moab its ruler (שפט) and princes (שרים).[147] These similarities, coupled with the fact that the oracles are placed next to each other, suggest that Amos was probably familiar with the traditional ethnic connection between Ammon and Moab (cf. Genesis 19, Deuteronomy 2).[148] The geographical proximity of the two nations probably contributed to the development of this fraternal tradition, which can be explored in more detail as we discuss the name that Amos used for the Ammonites.[149]

Amos called the Ammonites the בני־עמון 'the sons of Ammon', a designation that raises two questions: first, whether it is an endonym or exonym; and second, whether the name reflects a supposed eponymous ancestor like the Israelite Jacob. It should be recognized that בני + GN can serve a very generic role that reflects no indication of ethnic identity, as Isa 11:14 shows: "together they shall plunder the people of the east (בני־קדם)." However, if this is the case with respect to Ammon, then the בני + GN pattern was followed with remarkable consistency.

146. E. Puech, on the basis of the Greek evidence and comparisons with a parallel text in Jer 49:3, has rendered Amos 1:15 'Et Milkom ira en exil, ses prêtres et ses chefs ensemble, dit le Seigneur'. I do not find this convincing. The Greek witnesses generally translate מלכם as βασιλεις, and a reference to political figures is expected on the basis of the other oracles (E. Puech, "Milkom, le dieu ammonite, en Amos 1:15," *VT* 27 [1977] 117–25).

147. As most commentators agree, in this case שפט is synonymous with kingship and should not be viewed as evidence of some other political institution (Paul, *Amos*, 74; Mays, *Amos*, 40). Wolff (*Joel and Amos*, 163) views the institution as somewhat distinct from kingship but admits that "for all purposes . . . the official in question was a king."

148. If Psalm 83 dates to the Assyrian period, as seems likely, then Amos's familiarity with the Lot tradition seems assured. See the reference to the בני־לוט in Ps 83:6–8 and the associated discussion of A. A. Anderson in *The Book of Psalms* (2 vols.; NCBC; Grand Rapids, Mich.: Eerdmans, 1972) 2.595–98.

149. Geographical proximity (or distance) exerts an influence on human conceptions of self and also of others (cf. Hartog, *The Mirror of Herodotus*, 12–19).

From the eighth century to the postexilic period, the Ammonites were consistently identified in the prophetic literature as 'sons of Ammon' (בני־עמון), in contrast to Edom (not 'sons of Edom'), Moab (not 'sons of Moab'), Aram (not 'sons of Aram'), and so on.[150] Isa 11:14 is a good example of this pattern when it refers to "Edom, and Moab and the sons of Ammon." Likewise Jer 25:21 and Dan 11:41 list the same combination. And as Shalom Paul has pointed out, an Assyrian letter from Calah refers to the 'land of the sons of Ammon' (^{māt}*Ba-an-am-ma-na-aia*). The title בני־עמון for Ammon's people is therefore firmly established from the eighth century onward. The fact that the designation בני־עמון was consistently used by various foreigners suggests that it originated with the Ammonites themselves—that is, it was an endonym. This conclusion seems to be confirmed by an indigenous Ammonite inscription, which refers to the *bn ʿmn* (= Heb. בני־עמון).[151] In the absence of more plentiful data from the Ammonite evidence, our understanding of בני־עמון is aided by an examination of the biblical materials in Deuteronomy 2 and Genesis 19.

The Ammon/Moab tradition found in Deuteronomy 2 would appear to lie closer to the Amos tradition, because it adheres to the corporate migration model that the prophet preferred for Israel, Philistia, and Aram. Here Moab and Ammon (n.b., בני־עמון) are identified as the "sons of Lot" who migrated to their new homeland and dispossessed its inhabitants by the authority of Yahweh. Although this may strike us as an inconsistency, because the Lot forefather tradition does not immediately square with the corporate origin tradition that is emphasized in the text, this situation is perhaps no different from the Hosean tradition, where the forefather story and the corporate migration story appear to have existed with relative independence (see pp. 133–134). As Van Seters has noted, the Ammon/Moab origin tradition in Genesis 19 is quite different from the corporate migration described by Deuteronomy 2. The Genesis story stands much closer to the tradition in Genesis 38, in which a single ancestor, Judah, migrates to the region and settles there. This type of tradition cannot (easily) be squared with a corporate migration tradition, and so we must assume that these

150. All 21 references to Ammon in the prophetic literature refer to the "sons of Ammon." This is also the case in 85 of the remaining 107 references to Ammon.

151. Paul, *Amos*, 67–68. See also H. W. F. Saggs, "The Nimrud Letters, II: Relations with the West," *Iraq* 17 (1955) 134–35; H. O. Thompson and F. Zayadine, "The Tell-Siran Inscription," *BASOR* 212 (1973) 5–11.

represent alternative traditions which were preserved out of antiquarian interest by the Yahwist.[152] In the story of Genesis 19, the two incest-begotten sons of Lot, Moab and Ben-ammi, represent the eponymous ancestors of Moab and Ammon, respectively. As Westermann has pointed out, this story undoubtedly reflected the nature of relations between Israel and the Transjordanian states when the Yahwist's work was done.[153] But what is most interesting, I think, is that in Genesis 19 Ben-ammi is the ancestor of the בני־עמון, that is, that the ancestor's name attempts to account for the prevailing name used for the Ammonites, 'the sons of Ammon'. This would seem to suggest that, in the Yahwist's day, the name 'sons of Ammon' could not have reflected a patriarchal figure, Ammon, but was instead such an ossified reference to the Ammonites that the personal name of any supposed ancestor needed to reflect it (hence Ben-ammi). This does not completely solve the problem of what בני־עמון meant for eighth-century Amos, but it does show that one cannot assume that it reflects an eponymous ancestor. However, in Amos we seem to be dealing with an ethnic modality, because the title 'sons of Ammon' implicitly suggests an ethnic connection regardless of whether a particularly eponymous ancestor stood behind it. This ethnic designation was an endonym coined by the Ammonites themselves and was subsequently adopted by the surrounding nations, including Israel.

Given the ties between the Ammonite and Moabite oracles in Amos, the fact that the Ammonites were an ethnic entity implies that the Moabites were as well, perhaps sharing together the title "sons of Lot." If this is true and if we combine this with what we have already learned about Israel, Aram, and Philistia, then we may conclude that ethnic paradigms were a quite popular mode of identity in the peripheral communities of the eighth-century Levantine context.[154] The note-worthy exception seems to be Judah, unless of course the "Judah" tradition of Genesis 38 dates to an early period—a thesis that is difficult to confirm.[155] But none of these ethnic exemplars reflects the fervent ethnic intensity of Hosea's proto-Deuteronomic community.

152. Van Seters, *Prologue to History,* 238.
153. But the Yahwist may date much later than Westermann suggests (C. Westermann, *Genesis* [3 vols.; Minneapolis: Augsburg, 1984–86] 2.310–14).
154. The *Story of Sinuhe,* though much older, also supports this conclusion (see above, pp. 83–84). We can add to our list of ethnic entities in Amos the Ethiopians, whom Amos identifies as the 'sons of Cush' (בני־כשיים) in 9:7.
155. For discussion, see Westermann, *Genesis,* 3.46–57.

Before moving on to the Israel oracle in Amos, we should briefly review what has been accomplished during my examination of the "nations oracles" in Amos. I have suggested that the Aramean and Philistine oracles are adjacent to each other because both groups originated via ancestral migrations and that the Ammonite and Moabite oracles are adjacent to each other because the two groups shared common origins, perhaps as the ethnic progeny of an ancestor such as Lot. Whether this arrangement of the oracles was the result of an explicitly "intentional" effort on the part of Amos is a slightly different question that we cannot answer. After all, the human effort to convey intention frequently arranges words, phrases, and arguments in patterns that lie outside of our conscious awareness. Nevertheless, I believe that there is something significant about the arrangement of these oracles, one way or the other, and I believe that it is related to the question of the origin traditions of the nations involved.

This brings us at last to the Israel oracle of Amos 2:6–16, of which only 2:6–8, 14–16 is decisively authentic.[156] As commentators are quick to mention, the striking feature of this oracle is that, unlike the oracles that precede it, the basis of Amos's criticism is not Israel's bellicose activity but its internal penchant for social injustice. Very little attention has been given to the question of why Israel's failure is described in such unique terms, but I would suggest that two lines of inquiry are promising. First, it is natural to assume that Amos's criticism of Israel, despite its focus on social evils, stems from the same set of universal ethical standards that motivated the other oracles. There is, for instance, a natural correlation between selling people into exile, as the Philistines had done (1:6) and Israel's selling the needy into slavery (2:6). Aggressions against an international neighbor, like the instances denounced in each of the previous oracles, are congruent with Israel's social aggressions against the poor (2:7). The remaining criticisms, Israel's transgression of sexual norms (2:7) and its hypocritical practice of mixing religion with injustice (2:8), undoubtedly stemmed from the same universal principles that Amos espoused elsewhere.

Second, and I believe more important, the distinctive character of the Israel oracle is derived from the prophet's understanding of identity, particularly the difference between his conception of Israelite identity

---

156. See below, pp. 183–185.

and the identity of the nations around Israel. Consider the following table:

Table 3.1. The Judgment Scheme of Amos

Text	Addressee	Object of Oppression	Result
1:13–15	Ammon	Gilead	Destruction of Ammon
2:1–3	Moab	King of Edom	Destruction of Moab
2:6–16	Israel	Poor of Israel	Destruction of Israel

As one can see, Amos no more envisioned the destruction of Israel's poor along with the Northern state than he did the destruction of Gilead along with Ammon. Or to put it another way, although Amos viewed Ammon as an ethnic social modality that would be totally destroyed, his view of Israelite identity was different, primarily because he distinguished between various groups within Israel on the basis of socioeconomic factors. For Amos, it was not ethnic Israel that would be destroyed but rather the oppressive power structures of the nation that were persecuting the poor of Israel.[157] So in spite of his Judean roots, Amos sensed a shared identity with Israel that was different from his relation to Ammon and Moab. This no doubt stemmed from the very circumstance that prompted his prophetic ministry: the two peoples, Judeans and Israelites, shared Yahweh as a national deity. We should conclude from this that Amos probably envisioned a strong religious link between Judah and Israel, in spite of the fact that his Hosean contemporary seems to have harbored little interest in the South.

We should address two more questions that are raised by this oracle against Israel. First, why did Amos, more or less a contemporary of Hosea, fail to condemn Israel's cultic abandonment of Yahweh, as his Northern counterpart did? Although a precise answer to the question is difficult, the answer is undoubtedly related to the quite disparate views of identity embraced by the prophets Hosea and Amos. It seems possible that the religious behaviors that Hosea chastised were much less widespread than his polemic might lead us to believe. Perhaps the Baal

---

157. Here I agree in part with H. Reimer, who argues that all of the oracles envision only a partial destruction. However, I would argue that only the Israel oracle reflects the socioeconomic distinction necessary to argue for a partial destruction of the people, in this case the destruction of the oppressive upper classes of Israel (see *Richtet auf das Recht*, 63–64).

cult was such a minor part of the Israelite religious landscape (after all, Yahweh was the national God) that a prophet with other concerns, such as Amos, failed to notice much of it.[158] This is perhaps the strongest evidence that Hosea's perspective was both highly ethnic and highly peripheral. For Hosea, ethnicity was a distinctive feature of Israelite identity; for Amos, Israel's ethnicity was simply one more permutation of the same basic human identity.

The other question is a redactional one. Although Hosea was familiar with an Exodus/settlement tradition of sorts, in Amos 2:9–10 we have our first evidence that Israel's settlement of the homeland required that it displace and destroy the original Amorite inhabitants of the land. In our study of Israelite identity, we are naturally curious about how these Amorites figure within Israel's ethnic tradition and also what this conquest tradition tells us about Israel's origin traditions, and hence, about its identity. Are vv. 9–10 a redactional addition to the book of Amos? According to Mays, Reimer, Vollmer, and Wolff, vv. 10–12 should be considered a unit and treated as an addition, mainly because both the phrase את־ארץ האמרי לרשת and the forty-year wilderness experience in v. 10 are considered Deuteronomic.[159] The connection between v. 10 and vv. 11–12 is (1) the last two verses take up the change of address (from third person to second person) that is introduced by v. 10 and (2) they continue with the enumeration of Yahweh's generous activity on Israel's behalf. In other words, vv. 11–12 are redactional only by their association with v. 10, so the real question can be posed this way: is v. 9 redational and, if so, is v. 10 also redactional?

The idea that 2:9 is authentic has a respectable history in the study of Amos, and it is probably this momentum that has prevented more commentators from raising questions about it.[160] The phrase ואנכי השמדתי את־האמרי מפניהם has a Deuteronomistic ring to it, and the

---

158. Tigay has argued, on the basis of the onomastic evidence, that the biblical polemic far exceeds the actual cultic activity associated with non-Yahwistic deities (*You Shall Have No Other Gods*, 37–41).

159. Mays, *Amos*, 44; Reimer, *Richtet auf das Recht*, 28; Vollmer, *Geschichtliche Rückbliche und Motive*, 24–26; Wolff, *Joel and Amos*, 169–71.

160. Harper's commentary, which is more or less a compendium of Amos studies from the last century and a fountainhead for this one, assumes that v. 9 is authentic (Harper, *Amos and Hosea*, cxxxii, 54–59). Agreeing with Harper are: Mays, *Amos*, 50; Reimer, *Richtet auf das Recht*, 28; Vollmer, *Geschichtliche Rückbliche und Motive*, 24–25; Wolff, *Joel and Amos*, 87–89.

tradition about powerful Amorites is also familiar to the Deuteronomistic sources (Deut 1:27–28).[161] However, several features also distinguish the text from Deuteronomistic tradition. First, although the verb
שמד is used several times in the Deuteronomistic corpus (see esp. Deut
31:4), the verbs ירש and גרש are more common in references to the
conquest.[162] Second, as for the Amorites of 2:9, although Amos is in
good company when he associates them with "giants," the fact that he
extends this description to all Amorites rather than to portions of them
is unique in the Hebrew Bible.[163] Finally, 2:9 indicates that the Amorites were completely destroyed, "his fruit above and his roots beneath,"
which is at odds with the Deuteronomistic idea that a goodly portion
of the land's inhabitants escaped destruction. So it seems to me that 2:9
can only with difficulty be identified as a Deuteronomistic addition.

This brings us to Amos 2:10. The fact that Harper believes that
vv. 9–12 form a unit demonstrates that the change of address from
third to second person is not by itself sufficient evidence for dividing
an otherwise thematically related unit. And given that we have provided good reasons for keeping v. 9, we cannot too quickly cast aside
vv. 10–12. After all, even if the supposed redactor added them, he did
so under the guise that he created a new unit in 2:9–12. The real question is this: do the supposedly Deuteronomistic features of v. 10 war-
rant identifying it as redactional? The answer must be "no." The
argument that it is redactional presupposes that we have many sources
prior to and after Amos, and that when we compare v. 10 to all of these
sources it does not "fit the picture." However, as I am approaching the
text in this study, Amos is one of our earlier sources and can become,
with the other eighth-century prophets, a mother text for any number
of later traditions. After all, most of what we see in 2:10 is already
known to us from Hosea, except for the 40-year length of the wilderness experience. Thus, we ought to let vv. 9–10 tell us what Amos
knew about Israel's origins and history, all the while reminding our-

161. Ps 80:8, which appears to be of Northern origin, shows that the conquest
tradition was known in the North and that it was already integrated with the Exodus
tradition: "Thou didst bring a vine out of Egypt; thou didst drive out the nations and
plant it."

162. Usually, the Israelites possess the land (ירש) and Yahweh drives out (גרש) its
habitants. But other combinations occur. Cf. Deut 4:47; Josh 3:10; 24:8, 12, 18; Judg
11:21–22.

163. Mays, *Amos*, 50; Cf. 2 Kgs 14:9; Isa 2:13; Ezek 17:9; Job 18:16.

selves that we have not proved that vv. 9–10 are authentic. We have only outlined the reasons that suggest their probable authenticity.

What Amos 2:9–10 tells us is that the eighth-century Judean tradition of Israelite history included an Exodus from Egypt, an extended wilderness experience, and a conquest of the Amorite populations in the new homeland. Whether Amos would have connected this tradition with Judah as well is an interesting question that cannot be answered unequivocally, although the evidence from Hosea (which kept Israel and Judah at arm's length) would seem to suggest that he would not have done so. What is most interesting about this text, I think, is that while the Northern texts seem to have the Canaanites as Israel's chief opponent, this Southern text situates the Amorites in that role. This may explain the tendency in later texts to include both Canaanites and Amorites in their list of early Israelite opponents since, in a post-722 B.C.E. Judean context, scribes were forced to deal with both Southern and Northern traditions in close literary quarters.

At this point we can summarize our discussion of the "nations oracles." The five oracles in this complex reflect the prophet's universal standard of conduct, a standard that conformed to and was enforced by the sovereign and universal God, Yahweh. Yahweh had created the nations by settling them and by establishing their borders, and he had provided for their security and stability by enacting universal standards of international conduct (as reflected in the first four oracles) and social behavior (as reflected in the Israel oracle). The prophet envisioned a grand world order that operated according to these standards, and each of the nations he addressed had breached that order by seeking to "enlarge their borders" (1:13). Israel, the primary target of Amos's ministry, was juxtaposed with these nations to show that, as H. Reimer has put it, Israel was "kein besser Staat!"[164] But this comment ought to be tempered with the fact that Amos envisioned primarily the destruction of Israel's wealthy and oppressive classes rather than the nation as a whole.

We have also determined during this discussion that the international communities addressed by Amos probably shared the tendency to embrace ethnic components of identity to varying degrees of intensity, with the exception of Judah. And speaking of Judah—as a Judean,

164. Ibid., 68.

Amos was surprisingly laconic on the subject. In fact, if the standard redactional views of Amos are right, the only reference to Judah is by the Northern king, Amaziah, who tells Amos to go home. Was this reticence to speak of Judah a part of the prophet's rhetorical approach? This question must be taken up another time. But it now seems clear that, for Amos, Israel and Judah were linked by their common status as Yahwistic nations and that his notion of identity was, like Hosea's, primarily religious.

Woe to the Wealthy: Amos 6:1–7

In his recent article, H. C. Roberts has argued that in Amos's day political and socioeconomic problems fueled by the expansionist policies of Assyria and Aram created an environment of economic exploitation of the lower classes in eighth-century Israel.[165] The pressures wrought by this situation accentuated class differences in Israel's already stratified society, creating, at least from Amos's perspective, an atmosphere of competition between the wealthy upper class and the underclass. Therefore, despite the religious overtones, the climate of conflict in Amos should perhaps be related more closely to economic competition than to the religious competition that we see in Hosea. It is this sociological context that stands behind the text of 6:1–7.

The text has two redactional problems, the reference to Zion in v. 1 and the reference to Calneh, Hamath, and Gath in v. 2. Most scholars take the reference to Zion as a later Judean redaction, which makes sense for two reasons. First, Judah is noticeably absent from Amos, making a reference to Zion unexpected; and second, the remainder of the oracle addresses the wealthy of Samaria, not Judea.[166] For these reasons, I will assume that v. 1 originally addressed only the Northern Kingdom, not Judah. The reference to Calneh, Hamath, and Gath is often attributed to a time after Amos and is sometimes considered the work of his disciples.[167] This is because the period when Tiglath-pileser III threatened these cities, around 738–734 B.C.E., is

---

165. H. C. Roberts, "La época de Amós y la justicia social," *BT* 50 (1993) 95–106.

166. Rudolph, *Joel, Amos, Obadja, Jona*, 215.

167. Harper, *Amos and Hosea*, 141; Reimer, *Richtet auf das Recht*, 138; Wolff, *Joel and Amos*, 275.

well after the beginning of Amos's ministry (ca. 760 B.C.E.). However, as Wolff has noted, it is difficult to know when the prophet's ministry ceased in the first place.[168] This, joined to the fact that the ideology of 6:2 corresponds to ideology that is unmistakeably Amos's (cf. Amos 9:7), makes it difficult to attribute the text to someone other than the prophet.[169]

Several items related to the issues of ethnicity and identity arise in 6:1–7. First, this text indicates, as did the oracle in 2:6–16, that Amos identified with the poor lower classes of Israel rather than with their wealthy oppressors, "notable men" whom he sarcastically portrayed as enjoying the spices of life while "the destruction of Joseph" was before their eyes (6:1, 4–6). So Amos ought to be viewed as a peripheral prophet who "lacked status and social power" in relation to the central religious and political structures of Israel.[170] The "Woe!" of this text was therefore directed toward those who felt "secure on the mountain of Samaria" and who were "upon beds of ivory," not toward the poor of Israel who awaited deliverance on the "evil day" (i.e., the "Day of Yahweh" in 5:18–27).[171] Clearly, both here and elsewhere, Amos's concept of identity was tied primarily to religious and socioeconomic concerns, not ethnicity. Because of this, one cannot associate "ethnic stratification" with Amos's sociological views.[172]

Read in light of these socioeconomic distinctions, the text of 6:2 provides an additional insight into the prophet's concept of identity. The oracle says, concerning the wealthy in Israel:

> Are they better than these kingdoms [Calneh, Hamath, Philistia]?
> Or is their territory greater than your territory? O you who put far away the evil day, and bring near the seat of violence.

As was implicit in the oracles of 1:3–2:16, it is here explicit that Amos rhetorically blurred the ethnic distinctions between the upper-class oppressors of Israel and the foreigners who faced the punishment of

---

168. Ibid., 90.

169. Andersen and Freedman, *Amos*, 558–59; Mays, *Amos*, 114–15; Paul, *Amos*, 201–4.

170. R. R. Wilson, *Prophecy and Society in Ancient Israel*, 38, 270.

171. Mays, *Amos*, 116.

172. By "ethnic stratification" I mean that the obvious social stratification reflected in Amos is not along ethnic lines, as is the case with present socioeconomic conditions in the twentieth-century United States.

Yahweh along with them. Not only does this remind us that Amos was familiar with Israelite ethnicity but it also provides us with a more subtle insight. All along we have been pointing out that Hosea's peripheral community embraced a very intense kind of ethnicity, and this leaves us facing the implicit question of how the larger body of citizens in the Northern Kingdom thought about ethnicity. Although we cannot say what the average citizen would have thought, the rhetorical assault of Amos on the ethnicity of Israel's wealthy citizens could only have been effective if they too harbored a rather meaningful notion of ethnicity. Thus we should avoid the impression that Israelite ethnicity was important only to the proto-Deuteronomic movement; it was also important for the core political, religious and social structures of ancient Israel. Whether the poor and oppressed lower classes shared in these sentiments, however, is difficult to know.

In a different vein, there is a reference in our text to Joseph in 6:6, and this raises a number of questions. Did *Joseph* refer to the Northern Kingdom as a whole or to some restricted region within it? And did it imply a patriarchal figure? Because the polemical target in the surrounding context was Israel, most scholars, Harper, Paul, and Mays for instance, believe that the referent of יוסף was the Northern Kingdom.[173] Even Wolff, who correctly points out that יוסף/בית־יוסף normally refers to the central regions of the North, concludes that יוסף was often used polemically to highlight Israel's greatly reduced territorial limits.[174] But in either case we need to ask whether the patriarchal figure should also be associated with the name. I believe that there is substantial evidence to show that the most natural antecedent of יוסף would be not only a geographical region but also the ancestral figure known to us from Genesis 37–50. First, the fact that another eighth-century witness (Isa 9:20) pairs Ephraim and Manasseh as brothers implies that Amos is alluding to an ancestor tradition. Second, it is generally acknowledged that older strata of the Joseph traditions reflect a Northern provenience, which would require that they were current

---

173. Harper, *Amos and Hosea*, 112, 124; Mays, *Amos*, 89–90, 102; Paul, *Amos*, 165–66, 178.

174. The reference to בית יוסף in 5:5 is of no help here, since it is almost invariably viewed as a later addition. Harper connects it to the previous text in 5:4–5, which is also viewed as redactional (*Amos and Hosea*, 112; Wolff, *Joel and Amos*, 240).

during Hosea's ministry.[175] If this is true, the origin traditions of Israel already included more than one patriarchal figure during the ministry of Amos. This is an issue that we will be able to explore more completely in the context of Amos 7:10–17.

"You Shall Die in an Unclean Land": Amos 7:10–17

Until recently, this text has been viewed by nearly every scholar as belonging to the authentic corpus of Amos materials.[176] However, H. G. M. Williamson has recently argued that 7:9–17 is a Deuteronomistic redaction that seeks to interpret the plumb-line of 7:7–8 as Amos himself.[177] This is because the text not only interrupts (along with 8:4–14) the five visions recounted in 7:1–9:4 but also because it is clearly tied to the themes of the previous vision. I would respond that there certainly is an interruption of the vision series, but as even Williamson admits, there is no thematic interruption, and the collection process itself can account for this kind of phenomenon. What is perhaps more of a problem for Williamson's thesis is the fact that the so-called "Deuteronomic redaction" of Amos has left us precious little evidence, and almost everywhere in the collection the viewpoint is entirely different from the viewpoint found in the proto-Deuteronomic work of Hosea and the later Deuteronomistic editorial work in Jeremiah. Because of these observations, I am inclined to agree with the majority of commentators, who view 7:10–17 as authentic Amos material.

175. Two psalms of Northern provenience, Psalms 80 and 81, refer to Joseph as well as to Ephraim, Benjamin, Manesseh (Psalm 80), and Jacob (Psalm 81). See Davies, *Hosea*, 32; Anderson, *The Book of Psalms*, 2.581–87; A. Weiser, *The Psalms* (OTL; Philadelphia: Westminster, 1962) 547, 553. Anderson and Weiser assign Psalm 80 to a Northern context, but Anderson is not certain about Psalm 81, which Weiser regards as also Northern. Davies offers a few brief arguments in favor of Northern origins in his Hosea commentary. For more on the Northern origins of the Joseph tradition, see D. M. Carr, *Reading the Fractures of Genesis: Historical and Literary Approaches* (Louisville: Westminster/John Knox, 1996) 277–89, 300–302; D. B. Redford, *A Study of the Biblical Story of Joseph* (VTSup 20; Leiden: Brill, 1970); Van Seters, *Prologue to History*, 311–27; and Westermann, *Genesis*, 3.15–30.

176. Andersen and Freedman, *Amos*, 751–54; Harper, *Amos and Hosea*, cxxxii; Paul, *Amos*, 238–52; Wolff, *Joel and Amos*, 306–16; However, see Reimer, who argues that 7:10–17 is a later addition (*Richtet auf das Recht*, 215–25).

177. H. G. M. Williamson, "The Prophet and the Plumb-line: A Redaction-Critical Study of Amos vii," *OTS* 26 (1990) 101–21.

In this text, the peripheral character of Amos's prophetic work appears again in his conflict with representatives of the national religious and political system, Amaziah and Jeroboam, high priest of Bethel and king of Israel, respectively.[178] The prophet's Judean identity prompted Amaziah to urge Amos homeward,[179] but Amos responded, "The Lord said to me, 'Go, prophesy to *my people* Israel [italics mine].'" It is significant that Amos identified the Northern Kingdom as the people of Yahweh, since he undoubtedly held similar ideas about Judean identity. This reaffirms my observation that Amos saw a close connection between the Northern and Southern Kingdoms on the basis of their common identity as the people of Yahweh.[180] In the prophet's conceptual world, therefore, deity preference was regarded as an organizing principle in defining identity, but this religious principle of identity did not merge significantly with ethnic identity. Why were these two modes of identity so closely merged in Hosea and not in Amos? Perhaps ethnicity was not an important component of Judean identity during or prior to the eighth century B.C.E. This is a possibility that will be explored more thoroughly during our examination of Isaiah.

However, ethnicity was an important component of Northern identity, especially with respect to the notion of homeland. This is what gave the polemic of Amos its force: "you yourself shall die in an unclean land (על־אדמה טמאה), and Israel shall surely go into exile away from its land" (v. 17). The ideas expressed here correspond rather closely to those of Hos 9:3, with both texts indicating how closely Israelite identity was tied to the homeland and also how polluted foreign territory was by comparison (in both cases, foreign lands are טמא). But here again, several of Amos's ideas are quite distinct from Hosea's ideas. First, although the concept of land is closely related to the idea of covenant in many portions of the Hebrew Bible, including Hosea, the corpus of prophetic material from Amos explicitly conveys nothing about

178. The phrase "priest of Bethel" probably refers to the "high priest of Bethel" (Paul, *Amos*, 239). G. Pfeifer has argued that Amaziah did not act alone but sought to deport the troublesome Amos under the authorization of Jeroboam himself. That this is implied by the text seems to me very likely (Pfeifer, "Die Ausweisung eines lästigen Ausländers: Amos 7:10–17," *ZAW* 96 [1984] 112–18).

179. Pfeifer also argues that Amos's Judean identity played a part in this attempted expulsion. This seems to me to be self-evident from the text (ibid., 112).

180. There is also a strong tendency for Amos to use the perspective of his Northern audience in an ironic fashion, so that the benefits of their Yahwistic heritage are rhetorically minimized.

covenant ideology. And second, the relationship of Yahweh to the land was quite different in the theology of Amos. God as depicted by Amos was a more universal deity than in Hosea, so that the latter's notion of Israel dwelling on "Yahweh's land" (Hos 9:3) would probably have been too limited in the eyes of the Southern prophet, for whom Yahweh was the God of all lands. We might ask on the heels of this observation whether, in the absence of universality, Hosea would have viewed Yahweh as a "higher" or "more powerful" deity than the gods of the surrounding nations. I would suppose that the answer would be "yes," but it would be predicated in part on the somewhat speculative "excursus" at the end of this chapter.

As I have promised above, because the ancestral theme is here reintroduced by the reference in 7:16 to the 'house of Isaac' (בית ישׂחק), we can at this point return to the issue of the Joseph figure mentioned in connection with Amos 6:6. Since we should safely assume that Amos was familiar with the patriarchal figure Jacob, the references to Joseph and Isaac and the status of these two figures as patriarchs in later Israelite literature raise the question of how many patriarchal figures Amos knew.

Taking the problem of Isaac first, the manner in which 7:16 places Isaac in parallel with Israel reminds us of the Jacob/Israel parallels in Hosea and so invites the conclusion that Isaac was a patriarchal figure. There are a number of lines of evidence that suggest that this is the right conclusion to draw. First, J. Van Seters has observed that the "whole life of Isaac [in Genesis] is a rather pale reflection of the life of Abraham, and one can scarcely find in it any evidence of older traditions."[181] This probably indicates that at the time of the Yahwist's composition there was little or nothing left of Isaac apart from his identity as an ancient patriarchal figure. Such a situation would explain why, on the one hand, Isaac appears quite commonly as a name listed with Abraham and Jacob but, on the other hand, why he has so little impact in the prophetic corpus of the Hebrew Bible. It might also explain why his name appears in Amos as ישׂחק instead of יצהק, since the former now becomes an older spelling of the ancient patriarchal name. A second reason that the name of Isaac might refer to an ancestral figure is that it appears as a synonym for Israel but not, it seems, as a geographical name. This makes it unlikely, at least within our limited historical

---

181. Van Seters, *Prologue to History*, 268.

horizon, that the figure of Isaac developed from association with a particular region of the same name, as seems to have happened in the case of Ephraim, Manasseh, and some of the other figures in the Hebrew Bible. Third, where it can be examined with precision, בית almost invariably implies 'house of PN' in addition to 'house of GN', referring especially to the dwelling and/or progeny of the indicated PN.[182] To argue that "house of Joseph" or "house of Isaac" does not imply a forefather figure misses the point since, regardless of the phrase's supposed origins, *the language itself obviously did suggest a forefather figure. Otherwise, there would be no Isaac, son of Abraham.* Or, to say it another way, although one might imagine that the phrase *house of Isaac* could have originated as a geographical designation, it is difficult to imagine it remaining only this for long. Fourth, the probability that "Isaac" was a forefather figure is heightened by that fact that Hosea reflects a contemporary Jacob cycle which included the patriarch's marriage (12:12). The combination of Jacob's extended biographical cycle with this marriage tradition does suggest that we ought to expect additional family members, especially a father (Isaac) and/or a son (Joseph).

So, although we cannot speak about this with certainty, it does seem to me very likely that Amos knew at least three patriarchal generations—Isaac, Jacob, and Joseph. But these ancestral figures cannot necessarily be taken as evidence of a "patriarchal age" in the likeness of what we associate with the pentateuchal sources. In those sources we have a narrative that has been closely integrated and thematically unified within a chronological sequence. However, we cannot assume that this was the case in the eighth century because Abraham is not mentioned, the Isaac traditions are cryptic at best, and most scholars will agree that the Joseph narratives were secondarily connected to the Jacob traditions in the Pentateuch.[183] So one is hard pressed to find a "patriarchal age" here.

Summary

The combined evidence from Amos and Hosea shows that it was commonplace for ethnicity to play a role in the group identities of Israel and the surrounding nation-states. This mode of ethnopolitical

---

182. In fact, I can find no instance that unambiguously attests to the formula 'house of GN' without implying 'house of PN'.

183. See Westermann, *Genesis*, 3.22–28.

identity is most similar to the comparative materials from Greece and should be distinguished from the nonethnic modes of identity that predominated in the Egyptian and Mesopotamian sources. In spite of frequent sentiments of ethnicity among the smaller Levantine states, we observed that there was a great disparity in the intensity of these ethnonational sentiments as reflected in Amos and Hosea. Although it is an oversimplification to say that ethnicity played no distinguishing role in Amos's identity, particularly in light of his view that foreign lands were "unclean," it is substantially correct to say that, for Amos, ethnicity was only a mode of identity shared by various groups in the region and not a feature unique to any of them. Israel's migration from Egypt, which was for Hosea a primary element in Israelite identity, was for the Southern prophet only one more migration in the tradition of the Arameans, the Philistines, and others. This reinforces the conclusion that Hosea's community was a peripheral religious movement that displayed both an unusually heightened awareness of ethnic identity and an ardent desire to intensify ethnic boundaries in support of the national deity, Yahweh.

Although one might infer from our discussion of the surrounding nations that Judah also had ethnic traditions, the evidence for a distinctive Judean ethnicity is wanting in the Amos materials. We do not get the sense that there was a connection between the forefather figures—Jacob, Joseph, and Isaac—and the Southern Kingdom, nor is there evidence for a Southern eponymous counterpart, a "Judah" figure, unless one can demonstrate the antiquity of the tradition now preserved in Genesis 38.[184] The Southern prophet's fleeting references to Judean identity include a comment about the Davidic king and also numerous instances of implied connections between Judah and the Northern Kingdom, particularly when Amos refers to the Northern Kingdom as the people of Yahweh.[185] On the other hand, Hosea seems to have lacked any sense of common ground with the Judeans, and we should probably conclude from this that Southerners felt a greater affinity with the North than did the North with the South.

184. See discussion in Van Seters, *Prologue to History*, 207–9; Westermann, *Genesis*, 3.49–50.

185. The reference to the Judean king in Amos 6:5 reads in Hebrew, כדויד חשבו להם כלי־שיר, which is obscure in meaning but is usually rendered 'like David they invent for themselves musical instruments'. For a summary of the options, see Paul, *Amos*, 206.

This difference is easily explained, of course, by the fact that the Judeans were more than happy to rule (and tax) Israel, while the Israelites were less than satisfied to let them.

Up to this point, we have discussed various modes of identity— political, religious, ethnic, and so on—but we have not presented the essential ways in which these modes of identity were related to each other in the sources. How did our two prophets conceptualize the relationship between these various modes of identity? From Amos's point of view, although monarchic politics were entirely compatible with Israelite ethnicity, ethnicity played a comparatively minor role within Israelite identity. More important than Israel's ethnic identity was the problem created by the oppression of the poor; this threatened the sense of religious unity that the Israelites ought to have with God and with each other. The essential problem that Amos wrestled with was that Israel's wealthy classes had defined Israelite identity in such a way as to exclude the less fortunate from participation in the broader community. This problem was of an entirely different nature from the problems that Hosea tried to confront. There is no evidence that Amos attempted to link ethnic and religious sentiments, as did Hosea's party. This comes as no real surprise when we recognize that, from the Southern perspective, Yahwism was already present on both sides of the ethnic boundary that separated Israelites from Judeans. Ethnic distinctions could not have been very important for Amos anyway, because his discourse assumed that all of the nations shared a more fundamental and common position under the universal sovereignty of Yahweh. This view of the deity contrasted with Hosea's view. For Hosea Yahweh was more a localized than a universal deity, being a God with his own land, his own people, and his own primary sphere of activity. On the other hand, there is an implied sovereignty of Yahweh in the judgment that Hosea predicted via Assyria and Egypt, so in this respect the differences between Amos and Hosea must be viewed in part as rhetorical.

Ethnicity and Identity in Isaiah of Jerusalem

Isaiah serves as a bridge between the time of Hosea/Amos and the early seventh century B.C.E., after which a rather long break separates this eighth-century prophet from the next major prophetic witness, Jeremiah. While in the case of Hosea and Amos we have the luxury of possessing two generally "authentic" texts that contain a few later additions, this is obviously not true in the case of Isaiah. In Isaiah, a great deal of complexity is involved both in delimiting the various strata within the text and dating these strata to appropriate contexts. Because of this (and contrary to my approach in Hosea and Amos), my stance in Isaiah is that of a "minimalist," focusing attention primarily on the texts that are normally considered authentic.[186] As usual in our trade, however, there are several "borderline" texts that are so closely related to the topic that we cannot neglect them; the problems in these texts will have to be addressed in detail as they arise during the discussion.

Lest we cover the same ground a second time, I should like to outline several common elements (and differences) that can be identified in Isaiah and the other two eighth-century prophets. Despite the fact that the primary audiences of Isaiah and Amos were of two different sorts, Judeans and Israelites, even a superficial perusal of Isaiah's text will confirm the fact that the two Southern prophets should be viewed as stemming from a common Southern prophetic community. If we take Isa 1:10–17 as an example, we can see that Isaiah shared with the Tekoan Amos a common devotion to the poor, especially its orphans and widows, and that he blamed the troubles of this underclass on the ruling classes (קצינים) of the nation. For both prophets, the injustices of national society made cultic and ritual activities an exercise in hypocrisy that the deity would not accept.[187] Judgment and oppression would come upon the nation in each case. From this, we should conclude that class distinctions played an important role in Southern prophetic traditions and that, in contrast, this was not a primary concern for Hosea (at least in the corpus that he has left us). In spite of these similarities the rhetorical methods of the two Southern prophets differed chiefly in this: Amos belittled Israel by comparing it with foreigners, while Isaiah compared Judah with the morally reprobate populations of Sodom and Gomorrah. This is best explained by the

186. Isa 1:1–3, 1:10–2:1, 2:5–4:1, 5:1–24, 6:1–11, 8:1–18, 9:1–10:15, 14:24–32, 17:1–14, chaps. 18 and 20, 22:1–25, and chaps. 28–32. This list follows Soggin for the most part, but at points where he is unclear I have supplemented his work with R. E. Clements's work on Isaiah's text (J. A. Soggin, *Introduction to the Old Testament* [OTL; Louisville: Westminster/John Knox, 1989] 299–311; R. E. Clements, *Isaiah 1–39* [NCBC; Grand Rapids: Eerdmans, 1980] 2–8).

187. I agree with H. Wildberger that it is very difficult to suggest that Isaiah rejected cultic piety in principle. The juxtaposition of his cultic condemnation with his reprimand for social injustice shows clearly that it is religious hypocrisy that Isaiah condemns, not the cult itself (Wildberger, *Isaiah 1–12*, 39–40).

fact that ethnicity was not a primary feature of Judean identity, which necessarily precluded Isaiah's use of ethnic slurs.

This brings us to Hosea. Because Amos and Isaiah share many kinds of similarities, the differences that distinguish Amos from Hosea necessarily tend to differentiate Isaiah from the Northern prophet. There is nevertheless this similarity between Isaiah and Hosea: their common use of the concept of תורה ('law').[188] Here, as in Hosea, the term seems to refer to moral prescriptions regarding social behavior and, if we agree with Begrich's form-critical analysis of 1:10–17, then in both the Northern and Southern traditions the priests were responsible for the תורה instruction of the people.[189] But these observations are of a general kind and do not permit me to provide a detailed analysis of the relationship between the Northern and Southern תורה traditions. This will have to be worked out somewhere else.

A Struggle among Brothers: Isaiah 9:18–20

During our examination of Hosea and Amos, it was determined that the eighth-century Northern context knew of at least three patriarchal figures, Isaac, Jacob, and Joseph. Here we are fortunate not only because the text introduces us to two more Israelite ancestral figures but also because it clarifies their relationship to each and to the Judean traditions. The text is, with one exception that we will address, free of introductory problems and is uniformly embraced as Isaianic.[190]

> and the people are like fuel for the fire; no man spares his brother
> (אחיו) . . . each devours his neighbor's flesh (איש בשר־זרעו יאכלו),
> Manasseh Ephraim, and Ephraim Manasseh, *and together they are*
> *against Judah.*

188. See my previous discussion of Hos 4:1–19.

189. J. Begrich, "Geschichte Studien im A.T.," *TB* 21 (1964) 232–60. E. W. Davies has argued that a law code did not lie behind Isaiah's ethical concerns, since the activities he condemns were probably legal in a technical sense (e.g., mortgage foreclosures and debt-bondage). I would argue that here, as in Hosea, it is likely that an ethical lawcode akin to the Decalogue provided a religious form of social constraint beyond public legislation. This is suggested by Begrich's form-critical identification of Isa 1:10–17 as a priestly teaching, espcially in its use of the phrase האזינו תורת אלהינו. For the arguments of Davies, see *Prophecy and Ethics: Isaiah and the Ethical Tradition of Israel* (JSOTSup 16; Sheffield: JSOT Press, 1981) 113–19.

190. P. Auvray, *Isaïe 1–39* (SB; Paris: Gabalda, 1972) 128–29; Clements, *Isaiah 1–39*, 69; Duhm, *Das Buch Jesaia* (HKAT; Göttingen: Vandenhoeck & Ruprecht, 1968) 94–96; Kaiser, *Isaiah*, 1.136–37; Wildberger, *Isaiah 1–12*, 218–24.

The phrase in italics is viewed by Clements as a redactional addition by one who sought to point out more forcefully that the North's defeat arose because of its refusal to accept the Davidic monarchy.[191] I will address this claim soon, but the more common approach to this text is to identify a point at which Ephraim and Manasseh quarreled with each other and with Judah, an endeavor that is difficult according to Wildberger, because there is not enough specific information in the text to link it confidently with events that we know about.[192] Procksch's suggestion that it has in mind the conflict between Pekah of Manasseh (from Transjordan) and Pekahiah of Ephraim (from Cisjordan) has its merits (cf. 1 Kgs 15:25),[193] and chronologically speaking, this would correspond nicely with the Syro-Ephraimite War, thus suggesting an appropriate context for the text's reference to Judah. But even if this is not true, provided that the text was composed during or soon after the Syro-Ephraimite conflict—and it probably was—the reference to Judah seems appropriate enough in an eighth century Judean prophet. But the reference to Judah, even if it is redactional, is probably not a very late one.

I think that we can plainly see that the prophet has paired Ephraim and Manasseh not only because of the state of hostility between them but because of the prior relationship that he perceives them to have had with each other. Ephraim and Manasseh were אחים 'brothers' who were "eating one another's flesh" instead of living in peace, a situation not unlike the internecine struggles that occurred among the ethnic Hellenes of Greece. We need not attend to the details of this conflict or the events that might have been behind it because what this "brother" rhetoric means for our inquiry into Israelite ethnicity is more important. Because we can assume that Isaiah, like Amos, was familiar with the Isaac, Jacob, and Joseph figures of Northern lore, this reference to Ephraim and Manasseh as brothers, coupled with their later association as the sons of Joseph, makes it probable that we are actually dealing with four patriarchal generations in this eighth-century context: Isaac, Jacob, Joseph, and Ephraim/Manasseh. And if we deduce from this a patriarchal cycle of which Jacob was the centerpiece, the cycle would then extend over four generations and would tend, of course, to

191. Clements, *Isaiah 1–39*, 69.
192. Wildberger, *Isaiah 1–12*, 238.
193. O. Procksch, *Jesaja I* (Leipzig: Deichert, 1930) 106–7.

include fewer details about the cycle's first and fourth generations and greater detail about the second- and third-generation patriarchal figures. The materials available to us display exactly these features, since we have significant collections of material associated with both Jacob and Joseph but, at the same time, very little associated with Isaac, Ephraim, or Manasseh. The common notion among scholars that the original Jacob and Joseph traditions were of Northern provenience fits well into this explanation of the data.[194] For reasons that I have already enumerated (see p. 192), I would stress again that we should probably avoid the assumption that we are dealing with a supposed "patriarchal period" if by it we mean something like what is suggested by the pentateuchal sources. We would require a good bit more from our sources to make such a claim.

Having addressed the question of Ephraim and Manasseh, we turn to the problem of Judah. Despite my sense that the reference to Judah is probably authentic, the possibility that it is redactional is significant enough that I cannot claim this with conviction. If it is authentic, then Isaiah seems to have viewed the relationship between the Southern Kingdom and Ephraim/Manasseh with sentiments of kinship, since the struggle between the brothers, Ephraim and Manasseh, was presented in parallelism with the struggle between Judah and the two tribes. However, this pairing of Judah with Ephraim/Manasseh was not as deliberate as was the pairing of the two Northern groups themselves, and this makes it possible that the prophet never intended to imply ancestral connections between Judah and the North. Moreover, in the language of international politics, fraternal discourse was not uncommon in the ancient Near East, so that the older North–South political links through David might account for this language. However, the political use of fraternal language does not actually remove us from the realm of ethnicity since it was, after all, a rhetorical device with the precise purpose of creating stronger ethnic-like ties between two groups. What we can say with confidence, therefore, is that our text, whenever it was composed, viewed conflicts between the North and South as quite inappropriate in light of the common relationship that the two kingdoms shared with each other.

194. For bibliography on the Joseph traditions and their place in the pentateuchal materials, see p. 189 n. 175.

Assyria in the Eyes of a Judean: Isaiah 10:5–15

On the basis of the extensive primary sources that we examined in the previous chapter, we were able to sketch out some of the key Neo-Assyrian perspectives on identity, both with respect to the Assyrians themselves and also with respect to their imperial subjects. [195] We know that near the end of the eighth century, that is, the age of Isaiah, Assyrian ambitions of world domination were largely realized and Assyria's keen sense of superiority over its imperial subjects emerged. The new viewpoint was manifested in the sources by a tendency to count imperial subjects "as booty" rather than "as Assyrians." This competitive environment between core and peripheral modalities naturally intensified the sense of identity among the peripheral groups involved, and we can in fact demonstrate that some of Isaiah's most important ideas were a direct response to this peripheral experience, beginning with this text in Isaiah 10:5–15.

For the most part, recent exegetes are in agreement that vv. 10–12 are redactional, for both stylistic and ideological reasons. [196] My examination will therefore focus on 10:5–9, 13–15. As Clement has noted, this text "represents the surest and most reliable evidence that Isaiah did foretell a time when the Assyrians would be punished and overthrown by Yahweh." The terminus a quo for our text must be around 717, since the cities mentioned in v. 9 were by that time under Assyrian domination. These cities represent the steady march of Assyrian influence from North to South, with Judah the next obvious target. It was in this context that the Judean prophet Isaiah uttered this oracle of rebuke against Assyria. Since the prophet condemned the anti-Assyrian alliance against Sennacherib in 705–701, our text must date between 717 and 705.

Although Amos demonstrated that Southern prophetic circles often conceptualized foreigners in ethnic paradigms, there is no hint that

---

195. Although focused on slightly different issues, Machinist has already provided a valuable study of this issue (P. Machinist, "Assyria and Its Image in the First Isaiah," *JAOS* 103 [1983] 719–37). For a brief study of Neo-Assyrian administration and practice in the region, see B. Otzen, "Israel under the Assyrians," in *Power and Propaganda: A Symposium on Ancient Empires* (ed. M. T. Larsen; Mesopotamia 7; Copenhagen: Akademisk Forlag, 1979) 251–61.

196. Clements, *Isaiah 1–39*, 109–13; Duhm, *Das Buch Jesaia*, 99–100; Wildberger, *Isaiah 1–12*, 413–15. Kaiser retains v. 11 and Auvray retains the entire text (Auvray, *Isaïe 1–39*, 131–35; Kaiser, *Isaiah*, 1.136–37).

Isaiah understood Assyrian identity in an ethnic sense. In this text, the first-person speech of Assyria's king includes the phrase "are not my commanders all kings?" which shows at once that Isaiah's understanding of Assyrian identity was rooted in the institution of kingship, not ethnicity.[197] This comes as no surprise, since the comparative evidence from Assyria revealed the same monarchic perspective. The Neo-Assyrian sources show that Assyrian identity was not only monarchic but was monarchic to an arrogant extreme. The texts feature the repetitive royal claim that the king was "the great king, king of the universe, king of Assyria, king of the four corners of the earth." Such a claim would not have sat very well with Isaiah, who predicted that judgment would come upon all who were 'proud' (גאה), 'lofty' (רם), and 'lifted up' (נשא), a threat that applied not only to Judah but to the peoples in general."[198] For Isaiah, only Yahweh was the universal king that was 'high' and 'lifted up',[199] and any figure who sought this exalted position was necessarily a usurper that would be 'humbled' (עיני גבהות האדם שפל) and 'brought low' (ושח רום אנשים, Isa 2:11). As Huber has commented, "Not merely because of his cruelty, enjoyment of murder, etc., is it announced that the Assyrian must appear before the court, but because he rebelled against the place Yahweh determined for him and so is an offence to Yahweh's sovreignty."[200] Thus the Yahwistic universalism of Isaiah and Amos (which contrasted sharply with the particularism of Hosea) was not very patient with any modality, "peripheral" or "core," that failed to acknowledge Yahweh's lordship. And although Isa 10:12 is usually viewed as a later addition, it no doubt summarized Isaiah's sentiments: "the Lord . . . will punish the arrogant boasting of the king of Assyria."

One expression of the hubris for which Isaiah criticized Assyria was its inclination to boast about shifting international boundaries (10:13), a practice that Isaiah, like his compatriot Amos, viewed as an expression of rebellion against Yahweh's universal dominion. We have

197. Machinist, "Assyria and Its Image in the First Isaiah," 726–27.

198. See Isa 2:12 and Auvray's comments in *Isaïe 1–39,* 56. See also comments by J. S. Rogers, "An Allusion to Coronation in Isaiah 2:6," *CBQ* 51 (1989) 232–36.

199. See Isa 6:1.

200. "Nicht wegen seiner Grausamkeit, Mordlust usw. wird also dem Assyrer das Gericht angekündigt, sondern weil er gegen seine von Jahwe verfügte Bestimmung und damit gegen Jahwes Verfügungsgewalt verstieß." F. Huber, *Jahwe, Juda und die anderen Völker beim Propheten Jesaja* (BZAW 137; Berlin: de Gruyter, 1976) 50.

already seen in the Assyrian sources that the Assyrians were preoccupied with the problems both of extending their domain and of preserving stable border frontiers, but there is an essential difference of
perspective. As we saw in the "Synchronistic History" above (p. 43),
for the Assyrians it was the universal god Assur, not the universal God
Yahweh, that established the borders between nations and punished
transgressions of them. Given this, it seems possible, perhaps even
likely, that the eighth-century Judean preoccupation with borders and
boundaries, and with Yahweh's sovereignty over them, was a response
to similar theologies espoused by the Assyrians.

In addition to Assyria's penchant for border encroachments,
Isaiah's other complaint with the Mesopotamians was the disparity
that existed between Yahweh's plan for Assyria and the nation's own
plans. Yahweh had commanded Assyria to 'take spoil' (לשלל שלל) and
'to seize plunder' (לבז בז), but Assyria had instead chosen 'to destroy'
(לשמיד) and 'to cut off nations' (להכרית גוים). This grievance is an important one when we remind ourselves of Isaiah's view of Judah as an
economically stratified society. Although he envisioned the plunder of
the wealthy, he could not accept the perpetuation of Assyrian violence
against the nation as a whole.[201] For both Amos and Isaiah, Assyria was
not to destroy the underprivileged people of Yahweh but to punish the
oppressive upper classes of society.

Not only did Isaiah challenge Assyria's claim to universal domination, but he did so in juxtaposition to the powerful imagery of Yahweh's enthronement in chap. 6. This universal ideology and royal
imagery seems to be distinctive when we set in alongside the Northern
prophetic tradition as represented by Hosea. It reminds us much more
of Assyrian ideas about its god and king than it does of Israelite ideas
about Yahweh. In light of this, while it is much too strong a claim to
suggest that we have here the origins of Yahwistic kingship imagery, it
is clear that the peripheral experience of the Assyrian period brought
the kingship of Yahweh and his universal dominion to the theological
fore. Or to put this in slightly more theoretical terms, the Judean peripheral experience of the late eighth and early seventh centuries did
not produce a heightened sense of ethnicity but instead resulted in the

---

201. It is probably for this reason that the criticism of Assyria in 10:5–15 was juxtaposed to Isaiah's defense of Judah's impoverished population in 10:1–4. This might
also explain how two texts that are often viewed as a single unit, 5:8–24 and 10:1–4,
became separated in the collection. See Clements, *Isaiah 1–39*, 60–61.

intensification of Judean religious identity and, along with that, an ex-altation of its national God, Yahweh.

The Ethiopians: Isaiah 18:1–6

The eighth-century Israelite and Assyrian evidence, along with some classical sources, reflect the view that Ethiopia lay on the edge of the known world.[202] Whether Isaiah, like Hippocrates, would have attributed the phenotypical distinctives of the Ethiopians to their lo-cation on this geographical periphery is difficult to say.[203] But he was well aware that there were essential differences that separated these Ethiopians (כּוּשׁ) from the Judeans, namely, that they were מְמֻשָּׁךְ ('tall'), מוֹרָט ('smooth/hairless'), and נוֹרָא ('fearful').[204] Although Isaiah does not mention their darker skin tone, it is perhaps implied in his reference to their skin's smoothness.[205] The prophet's descrip-tion is remarkably similar to the description in Herodotus:

> These Ethiopians, to whom Cambyses sent them, are said to be the tallest (μέγιστοι) and fairest (κάλλιστοι) of all men. Their way of choosing kings is different from that of all others, as (it is said) are all their laws; they deem worthy to be their king that townsman whom they judge to be tallest and to have strength proportioned to his stat-ure. . . . Thank the gods who put it not in the minds of the sons of the Ethiopians to win more territory than they have.[206]

202. See the descriptions of Herodotus and Hippocrates in Hartog, *The Mirror of Herodotus*, 19–30. Throughout this discussion, *Ethiopia* refers not to the region associ-ated with modern Ethiopia but the region of the Sudan and Nubia just south of an-cient Egypt.

203. Hippocrates *Airs, Waters, Places*, 13–18. In this text we see a classical expres-sion of the early "climatic" explanation for human phenotypical attributes.

204. What is intended by the second term, מוֹרָט, is somewhat difficult. On the one hand, מרט often refers to a condition of baldness or to the process of removing hair (cf. Ezra 9:3, Neh 13:25, Isa 50:6), which would seem to indicate that our text is refer-ring to the relatively hairless skin of the Ethiopians. Others have attempted to connect this term with the dark skin color of the Ethiopians on the basis of 1 Kgs 7:45, where it is translated 'burnished', as in 'burnished bronze'. While it seems clear to me that the term refers to the smooth, hairless characteristic of Ethiopian skin, such a description undoubtedly brings to the reader's mind their dark skin hues as well.

205. Skin color is an obvious distinctive marker, and in the classical sources no author before Xenophanes applied a physical characteristic to Africans other than color. See F. M. Snowden, *Before Color Prejudice: The Ancient View of Blacks* (Cam-bridge: Harvard University Press, 1983) 10.

206. See Herodotus *Histories* 3.14, 21:

Thus it would seem that the ancient traditions are more-or-less unified in recognizing that the Ethiopians were tall, distinctive in appearance, and fierce in battle, with this last characteristic undoubtedly emphasized in Isaiah's mind because of the Ethiopian dynasty that had seized control of Egypt (the 25th Dynasty). These characteristics have a decidedly ethnic flavor, since they include quite pronounced inherited phenotypical characteristics, which would reinforce the already established tendency among the Southern prophets to conceptualize peoples through an ethnic paradigm.

The interesting issue reflected in Isaiah is the confusion of identity that resulted from the fact that the Ethiopians controlled Egypt during the latter part of the eighth century. The prophet's references to the "Nile," "vessels of papyrus," and "land the rivers divide" refer unmistakably to the regions normally associated with Egypt (cf. Isaiah 20). The Assyrian annals of Sargon II and Sennacherib reflect a similar awareness of the Ethiopian presence:

> Pharaoh of Egypt . . . which (land) belongs (now) to Kush (Ethiopia). . . . Hezekiah . . . had called (for help) upon the kings of Egypt and the bowmen, the chariot(-corps) and the cavalry of the king of Ethiopia, an army beyond counting—and they (actually) had come to their assistance.[207]

Both Assyrians and Judeans were well aware that the king in Egypt was ethnically Ethiopian and that an "outsider" ruled Egypt during this period. Although this Judean/Assyrian perception was no doubt heightened by the Ethiopians' distinctive phenotypical characteristics, their view of the Ethiopians should not obscure the fact that the Ethiopian kings seem to have viewed themselves as "more Egyptian" than native Egyptians. Both Piye (748–716 B.C.E.) and Shabako (716–702 B.C.E.) were often at pains to present themselves as Egyptian pharaohs in their royal titles, architectural pursuits, and religious commitments to Amun.[208] Furthermore, scholars have in fact tended to view these kings as cultural and religious conservatives,[209] a view born out in King Piye's claim that he restored traditional Egyptian religious life and that

---

207. *ANET* 286–87; and Luckenbill, *ARAB*, 2.30, 62, 193–95.

208. K. A. Kitchen, *The Third Intermediate Period in Egypt (1100–650 BC)* (2d ed.; Warminster: Aris & Phillips, 1986) 369–80.

209. Redford, *Egypt, Canaan, and Israel in Ancient Times*, 344; J. A. Wilson, *The Culture of Ancient Egypt* (Chicago: University of Chicago Press, 1965) 292–93; Frandsen, "Egyptian Imperialism," 169–70.

he rejected vassals who failed to meet Egyptian cultural standards (because they were "uncircumcised eaters of fish").[210] The Ethiopian kings had a similar contempt for the foreign Libyan element within Egypt, which they viewed as morally clumsy, ritually inept, and recreant in behavior.[211] As the reader may recognize already, there is a sense of irony here, because our failure to find ethnicity among native Egyptians in the previous chapter must be juxtaposed with this evidence that the Ethiopians tended to act like "ethnic Egyptians." So, although Judeans and Assyrians appear to have viewed the Ethiopian dynasty as ethnically distinct and "foreign" to the Egyptian milieu, the Ethiopian kings obviously felt themselves to be Egyptian. But this annulment of the ethnic distinction between Ethiopians and Egyptians was successful only to a point, as is illustrated by the fact that both Taharqa (698–664) and Tantamani (664–656) fled back to their Ethiopian homeland when Assyria brought to a close their control of Upper Egypt.[212]

The oracle in this text predicts judgment upon the Ethiopians, primarily because they sought to entice Judah (most likely, Hezekiah) to join a political alliance against Assyria. Isaiah was not very happy with this maneuver, perhaps because of certain pro-Assyrian sympathies but even more likely for religious reasons that I will outline below. It seems clear enough that his rejection of the Ethiopians was not rooted in any distinctive sense of Judean ethnicity.

Egypt in the Eyes of a Judean: Isaiah 19:1–15

The Ethiopians represented only one facet of the political matrix that vied for control of Egypt during the latter part of the eighth century and the early seventh century. As the Assyrian threat appeared on the horizon, the Libyan presence was also keenly felt. The western portions of the Delta were controlled primarily by a Libyan kingdom, and the contemporary 22d and 23d Dynasties were also associated with Libyan kings. Although the Ethiopian rulers called these kings "Libyans," to do so was something of a misnomer since the Delta's Libyan aristocracy had long since assimilated into Egyptian society.[213] At the same

210. Lichtheim, *AEL,* 3.80.
211. Redford, *Egypt, Canaan, and Israel in Ancient Times,* 344.
212. T. G. H. James, *An Introduction to Ancient Egypt* (San Francisco: Harper, 1979) 73–74.
213. W. W. Hallo and W. K. Simpson, *The Ancient Near East: A History* (New York: Harcourt Brace, 1971) 288.

time portions of the southern and eastern delta were governed by various chieftains and lesser princes, and none of the larger political modalities was fully able to tame these local rulers.[214] As we will see, Isaiah was clearly familiar with these political and cultural circumstances. But first a few preliminary observations about our text are in order.

The authenticity of this text is much debated, and it is customary to address the problem by recognizing three units within the text: vv. 1–4, 5–10, and 11–14 (v. 15 is for nearly everyone a later addition). Wildberger has claimed that the "politische Orientierungslosigkeit" described in vv. 1–4 and 11–14 represents the original oracle and that the "Naturkatastrophe" in vv. 5–10 is intrusive and therefore an addition. Kaiser and Duhm have rejected the entire oracle, Auvray has accepted it, and both Gray and Clements seem to be unsure about it.[215] In light of this, let us begin by setting aside vv. 5–10, which are of little consequence for this study anyway. Next we can exclude the questionable portions of vv. 1 and 3 for the same reason. This leaves us with a part of v. 1 as well as with vv. 2–4 and 11–14. A strong case can be made for the authenticity of all of these. Thematically, the political disintegration of Egypt reflected in vv. 1, 4, and 11–14 unites these texts as a single literary unit.[216] Historically this description of Egypt corresponds precisely to our understanding of the region in Isaiah's day. Furthermore, I can think of no reason that a later redactor would find this addition profitable, nor can one easily characterize the whole text as a late one.

Wildberger is probably correct when he dates this text sometime before the 25th Dynasty came to power in 716 B.C.E., since texts after that period recognize the new Ethiopian presence (cf. Isaiah 18 and 20). Given this context, we can outline specific circumstances that prevailed in the region.[217] Piye, the Ethiopian founder of what would

214. Ibid., 287–92; Redford, *Egypt, Canaan and Israel in Ancient Times*, 335. The best way to conceptualize this period is: (1) the demise of the Sheshonqids; (2) the rise of the Ethiopians; (3) the continuing presence of independent chiefdoms.

215. Auvray, *Isaïe 1–39*, 187–92; Clements, *Isaiah 1–39*, 166–67; Duhm, *Das Buch Jesaia*, 140–44; G. B. Gray, *Isaiah I–XXXIX* (ICC; Edinburgh: T. & T. Clark, 1912) 318–23; Wildberger, *Jesaja* (3 vols.; BKAT; Neukirchen-Vluyn: Neukirchener Verlag, 1978) 2.703–8.

216. However, there is no need to suppose that these texts were originally parts of the same prophetic oracle.

217. On this historical period, refer to Kitchen, *The Third Intermediate Period*, 348–77.

become the 25th Dynasty, ruled Egypt as an overlord. His underling
vassals were in three ranks. The highest rank included Osorkon IV in
Tanis and Bubastis (22d Dynasty), the uncertain successor of Input II
(Shoshenq IV?) in Leontopolis, two lesser pharaohs in Hermopolis and
Heracleopolis, and the hereditary princes in Athribis-with-Heliopolis.
The second rank was filled by Bakenranef's western kingdom (a remnant of the 24th Dynasty), the third was comprised of the four great
"Chiefs of Ma," and a large number of lesser rulers also participated in
governing the region. Obviously, there was a great deal of political and
cultural disorder within the Egyptian territory, and it was probably this
fact that prompted Isaiah to say in 19:14 that Yahweh had "mingled
(מסך) within her a spirit of confusion (רוח עועים)." This sense of political and cultural confusion is given a more detailed description in vv. 2
and 13.

> I will stir up Egyptians against Egyptians, and they will fight, every
> man against his brother and every man against his neighbor, city
> against city, kingdom against kingdom . . .

> The princes of Zoan have become fools, and the princes of Memphis
> are deluded; those who are the cornerstones of her tribes have led
> Egypt astray.

The princes of Zoan and Memphis were Osorkon IV (22d Dynasty)
and Bakenranef (24th Dynasty), respectively.[218] So Kitchen is substantially correct when he points out that Isaiah seemed to view rulers in
the nearby regions, particularly the 22d Dynasty at Tanis/Zoan, as the
primary representatives of Egyptian power, even when the primary
center of power was well removed from it.[219] The "cornerstones" of
Egypt's tribes (שבטים) were undoubtedly the various leaders of the
multifarious political and cultural modalities present at that time.[220]
This use of שבט ('tribe') is rather unusual because it is the only time in
the Hebrew Bible that the term is used of non-Israelite social modalities. Although this at first seems to provide a unique opportunity to

218. Bakenranef ruled from Sais but was recognized as the ruler of Memphis as
well (ibid., 376).
219. Kitchen, *The Third Intermediate Period in Egypt*, 373–74; Redford, *Egypt,
Canaan and Israel in Ancient Times*, 335–36.
220. Ibid., 335. The Hebrew singular פִּנַּת may be taken collectively or perhaps
emended to the plural, פִּנֹּת.

explore the term's significance in Israelite thought,[221] the complex Egyptian sociopolitical context makes it difficult to know whether the prophet's שבטים included larger modalities (such as the Tanites), smaller independent modalities (such as the "Chiefs of Ma"), or some combination of the two. Contrary to the suggestion of Clements, we cannot be sure that here we are dealing with "ethnic groups," and this means that our initial enthusiasm about שבט seems to be unwarranted.[222] But there is at least one conclusion that I think we should draw. If everywhere else שבט referred to Israelite and Judean modalities, then we must assume that, whatever Isaiah thought he saw in Egypt, it was similar to something that he perceived in the sociocultural features of Judah and Israel. Whether we should think here of "ancient" Judah and Israel or of the two contemporary kingdoms is another matter that is difficult to address.

What we can say with certainty is that, in Isaiah's eyes, Egypt's problem was the total collapse of a cohesive sense of identity. The references to Tanis and Memphis clearly point to the disappearance of an unambiguously "legitimate" Egyptian dynasty, and when he described the quarrel for political autonomy as the struggle of מצרים במצרים, Isaiah was depicting the various groups involved as "Egyptian" quite apart from the fact that many were supposedly of Libyan origin. As a result of this internecine struggle, "the spirit of Egypt (רוח־מצרים) within them" was to be emptied out. The significance of רוח־מצרים cannot be quickly arrived at using, as Gray does, a "stock" definition of רוח as opposed to נפש. Helpful generalizations about Hebrew anthropological terms, such as the ones provided in Wolff's *Anthropology*, are just that, and in a given context רוח, נפש, and לב can convey the same meaning.[223] The term רוח occurs twice in our text, here and also in 9:14, where Isaiah describes the "spirit of confusion" that Yahweh had

---

221. The term מטה, which is synonymous with שבט, is not used to refer to non-Israelite peoples. The anthropological term משפחה is also noticeably limited in its usage, referring to non-Israelite groups on very few occasions. See the "Table of Nations" in Genesis 10; Jer 1:15, 25:9; Zech 14:17. I will discuss משפחה at greater length in the next chapter.

222. Clements, *Isaiah 1–39*, 169.

223. H. W. Wolff, *Anthropology of the Old Testament* (Philadelphia: Fortress, 1974) 10–58. See, for example, the great lexical elasticity displayed by the Hebrew term לב/לבב, in F. H. von Meyenfeldt's *Het Hart in het Oude Testament* (Leiden: Brill, 1950). Portions of von Meyenfeldt's work were translated for me by A. Teeuwen.

given to Egypt. The continuing references to "foolishness," "stupid counsel," and "delusion" indicate that Egypt was losing its vital, unifying powers of reason (i.e., "the spirit of Egypt will be emptied out") and had been given over to a disruptive loss of rationality (i.e., "a spirit of confusion").[224] That Isaiah would depict the decline of Egyptian social order in this way suggests that he probably understood Egyptian history as an ancient tradition characterized by order and stability. He was undoubtedly familiar with Egypt's cohesive national character, its relatively continuous dynastic history, and its long and influential presence in the region. Isaiah predicted that, in the end, Egypt's political confusion would result in Assyrian domination: "a fierce king will rule over them" (v. 4).

The Egyptian materials that we have examined in the previous chapter show that Egypt's identity was primarily political, and the data from Isaiah only reinforces this perspective. This reaffirms the mounting evidence from Hosea, Amos, and now Isaiah that the identity of the larger Near Eastern powers, both in their own eyes and in the eyes of the Israelite prophets, was largely political. The exception to this rule seems to have been the tendency of Isaiah to understand Ethiopian identity in ethnic terms, but it must be remembered that, for their own part, the Ethiopians were anxious to portray themselves as the legitimate political heirs of Egyptian dynastic rule.

The Problem with Foreign Alliances: Isaiah 30:1–5 and 31:1–3

Hosea's distaste for Israel's international alliances is mirrored in several texts from Isaiah that criticize Judean sympathies with Egypt. As Clements has pointed out, these texts (Isa 30:1–5 and 31:1–3) are obviously related, though Wildberger would date 31:1–3 slightly later than 30:1–5.[225] With the exception of Kaiser, who views 30:3 as a late interpolation, commentators are united in viewing both texts as Isaianic.[226] The context reflected here is obviously one of the Egyptian-sponsored rebellions against Assyria, dating around either 713–711 or 705–701 B.C.E. Egypt was represented by "the princes of Zoan and Hanes," that is, the princes of Tanis and Heracleopolis. The remnants of

---

224. This use of רוח approximates Wolff's understanding of לבב/לב as the 'reasonable' aspect of humans. We might also see behind this a reference to Egypt's theology of the *Ba* as the vital force in the human spirit.
    225. Clements, *Isaiah 1–39*, 254; Wildberger, *Jesaja*, 3.1227–35.
    226. Kaiser, *Isaiah*, 2.286–87.

the 22d Dynasty were in Tanis, with which Judah was quite familiar, and Heracleopolis was at this point associated with the new Ethiopian dynasty of Shabako (the 25th Dynasty).[227]

The criticism offered in these oracles is straightforward: Judah had added 'sin to sin' (חטאת על־חטאת, 30:1) by "going down to Egypt for help" (31:1). This act was understood by the prophet as rebellion against the deity (הוי בנים סוררים) because, in doing so, Judah had substituted confidence (בטח) in foreign military power for confidence in Yahweh (ואת־יהוה לא דרשו). In my discussion of Hos 7:8–13, I suggested that Hosea rejected foreign alliances because he viewed them as 'covenants' (ברית) that threatened Yahweh's covenantal relationship with Israel. Although the Southern prophets lack any explicit notions of covenant ideology, Isa 30:1 implies that Hosea and Isaiah shared a common contempt for international military relationships because of their religious viewpoint. Isaiah's polemic presents the parallel accusation that Judah had sought לעשות עצה ולא מני ולנסך מסכה ולא רוחי (30:1). The first phrase, "to carry out a plan, but not mine," is clear enough. But the meaning of ולנסך מסכה is obscure primarily because this verb/noun combination occurs only here in the Hebrew Bible and because מסכה normally refers to 'molten images'. Most commentators have translated the phrase along the lines laid out by the RSV, 'to make a league' or 'an alliance',[228] which makes sense for several reasons. First, the LXX tradition actually translated ולנסך מסכה as συνθήκας ('covenant, agreement') which indicates, as Procksch has pointed out, that the Septuagint must have understood the Hebrew along the lines of σπονδὰς σπένδεσθαι 'to pour out a drink offering' during a covenant ratification ceremony.[229] Although there appears to be no concrete parallel to this use of drink offerings in Levantine treaty texts, the covenant renewal of Jacob in Genesis 35 does feature a libation.[230] All things considered, both the parallelism in 30:1 (ולנסך מסכה is parallel

227. Shabako moved north of Heracleopolis and took control of Memphis in his second year (715 B.C.E.), extending his rule to all of Egypt at the same time. Nonetheless, Osorkon IV continued to reign in Tanis as he had during Bakenranef's 24th Dynasty.

228. Clements, *Isaiah 1–39*, 243; Duhm, *Das Buch Jesaia*, 215; Kaiser, *Isaiah*, 2.285; Procksch, *Jesaia I*, 384–85; Wildberger, *Jesaja 28–39*, 1152. Auvray is less certain about this (*Isaïe 1–39*, 262–63).

229. Procksch, *Jesaia I*, 384–85.

230. One of the best illustrations of such a ceremony is found in the Sefire treaties (AIS I A 35–42).

with "carry out a plan") and the oracle's overall content favor that we read the text as the ritual ratification of a political alliance. One is at first tempted to suggest on this basis that Isaiah would have agreed with Hosea's condemnation of all foreign alliances,[231] but his oracles were silent on the question of alliances with Assyria and J. Høgenhaven has taken this as evidence that Isaiah endorsed the pro-Assyrian party.[232] This thesis may be true in part, but it cannot account for the whole matter, because Isaiah's criticisms of the Egyptian alliance in chaps. 30–31 do not appear to stem from his support for Assyria but from his prophetic conviction that it constituted rebellion against Yahweh. While Isaiah may have been very familiar with Assyrian propaganda and have resigned himself to its power, he obviously did so out of a respect for his sovereign God.[233] It would therefore seem that for both Isaiah and Hosea the issue of foreign alliances was more religious than political.

The Ancient Traditions in Isaiah of Jerusalem

J. Vollmer's examination of Isaiah's *Rückblicke* to ancient traditions is somewhat hampered by its tendency to presume the prophet's familiarity with the pentateuchal sources, and this is precisely the assumption that I have assiduously tried to avoid during this inquiry. But this problem turns out to be mostly academic because Vollmer has identified almost all of these *Rückblicke* as *nachjesajanischen*, so that they do not come into play here.[234] After all, it was not Israel's ancient tradition but its imminent end that stood in the center of Isaiah's prophetic proclamation.[235] I will therefore refer to his comments only as they relate to the specific texts that interest us. In relation to the issue of identity, Isaiah refers to two historical traditions that are particularly

231. Did Isaiah and Amos view Judah's relationship with Yahweh in the exclusive terms of Hosea? In contrast to Hosea's strong polemic against foreign deities, Isaiah and Amos offer no such polemic. In my view, the most likely explanation is that the universal status of Yahweh in Isaiah and Amos seems to have precluded the necessity of such an argument.

232. J. Høgenhaven, "The Prophet Isaiah and Judaean Foreign Policy under Ahaz and Hezekiah," *JNES* 49 (1990) 351–54; see also Clements, *Isaiah 1–39*, 11.

233. On Isaiah's familiarity with Assyrian propaganda and its military power, see Machinist, "Assyria and Its Image in the First Isaiah," 722–25, 728–29.

234. See Vollmer, *Geschichtliche Rückbliche und Motive*, 169–86.

235. Ibid., 187.

important to me, the first being his references to the Davidic monarchy and the second his allusions to the schism between the Northern and Southern kingdoms. These are naturally important issues because of the growing skepticism about the historicity of the David monarchy.[236]

Isaiah alluded to the Davidic tradition at several points, and only in one of these cases is there a question about the text's authenticity.[237] While Amos affirmed the artistic talents of the dynastic founder, Isaiah underlined his martial exploits against the Philistines (his victory at Mount Perazim in 28:21)[238] and against Jerusalem (successfully conquered in 29:1). We thus infer that the Judean prophetic tradition—and we would assume the people in general—was supportive of the Davidic monarchy. The importance of the Davidic period for Isaiah is especially clear in his oracle against Jerusalem's social and political climate (1:21–26), in which Yahweh promises:

> I will restore your judges (שֹׁפְטַיִךְ) as at the first and your counselors (יֹעֲצַיִךְ) as at the beginning. Afterward you shall be called the city of righteousness, the faithful city.

As Clements has noted, this cannot be a reference to the pre-Davidic period reflected in the book of Judges because for Isaiah the origins of Jerusalem lay with David's conquest of the city (29:1).[239] Instead, commentators have agreed that we must be dealing with a restoration of the ideal Davidic rule as it was in the beginning (כְּבָרִאשֹׁנָה ... אֲשִׁיבָה).[240] This restoration would feature leaders—judges and counselors—like the ones associated with the "golden age" of David.

This means that the conquest of Jerusalem and the founding of its ruling dynasty played the same role for Isaiah that the Exodus/Wilderness traditions played for Hosea. In both cases the *Ursprung* of the people represented a "golden age" in which the nation and the deity enjoyed prosperous relations. In spite of their obvious differences,

236. I have already referred to the recent discussion of G. N. Knoppers, "The Vanishing Solomon: The Disappearance of the United Monarchy from Recent Histories of Ancient Israel," *JBL* 116 (1997) 19–44.

237. Cf. Isa 1:26, 9:6, 28:21, and 29:1, with 9:6 being of questionable provenience. See the appropriate portions of Auvray, Clements, Duhm, Kaiser, Procksch, and Wildberger.

238. No doubt the tradition that informs 2 Sam 5:17–25.

239. Clements, *Isaiah 1–39*, 36.

240. Duhm, *Das Buch Jesaia*, 34–35; Gray, *Isaiah I*, 34; Wildberger, *Isaiah 1–12*, 70.

Isaiah and Hosea seem to have agreed that hope for the nation rested in a return to the "golden age." But their "golden ages" were entirely different, with one featuring origins outside of the land via deliverance from Egypt and the other featuring the conquest of a city within the land by a powerful military leader. To put this in terms laid out by Procksch some time ago, while Isaiah believed that a return to the monarchic ideal would restore Judah, Hosea viewed kingship as a misguided notion whose annulment was essential to the restoration of Israel.[241] In all of this, Hosea's concept of Israelite identity presents itself as ethnoreligious and in contrast with Isaiah's more political sense of national identity. This no doubt stemmed from the very different bases of identity envisioned by the two prophets, in one case (Hosea) a vision of identity that was grounded in the people's shared history with their national God, and in the other case (Isaiah) a vision of identity grounded in support for the divinely chosen monarchic dynasty. This monarchic focus would tend, in the case of Isaiah, to detract from an emphasis on the people and on their collective sense of identity in ways similar to the Mesopotamian and Egyptian evidence that we have already examined, wherein the constant preoccupation with kingship displaced an emphasis on the people themselves.

If the Davidic materials in Amos and Isaiah hint at the relationship that once tied North and South together, Isaiah's reference to the North–South schism in 7:17 made it explicit: "The Lord will bring upon you and upon your people and upon your father's house such days as have not come since the day that Ephraim departed from Judah." This evil omen was representative of the Southern perspective that the political schism had been a mistake and that it represented a threat to the security and identity of both nations, a view that was in stark contrast to Hosea's seeming apathy toward his Southern neighbors. All of this can be summarized with this proposition: if our three prophetic witnesses are suitable representatives of the eighth-century perspective, then the Judeans remembered the old United Monarchy with nostalgia and the Israelites with very little affection.[242]

241. Procksch, *Jesaia I*, 48.
242. In light of the fact that language often serves as an important marker of ethnic distinctiveness, it is instructive to note J. C. L. Gibson's observation that there was a marked difference in the eighth century between Judean and Israelite Hebrew. But we should strees that there is no evidence that would explicitly suggest that this was a strong marker of the distinctions between them in antiquity (Gibson, *Textbook of Syrian Semitic Inscriptions* [3 vols.; Oxford: Clarendon, 1971–82] 1.5–16, 21–24).

Summary:
Ethnicity and Identity in the Assyrian Period

Ethnic concepts such as forefathers and ancestral migrations played an important role in Israelite identity, and these Northern traditions were well known even to Southerners like Amos and Isaiah. This comes as no surprise, given the fact that in Amos we have evidence both of widespread tendencies toward ethnicity in the Levantine context and, at least in the case of the smaller states, of some knowledge about the ethnic traditions of the surrounding peoples. Therefore, Hosea's ethnicity is distinguishable not in type but in degree, since it appears to have been a more intense kind of identity with a firmer sense of boundary. However, these powerful sentiments were motivated not so much by ethnic concerns as by Hosea's desire to promote the agenda of his mono-Yahwist party. In essence, Hosea utilized a preexisting sense of Israelite ethnicity and intensified it through a heated polemic against other deities, which he identified as foreign. He therefore brings us neither to the root of Israelite ethnic identity nor to the beginnings of Israelite Yahwism; both of these predated him. Rather, his community was responsible for the merging (or remerging? or reemphasizing?) of these two modes of identity when it intensified ethnic sentiments in support of Israel's national god, Yahweh. "Foreignness" became the criteria for rejecting anything that threatened the mono-Yahwist community, and Hosea not only rejected "non-Israelite" deities like Baal, but he also criticized Jacob's ancient foray into Aram for a spouse, international political treaties, and even the nontheocratic institution of kingship. The extent to which Hosea's community sanctioned exclusive devotion to Yahweh is reflected in two related and powerful metaphors, marriage fidelity and an exclusive covenant relationship. All of this of course implies that the larger community that surrounded the mono-Yahwist sect did not adhere to these same intense boundaries, so that we must presume that Hosea's community was a peripheral one in the sociological sense. From this one should not conclude that Israel's sense of ethnicity entirely lacked meaningful boundaries, since the discursive strategies of both Hosea and Amos assume a general commitment by the people to Israel's ethnicity. Hosea's sense of ethnicity was simply stronger than most Israelites'.

Although it is difficult to unravel all of the factors that contributed to Hosea's unique perspective, I have suggested that the peripheral experience of Israel was perhaps an important one. As we will explore in more depth below, Hosea's community responded to this uncomfortable status by suggesting that Yahweh, not Assyria, was responsible for any military losses that might be suffered. In doing so, they replaced the specter of Assyrian domination with the vision of the rule of Israel's own God over his people and his land. As an expression of this ideology, Hosea endorsed unyielding loyalty to Yahweh and actively opposed alliances that might have symbolized dependence on sources other than Yahweh.

Returning to the ethnic features themselves—as I have said, the constituent parts of Israelite ethnic identity (its migration and forefather traditions) were assumed by, and therefore predated, our earliest prophetic sources. These ethnic traditions are similar to the Greek traditions described in chap. 2 and share with them the title *charter myths*, in that their essential purpose was to describe the origins of the peoples involved. It is important to assess the nature of the similarity here. The Greek traditions were of both aggregative and oppositional varieties. They were aggregative in the sense that the ethnic genealogies gradually accumulated new elements as groups were assimilated into the mix or as they needed to define the relationships between them with more precision. The oppositional elements of Greek ethnicity were for the most part relatively late developments because they stemmed from the pan-Hellenic effort to repulse the threat from Persia; in other words, the greatest sense of common identity among the various Greek peoples emerged when they faced a common outside threat. Similar ethnic patterns can be discerned in the Hebrew materials.

In the first place, there does appear to be an aggregative tendency to include the various Israelite ancestors and groups within a genealogical framework, since the Jacob and Joseph traditions appear to have existed somewhat independently of each other, only to be joined at a later point in time. Because the Jacob, Isaac, and Joseph figures do not function directly as eponyms for Israel, it seems to me that one could make the case that they have only secondarily been employed in their ancestral roles. The fact that Jacob does not figure in the ninth-century Song of Deborah perhaps indicates when the forefather tradition first appeared, or more precisely, when it was first adopted as an ancestral tradition. This remains a guess, however.[243] When we compare the

243. For a ninth-century dating of Deborah's Song, see my discussion in chap. 3 above.

eighth-century prophetic sources to the Song of Deborah, the aggregative tendencies in Israelite ethnicity stand out more clearly. In SDeb, there was an Ephraim but no Manasseh. In Isaiah, however, the two tribes appear, it seems, as brothers and as the common progeny of Joseph. Our examination of the "Moses blessings" (Deuteronomy 33) in the next chapter will provide us with a clearer vantage point on this aggregative process. In certain respects, these processes should be viewed as examples of what I call "concrete ethnicity"; in other words, the ethnic concepts serve to lay out and explain the relationships between existing groups that were in some sense already ethnic in character. This should be contrasted with "abstract ethnicity," the tendency to use ethnicity as a template to explain the character and origins of other groups. An example of this is Gen 10:22, which traces the origins of Assyria back to the forefather Asshur.

This brings us to the question of oppositional ethnicity and its place in the Israelite traditions. Perhaps in the Merneptah text, and certainly in SDeb and Hosea, the Canaanites figure as "the other" against which Israel defined itself. While in the first two sources this was largely a function of Canaan as a military opponent (if we take generous liberties with the Merneptah Stele), in Hosea the Canaanites should be associated primarily with the Phoenicians and with the religious threat from one of their chief deities, Baal. In other words, although SDeb implies that the Canaanites were the opponents of the Yahwists, this was a military struggle that became an ethnoreligious struggle only later when Hosea and his party sought to promote their mono-Yahwism.

More examples of oppositional ethnicity are found in the migration traditions of Israel's neighbors, particularly in the cases of the Arameans and the Philistines. Although these groups shared this type of legend with the Israelites, both were long-standing enemies of Israel and firmly separated from it via ethnic traditions. Migration origin traditions were also popular in archaic and classical Greece, and from this we should probably conclude that migration was a popular model in the eighth-century levant. This raises an important question. When we speak of a *model* are we then speaking of *abstract ethnicity,* that is, the use of ethnic models by one people to explain the origins of another? We may at first be tempted to think, along with the anthropologists, that we are dealing merely with "charter myths" that were invented to account for national origins of other peoples, but I have already pointed out that this is not very likely, because some of these migration traditions have at least a grain of truth behind them, particularly in the instance of the Arameans and Philistines. I also think that one could find any number of contexts that might lie behind the Israelite migration from Egypt, especially the circumstances that prevailed when the Asiatic Hyksos were forced out of Egypt. So in some of these cases our sources witness (perhaps in distorted fashion) to instances of concrete ethnicity that became the "charter myths" of these Levantine states.

I turn now to the question of Judean identity. Although Isaiah and Amos were familiar with the ethnic sentiments held by their Northern counterpart, they never expressed the idea that Judah somehow shared in that identity. The few indications of ethnicity in Amos and Isaiah were limited to descriptions of non-Judeans, and in Amos ethnicity did not even serve to distinguish the Israelite people from the Philistines, Arameans, and Ethiopians. Instead, Amos and Isaiah were concerned primarily with sociological, religious, and political modes of identity. Both Judean prophets were frustrated by the socioeconomic division that prevailed in society. The injustices associated with this situation were a primary cause of the coming judgment from Yahweh, which was presumably directed toward the upper classes rather than the "peasants." From a religious standpoint, the Southern prophets viewed Yahweh not only as a national god, although he certainly was that, but also as a universal deity. This emphasis clearly resulted from Judah's peripheral status under the Assyrians, as evidenced by the fact that Isaiah attacked the hubris of Assyria's king while he simultaneously averred that Yahweh was the true sovereign of the universe. Politically speaking, this sovereignty was tangibly expressed in his divine choice of the Davidic monarchy, which turns out to be an important component of Judean identity and one that distinguished it from Israelite identity. In spite of this difference between Israel and Judah, an important aspect of Judean ideology was its affiliation with the North, an affiliation that stemmed both from the period of Davidic rule in that region and also from a common Yahwistic heritage. As must now be clear, this sentiment of the South toward the North was not shared by many in the North toward their neighbors in the South.

In light of the comparative aspects of our inquiry, I suppose that it is appropriate at this point to ask specific questions about the provenience of the ethnic traditions in ancient Israel as we have outlined them up to this point. Was Israel's view of its own ethnicity, or of the ethnic identities of others, influenced in some way by the Greeks, Mesopotamians, or Egyptians? I think that we have confirmed without doubt that Isaiah's view of Israelite identity was very much influenced by Assyrian ideologies, but for both the Assyrians and the Judeans this sense of identity was more religious and political than it was ethnic. The ethnic traditions of the North, however, particularly the forefather and migration traditions, are a different matter and display certain similarities with the ethnic traditions from Greece, from the Old Babylonian period, and from the anthropological data that was discussed in our introduction. We will need to sketch out these similarities and differences with a view to identifying potential points of contact.

Israel's ancestral traditions were of three varieties. First, they included figures like Jacob and Isaac, whose names appear to have no immediate connection either with the nation of Israel itself or with a particular geographical region. In such cases, the traditions do not seem to have been contrived to explain the origins of Israel or groups within Israel but were secondarily appropriated as a tradition about *the* ethnic forefather. As Westermann points out, whether there is any kind of link between the traditions about Jacob and early Israel is difficult to say, given the evidence:

> If these texts, or even parts or motifs, or traces of them, actually go back to the period of the patriarchs, actually originated with those living persons Abraham, Isaac, Jacob, and Joseph, then the scholar must account for the path of these traditions from the period (2000–1400 B.C.E.) to the written works in the tenth, eighth, or sixth centuries. And this path is virtually inaccessible because 80% to 90% of it is oral tradition, and all we know of it is the written end product.[244]

While we might quibble with Westermann's characterization of the problem, I think that no one will question the fact that we face many difficulties in our effort to reconstruct and explain the history of these traditions, difficulties that for some will make the very idea of a connection between the Jacob tradition and early Israel a fanciful one. This seems to me too strong of an objection, because the Mesopotamian evidence has demonstrated the tendency to generate forefather traditions (during the Old Babylonian period) and to preserve these ancestral traditions—in a somewhat distorted form—for rather long periods of

---

244. C. Westermann, *Genesis: A Commentary* (3 vols.; Minneapolis: Augsburg, 1982–85) 2.36.

time (down into the Neo-Assyrian period). The Egyptian evidence from *Sinuhe* seems to indicate that kinship played an important role in the organization of Asiatic society during the second millennium. For these reasons I think that we should not quickly discard (or embrace) the Jacob traditions as a witness to life in early Israel, or, if you like, to life among the proto-Israelites.

This kind of tradition is clearly different from two other types of ancestral tradition. The first has the name of an ancestor, such as Ephraim or Manasseh, that is associated with a tribe or geographical region. Thus, one would imagine that the ancestor was contrived to account for the origins of the people or the territory. This is very close to what we have seen in the Greek evidence (Hellen was the forefather of the Hellenes) and also, to an extent, in the anthropological data (Tiv was the forefather of the Tiv people). Essentially, this brings us to a fork in the road, because the comparative evidence can lead us down one of two paths: one explains this kind of Israelite ethnicity through diffusion (they borrowed it from the Greeks or Phoenicians); the other explains it phenomenologically (similar kinds of traditions appear rather naturally among disparate groups). How does one choose? I have already explained that there are reasons to suspect contacts between the Greeks and Israelites via Phoenicia during the eighth century, and I have cited the third kind of ancestral tradition, the ancestral migration, that was known among the Greeks and among Israel's Levantine neighbors. With these migration traditions we face a similar problem because they too can be explained in two different fashions: first, as diffusions from some central point of origin, and second, as actual migrations that gave rise to the traditions. We could probably think of any number of ways to argue for either the diffusion model or the phenomenological model, but I do not think that either choice would be very conclusive, because our data are too cryptic. My own thought is that there is probably a mixture of the two involved in the origins and development of Israelite ethnicity.

Excursus:
Core and Periphery in the Assyrian Period—A Proposal

The Neo-Assyrian period brings to a close one of the most intense periods of peripheral experience that the Judeans and Israelites faced in antiquity. But our dialogue up to this point has been more with biblical scholarship than with ethnicity studies, so at this juncture I would like to interact briefly with the view of Wallerstein, now popular in many quarters of scholarship, that ethnic identity is created and nurtured when small peripheral social modalities live under the imperial pressures of a powerful core civilization.

First, in Hosea and in Amos we saw a tendency among the Levantine peoples to employ ethnicity as an organizing principle of identity. Because these neighboring groups shared a common status as "peripheral societies," this would come as no surprise to Wallerstein. But the Judean evidence shows that our support for Wallerstein must be qualified since it is far from certain that ethnicity played any role in Southern identity and, even if some ethnic sentiments existed, it is clear that they did not intensify during the eighth century. Instead, Judean identity was primarily organized around religious and political ideas, and these were the boundaries that intensified during the Assyrian period. In other words, it seems rather clear that competition between a core and periphery intensifies not only ethnic boundaries but any existing boundaries that serve to promote a sense of community and identity.

Regarding the "core" civilizations in Assyria and Egypt—neither the native evidence nor the Hebrew sources suggests that ethnicity played any significant role there, and this suits well the theoretical predictions of Wallerstein. The Israelite and Judean dynasties acted out their peripheral relationship with these core societies quite predictably as they sent and received envoys in their effort to forge some sense of national security. Probably one of the more interesting observations that we could draw from this is that Israelites and Judeans tended to view Egypt and Assyria as equals, in spite of the fact that during this period the glory of Egypt had long since faded. This exposes the rather potent effect of Israel's collective memory, which continued to consider Egypt the powerful core civilization that it had been but was no longer. Such an impression of Egypt is not entirely surprising if one considers the cumulative effect of Egypt's long domination of Asia and, over the years, its frequent military incursions by the likes of Thutmose III,

Amenhotep III, Ramses II, Merneptah, and Sheshonk I, to name a few.

It would be natural for any of the smaller peripheral states in the region, Israel and Judah being no exception, to seek the help of one core civilization when threatened by another. How did these states respond in the face of the powerful threat from Assyria? We can see two alternating diplomatic policies: first, an attempt to appease Assyria politically, and second, an effort to establish military alliances with Egypt and with the surrounding peripheral states. Given that these practices were quite conventional and clearly expected in such circumstances, we must ask ourselves again why Hosea and Isaiah took such a stalwart position against Israel's political effort to defend itself. In the paragraphs that follow, I will suggest an answer to this question.

We should begin with a reminder of the positions that have been staked out on this issue and the rationale that lay behind them. Our Northern prophet, Hosea, viewed both the payment of tribute (to appease foreign aggressors) and the use of military alliances (to defend against them) as a "mixing" with "foreigners" that would devour Israel's strength (7:8–9). This was because Yahweh had already proved his mastery over the core imperial powers in the Exodus event, and Israel needed only to safeguard its relationship with him. Isaiah was equally uneasy with similar policies in Judah but for somewhat different reasons. It was not only that Yahweh could defeat a core power but that he was a universal deity whose sovereign territory included the core powers. Thus Isaiah and Hosea traversed different roads to arrive at the same kinds of conclusions about political alliances with foreign powers. But I think that we can go a bit further in our analysis of these ideas.

Israel's position on the periphery of two great civilizations had dictated a history of defeat and subordination. In terms of military resources, it could compete with the martial power of these urban civilizations only when they were internally weakened. However, in terms of theological resources, it had Yahweh, who could resist any potential foe. This was a theological idea that represented hope for a people who, on simple material grounds, could never be optimistic about the chances of military resistance. This theological position had to be grounded in tangible policy, and for both Hosea and Isaiah this trust in Yahweh was best expressed in a rejection of help from all others. And there is more. In the view of these prophets, not only military victory but also military defeat was the result of Yahweh's activity or inactivity in the history of events. *This meant that it was no longer Assyria, the foreign power, who dominated Israel; it was Yahweh himself.* In other words, prophetic theology was a denial of foreign domination that could be summarized in two complementary theological propositions. First, the prophetic rejection of foreign political relationships was a theological response to the imperialistic policies of core urban civilizations toward peripheral regions, in this case Israel and Judah. With this strategy, the prophets exchanged Israel's frailty for Yahweh's martial powers, thus preserving Israel's importance in a world where, on other grounds, it remained an insignificant player.[245] Second, the theologies of divine retribution embraced by these prophets displaced the long-standing specter of foreign domination. Just as Yahweh's power was substituted for Israel's frailty in the first proposition, so also Yahweh's dominion was substituted for the domination of foreign powers in the second. In this theology, Israel was never at the mercy of foreign powers, either in times of potential threat or in times of imperial domination.

I consider this proposal somewhat speculative, since it is based on a combination of theory and data that are heavy on the theory side. In addition, I am quite hesitant to argue, as Wallerstein would, that Asiatic identities on the periphery of Egypt and Mesopotamia were *created* by the dominance of those core civilizations. Nevertheless, I believe that the data do tend to support the assertion, often made in ethnicity studies, that the domination of a peripheral social modality by powerful, imperialistic policies will transform the identity of that social group.

---

245. There is a long-standing debate concerning the origin of certain elements of Israel's warfare theology, particularly the tradition that Yahweh fights on behalf of Israel. Von Rad viewed this as late and Deuteronomic in origin, while others (F. M. Cross, P. D. Miller, M. C. Lind) view it as a more ancient concept. For a brief summary of the history and issues as well as a bibliography, see B. C. Ollenburger's introduction to the English edition of von Rad's *Holy War in Ancient Israel* (Grand Rapids, Mich.: Eerdmans, 1991).

Chapter Five

Ethnicity and Identity in the Judean Monarchy

The period between Isaiah and Jeremiah has produced a rather silent and therefore disappointing interim in our biblical sources.[1] While the Deuteronomistic History provides an account of this period, the history itself dates to the late Judean monarchy or the exile, so that there is a substantial period during the seventh century for which our firsthand literary sources are the Assyrian annals of Sennacherib, Esarhaddon, and Assurbanipal. Several Judean works serve as witnesses to the period that follows these Assyrian sources, particularly Deuteronomy and Jeremiah, and it is this later period that is of primary importance for this chapter. However, before I turn to these sources, in the interest of perspective I will tarry briefly on the subject of the years between Isaiah and the Josianic age.

When one speaks of *exile*, the sixth-century Judean exile almost invariably comes to mind, with the term less often reminding us of Israel's fate at the end of the eighth century. Despite our impression from the biblical sources, however, Sennacherib's annals inform us that a third important exile took place. According to the annals, 200,150 people were "counted as booty" by Sennacherib, and this number—if it referred to actual exiles—would be far in excess of anything encountered during the other two deportation experiences.[2] S. Stohlmann has carefully examined the available texts and concluded that the phrase "to count as booty" should not be equated with deportation and that the number deported was therefore considerably less than the high

---

1. However, I will argue below that much of Deuteronomy originated during this "silent period" between 722 B.C.E. and Josiah's reforms.
2. *ANET* 288.

number provided by Sennacherib.[3] Nevertheless, Stohlmann correctly surmised that this "hidden exile" was quite comparable to the two exiles more familiar to us. This noteworthy event, which was prompted by Hezekiah's rebellions against Assyria, began the long Assyrian domination of Judah that came to a close only during the reign of Josiah. For most of this period, Manasseh ruled Judah and seems to have submitted rather passively to his Assyrian overlords.[4] The fact that the Deuteronomistic Historian remembered Manasseh with disdain and contrasted him with both his major predecessor (Hezekiah) and his successor (Josiah) is evidence that a strong sentiment must have existed against Manasseh's policy, at least in some circles. Assyrian imperial tactics, which had included a "two-way" deportation policy in the North,[5] appear to have taken a different turn in the South, where a massive "one-way" deportation depopulated Judah.[6] Nevertheless, due to the influx of foreign groups into adjacent regions—to the north, south, and east—the frequency of foreign contacts increased markedly for the relatively isolated Judeans.

In addition to contact with these distant foreigners, and perhaps a more important population trend in the period, was the migration of Israel's citizens into Judah after 722 B.C.E. Deuteronomy and a number of other texts in the Hebrew Bible betray Northern origins and, although straightforward accounts of this migration process are wanting, it is quite clear that these literary and religious traditions arrived in the South via Northern refugees.[7] It is difficult to assess the tensions and problems that must have arisen from this situation. On the one hand, it seems clear that these refugees would have shared with their Judean counterparts many cultural patterns, a Yahwistic heritage, a concept of priestly torah (see above, pp. 148, 196), and probably certain cultic

3. Stephen Stohlmann, "The Judaean Exile after 701 B.C.E.," in *Scripture in Context II: More Essays on the Comparative Method* (ed. W. W. Hallo, J. C. Moyer, and L. G. Perdue; Winona Lake, Ind.: Eisenbrauns, 1983) 147–75.

4. J. A. Soggin, *A History of Ancient Israel* (Philadelphia: Westminster, 1984) 238–40; cf. *ANET* 291, 294.

5. By "two-way" I am referring to the practice of sending conquered populations to other areas of the empire while resettling foreign populations in their place.

6. Nadav Na'aman, "Population Changes in Palestine following Assyrian Deportations," *Tel Aviv* 20 (1993) 112–19.

7. Deut 18:6 is a prime example. It refers to Levites who had made their way into Judah from Israel.

rites and festivals.[8] Furthermore, the mono-Yahwist party represented by Hosea and his community would have been especially comfortable in the South, as seems evident in the fact that his brand of Northern literature took firm root in the South. On the other hand, Hosea and the epigraphic evidence confirm the presence of Baal worship in the North, both in central and peripheral contexts, and this cultic activity would probably have been at odds with Southern religious authorities as represented by Isaiah and Amos (although one must say that Amos has little to say in condemnation of the Northern Baal cult).[9] Competition for ecological resources and an ever-increasing underclass would have added to the growing tensions in Judah. In sum, Judean population trends during the late eighth and early seventh centuries included a marked increase of Israelite refugees within Judah and an increase of various foreign groups on Judah's immediate periphery and even within the state's borders.

This period of Assyrian domination featured a marked intensification of ethnic boundaries in Judean society, boundaries that were virtually invisible during the early days of the Assyrian period yet became quite pronounced by its end. Such a pattern is expected by the core-periphery model commonly espoused in ethnic studies proper, and I will show from the biblical data that this is not a coincidence.[10] In the eighth-century materials, the Assyrian presence was already exerting a quite noticeable effect upon the ideas of Hosea, Amos, and especially Isaiah. The long-term effects of Assyrian domination are even more profound when observed via their impact on Deuteronomy and Jeremiah.

In this chapter, I will focus on modes of identity, especially ethnic modes, that are present in these two important sources from the late Judean monarchy. In both Deuteronomy and Jeremiah we face not only the problem that some of the materials actually date to the early exile (or even later) but also the problem that isolating this exilic material is a rather arduous task at certain points. This make it more diffi-

8. R. de Vaux, *Ancient Israel* (2 vols.; New York: McGraw-Hill, 1965) 2.75.

9. On the epigraphic evidence, see J. H. Tigay, *You Shall Have No Other Gods: Israelite Religion in the Light of Hebrew Inscriptions* (HSS 31; Atlanta: Scholars Press, 1986) 47–89.

10. I am thinking here of Wallerstein's theories, but many ethnic theorists would see at least the partial truth of his core-periphery model. The biblical data actually correspond to his predictions only in part, as we will see.

cult to utilize as our sociohistorical boundary a rather crucial historical period—namely the exile. Therefore, although this chapter focuses on identity before the exile, it will necessarily entail materials and issues from the early exilic period, and this will be especially true during my comparative discussion of Deuteronomic lawcode, the Holiness Code, and the Book of the Covenant.

Deuteronomy

From a literary standpoint the book of Deuteronomy can conveniently be divided into five basic components: the historical prologue (chaps. 1–4), the parenetic introduction (chaps. 5–11), the lawcode (chaps. 12–26), blessings and curses (chaps. 27–30), and concluding remarks (chaps. 31–34). The two latter sections are quite complex and include some materials that are rather old and go back to the early "core" of Deuteronomy as well as some post-Deuteronomistic additions, which may or may not be old depending on the text involved. The other three sections of the book have literary problems of their own but are nonetheless more homogenous than sections four and five. In general, I adhere to the commonly held position that the underlying basis of chaps. 12–26 was a lawcode of Northern origin that dated no later than the eighth century B.C.E. and that, generally speaking, the text reached its present form in conjunction with Josiah's reforms late in the seventh century.[11] Following M. Noth,[12] I regard chaps. 5–11 as the original introduction to this lawcode and chaps. 1–4 as a later addition by the Deuteronomistic Historian that served to introduce his work.[13]

11. T. Römer has suggested that the original lawcode is principally represented by chaps. 12–18, with an introduction in chap. 6 and a conclusion in chap. 26 ("Le Deutéronome à la quête des origines," in *La Pentateuque: Débats et recherches* [ed. P. Haudebert; Lectio Divina 151; Paris: du Cerf, 1992] 67–68). On the Northern origins of Deuteronomy, see E. Nielsen, *Deuteronomium* (HAT; Tübingen: Mohr, 1995) 4; M. Weinfeld, "The Emergence of the Deuteronomic Movement: The Historical Antecedents," in *Das Deuteronomium: Entstehung, Gestalt, und Botschaft* (ed. N. Lohfink; BETL 68; Leuven: Leuven University Press, 1985) 83–87.

12. M. Noth, *The Deuteronomistic History* (2d ed.; JSOTSup 15; Sheffield: JSOT Press, 1991) 27–44.

13. The details of the redactional history of these texts is somewhat complex. In particular, see N. Lohfink's redactional analysis of Deuteronomy 5–11, in *Das Hauptgebot: Eine Untersuchung literarischer Einleitungsfragen zu Dtn 5–11* (AnBib 20; Rome: Pontifical Biblical Institute, 1963).

The dating of the first four chapters in Deuteronomy is rather difficult, despite F. M. Cross's defense of a preexilic edition of the Deuteronomistic History and the more recent defense by R. D. Nelson.[14] I have insufficient confidence in the idea to base a descussion on it. I must concede that Deuteronomy 1–4 might easily date to the early exilic period or perhaps even later. As I have said, I regard portions of chaps. 5–11 and 12–26 as Northern in origin. While noting the implications of this origin where it is important, I will focus on the function of chaps. 5–26 within the seventh-century Judean context and give attention to any relevant redactional problems. I will handle other issues in Deuteronomy and the various problems within the latter portions of the book (chaps. 27–34) as they arise. My discussion begins with an issue closely related to ethnic identity, the problem of the "forefathers" in Deuteronomy.

"The Fathers" in Deuteronomy

During my discussion of Hosea in chap. 3 above, I pointed out that the forefather migration tradition of the exodus and the Jacob ancestor tradition were two competing origin traditions that existed alongside each other in eighth-century Israel. The references to the fathers in Deuteronomy would therefore seem, at least on the surface, to reflect a rather advanced stage in the history of Israelite ethnic ideas because they include an additional patriarchal figure, Abraham, and because the patriarchal figures (Abraham, Isaac, and Jacob) are clearly joined to the forefather migration tradition. But this view is somewhat superficial, and I agree with several others that the patriarchal formulas ליצחק לאברהם וליעקב are likely to have been later additions that served to link the book of Genesis with Deuteronomy and the Deuteronomistic History.

It was J. Van Seters's 1972 article that first suggested the redactional status of this patriarchal formula,[15] but his seminal work has been superseded by the more detailed work of T. Römer.[16] Römer has

---

14. F. M. Cross, *Canaanite Myth and Hebrew Epic* (Cambridge: Harvard University Press, 1973) 217–90; R. D. Nelson, *The Double Redaction of the Deuteronomistic History* (JSOTSup 18; Sheffield: JSOT Press, 1983).

15. J. Van Seters, "Confessional Reformulation in the Exilic Period," *VT* 22 (1972) 448–59.

16. T. Römer, *Israels Väter: Untersuchungen zur Väterthematik im Deuteronomium und in der deuteronomistischen Tradition* (OBO 99; Göttingen: Vandenhoeck & Ruprecht, 1990).

pointed out that the patriarchal name-formula normally occurs in apposition to "the fathers" and that, when sufficient attention is given to the issue, it becomes quite clear that "the fathers" of Deuteronomy are not the patriarchs but the generation that came out of Egypt. He supports this claim by showing that this understanding of the fathers is precisely that of Hosea, Jeremiah, and Ezekiel, provided that one agrees with him that Jer 33:26 is late, which seems to me very likely.[17] According to Römer, the two texts that seem to create a problem for this thesis, Deut 9:27 and 34:4, do not follow the above pattern because of their redactional status, the former being associated with Exodus 32 and Numbers 14 as Deuteronomistic redaction and the latter being associated, along with Gen 50:24, Exod 32:13, 33:1, and Num 32:11, with the *Endredaktion* of the Pentateuch.[18] The fact that the preexilic prophetic collections do not refer to the Abraham tradition lends additional support to Römer's convincing thesis.

N. Lohfink has challenged Römer's conclusions, arguing that some of Deuteronomy's forefather references presuppose the patriarchs and that on other occasions the patriarchal names cannot be deleted without disturbing the text's integrity.[19] While Lohfink makes several fine points, he fails to address one of the more important issues, which is that both the earlier and contemporary sources—Hosea, Jeremiah, and Ezekiel—understood the forefathers to be the exodus generation, and it is this which makes Römer's assertions about Deuteronomy so convincing. This evidence, coupled with the consistent apposition of the father names with אבות, shows that Römer's thesis is probably correct in spite of Lohfink's detailed criticisms. The original "forefathers" of Deuteronomy were none other than the exodus generation and their children who conquered the land of Canaan.[20]

As I will show below during my discussion of the parenesis in Deuteronomy 5–11, these forefathers served an integral role in the Deuteronomic sense of identity. However, I want to discuss for a moment the role of the forefathers in the lawcode proper (Deuteronomy

17. As Römer notes, the text is concerned with the restoration of the Davidic kingship and Levitical priesthood and therefore should probably be associated with the exilic period (ibid., 481).

18. Ibid., 255–65.

19. N. Lohfink, *Die Väter Israels im Deuteronomium* (OBO 111; Göttingen: Vandenhoeck & Ruprecht, 1991). See especially pp. 27–47.

20. My conclusions agree with those previously published by J. Van Seters in *Prologue to History* (Louisville: Westminster, John Knox, 1992) 215–26.

12–26). Here their role is less pronounced but retains the essential parenetic character found in chaps. 5–11. Three elements are represented in this lawcode parenesis. First, Yahweh, as opposed to any other deity, was presented to Israel as the "God of your fathers."[21] This both demonstrated the antiquity of Israel's relationship with Yahweh and exploited the natural affinities of kinship to promote fidelity to Yahweh. He alone was the God of the people. Second, Yahweh's oaths to the fathers, which in the lawcode included promises of land, increased numbers, and mercy, were conditional and predicated on obedience: "None of the devoted things shall cleave to your hand . . . that the Lord may turn from the fierceness of his anger . . . and multiply you, as he swore to your fathers" (Deut 13:17).[22] Third, on one occasion the *nicht-kennen* formula was used with reference to the non-Yahwistic deities. This formula is more prominent in the parenetic introduction but on this occasion served the same polemical role, which was to point out that Israel should follow Yahweh because he was the deity known to the forefathers and, therefore, the proper deity for those who desire to live within the Israelite ancestral tradition. So in the Deuteronomic law, the forefather tradition served as a primary expression of ethnic sentiment and common origins, both in terms of ancestry and in terms of historical experience. The primary purpose of these ethnic expressions in Deuteronomy was to exploit the natural sentiment of kinship as a motivational factor in the effort to promote the Deuteronomic ideal of mono-Yahwistic fidelity. This ethnic forefather tradition comes into clearer focus when the lawcode's old parenetic introduction (chaps. 5–11) is examined.

Ethnicity and Identity in the Parenesis of Deuteronomy 5–11

In the present form of the text, Deuteronomy 5–11 serves as the primary statement of community identity in Deuteronomy. The literary history of this pericope has been explored most completely by N. Lohfink, and his work has yielded conclusions that are considered both definitive (that the Horeb experience and Decalogue are secondary) and speculative (that the basis of chaps. 5–8 rests in a Gilgal covenant text associated with Judg 2:1–5).[23] Part of the continuing

21. See Deut 12:1, 26:3–5.
22. Cf. Deut 19:8; 26:3–5, 15.
23. See N. Lohfink, *Das Hauptgebot,* especially his discussion of the "Gilgal text" on pp. 176–80.

confusion both here and with the rest of Deuteronomy stems from the fact that, although everyone speaks of the *Kern* of Deuteronomy, very little care is given as to whether this core refers to an older Northern edition or rather to the original Josianic Deuteronomy. In other words, even if Lohfink's analysis has successfully uncovered the various *schickten* in the text, these layers are not always associated with particular historical contexts, and this limits the usefulness of his conclusions. Because all of Lohfink's layers in chaps. 5–11 predate the Deuteronomistic additions to the work, I will assume that these chapters substantially reflect the edition of Deuteronomy that we associate with Josiah's reforms. I would like to discuss the vision of community identity put forward by Deuteronomy under six separate headings, as organized below.

The Formula 'Yahweh, Your God' (יהוה אלהיך). It is very easy, given the common translation of יהוה אלהך as 'the Lord your God', to overlook the fact that repetition of this phrase in Deuteronomy 5–11 served the role of emphasizing the personal name of the deity, Yahweh, and his claim to Israel's sole allegiance. In this respect, the traditional translation does grave injustice to the intent of the Deuteronomic legislation, since the central issue in Deuteronomy, as it was in Hosea, was the competition between the God Yahweh and other deities, such as Baal.[24] The Deuteronomic movement was attempting to replace any expressions of what it viewed as religious pluralism with mono-Yahwism, and many themes in Deuteronomy turn out to be ancillary to this main theme. So, for instance, although it is common to focus on the notion of covenant and its importance in Deuteronomy—and it was, no doubt, important—the primary function of the covenant was to promote the Deuteronomic preference for an exclusive relationship with Yahweh. And many phrases used in the book, such as the concept of Israel as a "holy people" and the claim that the people were "set apart" by Yahweh from among "all the peoples on the face of the earth," were designed to emphasize this special and therefore exclusive

24. We should note the work of B. Halpern, who concludes, correctly I think, that in the seventh century the term *Baal* served a collective function and referred, polemically speaking, to all foreign deities ("The Baal [and the Asherah] in Seventh-Century Judah: Yhwh's Retainers Retired," in *Konsequente Traditionsgeschichte: Festschrift für Klaus Baltzer zum 65. Geburtstag* [ed. R. Bartelmus; OBO 126; Göttingen: Vandenhoeck & Ruprecht, 1993] 115–54).

kind of relationship Israel ought to have with its deity. This is not to overlook the obvious fact that beyond the struggle of Yahwism against non-Yahwism there was also a struggle between "pure" Yahwism and corrupted Yahwism (i.e., Yahwism under foreign influence), and we will discuss this issue in more depth later. The influence of other deities, however, was a serious concern for the Deuteronomic party, and it turns out that ethnicity served an important role in their discursive effort to eliminate this religious competition, as we see in the book's use of Israel's forefather traditions.

The Forefathers.   The references to the forefathers, which I have discussed briefly already, were closely tied to the phrase יהוה אלהיך. In Deut 6:3, Yahweh was described as 'the God of your fathers' (יהוה אלהי אבתיך), and on many other occasions the fathers were recipients of oaths sworn by יהוה אלהיך (see Deut 6:10, 7:12, 8:18, 9:5, 10:22).[25] That Yahweh was the God of Israel is therefore reinforced by the long-standing relationship between the deity and the forefathers, and the tie between Yahweh and later generations was accomplished by extending this relationship to the progeny (זרע) of those fathers:

> yet the Lord set his heart in love upon your fathers (באבתיך) and chose their descendants (בזרעם) after them, you above all peoples, as at this day. (Deut 10:15)

So Yahweh had designated Israel as the ethnic community that would receive his love and protection, and this community was to be distinguished from the 'peoples' (עמים) and 'nations' (גוים) on Israel's nearby

25. It is very interesting that this combination occurs outside of Deuteronomy only in Exod 3:13–16; Josh 18:3; 2 Chr 13:12, 28:9, 29:5; Ezra 8:28, 10:11. According to most accounts, all of these texts postdate Deuteronomy except perhaps Exod 3:13–16. Van Seters, who has argued that the J narrative and with it the call of Moses in Exodus 3 are later than Deuteronomy, has recently suggested that the revelation of the divine name in that text was prompted by Ezekiel's claim that God appeared to Israel in Egypt as Yahweh. I would suggest that the revelation actually serves a two-fold purpose, first to solve a conundrum created by Ezekiel, and second, to relate J's narrative more closely to Deuteronomy. Just as the names Abraham, Isaac and Jacob were added to Deuteronomy to bring it into conformity with J, so J's narrative added the "God of the fathers" to connect Abraham, Isaac, and Jacob to the older "fathers tradition" of Hosea and Deuteronomy (Van Seters, *Prologue to History,* 227–45; idem, *The Life of Moses: The Yahwist as Historian in Exodus–Numbers* [Louisville: Westminster/John Knox, 1994] 47).

periphery (Moabites, Ammonites, etc.) by this special and exclusive status in relation to Yahweh. Yahweh was their own God and they were his special people. All of this was clearly an effort to promote Deuteronomy's mono-Yahwistic ideal by employing sentiments of kinship in support of that agenda, a tactic that the proto-Deuteronomic movement (as depicted in Hosea) had already perfected. There were a number of promises made in Deuteronomy to this ethnic community and these were predicated in most cases on Israel's faithfulness to Yahweh. Foremost of these examples would be the deity's promise of an Israelite homeland.

Land Theology.　As I pointed out during my discussion of Hosea, the concept of *land* often plays an important role in ethnic modes of identity. Among Yahweh's oaths in Deuteronomy was a promise to give the forefathers the land that he had sworn to them: "when the Lord your God brings you into the land which he swore to your forefathers" (Deut 6:10). The land's dimensions are provided in the text (11:24) and are said to stretch from the southern wilderness to Lebanon in one direction and from the Euphrates to the Mediterranean in the other.[26] As later texts came into play, these boundaries were represented with increasing precision, so that Dtr in Deut 1:7 attempted to clarify these borders, and the P text of Num 34:2–12 went into even greater detail. More important than the issue of the specific boundaries is the ideology behind Deuteronomy's concept of the land, which I will explore along two lines. First, attention should be given to the question of conditionality of the land-promise theme, and second, the provenience of Deuteronomy's land theology should be assessed.

　　L. Perlitt has attempted to argue that several layers of land theology exist in the book of Deuteronomy and that, furthermore, among these layers is a theology of unconditional land promise in the lawcode of Deuteronomy 12–26. For Perlitt, this idea is found in no other Old

---

26. Mayes, and Buis and Leclercq feel that the מדבר in view here is the Syrian wilderness rather than the dry southern regions of Palestine. However, Deut 1:7, which is clearly a more detailed explication of this text, interprets the מדבר as the נגב and ערבה, and this is also how both Nielsen and Braulik see it (A. D. H. Mayes, *Deuteronomy* [NCBC; Grand Rapids: Eerdmans, 1979] 217; P. Buis and J. Leclercq, *Le Deutéronome* [SB; Paris: Gabalda, 1963] 97; G. Braulik, *Deuteronomium* [2 vols.; Würzburg: Echter, 1986–92] 1.91; Nielsen, *Deuteronomium*, 127).

Testament literary context.[27] But there are serious problems with Perlitt's thesis, because 12:28 warned that the Israelites should 'be careful' to follow the commands outlined in the lawcode, " *in order that* (למען) it may go well with you and your children after you." This text provides us with a paradigm in that the command to "be careful" (שׁמר) can only be meaningful if punishment was envisioned, and the verb was used in this way on seven other occasions in the lawcode proper.[28] Also, the text warns that those who follow the example of the dispossessed nations would be 'utterly destroyed' (חרם; see 13:12–16), which again implies that Israel could lose the land as easily as the primeval inhabitants did. And finally, Hosea's proto-Deuteronomic land theology was clearly conditional, since he envisioned the punishment of Israel via Assyrian deportations. So it is difficult to believe, then, that the oldest levels of Deuteronomy were unconditional.[29] The land theology of the lawcode is clearly conditional, and this is even more explicit in the parenetic sections of Deuteronomy 5–11 (see Deut 8:19–20).

Concerning the provenience of Deuteronomy's land theology, we must begin with observations made in chap. 3 about Hosea and Amos. Hosea's particularism viewed Israel's territory as "Yahweh's land," while Amos had a more universal perspective in which all lands were under Yahweh's authority and were distributed to the corresponding peoples. Another observation was that, for Hosea, the religious corruption of Israel did not take place in Yahweh's land but instead took place on foreign soil during the Baal-Peor incident before Israel's settlement (Hos 9:10). This last feature is at variance with Deuteronomy, where the primary source of corruption was within the land through the influence of its primeval inhabitants. And in Deuteronomy the land was no longer "Yahweh's land" but was given to Israel and so became Israel's land:

> he will give the rain for your land (ארצכם) in its season, the early rain and the later rain, that you may gather in your grain and your wine and your oil. (Deut 11:14)

This was not only true in the parenetic materials of chaps. 5–11 but also in the lawcode proper, as seen in Deut 12:19 and 15:7. Further,

---

27. Perlitt, "Motive und Schichten der Landtheologie im Deuteronomium," *Deuteronomium-Studien* (Tübingen: Mohr, 1994) 108.
28. Cf. Deut 12:1, 32; 16:12; 17:10; 23:23; 24:8; 26:16.
29. My conclusion is in agreement with Van Seters, *Prologue to History,* 229.

although the text is Deuteronomistic and somewhat later, Deuteronomy 2 reflects similar notions, in that Yahweh's "land gifts" extended not only to Israel but also to its neighbors, Edom, Moab, and Ammon. In this respect Deuteronomy's land theology shares more in common with the universalistic perspectives of Amos than with the particularistic views of Hosea.

This should suggest to us something about the date and provenance of Deuteronomy, and we must remember that we are speaking here not only of the parenetic section but also of the earlier lawcode itself. Although the religious polemic is characteristic of Hosea, Deuteronomy's land theology is more like Amos's. Without getting into the form-critical isolation of the various sources, laws, and traditions that lie behind Deuteronomy, some of which could be very old, the best explanation for this similarity is that Deuteronomy's earliest composition should be located among or in conjunction with Northern refugees in Judah sometime after 722 B.C.E. and, given the fact that the language is consistent with Judean Hebrew of the seventh century,[30] the date should probably stand somewhere between the reigns of Hezekiah and Josiah.[31] The combination of Northern and Southern features in the book's land theology are explained by this hypothesis. These observations are important because, as I will show in the next section, they suggest an appropriate Sitz im Leben for some of the text's ethnic traditions.

The History of the People. As I have pointed out previously, a community's sense of history can be a very powerful component of ethnic identity, and this was no doubt true of the Deuteronomic community. Three primary events encapsulate the history of the people in Deuteronomy: the exodus, the wilderness, and the conquest of the land. These are presented as corporate experiences: in the cases of the exodus and wilderness traditions, as experiences of the forefathers; and in the case of the conquest, as the experience of their progeny (זרע). I

30. Mayes, *Deuteronomy*, 81.

31. A. Alt has already proposed that Deuteronomy originated in a Northern renewal movement after the fall of Samaria ("Die Heimat des Deuteronomiums," *Kleine Schriften zur Geschichte des Volkes Israels* [3 vols.; Munich: Beck, 1953–59] 2.250–75).The key difference between us is that, while he locates this Northern renewal movement in the North, I would suggest that it could easily have taken place in the South.

think that, due to the lack of evidence, it is unprofitable to attempt to uncover the origins of the exodus and wilderness stories, both of which may be quite old. But I think there is something that we can say about the conquest tradition and the historical context that may have given rise to it (or, at least, the historical context that made it popular in the time of Deuteronomy).

With the exception of Amos 2:9, the authenticity of which has been questioned, there is a notable absence of the conquest tradition in Hosea, Amos, and Isaiah. This evidence suggests two possibilities. First, if we assume for a moment that Amos 2:9 is an authentic eighth-century tradition, then we must conclude that the origin of the conquest tradition dated prior to the classical Deuteronomic period. But even if this were true, the tradition in Amos that the Amorites were completely destroyed during the conquest is at variance with the account of Deuteronomy, which added other opponents (Hittites, Canaanites, Hivites, etc.) and warned of the threat posed by the foreigners that were not destroyed (cf. Deut 7:1–5). Portions of this text from Deuteronomy are probably later Deuteronomistic additions (vv. 1b–2, 4–5), and this makes it difficult to know whether the additions date to the period just before or during the exile.[32] But from this data it is clear that both Deuteronomy and the Deuteronomists that followed were very interested in the conquest tradition. The second approach is that the text in Amos is redactional and that the conquest tradition actually originated with Deuteronomy. But whether we adopt the first or second approach to the problem, we can speculate that there were contextual issues that made this tradition fit so well into the agendas of the Deuteronomic and Deuteronomistic parties.

During my discussion of land theology in the previous section, I suggested that Alt was onto something when he suggested that the origins of Deuteronomy should be sought in the North, after 722 B.C.E., and I believe that the features of the conquest tradition also make sense in that context. The primeval inhabitants of the land would correspond to the foreign deportees transplanted by Assyria in the North. The conquest theology itself would challenge the remaining Yahwistic power—Judah—to restore the land's purity by evicting these inhabitants and restoring proper Yahwism. The most likely period for these

---

32. Nielsen, *Deuteronomium*, 94–97.

notions to arise would have been during the latter half of the seventh century, when Assyrian power over the west was waning.[33] As the ostracon of Yavneh-yam appears to show (and as the questionable testimony of the Chronicler tells us), Josiah may have taken the challenge of Deuteronomy seriously, since these sources suggest that he extended his control into the North around 630 B.C.E.[34] The influence that gave impetus to these early Deuteronomic materials would seem most likely to have come from the proto-Deuteronomic school of the North. Whether the proper Sitz im Leben should be Yahwistic circles in the North or the influence of Northern refugees in the South is a more difficult question to answer, although I tend toward the latter for this reason: it seems clear that in Deuteronomy there already existed the blend of Israelite and Judean identity that produced the Deuteronomic ideology of the term *all Israel*. I will offer additional comments relating to the provenience of Deuteronomy during my discussion of the 'sojourner (גר) and the 'foreigner' (נכרי).

Ethnic Separatism in Deuteronomy 5–11.   The ethnic component of identity in Deuteronomy's parenetic introduction is quite pronounced, as illustrated by Deut 7:1–3. Here the community was commanded to destroy the land's inhabitants and to practice endogamy. The command to avoid marriage with "Hittites, Girgashites, Amorites," and so on, seems incongruous with both the command to destroy these people and with the fact that none of these peoples seem to have existed in the seventh century B.C.E.[35] What this actually tells us, then, is that the Deuteronomic community had extended the principles of endogamy beyond the primeval inhabitants to the sphere of the surrounding foreigners. The text is hardly clear as to what groups this would have excluded or what exceptions may have existed. Ammonites? Moabites? Egyptians? Edomites also? More clarity is provided in the Deuteronomistic History and perhaps in Deuteronomy 23, and I

33. As suggested by G. von Rad, *Studies in Deuteronomy* (SBT 9; Chicago: Regnery, 1953) 61.

34. See J. C. L. Gibson, *Textbook of Syrian Semitic Inscriptions* (3 vols.; Oxford: Clarendon, 1971–82) 1.26–30. See also J. Naveh, "A Hebrew Letter from the Seventh Century B.C." *IEJ* 10 (1960) 129–39.

35. See chap. 2 above, pp. 34, 88–89, and later in this chapter, p. 273. See also similar comments by B. Schmidt, *Israel's Beneficent Dead* (Winona Lake, Ind.: Eisenbrauns, 1996) 139.

will discuss both of these below.[36] We should not think of these endog-
amous practices as originating with Deuteronomy because, as I pointed
out in chap. 3, they were reflected already in Hosea's criticism of Jacob's Aramean wives. But an even greater error would be to allow the
questions of endogamy and ethnic separatism to distract us from a
more important priority, namely, that these policies had the ultimate
aim of protecting Yahwism from the influence of foreign religious elements. Even in its most ethnic guise—"kill the Canaanites"—Deuteronomic identity was concerned primarily with religious identity rather
than ethnic purity.

"Brother Theology" in Deuteronomy

At this point we turn from the parenesis of Deuteronomy 5–11 to
texts and issues related to the lawcode proper. Certainly some of the
more natural expressions of ethnic sentiment in the book of Deuteronomy are the expressions that refer to the people of Israel as "brothers." The use of אח ('brother'), which occurs 48 times in Deuteronomy,
has been thoroughly examined in an article by L. Perlitt. Perlitt concludes that many uses of the term in Deuteronomy were secondary to
the older core of the book and that this *brotherhood* concept of identity
should be attributed to the creativity of the late seventh-century Deuteronomic movement. Specifically, he sees that in the original Deuteronomic law, as expressed in 13:6 for example, אח referred to one's blood
relatives, while רע ('friend') referred to one's neighbors.[37] However, redactional activity shifted this semantic relationship, so that in Deut
15:2ff., for instance, the addition of אח in apposition to רע moved the
former beyond the range of a blood-relative to the status of *der Nächste*.
Perlitt contends that the redactor made similar changes in conjunction
with אביון ('poor') and עברי ('Hebrew'), so that אח is equated not only
with the neighbor but also with *der Arme* and *der Hebräer*.[38] The primary evidence that supports this conclusion is therefore twofold:
(1) the semantic shift in אח that we have just noted; and (2) the presence of other terms that stand in apposition to אח (עברי, אביו, רע).
    Several texts that are normally attributed to the older core of Deu-
teronomy would at first seem to present a problem for Perlitt's thesis

36. See Judg 3:5, 1 Kgs 11:1–2.
    37. L. Perlitt, "Ein einzig Volk von Brüdern," *Deuteronomium-Studien* (Tü-
bingen: Mohr, 1994) 53–54.
    38. Ibid., 55–57.

(specifically Deut 15:2, 17:15, 23:20–21, and 24:14), since they place אח in opposition to out-groups and therefore imply national brotherhood rather than family consanguinity. Perlitt views these texts as quite different from the redactional use of אח, since for the redactor אח referred to 'Mitmensch', while אח in these texts actually referred to 'Mitisraelit', that is, "The brother in these [texts] is the non-foreigner, the Israelite."[39] However, the distinction that Perlitt sees here is slight, and although one might see fit to entertain his theory of a Deuteronomic *Bruderschicht*, the ethnic sense of brotherhood is clearly visible in the older portions of Deuteronomy:

> Of the foreigner you may exact it [outstanding debt]; but whatever of yours is with your brother your hand shall release. (Deut 15:3)

> You may indeed set a king over you . . . one from among your brethren you shall set as king over you; you may not put a foreigner over you, who is not your brother. (Deut 17:15)

These texts can hardly fail to imply notions of extended kinship and thus of Israelite brotherhood and ethnic sentiment. And there are related considerations that should be noted. First, although Hosea does not manifest *brotherhood* terminology, it does use covenant imagery (which is often rich in brotherhood imagery),[40] and it reflects ethnic sentiments among the Northern peoples. Second, Amos 1:9–11 appears to indicate that Edom was viewed as the "brother" of Israel and as a fellow participant in the ברית אחים, and it is difficult to imagine that Israel could have viewed the Edomite out-group as a brother without prominent notions of indigenous Israelite brotherhood. Third, below I will argue that the "Blessing of Moses" in Deuteronomy 33 reflects notions of brotherhood among the Northern tribal groups. All of this suggests that the ideology of Israelite brotherhood dates well before the era of Josiah's reforms.

Nevertheless, even if part of Perlitt's thesis is correct, I would suggest that Deuteronomy's expressions of ethnic brotherhood may have been amplified and fitted to a new agenda by the Josianic redactor.[41]

39. "Der Bruder ist demnach der Nicht-Ausländer, der Israelit." Ibid., 54, 56–57, 60–61.

40. M. Weinfeld, "Covenant Terminology in the Ancient Near East and Its Influence on the West," *JAOS* 93 (1973) 190–91.

41. The redactor should be identified with the initial redactional activity associated with Josiah's reform effort. This is because the brotherhood ideology of Deuteronomy had a marked influence on the prophetic work of Jeremiah (cf. 9:4, 12:6, 23:35).

The new agenda was vitally concerned with the extension of ethnic brotherhood into the everyday pattern of Judean life, so that natural affiliations of kinship would motivate community members to care for each other:

> And this is the manner of release: every creditor shall release what he has lent to his neighbor; he shall not exact it of his neighbor, his brother, because the Lord's release has been proclaimed. (Deut 15:2)

> If there is among you a poor man, one of your brethren, in any of your towns within your land which the Lord your God gives you, you shall not harden your heart or shut your hand against your poor brother. (Deut 15:7)

Whether we view it as Perlitt's later *Bruderschicht* or as original with the older core of Deuteronomy, the text contains an intentional manipulation of existing ethnic sentiments designed to promote not only the Deuteronomic religious agenda but also its social agenda. The motivations behind this agenda correspond to my notion that the origins of Deuteronomy should be sought in circles that sympathized with the plight of Northerners. First, it calls upon those in the South to accept each other, and also their fellow Yahwists from the North, as brothers. And second, it legislates proper care and compassion toward the less fortunate of these brethren, particularly the Northern refugees. In my view, the fact that brother theology existed already within Northern circles and yet was promulgated so actively in Deuteronomy shows that it was probably a new notion for the Southern Judeans.

The status of these "brethren" and their relationship to Northern refugees and toward non-Israelites is clarified by two issues in the law-code: first, the problem of flesh that "dies of itself" (14:21), and second, the case of a "Hebrew slave" in 15:12–18. These texts help to elucidate the concept of אחים precisely because they focus our attention on those who were not "brothers," namely, the 'sojourner' (גר) and the 'foreigner' (נכרי).

The Sojourner and Foreigner in Deuteronomy 14:21

This text brings several passages into the orbit of our discussion, specifically, texts from the Holiness Code (Lev 17:14–16, 22:8), the Book of the Covenant (Exod 22:31), and Ezekiel (4:12–15, 44:31). These texts relate directly to the whole question of the consumption of the נבלה ('carcass') and will help to clarify the tradition history of the

Deuteronomic statute. But what brings the text into our purview in the first place is that it distinguishes the Israelite from both the 'sojourner' and the 'foreigner' (גר and the נכרי), and this distinction will preoccupy us for the moment.

Implicit in Deut 14:21, which tells Israelites not to eat the נבלה but allows them to give it to the גר or sell it to the נכרי, are three social categories, two of which are close to each other. The first category is the Israelite community, normally represented as the אחים in Deuteronomy, and this category stands in contrast to both the גר ('sojourner') and נכרי ('foreigner'). The Israelites were not permitted to consume the נבלה in question because to do so would threaten the Deuteronomic ideal of "a people holy to the Lord their God."[42] The question that this raises is, in what sense were the גר and נכרי distinguished from each other and in what sense did they share a common status as outsiders? And what was their place within seventh-century Judean society?

D. Kellerman's suggestion regarding the גר is a common one, that a גר is best understood as one who leaves his homeland to place himself under the legal protection of another.[43] But this is a bit more technical than the term actually suggests. Such a sojourner might, of course, have a protected status among a host people, but only if the protection were actually provided (and the need for this legislation suggests that the concept of גר-protection was in question). More likely, the verbal root simply suggests that one had departed from the homeland and was dwelling among another people,[44] with the relative protection, rights, and opportunities afforded by the new conditions varying with the context. C. Bultmann is correct to recognize that in Deuteronomy the sojourner had "no means of gaining and securing their livelihood" and thus filled a rather vulnerable socioeconomic station.[45] This is why

42. This distinction is at variance with the conclusion of M. Rothschild, that the גרים were required to observe Israel's religion because of their presence in the land. This is not entirely the case in Deuteronomy, although the picture changes somewhat in the Holiness Code. See M. Rothschild, "Aliens and Israelites: Part I," *DD* 9 (1981) 196–202.

43. D. Kellerman, "*gēr*," *TDOT* 2.443.

44. BDB 157–58. This definition is in keeping with the conclusions of C. van Houten, *The Alien in Ancient Israelite Law* (JSOTSup 107; Sheffield: JSOT Press, 1991) 19.

45. "[Ü]ber keine Mittel zur Erzielung und Sicherung ihres Lebensunterhalts verfügt." C. Bultmann, *Der Fremde im antiken Juda: Eine Untersuchung zum sozialen Typenbegriff "ger" und seinem Bedeutungswandel in der alttestamentlichen Gesetzgebung* (FRLANT 153; Göttingen: Vandenhoeck & Ruprecht, 1992) 102.

Deuteronomy typically listed the sojourner with the equally piteous widows and orphans (Deut 16:11–14).[46] Another variation of the term גר is represented by the lifestyle of the Rechabites in Jer 35:1–11, who were not so much foreigners within Judah as they were indigenous nomads. In this way, the word גר functioned sociologically, rather than politically and ethnically, as a reference to one's nomadic *Lebensart*.

The גרים mentioned in Deuteronomy were probably of varied origin. Some were foreigners displaced by Assyrian imperialism, some were refugees from the Northern Kingdom, and some were probably of the indigenous, nonsedentary variety. But whatever the case, the curious question is this: why did the statutes of Deuteronomy so energetically protect the foreign גר and at the same time take such a firm stance against foreign peoples and influence in general? This becomes clear only when sufficient attention is given to the function of גר in Deuteronomy and to the historical contexts that gave rise to the text. Although it is common to think of the גר as "an intermediate position between a native (אזרח) and a foreigner (נכרי),"[47] this is a slightly oversimplified perspective. In Deuteronomy the גר could be an Israelite as well as a foreigner (see the Levites in Deut 18:6) and at certain points functioned within the community's religious life, as we see through his or her participation in the festival (חג שבעות) of Deut 16:9–11. At other points the גר was clearly an outsider and so was distinguished from the community, as in our text: "you shall not eat anything that dies of itself . . . you may give it to the alien (גר) . . . or you may sell it to a foreigner" (Deut 14:21). The various uses of גר in Deuteronomy are clarified by Table 4.1. Instead of viewing the גר as a 'resident alien', which has both ethnic and national overtones, we should instead recognize it as a social classification within which one finds both Israelites and non-Israelites. Among the גרים of foreign origin (categories #3 and #4) we find both those who were on the social periphery of the community and were assimilated into it (category #3)[48] and those who

46. We must remember, however, that the meaning of the English word *widow* does not correspond precisely to the Hebrew אלמנה. The former implies only that one has lost a husband, while the latter implies that one has lost a husband and has no family ties, so that the widow has no source of material wealth. See H. J. Boecker, *Law and the Administration of Justice in the Old Testament* (Minneapolis: Augsburg, 1980) 19.

47. Kellerman, "*Gēr*"; de Vaux, *Ancient Israel*, 2.74–75.

48. P. Schmidt has noted that the גר were composed chiefly of migrant guestworkers who were participating within the culture and were being assimilated to it. For

Table 4.1. The "Sojourner in Deuteronomy"

Category	Relation to Community
1. Landed Israelite (אזרו)	In
2. Unlanded Israelite (אחים/גר)	In
3. Non-Israelite on social periphery (גר)	In
4. Non-Israelite in geographical proximity (גר)	Out
5. Foreigner (נכרי)	Out

were foreign but chose to retain an independent sense of identity (category #4). It was the former that participated in the community's religious life and the latter who, like the foreigner, consumed unclean foodstuffs.[49] But even for the גר who sought membership status in the community, the statutes themselves show us that a boundary continued to exist, at least until his or her family's foreign status was concealed by the passage of time.[50]

The 'foreigner' (נכרי) in our text presents us with fewer problems than the גר. C. Bultmann suggests that the נכרי is one whose "origin is from outside the Israelite monarchy."[51] Although this was no doubt true, the minor place of kingship in Deuteronomy suggests that Bultmann is closer to the truth when he says that the נכרי has no natural link to the land and the national God, Yahweh.[52] But the foreigner envisioned here did possess certain ties to the local Judean milieu, as evidenced by his or her participation in the community's economic life.

---

this reason, it is no surprise that the Septuagint would come to view the גר as a 'proselyte' (P. Schmidt, "De Vreemdeling in Israel," *Collationes* 23 [1993] 237–40 [translated for me by George Tous van Neukirk]; de Vaux, *Ancient Israel*, 2.75).

49. For this reason I cannot agree with Weinfeld's suggestion that Deuteronomy's social polarity involves a contrast between אח and גר. Rather, in Deuteronomy, both the Israelite גרים and assimilated גרים would have been considered אחים (*Deuteronomy and the Deuteronomic School* [Oxford: Oxford University Press, 1972; repr., Winona Lake, Ind.: Eisenbrauns, 1997] 229). My conclusions regarding the גר mentioned in Deut 14:21are supported by the work of van Houten: "without a doubt, the alien referred to here is a non-Israelite" (*The Alien in Israelite Law*, 81).

50. J. Milgrom, "Religious Conversion and the Revolt Model for the Formation of Israel," *JBL* 101 (1982) 169–76.

51. "Herkunft von außerhalb der israelitischen Monarchien ist"; Bultmann, *Der Fremde in antiken Juda*, 93.

52. "[K]ein natürliches Band das Land und den Nationalgott Jahwe"; ibid., 100.

The problem addressed by the Deuteronomic law was therefore created by the proximity of the גר and the נכרי to the Israelite community proper, and it would appear that Deuteronomy was able to forge a compromise between its extreme nationalist position and its equally strong humanitarian leanings. This was accomplished by distinguishing between the foreigner who was economically vulnerable (the גר) and the foreigner who was an economically independent figure (the נכרי).[53] However, from a cultic standpoint, the text makes it clear that both foreigners and nonassimilating sojourners were rejected from participation.

This said, we can turn our attention more directly to Deut 14:21. The prohibition against consuming the נבלה is normally connected with the blood taboo of Deut 12:16.[54] The edible flesh was not necessarily wasted, since it could be given away or sold to non-Israelites. We might rightly expect, in light of Deuteronomy's fierce stance toward the land's primeval inhabitants, that this text reflects an aversion toward these non-Israelite groups. But even though the גרים were conceptually linked with the foreigners, they were nonetheless recipients of the free foodstuffs; there was also no apparent malice toward the foreign trading partners. This surprising outcome stems from the community definition provided in the text, that Israel was a "people holy to Yahweh." Deuteronomy was much more concerned with providing a clear definition of the Yahwistic community than it was antagonistic toward "foreigners," either those within Israel or those without. As we have pointed out, the primary distinguisher of identity in the Deuteronomic community was not so much ethnic (although it was) as it was religious, being tied especially to Israel's special status before Yahweh.

How does this data support my thesis that Deuteronomy's origins reflect both Northern and Southern influences after 722 B.C.E.? While a concern for the oppressed "widows and orphans" is characteristic of ancient Near Eastern law,[55] the inclusion of the גר is unique to the Hebrew Bible and does not seem to predate Deuteronomy.[56] This new

53. "Ökonomisch selbständige Gestalt"; Ibid., 102; van Houten, *The Alien in Israelite Law*, 82.

54. Braulik, *Deuteronomium*, 1.108.

55. Boecker, *Law and the Administration of Justice*, 54, 57, 76.

56. See van Houten, *The Alien in Israelite Law*, 34–41. Supposed similarities between the Greek *perioikoi* and *metoikoi* are just that, since neither corresponds very closely to the Hebrew גר. The *perioikoi* were hardly foreigners in the midst of Sparta,

consideration finds its proper context after the fall of Samaria when representatives of the North (and the humanitarian prophets of the South) pushed for legislation to protect the many Northern refugees living in the South. Although sociologically these refugees were גרים, because they were Yahwistic sojourners they were also 'brothers' (אחים). But because of the existential similarities between these Israelite sojourners and the foreign ones, the new protective legislation tended to create a blurred, and therefore permeable, ethnic barrier between them. This open-handed stance toward foreigners is for most scholars, I think, an unexpected surprise in light of Deuteronomy's more general antipathy toward outsiders.

If this legislation was concerned with establishing some sense of boundary between the Israelites on the one hand and the sojourners and foreigners on the other, then it is profitable to ask how long this effort was protracted within the Israelite sources, namely, within the other law collections. In another study, I have attempted to show that one can trace the concerns associated with the biblical נבלה laws chronologically from the D lawcode, through HC and BC, and ending with the P code.[57] My argument can be summarized as follows:

(1) The original law in DC prohibited the consumption of נבלה, presumably because of Deuteronomy's blood taboo. (2) HC altered this law by allowing the consumption of the נבלה so long as those doing so took precautions to prevent the pollution of the temple precinct. But this new policy raised questions about the נבלה that had been torn by unclean carnivores (טרפה), so HC also provided a ruling on this: it could be eaten. (3) BC followed HC in permitting the consumption of the נבלה but took exception with HC's טרפה ruling, which it attempted to overturn by prohibiting טרפה consumption. (4) Not surprisingly, P ignored BC's statute and followed HC's priestly tradition of permitting טרפה/נבלה consumption. However, the P legist recognized a potential problem created by this policy, namely, that the נבלה of altar animals, though unsuitable for the altar, contained fat products which might nonetheless carry a special cultic status. So P clarified the legal position of HC by prohibiting

and the Athenian *metoikoi* were ethnically Greek. See M. M. Austin and P. Vidal-Naquet, *Economic and Social History of Ancient Greece: An Introduction* (Berkeley: University of California Press, 1977) 78–79, 84–85, 95–97; Bultmann, *Der Fremde in antiken Juda*, 28–30.

57. D/DC = Deuteronomic Law Code; HC = Holiness Code; BC = Book of the Covenant; P = Priestly Code.

the consumption of animal fat when the נבלה or טרפה was of a spe-
cies suitable for the altar.[58]

As M. Douglas pointed out long ago, the dietary laws in the Hebrew
Bible served to lay out the indicia of one's participation in the Israelite
ethnic community,[59] and we can trace this problem through the history of the biblical נבלה laws from the preexilic period, through the
early and late exile, into the postexilic period. We see in the biblical
materials a long and healthy legal tradition dedicated to expressing Israelite identity according to the pursuit of ritual cleanliness, represented chronologically by the sources in D, HC, BC, and P.

According to the tenets of ethnic studies proper, an exilic experience should intensify existing ethnic boundaries because of efforts to
preserve group identity, and the above texts seem to sustain this prediction, because HC reflects an intense interest in clarifying the details of
the extant D lawcode, which was itself concerned with ethnic distinctiveness.[60] The law in HC was particularly concerned with clarifying
who came within the scope of the statute. HC at first seems at variance
with DC about this when it suggests that the גר was within the scope
of the dietary mandate, but as my previous discussion of the גר shows,
I do not think that this was the case. Instead, HC was clarifying the
principle that the assimilating גר (in contrast to the nonassimilating
גר) was equally culpable along with other Israelite citizens. This is basically my perspective on DC, because I see in Deuteronomy two different classes of גר, those who were assimilating and those who were not.
Nevertheless, there does seem to be a certain distinctiveness in HC's
perspective because in this law, as elsewhere, HC is very careful to include both the אזרח ('native born') and the גר as participants in Israel's
cultic community. This indicates, I think, that the intensification of
community identity in the early exilic period had the twofold effect of,
on the one hand, closing the ideological gap that separated the Israelites from the גרים who were assimilating to them and, on the other
hand, widening the rift that separated Israel from the nonassimilating

<hr/>

58. K. L. Sparks, "A Comparative Study of the Biblical נבלה Laws" *ZAW* 110
(1998; forthcoming).

59. On the close association of ritual purity and boundary maintenance, see
M. Douglas, *Purity and Danger: An Analysis of Concepts of Pollution and Taboo* (New
York: Praeger, 1966); D. L. Smith, *The Religion of the Landless: The Social Context of the
Babylonian Exile* (Bloomington: Meyer Stone, 1989) 139–51.

60. Ibid., 49–92.

sojourners (תושב). [61] As we will see, many of the patterns that we have observed in our discussion of the biblical נבלה laws apply also to the slave laws of the Hebrew Bible.

The Hebrew Slave in Deuteronomy 15:1–18

Scholarly interest in Deut 15:1–18 has generally been overshadowed by fascination with its parallel in Exod 21:1–11. This is primarily because the text from BC has been considered much older and because it is thought that the word עברי is not used as an ethnic term but as a sociological designation in Exodus 21. These facts suggest a link between עברי and the second-millennium B.C.E. sociological class known as the Ḥapiru, and this link is in turn believed to reveal something about the origins of ancient Israel. But all of this is predicated on the idea that Deuteronomy is later than and dependent upon BC, and my previous discussion of Deut 14:21 suggests that BC may postdate both Deuteronomy and HC. I will attempt to demonstrate that this chronological relationship also holds for Deut 15:1–18 and BC. Because עברי is clearly an ethnic rather than sociological designation in Deuteronomy 15, a successful venture on my part will establish that the term is also an ethnic designation in Exodus 21. This would make it difficult to establish a discernible connection between the ethnic term עברי and the second-millennium sociological term Ḥapiru.

With regard to the chronological relationship between the Hebrew slave texts in Deuteronomy 15 and Exodus 21, G. C. Chirichigno's recent monograph is representative of most studies that assume that the law in BC is older. [62] A notable exception to this trend is the discussion

---

61. M. Weinfeld has pointed out that while D was concerned primarily with the purity of the people, HC added an intense concern for the purity of the land, which of course necessitated the purity of everyone in the land, both natives and sojourners (*Deuteronomy and the Deuteronomic School,* 225–32). While this is partially true, why then did HC not bring the נכרי ('foreigners') under the scope of the law? The reason is that the statute in HC is concerned primarily with clarifying the boundaries that define the community.

62. G. C. Chirichigno, *Debt-Slavery in Israel and the Ancient Near East* (JSOTSup 141; Sheffield: JSOT Press, 1993). One can add to this list E. Otto, "Aspects of Legal Reforms and Reformulations in Ancient Cuneiform and Israelite Law," in *Theory and Method in Biblical and Cuneiform Law* (ed. B. M. Levinson; JSOTSup 181; Sheffield: JSOT Press, 1994) 160–96; F. Crüsemann, *The Torah: Theology and Social History of Old Testament Law* (Minneapolis: Fortress, 1996) 154–59. Crüsemann's sentiment is a common one: "Every study of the so-called Book of the Covenant (Exod 20:22–23:33)

of O. Loretz, who has argued that the law from BC (at least in its final form) should be associated with the postexilic period, suggesting that it was inspired by the earlier law from DC.[63] But in doing so, Loretz has put a great deal of weight on a presumed dependence of BC's law on the supposedly late sabbath institution, and it seems to me that there is no necessary dependence of the seventh-year release in Exodus 21 on such a general sabbath observance. There are perhaps better arguments for dating the BC law after DC, and here we can outline a few of them in a preliminary way. In the first place, I would suggest that the law in Exodus makes the most sense if it is read in light of the "brother theology" that, I have argued, originated with the Deuteronomic code and had its appropriate Sitz im Leben in the period after the fall of Samaria, when efforts were made to unify the Yahwistic peoples in the North and the South. After all, it does seem that the pentateuchal Yahwist already presumed this "brother theology" in his narrative work (cf. Exod 2:11), and this might suggest that the Yahwist was in fact dependent upon Deuteronomy. If this were true, the term עברי would everywhere be an ethnic one rather than a remnant of the sociological group known as the Ḥapiru.[64] That this is the proper conclusion is reinforced by a comparative study of the two laws (as Van Seters has recently demonstrated)[65] and by the fact that עברי itself was probably not an ancient term that developed from Ḥapiru but was instead, as I will try to show, a rather late development.

Now the fact that עברי functions as an ethnic term is nowhere more apparent than in Deuteronomy, where the text's ethnically-charged "brother theology" is linked in Deut 15:12 directly to the

---

can begin with the following assertions, which are recognized today as indisputable facts. . . . The Book of the Covenant is older than Deuteronomy and so is the oldest law book in the Old Testament" (p. 109).

63. See O. Loretz, *Habiru-Hebräer: Eine sozio-linguistische Studie über die Herkunft des Gentiliziums ʿibri vom Appellativum habiru* (BZAW 160; Berlin: de Gruyter, 1984) 122–46.

64. If BC postdates D and if עברי is an ethnic term in D, then it should without doubt be viewed as an ethnic term in BC. However, even those who accept the priority of BC sometimes conclude that עברי is an ethnic term in Exodus 21. See A. Alt, *Kleine Schriften zur Geschichte des Volkes Israel* (3 vols.; Munich: Beck, 1953–59) 1.278–332; Chirichigno, *Debt-Slavery in Israel and the Ancient Near East*; A. Levy-Feldblum, "The Law of the Hebrew Slave: The Significance of Stylistic Differences," *Beth Mikra* 31 (1985–86) 348–59.

65. J. Van Seters, "The Law of the Hebrew Slave," *ZAW* 108 (1996) 534–46.

עברי designation: 'your brother (אחיך), a Hebrew man (העברי) , or a Hebrew woman (העבריה)'. But if, as I am suggesting, עברי does not find its origins with the Ḥapiru, can anything more be said about the term's provenience outside of pointing out that it was an "ethnic" term?[66] It is very interesting to notice that the distribution of the term עברי in the Hebrew Bible is quite restricted. It is found primarily in the Joseph novella of Genesis 37–50, the Exodus narrative of Exodus 1–10, and the "Philistine narratives" of 1 Samuel.[67] The term also occurs in Gen 14:13 and Jonah 1:9. Perhaps this sparse representation does not stem from the term's antiquity as an almost forgotten ethnic term but from the fact that it developed later than many portions of the biblical materials. As O. Loretz has concluded, "the biblical sources for עברי are all to be dated in the postexilic period,"[68] and the term 'Hebrew' as a reference to Palestine/Israel does not show up in the extrabiblical materials until the Egyptian Saite/Persian period (664–500

66. Extensive bibliography is available on this subject. In addition to the sources cited below, see also the following: M. Anbar, "Le pays des Hébreux," *Or* 41 (1972) 383–86; M. Astour, "Le étrangers à Ugarit et le statut juridique de Habiru," *RA* 53 (1959) 70–76; R. Borger, "Das Problem der ʿapiru," *ZDPV* 74 (1958) 121–32; I. Cardellini, *Die biblischen "Skalven"-Gesetze im Lichte des keilschriftlichen Sklavenrechts* (BBB 55; Bonn: Hanstein, 1981) 243–51; M. P. Gray, "The Habirû-Hebrew Problem in the Light of the Source Material Available at Present," *HUCA* 29 (1958) 135–202; N. P. Lemche, "The Hebrew Slave: Comments on the Slave Law Ex. XXI 2–11," *VT* 25 (1975) 129–44; H. Parzen, "The Problem of the Ibrim in the Bible," *AJSL* 49 (1932/33) 254–61; D. B. Redford, "The 'Land of the Hebrews' in Gen XL 15," *VT* 15 (1965) 529–31; J. A. Soggin, "Heber der Qenit: Das Ende eines biblischen Personennamens," *VT* 31 (1981) 89–92; W. R. Wifall, "The Tribes of Yahweh: A Synchronic Study with a Diachronic Title," *ZAW* 95 (1983) 207–9.

67. Gen 39:14, 17; 40:15; 41:12; 43:32; Exod 1:15–19; 2:6–13; 3:18; 5:3; 7:16; 9:1, 13; 10:3; 1 Sam 4:6–9; 13:3, 7, 19; 14:11, 21; 29:3.

68. "[D]ie biblischen Belege für עברי sind alle in die nachexilische Zeit zu datieren"; I cannot offer a complete defense of this position within the scope of this work and so rely here on the efforts of others. In general, see Loretz, *Hapiru-Hebräer*. On Genesis 14, see J. Van Seters, *Abraham in History and Tradition* (New Haven: Yale University Press, 1975) 296–308. Even C. Westermann, who sees in the text some very ancient material, confesses that the present form of chap. 14 betrays its postexilic influence (*Genesis* [3 vols.; Minneapolis: Augsburg, 1985] 2.192). On the Joseph story, see D. B. Redford's very convincing arguments in *A Study of the Biblical Story of Joseph* (VTSup 20; Leiden: Brill, 1970). On the narratives of 1 Samuel, see pp. 346–53 of J. Van Seters, *In Search of History: Historiography in the Ancient World and the Origins of Biblical History* (New Haven: Yale, 1983; repr., Winona Lake, Ind.: Eisenbrauns, 1997). On the Exodus narratives, see Van Seters's recent work on the J narrative in *Prologue to History* and *The Life of Moses*.

B.C.E.).[69] Afterward, the term "Land of the Hebrew" was employed until the Roman period by various authors in reference to Palestine.[70] Is it a coincidence that the late Egyptian sources refer to Palestine as ʿybr and that the contemporary Hebrew texts consistently put this description in the mouths of foreigners, both Egyptians and Philistines?[71] What seems most likely is that the term עברי was an exonym borrowed by Israel from the surrounding peoples, especially Egypt, who used the term to refer to the region in which Israel lived.[72] In my view, the terminology probably arose from the name given by foreigners to the language used by the Israelites. This would explain why Israel's speech was labeled 'Hebrew', a term that seems to have no clear connection with either Judah or Israel. And although this perhaps brings us closer to solving the problem of עברי and its origins, it leaves us with the still-unsolved problem of the term's etymology, a problem that has consistently eluded an unequivocal solution.[73] But the suggestions offered here seem to explain both the lateness of the term and also its relative paucity in the biblical sources.

In light of this discussion, it becomes all the more attractive to consider the possibility that Deuteronomy 15 is our earliest witness to the use of עברי in the ancient sources. We can test this by assuming the priority of DC and seeing how the discussion goes. First, why was עברי used in Deuteronomy and why in conjunction with the term

69. Following Redford in this conclusion are M. Weippert, *Die Landnahme der israelitischen Stämme in der neueren wissenschaftlichen Diskussion* (FRLANT 92; Göttingen: Vandenhoeck & Ruprecht, 1967); and R. Giveon, "Hapiru," *LÄ* 2.952–55.

70. Redford, *A Study of the Biblical Story of Joseph*, 201–2.

71. As has been observed by N. P. Lemche, "The Hebrew and the Seven Year Cycle," *BN* 25 (1984) 68; see F. A. Spina's similar observation, in "Israelites as *gerim*, 'Sojourners,' in Social and Historical Context," *The Word of the Lord Shall Go Forth: Essays in Honor of David Noel Freedman in Celebration of His Sixtieth Birthday* (ed. C. L. Meyers and M. O'Connor; Winona Lake, Ind.: Eisenbrauns, 1983) 331.

72. Lemche suggests that the term *Hebrew* cannot be a late ethnic designation for Jews because it "is never used of postexilic Jews in the sections of the OT which expressly refer to this period." What he fails to notice is that this is precisely because the term is an exonym which Jews would be prone to use only when describing themselves in the mouths of others (N. P. Lemche, "The Hebrew and the Seven Year Cycle," 68).

73. Whether ultimately true or not, the common suggestion that עברי is related to the root עבר 'to go across' supports the notion of an exonym. Exonyms are generally coined in geographical and spatial terms. For other ideas on etymology, see R. J. Williams, "Review of R. A. Parker, *A Vienna Demotic Papyrus on Eclipse- and Lunar-Omina*," *JNES* 25 (1966) 69; Redford, *A Study of the Biblical Story of Joseph*, 201; and, of course, see Loretz, *Habiru-Hebräer*.

'brother' (אח)? As discussed above (p. 237), elsewhere in Deuteronomy אח was apposed to 'neighbor' (רע) and 'poor' (אביו) in an effort to employ ethnic sentiments in support of community solidarity
under Yahweh. The neighbor is a brother. The poor man beside you is
a brother. And similarly, it may be that Deuteronomy 15 has apposed
this brother theology with עברי in an effort to say, "the Hebrew, the
one who speaks your language, is your brother." In this way Deuteronomy brings into the discussion of ethnic boundaries one of the
more common ethnic markers, language. It is difficult to say precisely
how this might have worked. On the one hand, the Hebrew, Moabite,
Ammonite, and Phoenician languages were virtually identical. On the
other hand, dialectal differences may be observed between these languages and even within them, as the "shibboleth" text of Judg 12:6
shows.[74] So it is quite possible that dialectal features served to distinguish Israelites and Judeans from other peoples. I cannot stress enough,
however, the minor role that this probably would have played, given
West Semitic linguistic similarities. Furthermore, we must reckon with
the possibility that by the time Deuteronomy used the term עברי, its
semantic range had already extended beyond its original linguistic
denotation.

The distinction made between the Hebrew slave and the non-
Hebrew in this text is quite pronounced and brings us to the discussion
of the way the groups on each side of the ethnic boundary were treated.
The law in vv. 1–3 extended debt relief to all Israelites on a seven-year
cycle but excluded foreigners from the benefit. Similarly the manumission of slaves during the seventh year (vv. 12–18) was for Hebrews
only, implying that perpetual slavery was the lot of foreign slaves. We
may conclude that the laws were enacted to protect members of the
ethnic community. The problems that arose in connection with the
slave release in Jeremiah 34 show that this statute was both new (at
least in its implementation) and unpopular, and this fact should serve
to remind us that Deuteronomy's vision of Israel's ethnic community
was in truth a visionary ideal that many resisted. And this law was
perhaps easy to resist because, as Van Seters has pointed out, it was
composed more as a moral prescript to be implemented within the

---

74. See Gibson, *Syrian Semitic Inscriptions*, 1.5–8, 21–22; F. M. Cross and D. N.
Freedman, *Early Hebrew Orthography: A Study of the Epigraphic Evidence* (AOS 36;
New Haven, Conn.: American Oriental Society, 1952).

household rather than as a legal statute that would be enforced in the public forum.[75] The public setting of the manumission "covenant" described in Jer 34:15 was designed precisely to address this problem, but it ultimately failed to do so because there were no statutes to prevent reenslavement after manumission. As Van Seters points out, this problem was finally addressed in a definitive way by BC, which required that the ritual ear-piercing become a public ceremony at the Temple: "then his master shall bring him to God, and he shall bring him to the door or the doorpost; and his master shall bore his ear through with an awl; and he shall serve him for life" (Exod 21:6).[76] One can discern here a clear sense of progress in the effort to protect slaves within the ethnic community as the statutes moved from the original household law of DC, to a more public effort in Jeremiah, to an even more public effort on the part of the BC legist. Thus the proper order of the tradition here should be traced from DC through Jeremiah to BC.[77]

How might HC fit into this picture? As was the case with the נבלה, so too with the slave, we see that HC reflects an exilic intensification of ethnic sentiment. While Deuteronomy decreed manumission for Israelite slaves after six years, HC expanded the legislation to prescribe proper treatment of the slave before the time of manumission: "if your brother (אחיך) becomes poor . . . and sells himself to you, you shall not make him serve you as a slave" (Lev 25:39).[78] Instead of serving under the harshness of slave-like conditions (v. 46), the fellow Is-

75. Van Seters, "The Law of the Hebrew Slave," 535.
76. Ibid., 541.
77. As I pointed out in chap. 3, concern for social justice was a characteristic of the eighth-century Southern prophetic tradition. In Deuteronomy, the emphasis on social justice appears to stem from a combination of Southern and Northern influences. The concern for displaced Levites and other Northern גרים stems from Northern influence, but the basic and fundamental concern for "widows and orphans" is characteristic of the Southern prophetic tradition. For a discussion of social justice in Deuteronomy as it relates to this text, see J. M. Hamilton, *Social Justice and Deuteronomy: The Case of Deuteronomy 15* (SBLDS 136; Atlanta: Scholars Press, 1992).
78. Although HC says that manumission was to take place in the year of Jubilee, which would involve almost a lifetime of slave service, not six years, I view the Jubilee tradition as late and so assume agreement between the original HC law and the present text. The primary arguments for this are three: (1) the Jubilee tradition does not appear in any preexilic texts; (2) the Jubilee year appears to find its contextual home in Nehemiah's reforms (see Nehemiah 5), which are late; (3) the distinction made in HC between Israelites and foreigners makes little sense in the context of the Jubilee system. For concurring arguments, see Levine, *Leviticus*, 272–74; van Houten, *The Alien in Israelite Law*, 128.

raelite (אָחִיךָ) would serve as a hired servant (שָׂכִיר) and as a sojourner (here, תּוֹשָׁב).[79] The law itself presupposes that the community of Israel was not accustomed to distinguishing between the treatment of native slaves and non-Israelite slaves. So once again we are dealing, as in Deuteronomy, with an ideal picture of the community as conceptualized by those who produced HC, a community that embraced ethnic sentiments more deeply than the broader community that it hoped to influence. Having defended the ethnic kin from the harshness of their brethren, HC proceeded to address the additional problem that some Israelite slaves were not protected by the legislation because they were indentured to foreigners; that is, they were indentured to those who lacked the fundamental ethnic sentiments necessary to motivate proper treatment of the Israelite slave (25:47).[80] In such cases, the brother, uncle, cousin, or nearest kinsmen was responsible for freeing the indentured relative.[81] In this way HC attempted to clarify and extend the benefits of community membership as outlined in Deuteronomy. But the HC legist was not content with this effort to protect members within the community, for he also made a serious effort to clarify the actual parameters that defined community membership.

HC closely follows the pattern of Deuteronomy when it distinguishes between the 'surrounding nations' (הגוים סביבתיכם) and the 'sojourners' (התושב הגרים עמכם), on the one hand, and the ethnic 'brothers' (אחים) of Israel on the other (Lev 25:44–45). But there is a further development of this "sojourner" identity in HC that goes beyond the one provided by Deuteronomy. In Deuteronomy there was a threefold social classification scheme—brother, sojourner, and foreigner (נכרי/גר/אח)—in which the term גר served a dual semantic role, referring to both assimilating foreigners and nonassimilating foreigners. This situation is altered in HC, where the assimilated foreigner was

79. Van Houten has concluded that תּוֹשָׁב and גר are virtually synonymous in the Hebrew Bible (cf. Gen 23:4), however, she also concludes that in P the גר represented the permanent foreign resident while the תּוֹשָׁב referred to the temporary foreign resident (*The Alien in Israelite Law*, 125–26). In my view, the relationship is a bit more complicated than this, as I will show below.

80. Notice the absence of both גוי and נכרי in the statute. This is no doubt because, as outsiders, they could not fall under the jurisdiction of Israelite law.

81. The text's implicit connection between ethnic identity and the more narrow sphere of familial kinship conforms—as in Deuteronomy—to the sociobiological view of ethnic identity, which suggests that ethnicity is a rather natural extension of kinship. See Richard H. Thompson, *Theories of Ethnicity: A Critical Appraisal* (New York: Greenwood, 1989) 21–48.

designated גר and the nonassimilated foreigner תושב. That this was
the case becomes evident when we consider the following. First, I cannot agree with van Houten that the תושב was a temporary foreign resident in contrast to the גר, a permanent foreign resident. According to
Lev 25:45, the תושב could refer to people born in Israel's land, which
does not suggest a temporary residence status. Second, while at several
points HC suggests that the גר be treated as the native אזרח (Lev
19:34, 24:22) this was never true of the תושב. Third, the גר was consistently presented together with the native Israelite as part of the religious community,[82] as is particularly clear from Lev 20:2: "Say to the
people of Israel, any man from the people of Israel or of the strangers
(גר) that sojourn in Israel. . . ." In contrast, the תושב was never represented as a community participant and was, in fact, viewed as an outsider (זר) in Lev 22:10–13. So it is plainly evident that, although the
תושב and גר shared a common identity as foreigners in the midst of Israel (Lev 25:47), the two terms were significantly different for HC.
The intensification of ethnic sentiments that accompanied the exilic
situation required that a rhetorical distinction be created between
assimilating foreigners and nonassimilating foreigners, and this was
accomplished by preserving the term גר, which was becoming synonymous with our word 'proselyte',[83] and by coining a new term, תושב,
which served to identify foreigners who were merely residing (ישב)
within the community.[84] That this linguistic distinction originated at
the time of HC (and most likely with HC) is suggested by the fact that

82. Members of the Israelite community or the community itself are variously described as אזרח, בני־ישראל, and בית־ישראל. See Lev 16:29; 17:7, 10, 12, 13, 15;
18:26; 19:34; 20:2; 22:18; 24:16; 25:23.

83. By *proselyte* I mean only that a non-Israelite has assimilated to the Israelite
community as defined by the literature in question. In light of this, the recent conclusion of Rendtorff that the גר was "a person who lives more or less permanently among
the Israelites but does not become one of them" appears too simple. See his otherwise
helpful discussion in "The *Gēr* in the Priestly Laws of the Pentateuch," in *Ethnicity and
the Bible* (ed. M. G. Brett; Biblical Interpretation Series 19; Leiden: Brill, 1996) 77–87.

84. M. Smith briefly discusses the semantic development of גר from its early
meaning, 'resident alien', to its later meaning in the HC, 'proselyte'. However, he fails
to see that גר was beginning to serve a proselyte function already in Deuteronomy. But
it was the development of the term תושב by HC that actually served to limit the semantic range of גר to 'proselyte'. Although failing to see the development of גר and
תושב as outlined here, in an older study T. J. Meek recognized that גר was taking on
the meaning of 'proselyte' in HC ("The Translation of *Gēr* in the Hexateuch and Its
Bearing on the Documentary Hypothesis," *JBL* 49 [1930] 172–80).

all other uses of תושב are postexilic.[85] Regarding other texts, the BC corpus deals only with the question of the oppressed גר, אלמנה, and יתום and does not add very much to our discussion of תושב; however, it is interesting that Genesis 23, which brings Abraham into very close relations with the Canaanites and Hittites, used the term תושב—'non-assimilating sojourner'—to describe the forefather.[86] This is best understood as P's effort to modify an older tradition by placing some rhetorical distance between Abraham and the 'people of the land' (עם־הארץ).

The Status and Treatment of Foreigners in Deuteronomy 23:4–8

The distinction between Israelites and foreigners moves beyond the various statutory differences that we have discussed to a kind of ethnic separatism, as expressed in Deut 23:4–8:

> No *Ammonite or Moabite shall enter the assembly* (קהל) of the Lord; even to the tenth generation none belonging to them shall enter the assembly of the Lord forever; because they did not meet you with bread and with water on the way, when you came forth out of Egypt, and because they hired against you Balaam the son of Beor from Pethor of Mesopotamia, to curse you. Nevertheless the Lord your God would not hearken to Balaam; but the Lord your God turned the curse into a blessing for you, because the Lord your God loved you.

Three important questions are raised by the text. First, what is the 'assembly of Yahweh' (קהל יהוה), and does such a concept easily fit into the preexilic context? Second, why does the text distinguish between Edom/Egypt on the one hand and Ammon/Moab on the other? Third, if one attributes this text to the Deuteronomic code, how does its separatism square with the code's statutory support for the assimilating foreigner, the גר? I will adopt, as a starting point, C. Bultmann's recent monograph, which includes a thorough examination of this text. Regarding the problem of Ammonite/Moabite exclusion from the

---

85. Gen 23:4, Exod 12:45, Num 35:15, 1 Chr 25:15, Ps 39:13. The three pentateuchal texts are all from P, the Chronicler is postexilic, and according to Anderson, Psalm 39 is generally dated to the Persian period (A. A. Anderson, *Psalms* [2 vols.; NCBC; Grand Rapids: Eerdmans, 1972] 1.308).

86. The fact that Gen 23:4 refers to Abraham as a גר and a תושב does not negate my thesis. The term גר exhibits much greater lexical elasticity and is not as limited to the translation of 'proselyte' as the term תושב is to 'nonassimilating resident alien'.

assembly, Bultmann has concluded that, not only are the "historical-ethical" explanations provided in vv. 4–5 later additions, as has long been suggested,[87] but the entire Ammonite/ Moabite issue finds its contextual home in Neh 13:1–3: "no Ammonite or Moabite should enter the assembly of God" (קהל אלהים).[88] This would make the Ammonite/Moabite exclusions quite late. But Bultmann also sees evidence in both Deuteronomy and Lam 1:10 that a preexilic קהל יהוה did exist and that the exclusions placed on Edomites and Egyptians originated with Deuteronomy.[89] From this he concludes that the original statute concerned the terms under which Edomites and Egyptians could be included within the religious community, while a postexilic addition to the text permanently excluded Ammonites and Moabites.

There are several problems with this conclusion. First, the text in Nehemiah 13 was concerned not so much with Ammonites and Moabites as with the exclusion of foreigners in general: ויבדילו כל־ערב מישראל.[90] In other words, one can imagine the derivation of Nehemiah's ideas from ideas in Deuteronomy much more easily than one can imagine a postexilic redactor summarizing an antiassimilationist policy by adding specific references to Ammon and Moab in the assembly laws of Deuteronomy. I conclude from this that Deuteronomy 23's permanent exclusion (עד־עולם) of Ammon and Moab predates Nehemiah 13, and this establishes a terminus ad quem for the text during the middle of the fourth century B.C.E. Second, Bultmann's conclusion that the Egypt/Edom exclusions are older than the Ammonite/Moabite is doubtful because the Egypt/Edom exclusions are in fact not independent קהל exclusions. They are more properly viewed as modifications of the Ammonite/Moabite law and assume a period in which the Ammonite/Moabite exclusions had become a generalized exclusion of all foreigners—including Edomites and Egyptians. The most likely context for this would have been after Nehemiah's day, when the Ammon/Moab exclusion was interpreted in just this general fashion and

87. His evidence for this is the text's obvious relationship to Deuteronomy 1–4, which is a later addition to the original Deuteronomy, as well as the shifts in form of address that are present in the text (Mayes, *Deuteronomy*, 316–17).

88. See Bultmann, *Der Fremde im antiken Juda*, 103–19.

89. Ibid., 104, 119. Bultmann concludes that קהל יהוה "eine aktuelle Versammlung meint und nicht Gesamtbegriff für das Jahwevolk ist." He therefore assigns the Edomite/Egyptian exclusion to the seventh century B.C.E.

90. J. Blenkinsopp, *Ezra–Nehemiah* (OTL; Philadelphia: Westminster, 1988) 350–52.

when the large diaspora population in Egypt prompted a softening of Judean policy toward its southern neighbors. But notice the negative command, 'do not abhor' (לא־תעב), which is a rather subdued prescription in comparison with the Deuteronomic charge to 'love the sojourner' (ואהבתם את־הגר; see 10:19).[91] In this postexilic context, a certain rhetorical distance was preserved between ethnic Israel and its neighbors, even when the objective was to establish a "relaxed" stance toward them.

So far, this leads us to the conclusion that the Ammonite/Moabite exclusions predated Nehemiah and that the Edomite/Egyptian modification of the law postdated Nehemiah. But how much earlier than Nehemiah did the exclusions date? This brings us to Lam 1:9–10, a text that bemoans the trespass of the 'assembly' (קהל) by foreigners, and that is normally dated either just prior to the exile or just after its beginning.[92]

> O Lord, behold my affliction, for the enemy has triumphed! The enemy has stretched out his hands over all her precious things; yea, she has seen the nations (גוים) invade her sanctuary (מקדשה), those whom thou didst forbid to enter thy congregation (קהל לך).

As Hillers has noted, "the command referred to . . . is obviously Deut 23:3[4H], in view of the close verbal agreement."[93] The similar features between this text and the Deuteronomic statute are rather pronounced:

Lam 1:10:	בקהל לך	צויתה לא־יבאו
Deut 23:4:	לא־יבא עמוני ומואבי בקהל יהוה	

The verb צוה suggests that Lamentations has legal materials in mind, of which Deuteronomy 23 would be the most likely candidate. According

---

91. Lohfink suggests that this is a later addition to the present context due to its affinity for 10:18. Although this may be true, it is characteristic of Deuteronomic ideology and, as Mayes suggests, it is probably an old formulation (Lohfink, *Das Hauptgebot*, 223; Mayes, *Deuteronomy*, 211).

92. W. Rudolph says that the absence of references to the destruction of Jerusalem and the Temple in Lamentations 1 suggests a date sometime between 597 and 586 B.C.E. D. Hillers, on the other hand, dates the text just after the exile (W. Rudolph, *Das Buch Ruth, Das Hohe Lied, Die Klagelieder* [KAT 17; Gütersloh: Mohn/Gütersloher Verlagshaus, 1962]; D. Hillers, *Lamentations* [rev. ed.; AB 7A; Garden City, N.Y.: Doubleday, 1992] 9–10; C. Westermann, *Lamentations: Issues and Interpretation* [Minneapolis: Fortress, 1994] 130–31).

93. Hillers, *Lamentations*, 25.

to Bultmann, this evidence supports the conclusion that Deuteronomy's assembly law should be dated no later than the early exile, that
is, to the date of Lamentations. Two recent commentators on Lamentations, however, would question this conclusion. I. Provan has pointed
out that "the allusion to illegal entry into the temple could be understood in relation to the events of 597, 587 or 167 B.C.," and O. Kaiser
has suggested that Lamentations 1 might date as late as the fourth century B.C.E.[94] On the basis of our evidence, this conclusion is sound, for
Lam 1:10 has interpreted the Deuteronomic statute as a general exclusion of foreigners, and this would seem to be most closely associated
with the time of Nehemiah, or at least closer to it. Lam 1:10 cannot
therefore serve as evidence of an early Yahwistic 'assembly' (קהל). We
must instead try to identify a point at which the original Ammonite/
Moabite assembly exclusion might have arisen.

We have determined that the Ammon/Moab exclusion dates before Nehemiah, and the fact that Deuteronomy was very supportive of
assimilating foreigners (גרים) suggests that the law originated in a context that lay somewhere between the classical Deuteronomic period
and Nehemiah. I would suggest that the most suitable context would
have been soon after the exile's conclusion, when the various groups of
returnees attempted to reestablish a common context for worship, the
קהל. These groups returned to their ancestral lands and found that in
some cases they had been dispossessed by foreigners, particularly by the
Transjordanian peoples (cf. Jer 49:1–3). In this context, the Ammo-
nite/Moabite exception was necessitated precisely because the exiles
were faced with two conflicting circumstances: on the one hand, a legal
tradition that looked favorably upon assimilating foreigners; and on
the other hand, a situation in which specific foreigners—Ammonites
and Moabites—were a threat to the future of the community. The result was the assembly exclusion of Deut 23:3, to which vv. 4–5 were
subsequently added at some later point to explain the exclusion when
the original context that prompted it was forgotten.

The cultic exclusions of the Moabites and Ammonites were added
to a previously existing statute that excluded 'bastards' (ממזר) from the
assembly. The rare Hebrew term is an Aramaic loanword of the same

94. O. Kaiser, "Klagelieder," in *Das Hohelied, Klagelieder, Das Buch Ester: Über-*
setzt und erklärt (Göttingen: Vandenhoeck & Ruprecht, 1992) 104–9; I. Provan, *Lam-*
entations (NCBC; Grand Rapids, Mich.: Eerdmans, 1991) 13.

meaning and at once brings to mind the בנים זנונים ('sons of harlotry') and זרים בנים ('strange sons') described in Hosea 2 and 5. Braulik correctly surmises, along with Mayes, that these children were born of "foreign" cultic activities and were thereby the progeny of a foreign deity.[95] One potential threat to such illicit activity would therefore have been the "excommunication" of the resulting offspring. This analysis corresponds to the proto-Deuteronomic thought expressed in Hosea and fits well in the present literary context of Deuteronomy 23. Here again we see the powerful antipathy of the Deuteronomic community toward foreign cultic activity and also toward those who, by association with it, become "foreigners." In sum, the growth of the assembly exclusions in Deuteronomy 23 may be represented as follows: first, the religious exclusion of people involved in foreign cults; second, the ethnic exclusion of Ammonites and Moabites; third, the logical extension of the Ammonite/Moabite exclusion to all foreigners; and finally, an attempt to promote ethnic inclusion by providing special allowances for Egyptians and Edomites.

The Primeval Inhabitants as the Rhetorical Other

Up to this point, the "foreigners" I have discussed—Ammonites, Moabites, Edomites, and Egyptians—should be classified as "objective others"—in other words, as part of an actual social category that existed in the world of the Israelite community and from which the community felt a need to distinguish itself. Similar in certain respects but distinctly different in others is Deut 7:1–5, which commands the total annihilation of Palestine's original inhabitants (Hittites, Girgashites, Amorites, Canaanites, Perizzites, Hivites, and Jebusites) and prohibits marriages and covenants with them.[96] Mayes hints at the difference when he says, "The reference [to Hittites] is something of a problem, for the historical Hittite empire of the Late Bronze Age lay considerably north of Palestine" (and, I would add, considerably earlier

---

95. Braulik, *Deuteronomium*, 2.170; Mayes, *Deuteronomy*, 316.

96. Although this position would seem to be very compatible with the proto-Deuteronomic movement as represented by Hosea, who rejected foreign covenants, Nielsen (*Deuteronomium*, 94–97) has identified vv. 1b–2, 4–5 as part of the Deuteronomistic expansion of this text. This is, however, not the most common tack on the text. Lohfink regards it as one of the older portions of Deuteronomy 5–11 (*Das Hauptgebot*, 167ff.), and Mayes argues that at least vv. 1–3 are authentic (*Deuteronomy*, 181); and the first three verses are what interest me most.

chronologically). In chap. 2, we saw that the "Hittites," "Amorites," and "Canaanites" were probably archaic exonyms of Mesopotamian and Egyptian origin, and Mayes has suggested that the reference to "Hivites" (an otherwise unknown group) might actually reflect the term *Horite*, which is also an archaic Egyptian exonym. Of the other peoples mentioned here, the Jebusites[97] existed only in Israelite literature as the primeval inhabitants of Jerusalem, and the two other groups, the Perizzites and Girgashites, are also unknown outside of the Hebrew text. We can add to this list the giant Anakim of Deut 9:1–2.[98] Most likely, there were no extant groups in seventh-century Judah that corresponded directly to the various peoples listed here. Contrary to the "objective others" that confronted Judah during this period, we have here "rhetorical others" which served as a foil in the argument and theology of the Deuteronomic community. Consequently the primeval inhabitants of Canaan should be carefully distinguished from actual foreigners on the community's periphery.

This distinction is illustrated especially by Deut 20:10–18, in which the primeval populations *within the land* were to be completely destroyed (חרם), whereas the foreign populations encountered *in distant lands* were offered an opportunity to surrender and, even if they did not surrender, the resulting attack was directed only at the males.[99] In such cases the women of the conquered people could be taken as wives by the Israelites (Deut 21:10–14), provided that they observed a one-month "rite of passage" that furnished the liminal transition from a foreign to an Israelite identity.[100] The very different kinds of rules

97. Although occasionally called *Jebus* in the Hebrew Bible, second-millennium texts from El Amarna show that the city was known in Egypt by its West Semitic name, *Urusalim* (see W. L. Moran [ed.], *The Amarna Letters* [Baltimore: Johns Hopkins University Press, 1992] 328–29, 332–34).

98. The Anakim are described as a people גדול ורם.

99. In other words, Deuteronomy espouses standard military practice. Apparently, the Deuteronomic legislators were unwilling actually to endorse earlier practices in the region, such as the חרם undertaken by Mesha of Moab (see *ANET* 320).

100. On the Deuteronomic (and some would say pre-Deuteronomic) character of the law in Deuteronomy 21, see M. du Buit, "Quelques contacts bibliques dans les archives royales de Mari," *RB* 66 (1959) 576–81; Mayes, *Deuteronomy*, 300–301; Nielsen, *Deuteronomium*, 201–6. For classic discussions of liminality and ritual, see V. Turner, *The Ritual Process: Structure and Anti-structure* (The Lewis Henry Morgan Lectures, 1966; London: Routledge & Kegan Paul, 1969) 95–165; idem, "Liminal to Liminoid, in Play, Flow, and Ritual: An Essay in Comparative Symbology," *Rice University Studies* 6 (1974) 53–92.

that governed the treatment of distant foreigners as opposed to the primeval peoples probably stems from the fact that none of these primeval peoples existed in the Deuteronomic period, so we should probably conclude that for the Deuteronomic movement and its audience, Israel had succeeded in its quest to destroy the primeval nations of Palestine.[101] In spite of the fact that they no longer existed, these primeval groups served an important rhetorical function in both the military and religious spheres. As I have pointed out previously, von Rad long ago suggested that the decline of Assyrian power after 701 B.C.E. prompted conscription of a new Judean militia.[102] Although I cannot agree with many of the accoutrements of his idea, he is undoubtedly correct that the passing of Assyrian domination prompted the desire for and the need for a revived Judean military. Rhetorically speaking, the implied martial victories over the Anakim and others would have renewed confidence for these troops: "When you go forth to war against your enemies, and see horses and chariots and an army larger than your own, you shall not be afraid of them. . . ." (Deut 20:1).

But more important than the rhetorical function of these primeval groups in the military sphere was their function in the religious sphere. Deuteronomy thoroughly demonized and marginalized the primeval inhabitants of Palestine:

> you shall utterly destroy them, the Hittites and the Amorites, the Canaanites and the Perizites, the Hivites and the Jebusites, as the Lord your God has commanded; that they may not teach you to do according to all of their abominable practices (תועבה) which they have done in the service of their gods, and so to sin against the Lord your God. (Deut 20:17–18)

> take heed that . . . after they have been destroyed before you, and that you you do not inquire about their gods, saying, "How did these nations serve their gods?—that I may do likewise." You shall not do so to the Lord your God; for every abominable thing (תועבה) which the Lord hates they have done for their gods; for they even burn their sons and their daughters in the fire to their gods. (Deut 12:29–31)

101. We can now add another category to our previous chart. The primeval inhabitants represent a "rhetorical other," whose primary function in the literature was to be a destroyed enemy.

102. Von Rad, *Studies in Deuteronomy*, 60–61.

The operant description of these deviant primeval religious practices was תועבה 'abomination'. Other practices may be added to this Deuteronomic category, including the production and use of divine images (פסילים, 7:25), nonprophetic forms of intermediation (18:9–14), unclean foodstuffs (14:3), transvestism (22:5),[103] and cult prostitution (23:17–18).[104] The threat that these practices represented to the Deuteronomic reformers probably existed on two levels. On one level, the Josianic reform suggests that many of these practices were quite closely associated with the central Yahwistic cult prior to the reform. I am thinking here not only of Jerusalem but also of other temple sites where Yahweh was venerated. On another level, many of these "abominations" would have been practiced in the peripheral cult, so that post-D legislation found it necessary to warn against setting up images 'in secret' (ושם בסתר; 27:15).[105] The national reformers, religious progeny of Hosea and the proto-Deuteronomists,[106] brought their brand of aniconic, monotheistic Yahwism to the fore and with it a powerful, highly-charged ethnic identity that joined Yahweh's people together as אחים. As "rhetorical others," the primeval inhabitants of Canaan served three different but overlapping roles in this new Yahwistic community.

103. Although this was clearly a cultic offense, Mayes's suggestion that cultic transvestism was rejected because of its non-Israelite origins is uncertain. It is possible that the rejection stems from the implicit confusion of natural categories in a manner similar to that which Mary Douglas has isolated in P. Nonetheless, Römer has pointed out that transvestism played a significant role in the Mesopotamian cult of Ishtar. See M. Douglas, "The Abominations of Leviticus," *Purity and Danger* (London: Routledge & Kegan Paul, 1978) 41–57; Mayes, *Deuteronomy*, 307; W. H. Römer, "Randbemerkungen zur Travestie von Deut. 22,5," in *Travels in the World of the Old Testament: Studies Presented to Professor M. A. Beek on the Occasion of His 65th Birthday* (ed. M. S. H. G. Heerma van Voss; Studia Semitica Neerlandica 16; Assen: Van Gorcum, 1974) 217–22.

104. For a discussion of קדש/קדשה and its relationship to cult prostitution, see p. 149 n. 69.

105. Similar peripheral concerns are reflected in Jer 7:16–20 and 44:15–19. Jeremiah 44 is sometimes attributed to the Deuteronomistic redactor, but Jones and Holladay view it as Jeremianic. On the other hand, Jones suggests that the text is at points dependent on Dtr, which, provided that one dates Dtr to the exile, raises problems for Jeremianic origin. Nevertheless, the text probably approximates the religious context that confronted Jeremiah. See W. L. Holladay, *Jeremiah: A Commentary on the Book of the Prophet Jeremiah* (2 vols.; Hermeneia; Minneapolis: Fortress, 1989) 2.286–7; D. R. Jones, *Jeremiah* (NCBC; Grand Rapids, Mich.: Eerdmans, 1992) 447–56.

106. It is interesting that, for Hosea, the corruption of Israel took place outside of the land via Baal at Peor. For Deuteronomy, the corruption came inside the land at the hands of its primeval peoples.

First, by staging a national renewal and simultaneously identifying the unacceptable practices as primeval and non-Israelite, the Deuteronomic community placed a discursive wall between Israel and these foreign practices. Second, by associating the unwanted practices with the primeval inhabitants and by depicting these primeval peoples in the most negative terms—for example, they sacrifice children to their gods—the Deuteronomists cast a long, dark shadow upon all associated practices. Third, because the primeval inhabitants did not exist in seventh-century Judean experience, the Deuteronomic message seemed uniquely real, inasmuch as the fate of the evil Canaanites awaited unfaithful Israelites: "And if you forget the Lord God and go after other gods and serve them and worship them, I solemnly warn you this day that you shall surely perish. Like the nations that the Lord makes to perish before you . . . because you would not obey the voice of the Lord your God" (Deut 8:19–20). Nevertheless, despite the rhetorical nature of these ethnic boundaries, it is equally clear that at points they functioned well beyond the threshold of what we might call "rhetoric."

The Provenience of Ethnic Identity in Deuteronomy

Our discussion in the last few sections has emphasized the similarities that may be observed between ethnic concepts in Israel and in Greece as represented by Herodotus and some of the earlier archaic sources, especially with respect to the importance of forefather and ancestral figures. One of the comparative problems that we face, of course, is that similar kinds of traditions were also identified in the Old Babylonian materials and the comparative anthropological data, and this makes it difficult to argue in a definitive way that certain ethnic features in Israel can be explained by cultural diffusion. Nevertheless, my own opinion is that Deuteronomy (especially in its Deuteronomistic sections) shows signs of influence from Greece or perhaps from a common cultural arbiter between Israel and Greece. Such an exchange of ideas should be viewed as more likely in the case of Deuteronomy than in the eighth-century prophets, because Deuteronomy comes later in the period of growing contact between Greece and the Levant. On the other hand, I think that there is sufficient subtlety in the evidence to suggest that we are talking about probabilities rather than about practical certainties.

How do the ethnic features in Deuteronomy compare with ethnicity of the Greeks? The concept of eponymous ancestors, which played a major role in Hesiod, Herodotus, and Hosea, was not an important idea in Deuteronomy. On the other hand, ancestral migrations did play an important role in both Deuteronomy and the Greek materials, and in both cases we can cite evidence that the migrations moved from places of high culture (Egypt) to the new homeland. A number of other Greek features that were absent from the eighth-century prophetic tradition also played important roles in Deuteronomy. The Greek materials I examined in chap. 2 tend to portray peoples who were spatially and temporally peripheral: cannibalism, human sacrifice, strange cultic activities, unusual social customs, sexual deviancy, and nomadism were characteristic of these marginal peoples. Excepting cannibalism and nomadism, Deuteronomy clearly exhibited a tendency to conceptualize the primeval inhabitants of Palestine in these terms.[107]

As we proceed to the later Deuteronomistic materials in chaps. 1–4, the similarities with Greek ideology appear still greater. Deuteronomy 1 and 2, which represent later additions by the Deuteronomistic Historian, contain more advanced solutions to the problems of Israel's history and include itinerary,[108] genealogy, ethnographic notices, and serious attempts to systematize these into a comprehensive model, as shown in the accompanying chart (see Table 4.2). Notice that, unlike the primeval inhabitant lists of Deuteronomy proper, this material clearly distinguishes between the Amorite "hill-dwellers" and the Canaanites who live "by the seacoast" (Deut 1:7).[109] Horites were the original inhabitants of Edom and each culture, Israel, Ammon, Moab, and the Caphtorim, had its own name for the giant primeval inhabitants of its homeland, traditions that have affinities with the Greek traditions.[110] Each group, with the exception of the Caphtorim, had a forefather figure who served to provide an ethnic origin for the

107. E.g., human sacrifice (12:31), strange cultic activities (14:1), strange customs, (14:3ff.), and sexual deviancy (23:17–18).

108. On itinerary as a characteristic of Greek literary tradition and also for a helpful summary of the Greek antiquarian tradition, see Van Seters, *Prologue to History*, 78–103, 199–200.

109. Cf. Josh 13:1–7, as indicated by Mayes, *Deuteronomy*, 120. Although Mayes views the text as Deuteronomistic, Van Seters is probably correct that the allotment of the land in Joshua 13–22 should be attributed to the Priestly writer (Van Seters, *In Search of History*, 331–37).

110. Cf. Deuteronomy 1–3 and Hesiod's *Theogony* 50 and 185. These giants should be associated with the primeval "bronze race" described in *Theogony* 140–55, as West has demonstrated, in *Hesiod: Works and Days* (Oxford: Clarendon, 1978) 174.

Table 4.2. The Primeval Traditions of Israel's Neighbors

People	Dispossessed People	Primeval Giants	Forefather
Israel	Amorites	Anakim	Jacob
Edom	Horites	—	Esau
Moab	—	Emim	Lot
Ammon	—	Zamsummim	Lot
Caphtorim	—	Avvim	—

people in question. By laying things out in this way, Israel was following the very natural pattern of projecting its own ethnic mode of identity onto its neighbors (although we should not too quickly discount the idea that here Israel may have gleaned some of this information from the other groups that were nearby).

Despite these Greek-like features, Deuteronomy also exhibits the marks that distinguish it as an Israelite piece. Most significant is the fact that in the Deuteronomistic sections of the book Yahweh was the giver of the land for Edom, Ammon, and Moab, as well as Israel, and it was He who allowed them to dispossess the giant primeval peoples who preceded them. This idea finds its earliest witness in Amos: "Did I not bring up Israel from the land of Egypt, and the Philistines from Caphtor and the Syrians from Kir?" (Amos 9:7). So we see that both Deuteronomy and its Deuteronomistic expansions display a combination of features that are similar to the Greek materials but also display the unique stamp of the Israelite traditions. Were Israelite and Greek ideas about ethnicity and identity influenced by common sources? Ultimately, it is difficult to give an answer to this question in a categorical way. Nevertheless, I think that the answer is probably "yes," and I think that the common arbiter was Phoenicia.

Ethnic Boundaries in Deuteronomy

We have demonstrated that ethnicity was an important mode of identity for the proto-Deuteronomic, Deuteronomic, and Deuteronomistic communities. But there is another related question that is an important one. How rigid in actual practice were the boundaries associated with this ethnicity? I think that the Deuteronomic "ban theology" (חרם) would at first lead us to think that the boundaries were very rigid indeed.[111] However, things are not so simple, I think, and to

---

111. See Deut 7:1–3.

bring this out more clearly we need to examine in a more direct way the ethnic criteria of Deuteronomy (the definitions used to define community membership) as well as the indicia used by the community to make ready judgments about who was in and who was not.

In Deuteronomy, the most important criterion for community membership was one's status with respect to Yahweh, the national deity of Judah (and Israel). That the priority of this religious standard for group membership exceeded the ethnic requirement is quite clear, since it appears that a foreigner who joined himself to the national God (the assimilating גר) was quite readily accepted into the community. The foreigner who accepted this arrangement would necessarily have avoided non-Yahwistic "foreign" gods as well as any religious practices that were considered "non-Yahwistic" and were by association "foreign" practices. That Deuteronomy's preoccupation was more religious than ethnic is evidenced by the semantic range of גר ('sojourner'), which was broad enough to qualify people of almost any origin for a non-Israelite social position that invited cultural and religious assimilation.[112]

This emphasis on the religious criteria employed by the Deuteronomic community should not overshadow Deuteronomy's genuine expressions of ethnic sentiment. Deuteronomy was certainly interested in the common identity shared by Judeans and Israelites as the people of Yahweh and so attempted to integrate the two Yahwistic populations into one ethnic community. This was accomplished by intensifying existing Israelite ethnic sentiments, as first expressed in Hosea, and by extending them through a kinship theology of brotherhood (אחים) to all Judeans and Israelites. The criteria for ethnic inclusion thus hinged on one's status as a 'brother' (אח) and also on one's status as a fellow heir of the forefathers (אבים). This brotherhood community inherited an exclusive covenant relationship with the deity of their forefathers, resulting in their common status as "sons of Yahweh" (Deut 14:1).[113]

112. Here I tend to agree with P. Dion, who has commented that Israel's ethos in Deuteronomy was not inordinately hostile to foreigners (excepting the conquest theology) and that, furthermore, certain texts reveal a general appreciation for other cultures and an ethnographic interest in other peoples (P. Dion, "Deuteronomy and the Gentile World," *Toronto Journal of Theology* 1 [1985] 203–4). Cf. Deut 2:10–23, 3:9–11, 6:10–11.

113. But see the late addition in 5:1–3, which suggests that the covenant was not made with the forefathers but with later generations. Mayes suggests that this contradiction should not be taken strictly but instead reflects the author's intent to stress the covenant's continuing validity for his own generation (Mayes, *Deuteronomy*, 165).

Who would lead this ideal community? Although Mullen has shown that the Davidic kingship played a vital role in the definition of this Deuteronomic ethnic community,[114] it seems that kingship itself actually played a minor role in the Northern headwaters of Deuteronomic thought, as evidenced by its slender treatment in Deuteronomy (17:14–21)[115] and by the negative stance of Hosea toward the monarchic institution (Hos 13:10–11).[116] Instead, the primary leadership roles envisioned by Deuteronomy included the 'elders of the city' (זקני העיר) and 'judges' (שפטים),[117] with the religious leadership shared by levitical priests and prophetic intermediaries. Given the Davidic leanings of Amos and especially of Isaiah, we must assume that this nonmonarchic leadership perspective originated in Northern circles, a perspective that no doubt required adjusting in the Judean context. But no matter how one solves the issue of community leadership, it is clear that the community itself was to be housed in the land that Yahweh gave to them to possess, an idea that is similar to (but distinct from) Hosea's idea that the deity had brought Israel out of Egypt and into "Yahweh's land."

Leaving behind the question of *criteria*, perhaps more interesting with respect to ethnic boundaries in Deuteronomy is the question of *indicia*, the "ethnic markers" that provided a ready identification of those within the group and those who were outsiders. Given the overarching "nationalism" of Deuteronomy, any features that would readily identify a Judean would seem to have served such a purpose. We do have some evidence, via Assyrian inscriptions, that Judean practice included a distinctive wardrobe, particularly a headdress, which set them

114. E. Theodore Mullen, Jr., *Narrative History and Ethnic Boundaries: The Deuteronomistic History and the Creation of Israelite National Identity* (Semeia Studies; Atlanta: Scholars Press, 1993), 163–207.

115. In excursus 2 below, I will discuss the possibility that this text is postexilic in origin.

116. In fact, as Braulik has noted, Deuteronomy represents a "demokratisieren" which limits the powers of the monarchic institution. See Braulik, *Deuteronomium*, 2.127–8.

117. See Deut 16:18; 19:17; 21:6–17. The "heads of tribes (ראשי שבטים) are also mentioned in Deuteronomy, but only in later additions. The leadership role of the elders is so prominent in Deuteronomy that L. J. Hoppe has suggested that they were responsible for its composition ("Elders and Deuteronomy: A Proposal," *Église et Théologie* 14 [1983] 259–72). For more regarding the place and function of the elders in Deuteronomy, see J. Buchholz, *Die Ältesten Israels im Deuteronomium* (Göttinger Theologische Arbeiten 36; Göttingen: Vandenhoeck & Ruprecht, 1988).

apart from Philistines, Israelites, Phoenicians, Syrians, Arabs, and other groups in the region.[118] However, Moabites, Edomites, and Ammonites are not represented and, furthermore, we cannot be sure that the samples provided are representative of the respective population groups. Linguistically, we know that the West Semitic dialects in the region were distinctive, so that in both its early Israelite context and in its later Judean context, the ethnic community envisioned by Deuteronomy might have utilized language as an ethnic marker.[119] But perhaps more functional in the role of indicias were several legal statutes in Deuteronomy, particularly its culinary legislation (the community eats clean foodstuffs), its centralization of the cult, and perhaps its Sabbath regulations.[120] The origins of the latter have at times been associated with Ezekiel (20:12–20, 46:1),[121] but Perlitt and Mayes agree that our Decalogue text (and with it the Sabbath law) dates no later than the Deuteronomistic movement, and according to Lohfink its features fit that redaction (שמר + עשׂה in vv. 12–15).[122] In addition to Sabbath-keeping, adherence to regulations that centralized the cult would have been a distinctive practice, since foreigners would not have adhered to them, nor would many Judeans have done so. We cannot be sure about the impact of either Sabbath or dietary practices on Israelite identity, since it is difficult to know the extent to which these practices were unusual among Israel's neighbors. It is nevertheless plausible that these activities functioned as ethnic markers for the Deuteronomic community. In addition to these "positive indicia," Deuteronomy also displays a number of "negative indicia," practices and customs that readily indicated that one was operating outside of the bounds established by the community. These practices included the worship of foreign deities

118. See M. Wäfler, *Nicht-Assyrer neuassyrischer Darstellungen* (2 vols.; AOAT 26; Neukirchen-Vluyn: Neukirchener Verlag, 1975) 1.39, 65–67, 75, 117, 123, 157. As Kamp and Yoffee have noted, clothing styles often symbolize ethnic identity (K. A. Kamp and N. Yoffee, "Ethnicity in Ancient Western Asia during the Early Second Millennium B.C.: Archaeological Assessments and Ethnoarchaeological Prospectives," *BASOR* 237 [1980] 85–104).

119. Gibson, *Syrian Semitic Inscriptions*, 1.5–8, 21–22; Cross and Freedman, *Early Hebrew Orthography*.

120. See Deut 5:12–15, 12:1–14, 14:3–21. Sabbath-keeping comes to the fore during the exile beginning with Ezekiel. Whether it served any distinguishing role in defining Israelite identity prior to the exile is debatable.

121. De Vaux, *Ancient Israel*, 2.476.

122. Lohfink, *Das Hauptgebot*, 64–70; Mayes, *Deuteronomy*, 161–69; Perlitt, *Bundestheologie im Alten Teztament*, 81–91.

(like Baal) as well as participation in activities that were associated by Deuteronomy with non-Yahwistic cults, such as divination (Deut 18:9–14) and "death cult" rituals (Deut 14:1).[123]

From our historical vantage point, there is probably little about these prohibited practices that was essentially "non-Israelite." Instead, certain norms became associated with proper Yahwism by the proto-Deuteronomic party and, because Yahweh was the national deity, all unapproved practices became "foreign" by default. Furthermore, there is nothing exceptionally "powerful" about the indexes outlined by Deuteronomy, especially in regard to the "ethnic" aspect of Israelite identity. It is very difficult to imagine how these indexes could actually be employed to distinguish Israelites from foreigners on a day-to-day basis. Instead, it appears that the objective of Deuteronomy was not so much to distinguish foreigners from Israelites/Judeans as it was to distinguish proper Yahwism from either improper Yahwism or non-Yahwistic (i.e., foreign) activities. If this is the case, we should expect that the foreign/Israelite dichotomy in Deuteronomy was mostly rhetorical and polemical, and we should also expect that the boundaries that excluded foreigners were not as firm as Deuteronomy's "holy war" might suggest.

* * * * *

Excursus 1:
The Tribal List in the "Blessing of Moses" (Deuteronomy 33)

It has until recently been a tendency to see in this text a compilation of several separate tribal sayings (*Stämmespruche*), but S. Beyerle's monograph has questioned whether one can identify common generic elements within them or a common Sitz im Leben behind their composition.[124] But even in lieu of these things, there is nevertheless some truth to the idea that these were "tribal sayings" of a sort, even if on formal grounds they are more properly identified as "prayers," "blessings," or some other form. Thus the text originated, at least in part, as a series of independent blessings or sayings that were only subsequently combined into a list. The collection itself was compiled by nesting

---

123. T. J. Lewis, *Cults of the Dead in Ancient Israel and Ugarit* (HSM 39; Atlanta: Scholars Press, 1989) 100–101; J. C. de Moor, *An Anthology of Religious Texts from Ugarit* (Nisaba 16; Leiden: Brill, 1987) 80–81.

124. S. Beyerle, *Der Mosesegen im Deuteronomium: Eine text-, kompositions- und formkritische Studie zu Deuteronomium 33* (BZAW 250; Berlin: de Gruyter, 1997) 274.

these independent sayings within an older *Rahmen* psalm, which can be reconstructed by connecting 33:1–5 with 33:26–29.[125] I do not feel very optimistic about the prospects for reconstructing the independent tradition histories of each saying (although Beyerle has attempted to do so), but I am very interested in the original compilation of the list, its date, and also the redactional history that followed. Most of the components of the text are thought to be of Northern origins and consequently are normally dated no later than the eighth century, or perhaps earlier, and my discussion of the text will support this conclusion.[126]

Assessment of the "Blessing of Moses" requires clarification of several questions. How does this tribal list compare to other tribal lists in the Hebrew Bible, and what does this tell us? How firmly can we identify the historical provenience of the text and its constituent parts? And where does this text fall within the redactional history of Deuteronomy? Most tribal lists in the Hebrew Bible include twelve tribal units and follow one of the two patterns represented by Genesis 49 and Numbers 1. By comparison, this list would appear unusual, because it eliminates Simeon and is the only text that includes both Levi and Ephraim/Manasseh. H. Seebass has attempted to argue, albeit unsuccessfully in my view, that Simeon actually appears in the list as "Jeshurun."[127] Von Rad and others have attempted to explain the absence of Simeon as arising from the fact that no independent saying existed for that tribe, but this seems an unnecessary effort if we can explain its absence on other grounds.[128] The saying associated with Judah in 33:7 also presents a few problems. It entreats the deity to bring Judah to "his

125. Braulik, *Deuterononomium*, 2.238–44; Mayes, *Deuteronomy*, 396; Von Rad, *Deuteronomy*, 205.

126. Beyerle, *Der Mosesegen im Deuteronomium*, 279; C. J. Labuschagne, "The Tribes in the Blessing of Moses," *OTS* (1974) 98; H-P. Mathys, *Dichter und Beter: Theologen aus spätaltestamentlicher Zeit* (OBO 132; Göttingen: Vandenhoek & Ruprecht, 1994) 171; Nielsen, *Deuteronomium*, 299.

127. Seebass has attempted to show that "Jeshurun," mentioned in 33:5, 26, is actually a reference to the missing tribe of Simeon. This suggestion is problematic because both references in this text belong to the psalmic framework of the blessing and, moreover, because in the few occurrences of the term elsewhere in the Hebrew Bible, Jeshurun functions as a synonym for Israel/Jacob (H. Seebass, "Die Stämmeliste von Dtn. XXXIII," *VT* 27 [1977] 158–69).

128. G. von Rad, *Deuteronomy* (OTL; Philadelphia: Westminster, 1966) 204–8; Mayes, *Deuteronomy*, 396–97; but see the discussion of Labuschagne, who argues that some of the sayings are independent in origin and others are part of the original composition ("The Tribes in the Blessing of Moses," 97–112).

people," which might be profitably connected with any number of historical contexts. Beyerle has suggested that it should be associated with the Babylonian exile and thus may date some time after the Cyrus edict, but this is not a common viewpoint.[129] More often the clause is taken as evidence of the text's Northern provenience because it calls for Judah to join with the Northern tribes, most likely sometime before the Syro-Ephraimite war.[130] This date corresponds with D. A. Robertson's analysis of the text's linguistic features and makes sense of the second half of the saying, which requests help in the struggle against Judah's adversaries.[131]

The uniqueness of the text is heightened if one is prepared, as I am, to follow Labuschagne, Mayes, and others in the suggestion that the Levitical blessing in vv. 8–10 is a later addition.[132] If one does this and then recognizes that the text actually contains a "Joseph blessing" rather than separate blessings for Ephraim and Manasseh, then it becomes clear that we are dealing with a list of only ten tribes: Reuben, Judah, Benjamin, Joseph, Zebulun, Issachar, Gad, Dan, Naphtali, and Asher. This list probably stands somewhere between the tribal list found in the older Song of Deborah (which also contains ten tribal

---

129. Beyerle, *Der Mosesegen im Deuteronomium*, 108–12, 285.

130. On the association of this text with the Assyrian threat, see Nielsen, *Deuteronomium*, 300.

131. D. A. Robertson, *Linguistic Evidence in the Dating of Early Hebrew Poetry* (SBLDS 3; Missoula, Mont.: Scholars Press, 1972) 49–56. Buis and Leclercq, following previous suggestions by F. M. Cross and D. N. Freedman, dated the text as early as the eleventh century (*Le Deutéronome*, 206).

132. Labuschagne, "The Tribes in the Blessing of Moses," 101; Mayes, *Deuteronomy*, 402; F. M. Cross and D. N. Freedman, "The Blessing of Moses," *JBL* 67 (1948) 202–3. Nielsen views only a part of the Levi blessing as redactional (*Deuteronomium*, 294–303). Mayes outlines the reasons for viewing the Levi saying as a later addition as follows: (1) the Levi blessing is unusually long; (2) the descriptions in v. 11 and the linguistic variations between vv. 8–10 and v. 11 argue that 8–10 is an addition; (3) the text of vv. 8–10 includes relatively late features, such as the definite article, the sign of the definite object, and relative pronoun; (4) If one removes vv. 8–10, then v. 11 fits very well as the original ending of the short Judah saying, which would then read as follows:

And this he said of Judah:
Hear O Lord, the voice of Judah and bring him in to his people.
With thy hands contend for him, and be a help against his adversaries.
Bless, O Lord, his substance, and accept the work of his hands;
Crush the loins of his adversaries, of those that hate him, that they rise not again.

groups)[133] and later tribal lists that contain twelve groups and that clearly differentiate Simeon from Judah and Ephraim from Manasseh. This theory supports the usual dating of the collection to the eighth century, since we have concluded that the Song of Deborah is likely a work, at least in its final form, from the ninth century B.C.E.[134] Because Judah is not listed in Deborah's Song, we can conclude that it was a latecomer to the tribal list tradition, which makes sense given the potentially old tradition that Judah's origin was not tied to the other tribes.[135] One can also conclude, I think, that the Levites were added to the list even later, probably when they were granted tribal status to protect them during the vulnerable period reflected in Deuteronomy, a context that we have already discussed.[136] The incorporation of the collection into Deuteronomy was probably done by the Deuteronomistic Historian, since it was he who introduced the account of Moses' death in chap. 34, and this necessarily comes after both the "Blessing of Moses" (chap. 33) and the "Song of Moses" (chap. 32), as we see elsewhere in the Hebrew scriptures.[137]

This list of tribal blessings greatly enhances the view of eighth-century Israelite identity that was gleaned from the prophetic sources and to a certain extent reveals just how limited those sources turn out to be, at least in some respects. The tribal list in the "Blessing of Moses" (Deuteronomy 33) seems to imply additional patriarchal-type figures who should be associated with the individual tribes. I have pointed out above that Joseph, Ephraim, and Manasseh were already associated with each other via genealogy during the eighth century, and this relationship is reflected in Deut 33:13–17. We can expect, then, that genealogy played an important role in the list, as is more clearly evinced in 33:24, where the tribe of Asher was 'blessed beyond sons' (ברוך מבנים אשר) and was enjoined to become the favorite among his brothers (יהי רצוי אחיו). Geographically, the text often re-

133. For additional comments on the relationship between this list and the Song of Deborah, see Buis and Leclercq, *La Deutéronome*, 205–6.

134. See above, pp. 110–113. J. Van Seters has attempted to trace the history of the Machir and Gilead traditions within the biblical tradition, a discussion that includes, of course, the Song of Deborah (see his *Life of Moses*, 447–48).

135. See Genesis 38 and discussion in Van Seters, *Prologue to History*, 278–80.

136. For a brief overview of issues related to the Levitical priesthood and the priesthood in general, see J. M. O'Brien, *Priest and Levite in Malachi* (SBLDS 121; Atlanta: Scholars Press, 1990) 1–26.

137. Cf. Genesis 27:27–40; 48–49; 2 Samuel 22–23.

fers to the regions associated with each tribe, so that Gad "chose the best of the land for himself," Issachar and Zebulun "suck the affluence of the seas," Naphtali possessed "the lake and the south," and Dan "leaps forth from Bashan."[138] Implicit in these comments is a sketch of certain social modalities, 'tribes' (שבטים) according to the final form of the text, in which each group shared a common territory and was understood as the progeny of an eponymous ancestor. We cannot be sure that the compiler (or compilers) of the text would have extended these social features to every group mentioned in the blessing nor can we recklessly assume that these "tribal" ancestors were brothers to each other by virtue of a common lineage through Jacob, although this was certainly the case by the late seventh century. Nevertheless, it seems clear that the text was informed by certain genealogical notions and that a degree of ethnic sentiment was present within the community that produced this text.

That the list provides more detail than either Hosea or Amos should come as no surprise, since they were hardly exhaustive source materials. And what we actually have in Deuteronomy 33 is more or less in step with the ethnic sentiments of the eighth-century prophetic traditions, particularly in the high status that it gives to Joseph compared to Ephraim/Manasseh. The reference to Judah cannot necessarily be viewed as evidence of an ethnic connection between Israel and Judah (which would seem to be contrary to the views of Hosea, Amos, and Isaiah), since the call to "bring him [Judah] in to his people [Yahweh's people]" may stem from the common Yahwistic heritage of Judah rather than any supposed ethnic ties.[139] In this regard, the blessing has something in common with the Song of Deborah, where the primary tie between the groups was also religious, and it stands apart from the clear genealogical schematics that are characteristic of later tribal lists. As we examine the Song of Deborah and recognize the process of growth within the "Blessing of Moses" and within later tribal lists, the aggregate character of the Israelite ethnic tradition reveals itself. The ancient tradents adjusted the tribal-list tradition in an

138. Cf. Deut 33:18–23. Naphtali's region, "the lake and south," might also be translated 'the west and south'.

139. However, it should be remembered that, although ethnic sentiments for Judah were rather shallow when the blessing was composed, there can be little doubt that both the Deuteronomic movement and later Deuteronomistic editors understood Judah as ethnically related to the other tribes listed here.

ongoing effort to account for the introduction of new groups, the passing of old groups, and at the same time to preserve a certain number (10 or 12) of groups within lists. This aggregative tendency is very similar to patterns that we have noted in Greek ethnic behaviors.

*   *   *   *   *

Excursus 2:
The Deuteronomistic History

The fact that I am already addressing a formidable body of biblical literature here precludes thoroughly evaluating the Deuteronomistic History, but this desideratum is partially compensated by two factors. First, we have already discussed the book of Deuteronomy in detail, and much of the ethnic ideology reflected in it is characteristic of the history that follows. Second, E. T. Mullen has devoted a monograph to the topic of ethnicity in Dtr, so that much of the appropriate "spade work" has already been done.[140] I will briefly summarize the work of Mullen, offer criticisms where appropriate, and then point out a few additional details that require attention.

In my view, Mullen's work tends to focus much more on the definition of the Israelite community than on the place and function of ethnic sentiments within that definition. Because of this, although Mullen provides a careful analysis of religious identity in Deuteronomy, one will notice his rather thin treatment of some important issues that are integrally related to ethnicity. Questions about the forefathers, the patriarchs, "brother theology," holy war, and ethnic separatism, among other things, are largely unexplored. This tendency characterizes his treatment of the history as a whole, which in my view means that a there is more work to be done on the issue of ethnic identity and its place in the Deuteronomistic History. Nevertheless, Mullen's emphasis on the essentially religious boundaries that define Deuteronomic identity is fundamentally correct, because my study also suggests that Deuteronomy's primary concern was religious and Yahwistic, with ethnic sentiments playing a secondary role in support of those priorities.

Outside of a complete analysis of the source, there are two key issues raised by the Deuteronomistic History that should be discussed.

140. Mullen, *Narrative History and Ethnic Boundaries.*

First, Mullen's work identifies kingship as a central tenet of Deuteronomistic identity, and this is certainly correct. However, he tends to read this ideology also into Deuteronomy, which is not necessarily accurate. As in proto-Deuteronomic Hosea, kingship in Deuteronomy plays a very secondary role and serves no primary purpose in the community defined by the text. Furthermore, Bultmann has suggested that even the brief treatment of kingship in Deuteronomy 17 is secondary and addresses a much later, fifth-century, postexilic context.[141] We might debate with Bultmann on this point, but it remains clear that for Deuteronomy it was the local elders (זקנים) who filled the primary leadership role in the civic arena.[142] One important transformation of Deuteronomy's ideology in the history that followed was therefore the integration of monarchic ideology into it, and this emphasis on kingship no doubt stemmed from Judean (Davidic) influences on the previously "kingless" Deuteronomic movement.[143] The second adjustment made by the Deuteronomistic History was the extension of Deuteronomy's "rhetorical other" to the realm of the "objective other." J. Van Seters has pointed out that the history often combines Deuteronomy's primeval inhabitants with actual groups on Israel's periphery.[144] For instance, in Judg 3:5, the Philistines and Sidonians are included with the primeval inhabitants, the Canaanites and Hivites, even though it is hard to see how these primeval inhabitants might have fit into the context. Similarly, 1 Kgs 11:1–2 condemned Solomon for his associations with Moabite, Ammonite, Edomite, Egyptian, and Hittite women, even though the Hittites could not have served as a meaningful objective referent either in the day of Solomon or the day of the Deuteronomistic Historian. This rhetorical strategy connected existing groups with Israel's much detested ancient enemies and in doing so heightened the sense of ethnic distinction between Israel and its neighbors.

---

141. Bultmann, *Der Fremde in antiken Juda*, 145–57.

142. See especially Buchholz, *Die Ältesten Israels im Deuteronomium*; and L. J. Hoppe, "The Levitical Origins of Deuteronomy Reconsidered," *BR* 28 (1983) 27–36.

143. The fact that Dtr contains traditions that opposed kingship (see 1 Samuel 8) might suggest that a preexilic edition of the work was prepared by those associated with Deuteronomy, i.e., those who held a more negative view of kingship than that which exists in the final form of the Dtr.

144. J. Van Seters, "The Terms 'Amorite' and 'Hittite' in the Old Testament," *VT* 22 (1972) 68.

Jeremiah

I will examine several texts from Jeremiah that supplement what we have learned during our examination of Deuteronomy. These texts address three issues: (1) the place of Israel in Judean thought during the late monarchy; (2) the place of circumcision in Israelite identity; and (3) the ideological struggle between the exiles and the Palestinian remnant. Before examining these texts, I would like briefly to characterize Jeremiah's relationship to Deuteronomy and the reforms associated with Deuteronomy. Although Jer 7:4–11 appears somewhat critical of Josiah's reform effort, there is evidence that, in principle, Jeremiah supported the reform itself. E. Holt has argued—and it seems to me self-evident—that Jeremiah stood along with Deuteronomy in the prophetic tradition of Hosea, within the "stream of consciousness flowing from the north via Judah to Babylon."[145] According to Dtr (2 Kings 22) and Jeremiah, the prophet enjoyed the support of two families that were heavily involved in the reform, and he received protection from them before the exile took place. The same families also served Jeremiah as messengers after the exile.[146] On the other hand, the data one gleans from Jeremiah is surprisingly thin on the issue of the reform. The most logical explanation for this, says W. L. Holladay, is that Jeremiah was only five years old when Josiah's reforms took place in 622 B.C.E. The paucity of Jeremiah's comments about the reform therefore stem from the fact that it occurred many years previous to his ministry.[147] From such a vantage point, the problem of Jeremiah's relationship to the reform is largely secondary. What is clear from Jeremiah is that he granted the charter reform document, Deuteronomy, a central and authoritative role in his evaluation of Judean society.[148]

Israel and Judah in the Temple Sermon (Jeremiah 7:12–20)

A number of scholars have followed Mowinckel's conclusion that Jer 7:12–20 is a product of the Deuteronomistic redactor and there-

---

145. E. K. Holt, "The Chicken or the Egg—Or: Was Jeremiah a Member of the Deuteronomist Party?" *JSOT* 44 (1989) 109–22.

146. See Jer 26:24 and 29:3.

147. Holladay, *Jeremiah*, 1.1.

148. See H. Cazelles, "Jeremiah and Deuteronomy," *A Prophet to the Nations: Essays in Jeremiah Studies* (ed. L. G. Perdue and B. W. Kovacs; Winona Lake, Ind.: Eisenbrauns, 1984) 89–111. See also J. P. Hyatt's article by the same name, "Jeremiah and Deuteronomy," and in the same volume, pp. 113–27.

fore does not originate with the prophet.[149] E. W. Nicholson is correct to point out that the text shares many features with the Deuteronomistic History and also with other Jeremianic texts that are normally associated with the Deuteronomistic redaction of Jeremiah.[150] On the other hand, O. Eissfeldt, A. Weiser, W. L. Holladay, and others have long argued that Jeremiah used prose sermons that had a Deuteronomistic style, suggesting that prose features must be used with care to isolate secondary material in the collection.[151] For instance, regarding this text, Holladay points out that numerous features in the text are characteristic of Jeremiah's poetry and that the terminology used here, while overlapping with the terminology of Deuteronomy, is hardly Deuteronomistic.[152] But he arrives at this conclusion by minimizing each feature that is Deuteronomistic, such as the phrase "walk after other gods," and by failing to deal with the fact that 7:1–15 is nested within a much larger pericope, 7:1–8:3, which is "filled with D phraseology, and is in D's characteristic style."[153] In my view, while it is possible that this text goes back to the Jeremiah tradition, the presence of Deuteronomistic features within it robs us of any confidence. We must assume, therefore, that the text may have been formulated as

149. S. Mowinckel, *Zur Komposition des Buches Jeremia* (Kristiania: Dybwad, 1914) 31; W. Rudolph, *Jeremiah* (HAT; Tübingen: Mohr, 1958) xvi–xvii, xix, 51–52. Weinfeld, *Deuteronomy and the Deuteronomic School*, 325, 352. See also the idiosyncratic work of Carroll, who suggests that there was no Jeremiah (R. P. Carroll, *Jeremiah* [OTL; Philadelphia: Westminster, 1986] 38–49).

150. E. W. Nicholson, *Preaching to the Exiles* (Oxford: Blackwell, 1970) 34, and esp. 68–69.

151. W. L. Holladay, "A Fresh Look at 'Source A' and 'Source B' in Jeremiah," *VT* 25 (1975) 394–412; "Prototype and Copies: A New Approach to the Poetry-Prose Problem in the Book of Jeremiah," *JBL* 79 (1960) 351–67. See also O. Eissfeldt, *The Old Testament: An Introduction* (New York: Harper & Row, 1965) 352–53; A. Weiser, *Das Buch des Propheten Jeremia* (2 vols.; ATD; Göttingen: Vandenhoeck & Ruprecht, 1952–55) 1.60–61.

152. Holladay points out that the *Hiphil* of יטב is not Deuteronomistic. Neither is the pairing of דרכים and מעללים. The triad of "stranger, orphan, and widow," is characteristic of Deuteronomy, not Dtr. The phrase "walk after other gods," is Deuteronomistic, but its component parts are found in the undeniably Jeremianic texts (cf. 2:5, 23, 36; 5:19). Also, "the house that bears my name" is distinctly Jeremianic. See Holladay, *Jeremiah*, 1.240. In support of this view, see also Jones, *Jeremiah*, 142–46; Georg Fohrer, "Jeremias Tempelwort," *Studien zur alttestamentlichen Prophetie (1949–1965)* (Berlin: Alfred Töpelmann, 1967) 190–98.

153. J. P. Hyatt, "The Deuteronomistic Edition of Jeremiah," *A Prophet to the Nations: Essays in Jeremiah Studies* (ed. L. G. Perdue and B. W. Kovacs; Winona Lake, Ind.: Eisenbrauns, 1984) 254.

late as the early exilic period. This conclusion is only partially relevant for my work here, since I am primarily concerned with sources that describe how Judah viewed Israel during the late monarchy, and this text can adequately serve that role.

I have argued that one of the central purposes of Deuteronomy was to establish a unity among people who worshiped Yahweh, specifically a unity between Judah and the remnants of Israel. Although Deuteronomy makes no distinction between the two entities, the Temple Sermon shows us that, even in the late Judean monarchy, the distinction between the North and South had not been forgotten:

> Go now to my place that was in Shiloh, where I made my name dwell at first, and see what I did to it for the wickedness of my people Israel. . . . Therefore I will do to the house which is called by my name, and in which you trust, and to the place which I gave to you and to your fathers, as I did to Shiloh. And I will cast you out of my sight, as I cast out all your kinsmen, all the offspring of Ephraim. (Jer 7:12, 14–15)

On the one hand, the Northern temple site at Shiloh was accepted as a part of the common Judean/Israelite tradition.[154] In this respect, the religious identity of Israel and Judah had become one, as was the design of Deuteronomy. On the other hand, the phrase 'my people Israel' (עמי ישראל) in v. 12 appears to refer exclusively to the North, as is the case more explicitly in v. 15: 'all of your brothers (אחיכם), all the off-spring of Ephraim (זרע אפרים)'. The relationship between Israel and Judah is entirely ethnic at this point, since Ephraim is the brother (אח) of Judah. So the major goal of Deuteronomy's "brother theology"— the ethnic unification of Israel and Judah—was ultimately achieved. Still, in Jeremiah the term "Israel" served two differing functions, at times referring to the Northern Kingdom and at other times referring to the united people of Yahweh.

The ethnic connections between Israel and Judah naturally bring to mind their common forefather, Jacob. At this point, we are able to sketch an outline of this figure and his place in Israelite ethnicity. In chap. 3, I noted that the Israelite forefather Jacob was viewed unfavorably by Hosea (and we assume, by the proto-Deuteronomists) and that

---

154. Whether the temple was destroyed in the eleventh century or as late as the eighth century is irrelevant, since the major point of this text is that it was in ruins. For a discussion of the date of destruction of Shiloh's temple site, see J. Day, "The Destruction of the Shiloh Sanctuary and Jeremiah 7:12–14," *VT* 30 (1970) 87–94.

he appeared to have no connection with Judean identity as represented by Amos and Isaiah. In this chapter we saw that, despite Deuteronomy's efforts to connect Judah and Israel as a common ethnic people, the forefather Jacob played no vital role in this endeavor. Instead, this ethnic connection was accomplished via Deuteronomy's "brother theology" and an appeal to the forefathers. Finally, in Jeremiah we see that later in the seventh century the referent of "Jacob" became somewhat ambiguous, at times referring to the Northern Kingdom, at other times addressing Judah, and on still other occasions addressing the two as a single unit.[155] In other words, while it might be natural to assume that the brotherhood of Israel and Judah was accomplished by an appeal to their common ancestor named Jacob, the opposite is true. It was Deuteronomy's "brother theology" that preceded the connection of North and South via the forefather Jacob.

In sum, during the late monarchy and early exile, the Israel and Judah traditions were at points united and at other points divided, primarily because the example of Israel's failure continued to serve Jeremiah and others as an instructional paradigm in the South. As we will see, during and after the exile Judah served as its own example, and the historical distinction between Israel and Judah, while still known in the sources, retreated into the rhetorical background.

The Exiles and the Judean Remnant in Jeremiah 24

The clear, Ezra-like distinction that Jeremiah 24 makes between the exiles, who are promised success, and the Judean remnant, which is promised ruin, has naturally prompted the suggestion that this text is postexilic.[156] But beyond this fundamental similarity between our text and the situation after the return, the evidence for such a conclusion is wanting and the idea has not been widely embraced. Still, we must deal with the question of whether the text can be dated to the context it purports to address, namely, the Judean situation between the exile of 597 and the final destruction of the Temple in 586 B.C.E. The scholarly support for the text's authenticity—Rudolph, Holladay, and Jones—is formidable. Jones has summarized the more impressive arguments, pointing to the text's "stong marks of the Jeremiah

155. Cf. Jer 2:4 (Judah); 5:20 (Judah? Israel?); 10:16 (Judah/Israel); 10:25 (Israel).
156. H. G. May, "Towards an Objective Approach to the Book of Jeremiah: The Biographer," *JBL* 61 (1942) 148–49; Carroll, *Jeremiah*, 482–88.

tradition."[157] Specifically, he points out the following: (1) the vision is recounted in first person (cf. Jer 1:11–13); (2) גלות is characteristic of Jeremiah (cf. 28:4, 29:22, 40:1); (3) the phrase "for good" is Jeremianic (14:11, 21:10, 39:16, 44:27); (4) "build . . . tear down" is an echo of 1:10; and (5) the terms זועה ('horror'), חרפה ('reproach'), and קללה ('curse') are not characteristic of Dtr. To this we can add Holladays observation, "How likely are we to have a pseudepigraphic vision report in the book? A sermon on the sabbath (17:19–27) or prophetic torah (23:34–40) is one thing, but an autobiographical vision report is surely less likely."[158] Although this last claim is debatable, I think that all of the above combined evidence demonstrates the decidedly supportive stance that most scholars have taken toward the Jeremianic origins of Jeremiah 24.[159]

The strongest arguments against the Jeremianic origin of chap. 24 are probably the arguments of C. R. Seitz, who postulates a non-Deuteronomistic "exilic redaction" that has affinities with the Ezekiel tradition. He points out that Ezekiel, like the present text, held the exiled Jehoiachin in high esteem and pronounced judgment on Zedekiah and the Judean remnant (see Ezekiel 17, 19, 20). This is in stark contrast to what Seitz sees elsewhere in Jeremiah, where the prophet was actually a supporter of Zedekiah and pronounced evil omens on Jehoiachin (cf. Jer 22:19, 26; 36:30–31; 37:21; 38:14–28). This being the case, in the view of Seitz Jeremiah 24 is in tension with the rest of Jeremiah but fits nicely with Ezekiel. The natural conclusion to draw, he says, is that Jeremiah has undergone an exilic redaction by the Ezekiel school and that this redactional material included Jeremiah 24. There are, of course, other important elements in Seitz's argument, but they are only helpful if his major point can be sustained. However, a careful examination of the texts cited by Seitz will show that it cannot be.

First, a number of texts that Seitz uses to support his view of Jeremiah are often regarded as Deuteronomistic (e.g., Jer 22:26, 36:30–31).[160] Second, the texts do not supply the data that Seitz suggests they do: Jeremiah was hardly supportive of Zedekiah but rather warned

157. Jones, *Jeremiah*, 317–18.

158. Holladay, *Jeremiah*, 1.655.

159. But see especially W. McKane, who does not support the notion of Jeremianic authorship (*Jeremiah* [ICC; Edinburgh: T. & T. Clark, 1986] 597–617).

160. Hyatt, "The Deuteronomic Edition of Jeremiah," 258, 261; Nicholson, *Preaching to the Exiles*, 42; W. Thiel, *Die deuteronomistiche Redaktion von Jeremia 26–45* (WMANT 52; Neukirchen-Vluyn: Neukirchener Verlag, 1981) 49–51.

Zedekiah of impending judgment and suggested that he take appropriate actions to avoid this judgment (Jeremiah 37; 38:14–28). Third, after 597, Jeremiah predicted a long, three-generation exile (27:7), and the resulting message was the same for both the Judean remnant and the exiles.

> *To the Judeans (Jer 27:16–17)*: Thus says the Lord: "Do not listen to the words of your prophets who are prophesying to you, saying, 'Behold, the vessels of the Lord's house will now shortly be brought back from Babylon,' for it is a lie which they are prophesying to you. Do not listen to them; serve the king of Babylon and live. Why should this city become a desolation?"
>
> *To the Exiles (Jer 29:4–7)*: Thus says the Lord of hosts, the God of Israel, to all the exiles whom I have sent into exile from Jerusalem to Babylon: "Build houses and live in them; plant gardens and eat their produce. Take wives and have sons and daughters; take wives for your sons, and give your daughters in marriage, that they may bear sons and daughters; multiply there, and do not decrease. But seek the welfare of the city where I have sent you into exile, and pray to the Lord on its behalf, for in its welfare you will find your welfare."

These verses show that in Jeremiah's view there was no immediate hope for any of the parties involved: not for the exiles and not for the Judean remnant. The only appropriate response was submission to the overwhelming sovereignty of Yahweh as expressed through Babylonian imperialism. Therefore, while Seitz's thesis remains plausible, it fails to best the view that chap. 24 is Jeremianic.

It is common to set aside vv. 6–7, 9–10 as belonging to the Deuteronomistic redaction, but because this assessment is debatable I will isolate the more certain materials by focusing attention only on vv. 1–5 and 8.[161] The vision distinguishes between "good figs, very good," that is, the exilic community; and "bad figs, very bad, so bad that they cannot be eaten," that is, the remnant community in Judah, in this case summarily including Judean refugees in Egypt. While the text at first seems to cast moral aspersions on the Jerusalem remnant and moral compliments on the exiles, it is generally agreed that this is not the intention of the text.[162] Rudolph and Raitt have pointed out that

---

161. Carroll, *Jeremiah*, 1.655; W. J. Wessels, "Jeremiah 24:1–10 as a Pronouncement of Hope?" *OTE* 4 (1991) 399.

162. Carroll, *Jeremiah*, 1.657–60; Jones, *Jeremiah*, 319; Wessels, "Jeremiah 24:1–10 as a Pronouncement of Hope?" 401.

Jeremiah withheld his proclamation of future hope until after the exile took place.[163] This suggests that the focus should not be placed on the exiles themselves and on their superior moral qualities but on the meaning of the exile in Jeremiah's theology. As Raitt says, "Jer 24 never says that God is going to treat the Golah with favor because they are good . . . the 'good' finds its primary rootage in the intention of Yahweh's action: 'I will regard them as good.'" The theology informing Jeremiah's perspective was no doubt the theology that informed Deut 30:1–6, which promised that the exilic curse would be followed by a return to the land and to authentic Yahwism via the direct intervention of the deity: "And the Lord your God will circumcise your heart and the heart of your offspring, so that you will love the Lord your God with all your heart and with all your soul, that you may live." But for Jeremiah these predictions were relevant only for those who faced the purifying experience of the exile, as evidenced by his vision in chap. 24.

It is difficult to isolate the perspectives and concerns that contributed to this theological view of the exile. The primary problem in any discussion of exile-theology and its development is the fall of Samaria, because that event makes it hard to distinguish preexilic ideas about exile-theology (derived from the Assyrian deportation experience) from ideas that were prompted by the Babylonian exile itself. But this difficulty aside, it is quite clear that the conflict between the exiles and the Judean remnant, commonly associated with the restoration after Cyrus, began much earlier, during the period that immediately followed the exile. We will trace these theological trajectories into the book of Ezekiel during our discussion of the exile in the following chapter.

Judgment on the Circumcised Nations: Jeremiah 9:24–25

The Jeremianic origins of this text have not been questioned, but the text presents a few minor problems. The RSV is influenced by the inferior Greek translation and somewhat obscures the conclusion of v. 25.[164] J. A. Thompson reads the text as follows:

---

163. T. M. Raitt, "Jeremiah's Deliverance Message to Judah," *Rhetorical Criticism: Essays in Honor of James Muilenburg* (ed. J. J. Jackson and M. Kessler; Pittsburgh: Pickwick, 1974); Rudolph, *Jeremia*, 172–73.

164. 𝕲 and 𝔐 do not correspond precisely at the end of 9:25. The Greek reads ἐπὶ πάντας περιτετμημένους ἀκροβυστίας αὐτῶν 'I will visit upon all who are circumcised their uncircumcision', while the Hebrew reads ופקדתי על־כל־מול בערלה 'I will

> Look! Days are coming—Yahweh's word—when I will punish all
> who are circumcised physically: Egypt, Judah, Edom, Ammon,
> Moab, and all whose temples are shaved who live in the steppelands,
> for all these nations are uncircumcised —and all the house of Israel is
> uncircumcised in heart.

J. M. Sasson has examined the evidence for circumcision in the ancient
Near East and has concluded that the practice, which followed various
cultural permutations,[165] dated back at least to the early third millennium.[166] However, its place in the biblical sources is not so pronounced. Circumcision's earliest appearance in the Hebrew Bible—
except perhaps Genesis 34—is in Deut 10:16 and 30:6, both of which
are concerned not so much with the practice itself as with Israel's internal religious disposition: was Israel "circumcised" in the heart?[167] For
Deuteronomy, to be uncircumcised in the heart was to be religiously
"stubborn," and this image was taken up by Jeremiah at several points,
the present text included. However, despite its association with Israelite religious affections, circumcision was not a distinctly Israelite cultural feature in this text or in the Deuteronomic texts that preceded it.
The surrounding peoples—Egyptians, Moabites, Ammonites, and so
on—practiced the same ritual.[168] That these "circumcised" cultures
felt a common bond with each other and, at the same time, harbored a
sense of superiority toward the uncircumcised peoples around them
seems clear from texts in Ezekiel 28, 31, and 32. These texts predicted

---

visit upon all who are circumcised in the flesh'. In v. 26, ᵷ reads Ιδουμαίαν ('Idumean')
for the Hebrew יהודה ('Judah'= Ιουδαίαν). In both cases, ℳ is to be preferred. The
Greek translation in v. 25 is a theological interpretation of the text and in v. 26 Judah's
second place in the list prompted translators to suggest 'Idumea' in its place.

165. The surgical procedure seems to have varied in Israel and Egypt. In Israel the
entire prepuce was removed, while in Egypt a dorsal incision in the foreskin liberated
the glans penis. See J. M. Sasson, "Circumcision in the Ancient Near East," *JBL* 85
(1966) 474.

166. Ibid., 473–76.

167. The dating of Genesis 34 is problematic. As observed by Westermann, the
text in its present form appears to presuppose the commands in Deuteronomy 7 and
also has an affinity for the language of P. Westermann nonetheless postulates a very old
tradition behind the text that included as its fundamental basis the issue of circumcision. Still, the text does not indicate that circumcision was a uniquely Israelite practice,
only that some of the land's inhabitants did not follow the practice. See Van Seters,
Prologue to History, 277–78; Westermann, *Genesis*, 2.535–37.

168. The bond envisioned here perhaps goes beyond the rite itself. Rudolph has
suggested, probably correctly, that the nations listed in this text participated together
in an anti-Babylonian coalition (*Jeremia*, 70–71).

282 Ethnicity and Identity in the Judean Monarchy

the demise of various peoples and also scandalized their afterlife with these predictions: those who were circumcised would "lie among the uncircumcised," and those who were uncircumcised would go down to Sheol in their uncircumcision. Among the circumcised were the Egyptians and Edomites; among the uncircumcised were the Assyrians, Elamites, Sidonians, and the peoples of Meshech and Tubal. The clear inference from this text is that one should be pitied if he is either uncircumcised or if he is compelled to associate with the uncircumcised. We should derive from this the conclusion that circumcision served no unique role in the Israelite sense of identity prior to the seventh century B.C.E. Israel was instead a part of the broader cultural community that followed the practice.[169]

The terms that are semantically related to circumcision—ערל, ערלה, and מול—are narrowly distributed in the Hebrew text. One can deduce from the biblical sources a certain development in the attitudes and ideas related to circumcision. In the earliest sources from Deuteronomy and Jeremiah, circumcision was a common rite practiced by many of Israel's neighbors, and those who failed to practice it were considered culturally inferior. At this same historical juncture, circumcision, which by its nature involved the exposure of sensitive tissues, became symbolically related to the heart that was responsive to Yahweh. In the exilic context, Ezekiel appears to have come face to face with Israel's distinctiveness in regard to the practice of circumcision, as suggested by his list of exilic neighbors who did not practice the rite (Assyria, Elam, Tubal, Meshech, etc.). Finally, after the exile, circumcision became a unique aspect of Israelite identity, no doubt the result of the Jews' long stay in Mesopotamia. In this late period, circumcision became a sign of community membership (Genesis 17), and assimilating foreigners were required to undergo the ritual: "And when a stranger (גר) shall sojourn with you and would keep the Passover to the Lord, let all his males be circumcised; then he may come near and keep it; he shall be as a native of the land. But no uncircumcised person shall eat it" (Exod 12:48). In sum, prior to the exile, circumcision as a distinctive mark of Israelite identity had not yet emerged.

169. Holladay has noted that "the most remarkable single feature of the passage is the listing of Judah second, after Egypt and before Edom." This arrangement is perhaps due to geographical concerns, but it might also reflect the lack of distinction between Judah and Egypt in regard to circumcision (see Holladay, *Jeremiah*, 1.319).

Summary:
Ethnicity and Identity in the Judean Monarchy

The proto-Deuteronomic traditions that originated with Hosea took root in the South and continued his original mission, to establish Israel as a mono-Yahwist community. In the process, the Deuteronomic movement intensified existing ethnic sentiments—especially in its development of "brother theology"—and employed them in support of its religious agenda. But the agenda should not be characterized only by its support for Yahweh, since there was a decidedly humanitarian concern in Deuteronomy as well, especially in its effort to protect Northern refugees, which the community considered to be the ethnic brothers of the Judeans. It is to a certain extent natural that the discourse employed to achieve these aims included a decidedly caustic ethnic exclusiveness, but there were mediating features that suggested that the separatism was largely polemical. We can cite three characteristic examples.

The first is that Deuteronomy embraced a very supportive stance toward foreign "sojourners" (גרים). This tendency probably emerged alongside the effort to protect Israelite sojourners from the North and stemmed from the obviously close sociological association that existed between Israelite sojourners and non-Israelite sojourners. As a result, non-Israelite sojourners were able to assimilate to the Israelite religious community rather easily, although it is clear that some of the sojourners chose not to do this. The second feature is that in Deuteronomy the primary criterion for community membership was religious—a commitment to Yahweh—and not ethnic, and this explains why foreign sojourners could so easily be assimilated; assimilation required only one's commitment to Yahweh. All of this suggests that the ethnic sentiments of Deuteronomy were more rhetorical than actual, and this interpretation of the data is supported by the third feature of Deuteronomic ethnicity. We could identify no clear and useful indicia that existed to help the community readily distinguish between insiders and outsiders. This supports our thesis that Deuteronomy's ethnic concern was much more the establishing of a sense of ethnic kinship among Israelites and Judeans than it was the excluding of foreigners from participation within the community. Ethnic exclusivity came to the fore only in a few legal statutes that excluded 'foreigners' (נכריות that had no interest in community participation), nonassimilating sojourners (גרים within Israel that had no interest in community participation), and 'bastards'

(ממזר that were born of foreign cultic activities). In other words, Deuteronomy invited religious and cultural assimilation as long as one was interested in doing so and as long as one avoided contacts with foreign deities and foreign religious practices. Only in later periods did additions to Deuteronomy place specific limitations on community participation by Ammonites, Moabites, Edomites, and others.

Our comparison of Deuteronomy with the later law codes in HC, BC, and P was also highly instructive. The sources reflect a healthy legal tradition that was dedicated to clarifying the details of previously existing statutes, which were themselves concerned with Israel's ethnic distinctiveness. This legal tradition and its effort to clarify Israelite identity and ethnicity began with the preexilic Deuteronomic movement and continued through the exile (HC and BC) until the postexilic P corpus made its appearance. The legal materials reflected a marked intensification of ethnic identity during the early exilic period, in which the Holiness Code became preoccupied with establishing clear boundaries between foreigners who were assimilating into the Israelite community (גר) and those who remained outside of it (תושב).

During the course of our discussion, several other secondary items were explored. First, Jeremiah shows that, early in the exilic experience, a schism developed between the exiles and the people left behind in Judea, and this schism centered on the question of who represented the true heir of Israel and its land. Second, the term עברי ('Hebrew') was examined. It was determined that this ethnic designation originated late in the history of Israel as an exonym that Israel borrowed from the surrounding peoples. The term was probably coined as a description of the language spoken by the Israelites. Third, the tribal list in the "Blessing of Moses" (Deuteronomy 33) was examined and its approximate date established. The list is best understood as an eighth-century, ten-tribe list that stands between the ten-tribe list in the Song of Deborah (Judges 5) and later tribal lists, which contain twelve tribes. However, in its present form, the "Blessing" has been updated to include the full complement of twelve tribal names, albeit with a scheme not found in any other twelve-tribe list of the Hebrew Bible.

In spite of the obvious similarities that we can observe among the Hebrew sources that we have examined during our study thus far, it has become clear that the path from the late eighth to the early sixth centuries included a marked increase in the complexity and intensity of Israelite ethnic ideology. From a comparative standpoint, these ethnic features relate more closely to the Greek materials than to any others.

Chapter Six

Ethnicity and Identity
in the Exilic Period

Due to traditiohistorical concerns, we have already discussed portions of the exilic material available to us. Specifically, this included several texts from Ezekiel, legal materials in the Holiness Code, and also portions of the Deuteronomistic redaction of Jeremiah. These materials reflect a marked intensification of ethnic sentiments in the exilic community, a characteristic that became most evident during our comparison of the Deuteronomic legislation and the Holiness Code. Also clear from these sources was the fact that early in the exile an ideological conflict erupted between the exilic community and the Jerusalem remnant. In this chapter I will extend the discussion of these issues by focusing attention on three primary areas.

First, during our discussion of the relevant texts, we will give attention to the secondary literature that highlights sociological and theological aspects of the exilic experience.[1] Second, although I have already examined several texts from Ezekiel, I will present additional texts from this source that will help to flesh out our understanding of ethnicity and identity during the early exilic period. And finally, an examination of texts from Deutero-Isaiah will complete my study of the exile, since this source brings us to the close of that chapter in Israel's history.

---

1. I am thinking here primarily of D. L. Smith's recent work, *The Religion of the Landless: The Social Context of the Babylonian Exile* (Bloomington: Meyer/Stone, 1989). We can add to this the works of R. W. Klein, *Israel in Exile: A Theological Interpretation* (Philadelphia: Fortress, 1979); E. W. Nicholson, *Preaching to the Exiles* (Oxford: Blackwell, 1970); T. M. Raitt, *A Theology of Exile* (Philadelphia: Fortress, 1977); C. R. Seitz, *Theology in Conflict: Reactions to the Exile in the Book of Jeremiah* (BZAW 176; Berlin: de Gruyter, 1989).

Ezekiel

On the surface, the book of Ezekiel presents us with the most properly organized prophetic collection of the Hebrew Bible. Chapters 1–24 detail oracles against Jerusalem and Judah, chaps. 25–32 oracles against the nations, and chaps. 33–48 include oracles of salvation.[2] Nevertheless, the book shows many signs of redactional activity (among them, this clear organization) and also presents numerous text-critical problems.[3] These issues will be handled only as they relate to the specific texts in question. As the reader may already have recognized, my discussion tends to assume the long-standing association of Ezekiel with the Holiness School of early P, an association that I view as contextual, chronological, and ideological. I feel that that the discussion in the previous chapter and also in this chapter only adds support to this common perspective.

The Exiles and the Judean Remnant in Ezekiel 11:1–25, 33:23–24

Despite the fact that Ezekiel 11 has been secondarily added to its present location in the "Temple Vision" (Ezek 8:1–11:25), it is generally agreed that its proper temporal setting is still Ezekiel's ministry, not some later context.[4] The text falls into two parts, vv. 1–13 and 14–21, each associated with its own separate Sitz im Leben but related to the other in content, which is why the editor joined the two. The end of the chapter (vv. 22–25) belongs to the larger pericope of Ezekiel 8–11.[5] Although Zimmerli's perspective, that there are "strong grounds for its composition in the time when Jerusalem was still standing," is a common one, the reference in v. 10, "I will judge you at the border of Israel," no doubt refers to the events at Riblah in 587 B.C.E. (cf. 2 Kgs 25:20–21) and therefore suggests that the original text was expanded at that time.[6] The other text, Ezek 33:23–24, refers to "the inhabitants of

2. J. A. Soggin, *Introduction to the Old Testament* (OTL; Louisville: Westminster, John Knox, 1989) 358.

3. J. W. Wevers, *Ezekiel* (NCBC; Grand Rapids, Mich.: Eerdmans, 1969) 36–39; W. Zimmerli, *Ezekiel* (2 vols.; Hermeneia; Philadelphia: Fortress, 1979–83) 1.71–77.

4. G. A. Cooke, *Ezekiel* (ICC; Edinburgh: T. & T. Clark, 1951) 121; W. Eichrodt, *Ezekiel* (OTL; Philadelphia: Westminster, 1970) 112–19; Wevers, *Ezekiel*, 78–79; Zimmerli, *Ezekiel*, 1.230–31, 257.

5. See Zimmerli's reconstruction, ibid., 1.233–34.

6. Cooke, *Ezekiel*, 121; Wevers, *Ezekiel*, 76; Zimmerli, *Ezekiel*, 1.259.

these waste places" and consequently must date after 587 B.C.E. Taken together, these texts provide us with a glimpse into the conflict between the Judean remnant and the exiles as seen through the eyes of the exiles themselves, a debate already familiar to us from Jeremiah.

As we saw in the previous chapter, the conflict between the Judean remnant and the exilic community began after 597 B.C.E. and was a topic of dispute even in Palestine itself. Jeremiah, and no doubt some others in Judah, viewed the exilic community as the true heir of Israel's future. Ezekiel, like his prophetic predecessor, previewed for his audience the coming destruction that awaited the evil Judean remnant (11:1–13).[7] A later addition in vv. 9–11 records the fulfillment of this prophecy at Riblah, here called "the border of Israel," which shows clearly that Ezekiel's concept of homeland included all of the territory previously controlled by Judah and Israel. The heart of the debate between the two factions is recorded in 11:14–21. On the one hand, in language clearly influenced by preexilic Deuteronomic language, the inhabitants of Jerusalem were saying of the exiles, 'They have gone far from the Lord; to us this land is given for a possession' (הארץ למורשה לנו היא נתנה). For the homeland remnant, the exiles were outside of the land and therefore outside of Yahweh's purview.

Ezekiel's perspective was also influenced by Deuteronomy, particularly its "brother theology," but in his view only the exilic community (and not the Judean remnant) represented the true community of Israel: "Son of man, your brethren (אחיך), even your brethren, your fellow exiles (אנשי גאלתך), the whole house of Israel (כל־בית ישראל)." The prophet's use of apposition makes clear that the exiles were his ethnic brothers and the sole representatives of Israel. But he added to this Deuteronomic theology several ideas that we have come to associate more closely with the Deuteronomistic developments of the early exile:

> Therefore say, "Thus says the Lord God: 'Though I removed them far off among the nations, and though I scattered them among the

---

7. D. J. Halperin interprets this text as a judgment oracle against the exiles rather than against the Judean remnant community, primarily because he sees a parallel between the punishment "at the border of Israel" in 11:10–11 and the wilderness judgment of the exiles Ezek 20:36–38. In my view, the two texts share some similarities but do not address the same audiences. The evil city in view here is clearly Jerusalem, as the contextual pointers in 11:1, 22–25 show (D. J. Halperin, *Seeking Ezekiel: Text and Psychology* [University Park: Pennsylvania State University, 1993] 74–79).

countries, yet I have been a sanctuary to them for a while in the countries where they have gone.'" Therefore say, "Thus says the Lord God: 'I will gather you from the peoples, and assemble you out of the countries where you have been scattered, and I will give you the land of Israel.' And when they come there, they will remove from it all its detestable things and all its abominations. And I will give them one heart, and put a new spirit within them; I will take the stony heart out of their flesh and give them a heart of flesh, that they may walk in my statutes and keep my ordinances and obey them; and they shall be my people, and I will be their God. But as for those whose heart goes after their detestable things and their abominations, I will requite their deeds upon their own heads, says the Lord God." (Ezek 11:16–21)

As we see in this text, in at least one sense, Deuteronomistic theology was a necessary development of Deuteronomic theology because it helped to transfer the land-promise theme from the Judean context to the exilic context in Babylon. For both Ezekiel and Jeremiah, this was an important development because the future of Israel lay with the exilic community, and this was precisely because Yahweh had promised to secure what was missing prior to the exile, "a heart committed to covenant fidelity," and he had promised to do this primarily for the exiles.

We see, then, that early in the exilic experience, even prior to the fall of Jerusalem, the exilic community and their supporters in Judah understood that the exiles *were Israel*. This represents a transformation of the ethnic identity and sentiment found in Deuteronomy. While Deuteronomy utilized ethnic sentiments and "brother theology" in part to support its agenda of inclusiveness, here Ezekiel employs אח with precisely the opposite goal: to distinguish between his fellows and the Judean remnant. In doing so he removed the "obvious" ethnic ties that had previously joined the exiles to their Judean counterparts. Consequently, while we might rightly ask ourselves why Ezra and Nehemiah displayed so little affection for the people they met upon returning to Judah, we need not look to that late period for an answer. These exclusivistic sentiments originated among the exiles (and their Judean supporters) even before the first Temple was destroyed.

After the fall of Jerusalem, the debating factions continued their ideological struggle. One of the more interesting claims of the Judean faction was recorded in Ezek 33:23–24:

> The word of the Lord came to me: "Son of man, the inhabitants of these waste places in the land of Israel keep saying, 'Abraham was only one man, yet he got possession of the land (אֶת־הָאָרֶץ וַיִּירַשׁ); but we are many; the land is surely given us to possess (לָנוּ נִתְּנָה הָאָרֶץ לְמוֹרָשָׁה).'"

As in Ezekiel 11, the claims of the remnant community seem to reflect Deuteronomic terminology. But the reference to the patriarchal figure sets this text apart from Ezekiel 11 and is important because, if one grants that Jer 33:26 is part of the exilic Deuteronomistic redaction of Jeremiah, then it becomes our earliest prophetic witness to the patriarchal figure Abraham. Because most commentators mistakenly assume that the pentateuchal sources are early, they fail to ask the important question that the text raises: what was the state of the Abrahamic tradition in the early exilic period and how does this compare with the tradition in the pentateuchal materials? The works of J. Van Seters and of T. Römer are helpful in this regard.[8]

Römer is correct that the Abraham tradition that appears here should be viewed as a *nichtexilierten* tradition that originated within the Judean remnant community.[9] The text has connections with Deuteronomic language (הָאָרֶץ, נתן, ירשׁ) and finds its chief parallel in Genesis 15.[10] All of these data must be addressed. Van Seters has suggested that the theology that informs the Judean remnant's perspective in Ezek 33:24 should be distinguished from the theology assumed by Ezekiel, the exodus-settlement tradition. While the Judeans preferred an unconditional arrangement in which they, like Abraham, simply took possession of the land, Ezekiel assumed the conditionality of land inheritance as expressed in Deuteronomy. This is why, according to Van Seters, Ezekiel's response to the Judeans focused on their violence and idolatry: they had failed to meet the preconditions for land possession.[11] If true, this suggests that the Abraham tradition and the exodus-settlement tradition were still independent origin traditions during the

---

8. J. Van Seters, *Prologue to History* (Louisville: Westminster, John Knox, 1992); idem, *Abraham in History and Tradition* (New Haven: Yale University Press, 1975); T. Römer, *Israels Väter: Intersuchungen zur Väterthematik im Deuteronomium und in der deuteronomistischen Tradition* (OBO 99; Göttingen: Vandenhoeck & Ruprecht, 1990).

9. Römer, *Israels Väter,* 514–16.

10. Ibid., 515–17; C. Westermann, *Genesis* (3 vols.; Minneapolis: Augsburg, 1985) 2.224.

11. Van Seters, *Prologue to History,* 239–40.

early exilic period. Although I agree that they were probably independent traditions, I would offer several refinements to this discussion.

I want to begin with a discussion of the Abraham tradition as understood by the Judean remnant in Ezek 33:24. First, contra Van Seters, it seems to me unlikely that the Judeans viewed Abraham's possession of the land as *unconditional* and at the same time expressed their view in language highly reminiscent of Deuteronomy, which was itself a source in which land possession was highly *conditional*.[12] There are several texts that suggest that, at least in some quarters, the remnant community viewed themselves as meeting any and all relevant conditions. Ps 44:17–19 reflects this:[13]

> All this has come upon us, though we have not forgotten thee, or been false to thy covenant. Our heart has not turned back, nor have our steps departed from thy way, that thou shouldst have broken us in the place of jackals, and covered us with deep darkness.

Perhaps more important in this regard is Isa 6:11–13, a text that, as S. Japhet has noted, could not have escaped the attention of the Judean remnant community:[14]

> Then I said, "How long, O Lord?" And he said: "Until cities lie waste without inhabitant, and houses without men, and the land is utterly desolate, and the Lord removes men far away, and the forsaken places are many in the midst of the land. And though a tenth remain in it, it will be burned again, like a terebinth or an oak, whose stump remains standing when it is felled. The holy seed is its stump."

In a post-586 Judean context, this passage would have reinforced the notion that they as the remnant were the 'holy seed' (זרע קדש) and that the exiles had been moved "far away." In this text, hope lay with the

---

12. See my discussion above (pp. 225–228); and also Van Seters, *Prologue to History*, 239–39, 232–33.

13. See Klein, *Israel in Exile*, 18–19. According to Klein, Psalm 44 must date just after the exile for the following reasons: (1) Israel's armies have been beaten; (2) her foes have plundered her; (3) many people have been killed while others have been scattered among the nations; (4) her neighbors view her with scorn.

14. S. Japhet, "People and Land in the Restoration Period," in *Das Land Israel in biblischer Zeit: Jerusalem-Symposium 1981 der Hebräischen Universität und der Georg-August-Universität* (ed. G. Strecker; Göttinger Theologische Arbeiten 25; Göttingen: Vandenhoeck & Ruprecht, 1983) 107–8.

Judean remnant community, and this is virtually identical with the theology that informed the Judean side of the debate in Ezekiel 11 and 33:24.[15] What seems most likely is that the Judean remnant, faced with its own crisis—anarchy, poverty, religious chaos, political domination, ecological competition with the surrounding peoples, and ideological competition with the exiles[16]—produced (or enhanced) a forefather tradition that stood on the shoulders of the previously dominant theological (and therefore Deuteronomic) ideas. The need for this new tradition was prompted by the fact that Deuteronomy only partially corresponded to the remnant situation. Unlike the exodus generation, these Judeans were already in the land and yet were at the same time dispossessed. It is therefore reasonable to assume that, unlike the exodus-settlement tradition, the Abraham forefather was a dweller of the land who finally came to possess it. In addition to this land-inheritance theme, the Judeans appear to have inherited or created traditions about Abraham's posterity, for the phrases "he was one" and "we are many" would seem to presuppose this.[17] So, although for our purposes the Abraham tradition first appears in Ezekiel, the reference to a posterity tradition makes it likely that the Abraham figure was not an ex nihilo figure but that some traditions associated with him preceded the land-possession tradition that we find in Ezekiel.

The Register of the House of Israel: Ezekiel 13:8–9

In addition to tensions between the exilic community and the people in Judea, the prophet had to deal with internal pressures experienced by the exiles themselves. The larger context of 13:8–9, that is, Ezek 13:1–23, depicts the ongoing prophetic dispute between Ezekiel and the false prophets and prophetesses of the exilic community. It is sometimes suggested that 13:9 is a later addition, especially by scholars who believe that Ezekiel 13 dates before 586 B.C.E.[18] But the allusion to a Judean restoration in this verse cannot be denied to the pre-586 exilic community, since a return home applied to them as easily as to later exiles. It is in fact difficult to say whether the text dates prior to or

15. Ezek 11:14–15.
16. See Lam 1:3–4, 10, 17; 2:20; 4:10; 5:1–14; Ezekiel 35, 36:1–7.
17. Japhet, "People and Land in the Restoration Period," 108.
18. V. Herntrich, *Ezekielprobleme* (BZAW 61; Giessen: Alfred Töpelmann, 1933) 99; Wevers, *Ezekiel*, 85.

after the fall of Jerusalem; so Zimmerli is correct when he says that the question of date must remain open. [19]

The judgment that was pronounced on these false prophets was threefold: (1) they would be excluded from the 'council of the people' (סוד עמי); (2) they would be excluded from the 'register of the house of Israel' (כתב בית־ישראל); (3) they would not return to the land of Israel. In essence, it is usually understood that here the false prophets were stripped of their community citizenship. What interests me at this point is how this Judean community was defined in the early exilic period. First, exclusion from the סוד עמי was not an exclusion from the community as a whole but rather, as I. M. Duguid has pointed out, from the inner circle that claimed to lead via its intimate contact with the deity. [20] Upon losing his prized position of community leadership, a prophet was next removed from the document that identified him as part of the larger Israelite community, from the כתב בית־ישראל. Although Zimmerli and Eichrodt have attempted to associate this "register" with the one alluded to in Jer 22:30 (which seems to me highly questionable), [21] it should not be associated with any preexilic practice. If it was a very old "tribal roll," as suggested by Zimmerli, we would expect a Hebrew technical term in reference to it. Instead, we have here Aramaic כְּתָב, which suggests that the כתב בית־ישראל was a development of the exile.

As commentators have long pointed out, we cannot fail to posit a relationship between the כתב בית־ישראל in our text and the list of returning exiles provided in Ezra 2 and Nehemiah 7. Several questions arise from these postexilic lists. Were they an authentic record of the first returnees? What was the function of the lists? What was their relationship, if any, to the כתב בית־ישראל of Ezek 13:9? The question of authenticity is a difficult one. On the one hand, Rudolph has argued that the Golah list is authentic because it shows signs of growth, particularly in that there are shifts from 'sons of . . .' (בני) to 'men of . . .' (אנשי) and in that the priestly list was separate and added after the

---

19. Zimmerli, *Ezekiel*, 1.298.

20. See Jer 23:18 and I. M. Duguid, *Ezekiel and the Leaders of Israel* (VTSup 56; Leiden: Brill, 1994) 100–101.

21. The text says of Jehoiakin, "Write this man down as childless . . . ," which, if it is a reference to such a document, is a very vague one. See Eichrodt, *Ezekiel*, 166; Zimmerli, *Ezekiel*, 1.294.

Temple was built.[22] To this argument for authenticity we can add D. Smith's observation that, although the "sons of Hakkoz" were unable to authenticate their priestly pedigree in the return list (Ezra 2:61–63, Neh 7:63–65), in Ezra, Nehemiah, and Chronicles they are nonetheless serving as priests (cf. Ezra 8:33; Neh 3:4, 21; 1 Chr 24:10).[23] Although this suggests, of course, that the list predates the composition of Ezra and Nehemiah, contrary to Smith's conclusion, it does not ensure that the list dates before the historical period of their ministries. There are in fact good reasons for regarding the Golah list as late, at least in its final form. J. Blenkinsopp for instance, although he does not agree with Torrey that the list is pure fabrication, nonetheless points out that "the numbers [of returnees] are too high" and that the Golah list was "certainly compiled after the settlement since it names localities in which immigrants settled."[24] Taken together, this evidence would seem to argue for a composition, broadly speaking, after the return under Zerubbabel (because it assumes the settlement) and before the writing of Ezra and Nehemiah (because of the status of the Hakkoz household). Within these parameters, the data further suggest that the list was compiled over a period of time and that it was probably updated periodically to account for several repatriations.[25] The sources used to compile the list might easily have existed prior to the return, but this possibility is difficult to assess. In sum, regardless of whether it actually goes back to a specific source associated with Zerubbabel's return, the Golah list itself witnesses to a postexilic phenomenon that

22. W. Rudolph, *Esra und Nehemia* (HAT; Tübingen: Mohr, 1949) 16–20.

23. Smith, *The Religion of the Landless,* 104.

24. Blenkinsopp, *Ezra–Nehemiah: A Commentary* (OTL; Philadelphia: Westminster, 1988) 83. Similar sentiments are expressed by L. W. Batton, *Ezra and Nehemiah* (ICC; Edinburgh: T. & T. Clark, 1913) 71–74; D. J. A. Clines, *Ezra, Nehemiah, Esther* (NCBC; Grand Rapids, Mich.: Eerdmans, 1984) 43–45. For the view that the list is fabricated, see C. C. Torrey, *The Composition and Historical Value of Ezra–Nehemiah* (BZAW 2; Giessen: Alfred Töpelmann, 1896) 39–50. Notice that Ezra 2:1 calls the population 'the people of the province' (בני מדינה), which, as S. Japhet has noted, probably betrays the actual point of departure for the list ("People and Land in the Restoration Period," 113).

25. Blenkinsopp, *Ezra–Nehemiah,* 83, 85; Clines, *Ezra, Nehemiah, Esther,* 44. That this was the case seems assured by the fact that the leaders mentioned at the head of the Golah list of Ezra 2:1–2 and Neh 7:5–6—Zerubbabel, Joshua, Nehemiah, Azariah/Seriah (= Ezra/father of Ezra; cf. Ezra 7:1), Bigvai—cover a much broader historical period than the phrase "those who came up at the first" (Neh 7:5) might suggest.

included the compilation and transmission of such sources. The function of the Golah list as used in Ezra and Nehemiah is quite clear. As S. Japhet has noted, the list answered the question, who is the "true Israel?" The answer to this question reflected the strong ethnic sentiments present within the postexilic community:

> The following were those who came up from Telmelah, Telharsha, Cherub, Addan, and Immer, though they could not prove their fathers' houses (בית־אבותם) or their descent (זרעם), whether they belonged to Israel (אם מישראל הם): the sons of Delaiah, the sons of Tobiah, and the sons of Nekoda, six hundred and fifty-two. Also, of the sons of the priests: the sons of Habaiah, the sons of Hakkoz, and the sons of Barzillai (who had taken a wife from the daughters of Barzillai the Gileadite, and was called by their name). These sought their registration among those enrolled in the genealogies שׁתבם (המתיחשׂים), but they were not found there, and so they were excluded from the priesthood as unclean. (Ezra 2:59–62)

Although it is possible, as Mowinckel suggested, that we are dealing here at least in part with a fictionalized lineage system,[26] it was nonetheless believed that one was a true Israelite only when he/she could demonstrate an ethnic origin within the people of Israel and only when this pedigree could be established with written documentation. The necessity of such a pedigree rested in the special emphasis that these postexilic sources placed on ethnic purity (Ezra 9:1–2, 11–12):

> The land which you are entering, to take possession of it, is a land unclean with pollutions of the peoples of the lands, with their abominations which have filled it from end to end with their uncleanness. Therefore give not your daughters to their sons, neither take their daughters for your sons, and never seek their peace or prosperity, that you may be strong, and eat the good of the land, and leave it for an inheritance to your children for ever.

> The people of Israel and the priests and Levites have not separated themselves from the peoples of the lands with their abominations. ... For they have taken some of their daughters to be wives for themselves and for their sons; so that the holy race has mixed itself with the peoples of the lands.

The Golah community of Ezra considered ethnic pollution to be a primary cause of the exilic experience and, because of this, the commu-

---

26. S. Mowinckel, *Studien zum Buche Ezra–Nehemiah* (3 vols.; Oslo: Universitetsforlaget, 1964) 1.75.

nity was preoccupied with the notion of ethnic purity. Japhet has suggested that this concern for ethnic purity precluded the notion of proselyte conversion.[27] However, even in Ezra there is room for the willing outsider (Ezra 6:19–21).

This observation makes it very difficult to link the כתב בית־ישראל of Ezekiel 13 directly with the Golah lists of Ezra/Nehemiah. Ezekiel stands very close to the Holiness Code, and both of them reflect support for the proselyte גר and for his protected status within the Israelite community. Although ethnic purity was becoming an issue for HC, its openness to foreigners precludes a document that functions like the genealogical Golah lists of Ezra/Nehemiah. Instead, the purpose and function of the כתב ביתישראל must be sought in the situation faced by Ezekiel and the early exilic community. As we saw during our discussion of Ezekiel 11 and 33:23, the exilic community faced a predicament: the Judeans who did not go into exile were seizing the property of the departing exiles. Nevertheless, the hope of restoration expressed in Ezekiel and Jeremiah assumed that these exiles would some day return to these ancestral lands. In such a context, the כתב בית־ישראל of Ezek 13:9 is best understood as a record of family landholdings, and it is for this reason that the disenfranchised prophets of Ezekiel 13 were also told that they would not return to Israel, since this naturally followed from the fact that elimination from the records meant the loss of ancestral property.

Therefore, the function of the exilic כתב בית־ישראל was distinct from the function of the postexilic Golah list in Ezra/Nehemiah, and this fact rules out a direct link between the documents. However, it does not mean that there is no link between them. A. Alt long ago suggested that the Golah lists were derived from attempts to define the property rights of returning exiles and, although it is partly conjecture, this view suggests that a straight line can be interpolated between the two types of documents.[28] The original property lists would have been constructed in part according to the social organization of the exiles, which appears to have centered on the "heads of families," the elders (זקנים).[29] Assuming, then, that the exiled groups were moved and then

27. Japhet, "People and Land in the Restoration Period," 117.
28. A. Alt, *Kleine Schriften zur Geschichte des Volkes Israel* (3 vols.; Munich: Beck, 1953–59) 2.334–35.
29. See Duguid, *Ezekiel and the Leaders of Israel*, 110–11. Cf. Jer 29:1; Ezek 7:26, 8:11, 14:1, 20:1–3. We therefore see a similar pattern after the fall of the Northern

settled together, we should conclude that the property records were organized first by location within Judah and then by family. During the
course of the exile, these lists would have been frequently updated to account for changes in family circumstances, deaths, and so on. However,
after the exile, competition between the returning exiles and the people
living on their ancestral property intensified ethnic sentiments; these
property documents then served a new role in defining the ethnic community.[30] Not only did they serve as a record of ancestral properties,
but by extension they served to authenticate one's identity as a Jew. And
in these documents the restored community was none other than the
ethnic Israelites that returned from Babylon.

Restoring the Community in Ezekiel 40–48

As Ezek 13:9 shows, from the onset of their exilic experience, the
community in Babylon organized itself for a return to the land. They
viewed themselves as the true heirs of God's promises to the forefathers
and the future inheritors of the homeland. The imagination and en-
ergy devoted to the coming return was nowhere more animated than
in Ezekiel 40–48, which provided a vision of the reconstituted community in its motherland. Specifically, there are three issues that I will
examine.

First, it is important to recognize that the whole complex of chaps.
40–48 reflects a rather "lively history of growth."[31] In addition to the
"guidance vision" that provides the core of the materials,[32] the text has
been expanded by Ezekiel's followers and shows signs of editorial activ-

---

Kingdom and in the exile. In both cases, the demise of monarchic political leadership
resulted in a new emphasis on "lay leadership," i.e., the elders. See also J. Buchholz,
Die Ältesten Israels im Deuteronomium (Göttinger Theologische Arbeiten 36; Göttingen: Vandenhoeck & Ruprecht, 1988).

30. That this was the case is perhaps evidenced by the fact that the Golah list in
large part provided the regional origins of peoples rather than their ancestral heritage.
Its use to authenticate ethnic origins was secondary to its original purpose.

31. Zimmerli, *Ezekiel,* 2.547. Here and below I rely heavily on the literary analysis
of Zimmerli, who in turn was heavily dependent on H. Gese's work, *Der Verfassungs-
entwurf des Ezechiel (Kap. 40–48) traditionsgeschichtlich untersucht* (Beiträge zur His-
torischen Theologie 25; Tübingen: Mohr, 1957).

32. Ezek 40:1–37, 47–49; 41:1–15a; 42:15–20; 43:1–11. See Zimmerli's summary
in *Ezekiel,* 2.547–48. For more detail, see the appropriate sections of his commentary.

ity into the late exile and, in a few cases, into the postexilic period.[33] As S. Tuell has noted, we should not view this growth as isolated layers but as a continuous tradition of deliberative reflection on the Vorlage that preceded each layer.[34] The vision included a restoration of the Temple, of the religious leadership, of Israel's ancestral property, and also of the Davidic monarch, who in Ezekiel was represented as the 'prince' (נשׂיא).[35] The continuous editorial interest in this material (Ezekiel 40–48) shows that throughout the exile a primary element in the identity of the Golah community was, on the one hand, their status as a displaced community, and on the other, their status as a community that was "homebound." It was precisely this preoccupation with going home that served to intensify feelings of Judean distinctiveness in the Babylonian context, and this no doubt contributed to the intensification of ethnic sentiments and prevented wholesale assimilation in that foreign context.

The second issue that arises from this text is the tribal list in Ezekiel 48 and the associated division of the land. The chapter actually includes two tribal lists, one in vv. 1–29 and a later addition in vv. 30–35, and we will discuss both of them. Because we have already discussed the development of the tribal list tradition in the Song of Deborah and Deuteronomy 33, we are now in a position to offer a chronological history of the tradition as revealed in the biblical sources (see Table 5.1). The oldest tradition, reflected in the Song of Deborah, should be dated no later than the early ninth century on the basis of its linguistic features, as we have previously discussed. That this list was a "tribal list" is debatable, since neither מטה nor שבט occurs in the text, but the list nonetheless includes ten groups that later sources identified as "tribes." The earliest form of the Blessing in Deuteronomy 33, which dates to the eighth century, was also a ten-tribe list. It eliminated Machir and Gilead and added Joseph and Judah. The Joseph blessing mentions two units, Ephraim and Manasseh, but it nonetheless serves as one tribal unit in the text. In the seventh century, a Deuteronomic edition of the Blessing was prepared that, in accordance with Deuteronomy's support for the Levites, updated the collection of

33. See Zimmerli's discussions of Ezek 41:15b–21; 43:13–27; 44:4–5, 6–31.

34. S. Tuell, *The Law of the Temple in Ezekiel 40–48* (HSM 49; Atlanta: Scholars Press, 1992) 175. That the growth visible in the text is closely related to what preceeded it has also been carefully worked out by Gese and Zimmerli.

35. Duguid, *Ezekiel and the Leadership of Israel*, 10–90, 133–43.

Table 5.1 Tribal Lists in the Hebrew Bible

Song of Deborah (Judges 5) 9th century	Blessing of Moses A (Deut 33) 8th century	Blessing of Moses B (Deut 33) 7th century	Ezekiel 48:1–29 6th century	Ezekiel 48:30–35 6th century
1. Ephraim		1. Ephraim (5)	1. Ephraim (5)	
2. Benjamin	1. Benjamin (3)	2. Benjamin (4)	2. Benjamin (8)	1. Benjamin (5)
3. Machir				
4. Zebulun	2. Zebulun (5)	3. Zebulun (7)	3. Zebulun (11)	2. Zebulun (9)
5. Issachar	3. Issachar (6)	4. Issachar (8)	4. Issachar (10)	3. Issachar (8)
6. Reuben	4. Rebuen (1)	5. Reuben (1)	5. Reuben (6)	4. Reuben (1)
7. Gilead				
8. Dan	5. Dan (8)	6. Dan (11)	6. Dan (1)	5. Dan (6)
9. Asher	6. Asher (10)	7. Asher (12)	7. Asher (2)	6. Asher (11)
10. Naphtali	7. Naphtali (9)	8. Naphtali	8. Naphtali (3)	7. Naphtali (12)
	8. Judah (2)	9. Judah (2)	9. Judah (7)	8. Judah (2)
	9. Gad (7)	10. Gad (9)	10. Gad (12)	9. Gad (10)
	10. Joseph (= Ephraim, Manassah) (4)	(Joseph)	(Joseph)	10. Joseph (4)
		11. Manasseh (6)	11. Manasseh (4)	
		12 Levi (3)	(Levi)	11. Levi (3)
			12. Simeon (9)	12. Simeon (11)

Note: Numbers in parentheses represent the actual order within that tribal list.

blessings to grant tribal status to Levites. But the addition of Levi made it impossible to follow the ten-tribe tradition. Because eleven was not an "acceptable" number, the editor was satisfied to view the two Joseph groups, Ephraim and Manasseh, as a suitable solution.[36] The result was the twelve-tribe scheme which became standard from that point on. The lists in Ezek 48:1–29 and 48:30–35 witness the two latest forms of the tribal list. Because of the addition of Simeon to these lists,[37] the twelve-tribe pattern could only be preserved by eliminating one of the other tribal groups. One method of accomplishing this, illustrated in the first text, was to distinguish Levi from the other tribes. In this case,

36. For a similar numerological convention, see pp. 74–75.

37. It is often presumed that Simeon, which appears in tribal lists of the Pentateuch (which is also presumed early), was an older tribe that was absorbed into Judah. Although the history of the group is far from clear, the evidence suggests that Simeon was one of the youngest tribes, appearing in the lists only during the exile and afterward. Arriving at the same conclusion along a different path is B. Halpern, *The Emergence of Israel in Canaan* (SBLMS 29; Chico, Calif.: Scholars Press, 1983) 129.

the allotment of the Zadokites/Levites was considered the 'portion of Yahweh' (התרומה אשר תרימו ליהוה), which of course made that allotment distinct from the other twelve tribal allotments. A similar effort is made in Numbers 1 and Judges 15–19, where the Levites were not numbered with the tribes because of their appointment to temple service. The other method of compensation, as seen in the second text (Ezek 48:30–35), was to count Ephraim and Manasseh as one tribe, Joseph. This practice was followed whenever brief tribal lists preempted the first compensation method (to distinguish Levi), as seen in several other texts.[38] On the basis of this evidence it appears that the classical tribal schemes that we find in the Tetrateuchal sources should be dated more closely to the exile than to some of the earlier periods frequently suggested.

The later dating of tribal schemes also raises several issues regarding the division of the land itself and the establishment of its limits and borders (Ezek 47:13–48:29). Ezekiel 48 is exilic but was composed after Ezekiel himself and should instead be associated with the "Ezekiel school."[39] As Tuell, has noted, the tribes listed here did not exist during or after the exilic period, so that the tribal plan would seem to be infeasible.[40] In this sense the text is perhaps best described as a "utopian vision"[41] that demonstrates the long-standing grip of tribal identity on Israelite expressions of identity. Here we should not think of "tribal identity" in the sense of concrete social modalities but as the notion that an ideal restored community must necessarily be composed of twelve tribal units. Zimmerli has reconstructed the tribal arrangements as depicted by the text.[42] The tribal regions run north and south of the sacred precinct, which was a royal/priestly תרומה to Yahweh that surrounded Jerusalem. To the north lay Judah, and then beyond it Reuben, Ephraim, Manasseh, Naphtali, Asher, and Dan, respectively. To the south lay Benjamin and then Simeon, Issachar, Zebulun, and Gad.

38. Gen 35:22–26, 49:1–28; Exod 1:2–4; Deut 27:11–14; 1 Chr 2:1–2.

39. As evidenced by the lack of any urgency concerning the return to the land and also by the fact that the late-exilic critcisms of the Levites do not come into play here (Zimmerli, *Ezekiel*, 2.542).

40. Tuell, *The Law of the Temple in Ezekiel 40–48*, 170–71.

41. Cooke, *Ezekiel*, 524; Eichrodt, *Ezekiel*, 591; J. D. Levenson, *Theology of the Program of Restoration of Ezekiel 40–48* (HSM 10; Missoula, Mont.: Scholars Press, 1976) 115–16; Wevers, *Ezekiel*, 231.

42. See Zimmerli, *Ezekiel*, 2.535–37.

The picture was purely schematic and made no attempt, as would later texts, to reconcile the individual tribes to their historical locations. This was not the case in the historiographic texts of Deuteronomy 3 and Numbers 32. In these texts, both the Deuteronomist and the Yahwist were concerned precisely with the specific regions that should be associated with the various tribal groups.[43] Under the influence of these sources, P's later depiction of the tribal allotment was even more precise in assigning the tribes to an appropriate geographical setting.[44]

The other related issue in this text is the description of land boundaries in Ezekiel 47–48. The borders described there correspond to the P delineations in Numbers 34 and Joshua 15 but differ from P in that they extended beyond Sidon to the north and did not include Transjordan, a territory long associated with Israel.[45] Aharoni has suggested that these boundaries correspond to the old Egyptian holdings in Syria–Palestine, while Tuell, on the other hand, has suggested that they should be associated with the Persian satrapy of Abar-Nahara.[46] The exilic date of the text seems to preclude both options. More likely, the boundaries should be connected with the nations oracles in chaps. 25–28. There the Transjordanian states Ammon and Moab were given to the "people of the East," while more trenchant predictions were offered for Tyre and Sidon, who would "never be found again" (Ezek 26:21). This would account for the borders described in the text, since Transjordan would one day be under foreign control, and the uninhabited Phoenician region could then fall under Israelite control.

The final concern raised by Ezekiel 40–48 is the apparent conflict between 47:22–23 and 44:6–9. The two texts read as follows:

> You shall allot it as an inheritance for yourselves and for the aliens who reside among you and have begotten children among you. They

43. For a discussion of these texts, see Van Seters, *The Life of Moses: The Yahwist as Historian in Exodus–Numbers* (Louisville: Westminster, John Knox, 1994) 436–50.

44. Cf. Joshua 13–19; Judg 1:1–2:5, 2:22–3:4. For a discussion of these texts, see J. Van Seters, *In Search of History: Historiography in the Ancient World and the Origins of Biblical History* (New Haven: Yale University Press, 1983; repr., Winona Lake, Ind.: Eisenbrauns, 1997) 324–46.

45. J. Van Seters has assigned Joshua 15, along with a large portion of both Joshua and Judges, to P. He has done this because the tribal allotment process in Joshua 14–19 differs from that of Dtr, follows patterns in P, and uses P's allotment terminology (ibid., 324–46); on Israel's ancient ties to Transjordan, see especially the Mesha Stela in *ANET* 320.

46. Y. Aharoni, *The Land of the Bible: A Historical Geography* (Philadelphia: Westminster, 1967) 61–70; Tuell, *The Law of the Temple in Ezekiel 40–48*, 156–74.

shall be to you as native-born sons of Israel; with you they shall be allotted an inheritance among the tribes of Israel. In whatever tribe the alien resides, there you shall assign him his inheritance, says the Lord God. (Ezek 47:22–23)

And say to the rebellious house, to the house of Israel, "Thus says the Lord God: 'O house of Israel, let there be an end to all your abominations, in admitting foreigners, uncircumcised in heart and flesh, to be in my sanctuary, profaning it, when you offer to me my food, the fat and the blood. You have broken my covenant, in addition to all your abominations. And you have not kept charge of my holy things; but you have set foreigners to keep my charge in my sanctuary.' Therefore thus says the Lord God: 'No foreigner, uncircumcised in heart and flesh, of all the foreigners who are among the people of Israel, shall enter my sanctuary.'" (Ezek 44:6–9)

In tone and spirit, these texts appear to address two quite different contexts. The former, which reflects the stance of the Holiness Code precisely, is highly supportive of the foreigner who is seeking community assimilation. This suggests a date during the early exilic experience. The texts that sound like the second text (Ezek 44:6–9) may quite easily date to the postexilic period.[47] Furthermore, 44:6–9 has a number of features that are not characteristic of Ezekiel (נכר and 3d-person plural address)[48] and fits best into the context of Neh 13:4–9, which describes how the foreigner, Tobiah the Ammonite, was thrown out of the Temple. Prior to the exile, there was very little polemic of this nature and, barring animated creativity, the exile itself presented no real opportunity for such an "abomination" to arise. We must therefore conclude with Zimmerli that Ezek 44:6–16 is a postexilic addition to the prophetic collection.[49] Nevertheless, it is possible that the sentiments in this text were shared by some who lived during the exilic period.

47. Deuteronomy 23 and Lev 22:25. Regarding Deuteronomy 23, see my previous discussion (pp. 253–258). With respect to Lev 22:25, which legislates against taking sacrificial foodstuffs from a foreigner's hand, see K. Ellinger, *Leviticus* (HAT; Tübingen: Mohr, 1966) 300; A. Cholewinski, *Heiligkeitsgesetz und Deuteronomium* (AnBib 66; Rome: Pontifical Biblical Institute, 1976) 77–78.

48. Zimmerli, *Ezekiel*, 2.453; Wevers, *Ezekiel*, 219–20. But see Fohrer, who argues that the text comes from Ezekiel, that it has been influenced by Deuteronomy 23 and IIC, and that it deviates from the younger P (G. Fohrer, *Ezechiel* [HAT; Tübingen: Mohr, 1955] 246–47).

49. Zimmerli, *Ezekiel*, 2.454–55.

The Foundations of Restoration: A New Heart
(Ezekiel 36:16–38)

Although the details of the restoration were provided in Ezekiel 40–48, according to the final form of Ezekiel, the foundational theology that made this restoration possible was a change in the fundamental religious receptivity of Israel. This change should be closely identified with the 'new covenant' (ברית חדשה) mentioned in Jer 31:31–34, as Fohrer has pointed out.[50] The potential influence of a 'new covenant' idea on community identity is evidenced by the much later rift that it created between the Essenes and Christians, on the one hand, and the rest of Judaism, on the other.[51] Although some recent studies have questioned the Jeremianic origins of Jer 31:31–34,[52] it is generally believed to share features with the authentic corpus.[53] Thus, we should conclude that the new covenant tradition dates no later than the early exilic period, probably earlier. The previous weakness of Israel's covenant relationship with Yahweh, according to this new covenant tradition, rested in the fact that Israel was unable to remain faithful to him because their internal religious disposition, their 'heart' (לב/לבב), was deficient. The impasse could only be broken by means of a new covenant that changed the heart of Israel and secured its fidelity to the covenant. Although it is not entirely clear in this early expression of the new covenant theme, subsequent developments by the Deuteronomistic school unambiguously connected this new covenant promise with the exilic community:

> Behold, I will gather them from all the countries to which I drove them in my anger and my wrath and in great indignation; I will bring them back to this place, and I will make them dwell in safety. And they shall be my people, and I will be their God. I will give them one heart and one way, that they may fear me for ever, for their

50. Fohrer, *Ezechiel*, 205.

51. G. Vermes, *The Dead Sea Scrolls* (New York: Penguin, 1987) 37–38, 42, 81.

52. Nicholson, *Preaching to the Exiles*, 82; W. Thiel, *Die deuteronomistische Redaktion von Jeremia 26–45* (WMANT 52; Neukirchen-Vluyn: Neukirchener Verlag, 1981) 27–28.

53. W. L. Holladay, *Jeremiah : A Commentary on the Book of the Prophet Jeremiah* (2 vols.; Hermeneia; Minneapolis: Fortress, 1989) 2.197; D. R. Jones, *Jeremiah* (NCBC; Grand Rapids, Mich.: Eerdmans, 1992) 399–400; Rudolph, *Jeremia*, 201–4; A. Weiser, *Das Buch des Propheten Jeremia* (2 vols.; ATD; Göttingen: Vandenhoeck & Ruprecht, 1952–55) 2.285–88.

own good and the good of their children after them. I will make with them an everlasting covenant, that I will not turn away from doing good to them; and I will put the fear of me in their hearts, that they may not turn from me. I will rejoice in doing them good, and I will plant them in this land in faithfulness, with all my heart and all my soul. (Jer 32:37–41)

It was this exilic development of the new covenant theme that stood behind Ezekiel 36.

Although it is sometimes thought that Ezekiel 36 originated with the prophet himself,[54] the tradition is usually assigned to the late exile, when the *Heimkehr* was imminent.[55] Every element within the text links to ideas found in the earlier Deuteronomistic additions to Jeremiah and Deuteronomy. Taken together, these three sources—the supposedly authentic Jeremiah text (Jer 31:31–34), the Deuteronomistic redaction of that book (Jer 32:37–41), and Ezek 36:16–38—show that the concept of a new heart was an influential idea throughout the exilic period. This concept naturally facilitated a sense of distinctiveness in exilic identity, since the exiles—and not those left behind in Judea—had experienced the change of heart wrought by Yahweh himself. That this was the case among the exiles is still more evident in some of the texts that we will examine from Deutero-Isaiah.

The History of Israel in Ezekiel 20

In comparison with our previous discussion, Ezekiel 20 is extraordinary in that it clearly outlines the sacred history of Israel in four stages, followed by the exile: the exodus (vv. 5–9), the first wilderness generation (vv. 10–17), the second wilderness generation (vv. 18–26),[56] the residence in Canaan (vv. 27–29), and the exile (vv. 30–38).[57] As Van Seters and Römer have pointed out, there is no room for a patriarchal generation in this scheme.[58] But this is not surprising since

54. Cooke, *Ezekiel*, 385–86.

55. Zimmerli, *Ezekiel*, 2.245–46; Wevers, *Ezekiel*, 190–91.

56. That there are two wilderness generations here seems clear (Wevers, *Ezekiel*, 117–18; Zimmerli, *Ezekiel*, 1.410).

57. See a brief but similar historical outline in Jer 2:2–8. The outline that stands behind Ezekiel's work, especially in its recognition of two wilderness traditions, reflects a rather advanced stage of historical reflection. The traditions that inform the prophet here are no doubt those taken up by the Yahwist in his historiographic effort.

58. Römer, *Israels Väter*, 495–506; Van Seters, *Prologue to History*, 233–35.

Ezekiel 20 appeared several years before our first contact with the Abraham tradition in Ezekiel 33.[59] On the other hand, as Zimmerli has pointed out, Ezek 20:5 comes quite close to making a connection between the patriarchal figure and the Exodus generation: "On the day when I chose Israel, I swore to the seed of the house of Jacob, making myself known to them in the land of Egypt. . . ." But even if this does represent a tendency to combine the two origin traditions, the process must have been in its nascent stages, and the phrase זרע בית יעקב makes the whole proposition less likely, since a reference to the "house of Jacob" is slightly more ambiguous than something like 'the seed of Jacob' (זרע יעקב).

The remarkable feature of this historical *Rückblick* is that Israel's history is portrayed in entirely negative terms. There is no wilderness "golden age" like the one described by Hosea (9:10, 13:5), no period of faithfulness like the wilderness period in Jeremiah (2:2). The reason for this new historical perspective is perhaps foreshadowed by my previous discussion of Ezekiel 36. If Ezekiel's Israel was in need of a "new covenant," then this necessarily dictates that its prior history was entirely negative, at least rhetorically speaking. That this was Ezekiel's perspective on the matter is indicated by 20:38: "I will purge out the rebels from among you, and those who transgress against me." Only after this basic change in Israel's corporate constitution could Yahweh return them to the land (vv. 40–44).

In addition to his somewhat unique historical perspective, Ezekiel's polemic in this text is also unusual. Although like Jeremiah he includes the expected polemic against idolatry, on five occasions in this text he reprimands the exiles for profaning the 'sabbaths' (שבתות).[60] Here the custom of sabbath-keeping moves well beyond its previous importance; it has become a 'sign' (אות) of the relationship between Israel and its god, Yahweh. The appearance of this new emphasis within a foreign context, coupled with the 'sign' terminology, suggests that we are dealing here with an ethnic marker or indicium that clearly distinguished the "seed of the house of Jacob" from the surrounding peoples.[61] And as in Deuteronomy, this ethnic marker was closely associated with religious identity and thus marked the exiles not only as

59. Zimmerli dates the text to 591 B.C.E. (*Ezekiel*, 1.406).

60. Jeremiah also showed some concern for sabbath-keeping (Jer 17:21–27), but it played no central role in his prophetic criticisms.

61. Cooke, *Ezekiel*, 216–17.

Jews, but especially as the people of Yahweh. After the exile, sabbath-keeping continued to serve in this role and became one of the more important practices that identified an assimilating foreigner, as one can see in Isa 56:6–8.[62]

Deutero-Isaiah

If we follow the most common approaches to the book of Isaiah, Isaiah 40–55 brings us to the late exilic period and to the ministry of Deutero-Isaiah, who worked several decades after the ministry of Ezekiel, during a time when the return to Palestine was imminent.[63] We are fortunate to have two prophetic sources from the exilic period and even more fortunate that one dates to the early exile and the other to its end. This provides us with the material necessary to trace the development of Israelite thought through that brief parenthesis in Jewish history and to draw conclusions relating to the problems of ethnicity and identity. As D. Baltzer has demonstrated, there are many links between the concepts expressed in Ezekiel and those found in Deutero-Isaiah.[64] At certain points Deutero-Isaiah's development of these themes was minimal, but in some cases he quite transformed the ideas that he inherited from the earlier prophet.[65] There are four issues that are of interest for my work in Deutero-Isaiah, and these may be profitably compared to issues that were raised by the Ezekiel tradition: (1) the Abraham forefather figure, (2) the place of the "new covenant" in Deutero-Isaiah, (3) the foreigner in Deutero-Isaiah, and (4) the problem of the "Servant Songs." We will begin with the Abraham tradition.

---

62. For a discussion of the sabbath tradition, see H. A. McKay, *Sabbath and Synagogue: The Question of Sabbath Worship in Ancient Israel* (Religions in the Graeco-Roman World 122; Leiden: Brill, 1994).

63. Although the central topic of B. Schramm's monograph is Trito-Isaiah and the postexilic period, the book offers a very useful summary of the scholarly debate about Deutero- and Trito-Isaiah, both with respect to issues of composition and with respect to the relationships that we might draw between the two sections (Schramm, *The Opponents of Third Isaiah: Reconstructing the Cultic History of the Restoration* [JSOTSup 193; Sheffield: JSOT Press, 1995] 11–111).

64. D. Baltzer, *Ezechiel und Deuterojesaja: Berührungen in der Heilserwartung der beiden großen Exilspropheten* (BZAW 121; Berlin: de Gruyter, 1971).

65. For instance, their ideas about a "new exodus" from Babylon are quite close. On the other hand, the prophets differ markedly in the details of their deliverance theology (ibid., 24–26, 98–99).

Abraham in Deutero-Isaiah: Isaiah 41:8–10, 51:1–3, 54:1–3

In this section, I have three primary concerns: first the question of the Abraham tradition's development between the early exile (Ezekiel) and the late exile (Deutero-Isaiah); second, the relationship of this development to the land-promise theme; and third, the relationship between this patriarchal tradition and the exodus origin tradition. In Isa 41:8–10, 51:1–3, and 54:1–3, it becomes clear that the Abraham of Deutero-Isaiah was a more clearly developed character than the early-exilic figure known to the Judean remnant and to Ezekiel (see pp. 289–291). In Deutero-Isaiah the tradition is no longer expressed in Deuteronomistic language, and all the major features of the pentateuchal tradition are reflected in the materials. Abraham's wife (51:2, 54:1), his relationship to Jacob (41:8), the promise of progeny and blessings (51:2, 54:1–3), the issue of barrenness (51:3, 54:1), and the theme of personal righteousness (צדק in 51:1) are all quite pronounced, and the theme of land promise is clearly implied in 51:3, "For the Lord will comfort Zion; he will comfort her waste places." Even more explicit in this regard is Isa 54:3: "your descendants [those of Sarah, Abraham's wife] will possess the nations and will people the desolate cities." All of this evidence suggests that the patriarchal tradition that stood behind these texts was much more complex than the tradition reflected in Ezek 33:24 and that ownership of the tradition had shifted from the Judean remnant community to the exilic community. The tradition should not be viewed, as Römer has suggested concerning Isa 51:1–2, as *nichtexilierten* in origin but as a predominantly exilic development.[66] After all, is it an accident that the Abraham of the Yahwist comes to possess Canaan not from within the land, as in the Judean tradition reflected in Ezek 33:24, but after his trek from Mesopotamia (cf. Genesis 12)?[67] Furthermore, the fact that Abraham's trip via Haran mirrors the "new exodus" envisioned by Deutero-Isaiah suggests that the ideas of the prophet and of the Yahwist stand close together because both see the exilic community as the heir to the Abrahamic land promise.[68]

66. Römer, *Israels Väter*, 516, 535–36.

67. J. Van Seters argued several years ago that the statement in Gen 15:7, "I am Yahweh your God who brought you out from Ur of the Chaldeans to give you this land to possess it," is a reformulation of the common exodus formula, "I am Yahweh your God who brought you up out of the land of Egypt" (see "Confessional Reformulation in the Exilic Period," *VT* 22 [1972] 448–59).

68. For a discussion of this theme in Deutero-Isaiah, see Baltzer, *Ezechiel und Deuterojesaja*, 12–23; Van Seters, *Prologue to History*, 241–42, 250, 299.

Not only can we observe a certain degree of growth and development in the patriarchal story, but we can also recognize new exilic efforts to relate it to previous Israelite traditions. For example, in the sources that we have examined so far, the patriarchs and the forefathers of the exodus have existed side by side as two apparently independent origin traditions. But in contrast to the earlier sources that we have examined, Deutero-Isaiah mentions not only the departure from Egypt but also the arrival in Egypt (Israel "went down at first into Egypt," 52:4).[69] This can be explained as an apparent effort to make space for the patriarchal traditions that found their proper setting in the period before the sojourn in Egypt. The only text that predates Deutero-Isaiah and that also shares a similar viewpoint is the Deuteronomist's so-called "little credo" addition in Deut 26:5–9:

> And you shall make response before the Lord your God, "A wandering Aramean was my father; and he went down into Egypt and sojourned there, few in number; and there he became a nation, great, mighty, and populous. And the Egyptians treated us harshly, and afflicted us, and laid upon us hard bondage. Then we cried to the Lord the God of our fathers, and the Lord heard our voice, and saw our affliction, our toil, and our oppression; and the Lord brought us out of Egypt with a mighty hand and an outstretched arm, with great terror, with signs and wonders; and he brought us into this place and gave us this land, a land flowing with milk and honey."

It seems that this early-exilic text is the first to combine the patriarch origins with the exodus, but in doing so it attests to a tradition that stands somewhat apart from what was known in Genesis. As Van Seters has pointed out, it recognizes no patriarchal sojourn in Canaan.[70] To this Mayes adds that the "wandering Aramean" cannot readily be identified with Jacob (although such an identification seems likely to me).[71] And even though one would expect it in such a confessional summary, there is no room in this text for the Abraham figure (or for Isaac). All of this suggests that the effort to combine the patriarchal and exodus traditions was probably in its nascent stages during the early exile, as is perhaps suggested by the fact that the roughly contemporary source Ezekiel 20 was apparently unaware of or uninterested in

69. See, for example, my discussion of Ezekiel 20, above, pp. 303–304.

70. Van Seters, *Prologue to History*, 216.

71. A. D. H. Mayes, *Deuteronomy* (NCBC; Grand Rapids, Mich.: Eerdmans, 1979) 334–35.

the connection. This means that Deutero-Isaiah was informed by a more complete patriarchal/exodus tradition, one in which Abraham was a prominent figure. According to Van Seters the appearance of this tradition in Deutero-Isaiah should be associated with historiographical efforts during the exilic period, namely the history of the Yahwist, which sought to combine the patriarchal traditions with the older exodus-settlement tradition of Deuteronomy. This theory does find some support in what we are saying here, since the Abraham tradition seems to have been largely unknown to the historical summaries in Ezekiel 20 and Deut 26:5–9 and, on the other hand, to have exerted considerable influence on the late-exilic work of Deutero-Isaiah.

In addition to the question of the patriarchal tradition and its relationship to the Exodus tradition, the theme of 'righteousness' (צדק) that appears in connection with Abraham in Isa 51:1–2 and in 51:7 is also important. These texts are usually associated with the "new covenant" of Jer 31:31–34 and read as follows:[72]

> Hearken to me (שמעו אלי), you who pursue righteousness (רדפי צדק), you who seek the Lord; look to the rock from which you were hewn, and to the quarry from which you were digged. Look to Abraham your father and to Sarah who bore you. . . . (Isa 51:1–2)

> Hearken to me (שמעו אלי), you who know righteousness (ידעי צדק), the people in whose heart is my law; fear not the reproach of men, and be not dismayed at their revilings. (Isa 51:7)

The similarity between these excerpts is quite pronounced. If one assumes a correspondence between those who "pursue righteousness" and those who "know righteousness," which seems to me quite reasonable, then Abraham takes on a unique role in the prophet's understanding of the new covenant tradition and the "heart" associated with it. Abraham is the "rock" from which new covenant Israelites are "hewn," the paradigm of those who have the law (תורה) in their heart (לבב/ לב).[73] From this one should conclude that Deutero-Isaiah was responsible for the integration of two important streams of tradition, the his-

---

72. P. E. Bonnard, *Le Second Isaïe: Son disciple et leurs editeurs—Isaie 40–66* (Ébib; Paris: Gabalda, 1972) 251; C. Westermann, *Isaiah 40–66* (OTL; Philadelphia: Westminster, 1969) 236; R. N. Whybray, *Isaiah 40–66* (NCBC; Grand Rapids, Mich.: Eerdmans, 1975) 157.

73. As seen in formulaic expressions: (1) you who pursue righteousness = like Abraham; (2) you who know righteousness = law in heart.

torical tradition of the patriarch and the theological tradition of Jeremiah's new covenant. These texts would seem to imply two competing elements within Deutero-Isaiah's immediate context, those who had the "law in their heart" and those who did not. Specifically, I think that we should see behind this debate the texts in Genesis 12 and 15, in which the forefather Abraham was declared 'righteous' (צדקה) because he trusted (האמין ביהוה) Yahweh's promise of a progeny and a homeland, two promises that were fulfilled only after the patriarch's departure from his home in Mesopotamia. In a similar way Deutero-Isaiah called upon Israelites with a heart like Abraham's to believe that Yahweh would "comfort Zion . . . and make her wilderness like Eden" (Isa 51:3). These observations support the recent conclusion of N. K. Gottwald that Deutero-Isaiah's work must be understood chiefly as an effort to enlist support for a program of return to Judah.[74] The close link between "faith-righteousness" and "salvation" that emerges in Deutero-Isaiah also fits this agenda, since only a return to the homeland by faith would secure the salvation (or restoration) of the people of Israel.[75] On the other hand, there are other texts in Deutero-Isaiah that suggest the prophet's interest was not in Israel alone.

A Light to the Nations: Isaiah 42:6–7, 44:5, and 49:1–6

As they are commonly understood, the Isa 42:6–7, 44:5, and 49:1–6 texts encapsulate an advanced stage of ethnic inclusiveness that we have not observed in the older Hebrew sources. Yahweh's servant, who for the time being remains anonymous, has been given as "a light to the nations (גוים), to open the eyes that are blind" (42:6–7). According to Whybray the text does not refer to "missionary work" but instead to the fact that Yahweh's universal rule, so prominent in Deutero-Isaiah, will oblige foreigners to accept His sovereignty.[76] Similarly, H. M. Orlinsky suggests:

---

74. N. K. Gottwald, "Social Class and Ideology in Isaiah 40–55: An Eagletonian Reading," *Semeia* 59 (1992) 43–58. For a critique of Gottwald's article, see responses in the same *Semeia* volume.

75. C. R. North, *The Second Isaiah* (Oxford: Clarendon, 1964) 93, 95, 118. See also G. von Rad's discussion of צדקה/צדק in his *Old Testament Theology* (2 vols.; New York: Harper & Row, 1962–65) 1.370–83.

76. Whybray, *Isaiah 40–66*, 75; contra G. A. F. Knight, *Servant Theology* (Grand Rapids, Mich.: Eerdmanns, 1979) 48–49.

In a word: Israel will be "a light to the nations" in the sense that Israel will dazzle the nations with her God-given triumph and restoration; the whole world will behold this single beacon that is God's sole covenanted people. Israel will serve to the world at large as the example of God's loyalty and omnipotence.[77]

The observations of Whybray and Orlinsky are no doubt accurate to a certain extent. But the "covenant to the people" in 42:6 is almost always interpreted as a collective reference to the peoples, not to Israel, and this seems to have implications beyond the ones envisioned by Orlinsky.[78] Orlinsky is rather adamant in his assertion that Deutero-Isaiah was not really concerned with the salvation of people outside of the Israelite community. He does concede that the text of Isa 49:6 ("so that my salvation may reach to the end of the earth") might be taken, at least at face value, as a call to "bring God's teachings to the heathen nations and thereby afford the entire world the rewards that derived from acknowledging Him as their Deity."[79] But according to Orlinsky, this reading would not account for the surrounding context, in which the text explicitly states that God had destined the prophet to restore only the people of Israel, not their foreign neighbors.

But in my view this seems to be a convenient case of eisegesis, because the explicit point of 49:6 is that it was "too small a thing" for Yahweh's servant to restore only the "tribes of Jacob," and this implies that something other than ministry to Israel is in view, as is explicitly stated at the end of the verse: "I will give you as a light to the nations, that my salvation may reach the end of the earth." So in both Isaiah 42 and 49 there are good reasons for supposing that the prophet was interested not only in Israel but in foreigners as well, and, as we will see, there are also important reasons for supposing that his interest in foreigners was of a spiritual nature.

---

77. H. M. Orlinsky, *Essays in Biblical Culture and Bible Translation* (New York: KTAV, 1974) 186.

78. W. Grimm, *Deuterojesaja: Deutung, Wirkung, Gegenwart—Ein Kommentar zu Jesaja 40–55* (Calwer Bibelkommentare; Stuttgart: Calwer, 1990) 145–46; North, *Second Isaiah*, 112; Westermann, *Isaiah 40–66*, 100.

79. Orlinsky, *Essays in Biblical Culture and Bible Translation*, 169. Similar sentiments are expressed by N. H. Snaith, "The Servant of the Lord in Deutero-Isaiah," in *Studies in Old Testament Prophecy: Presented to Theodore H. Robinson on His Sixty-Fifth Birthday* (ed. H. H. Rowley; Edinburgh: T. & T. Clark, 1950) 187–200.

In addition to the very explicit statements that we have just discussed, there are three important lines of evidence that lend support to the conclusion that Deutero-Isaiah had in mind more than the effort to dazzle the nations with Yahweh's power or to extend Yahweh's rule over the nations. In the first place, I think that we should not overlook the blindness motif (עור) that was utilized in both Isaiah and Deutero-Isaiah to emphasize the spiritual poverty of the people.[80] The servant's role was to restore Israel by healing its blind eyes and by "turning the darkness before them into light" (49:16). But Deutero-Isaiah did not limit this ministry of enlightenment to Israel alone, as seems clear from Isa 49:6–7: "I have given you as a covenant to the people (עם), as a light to the nations (גוים), to open the eyes that are blind, to bring out the prisoners from the dungeon, from the prison those who sit in darkness." An almost identical description of the servant's ministry was offered in Isa 49:6, where the servant was given as a 'light to the nations' (לאור גוים) so that the salvation of Yahweh could reach the 'ends of the earth' (עד־קצה הארץ). Whybray's argument that "salvation" refers here "not to spiritual blessings but to Yahweh's coming victory over Babylon" cannot hold, in my view, because the motif of light and restored sight is a spiritual motif, not a political one.[81] And if these texts have in mind "spiritual blindness," as seems to be the case, then we should conclude that the servant's charge was not only to extend Yahweh's political jurisdiction (his תורה) to the "coastlands" (42:4) but also to extend spiritual freedom to all peoples—that is, to invite religious assimilation.[82]

A second feature that implies the prophet's spiritual interest in non-Israelites is the connection between Deutero-Isaiah's thought and the Abrahamic promise in Gen 12:1–9. J. Van Seters has pointed out

80. Isa 6:9–13, 42:18–25. S. R. Driver interprets the text primarily in spiritual terms (*Introduction to the Literature of the Old Testament* [New York: Meridian, 1956] 232).

81. Whybray, *Isaiah 40–66*, 139. Bonnard interprets the text along the lines of Israel's mission to the nations in *Le Second Isaïe*, 221–22.

82. Whybray, *Isaiah 40–66*, 126; North, *Second Isaiah*, 112–13. According to Bonnard, what the text envisions is Cyrus' defeat of Babylon, followed by the conversion of the liberated peoples to Yahweh. Westermann disagrees: "the opening of the eyes of the blind and the freeing of prisoners are intended to typify human suffering . . . the reference is not specifically to the blindness of Israel, a subject treated by Deutero-Isaiah in another context" (Westerman, *Isaiah 40–66*, 100). See also Grimm, who believes that here a new exodus of Israel will take place before the eyes of the peoples (*Deuterojesaja*, 145–46).

that the foreign nations of Gen 12:1–3 were blessed through their association with the 'great nation' (גוי גדול)[83] that God would make of Abraham.[84] The language of this promise speech was taken from royal terminology like the terminology associated with the Jerusalem monarchy,[85] and this suggests the original Sitz im Leben that lay behind the text. As in Assyrian royal ideology, in which the nations that honored the monarch received the expected blessings, so too the nations that honored the seed of Abraham were to be blessed. Deutero-Isaiah's vision of the future is also heavily colored with Zion theology and with the restoration of Jerusalem. Furthermore, like the Yahwist, the prophet carried forward a very corporate and royal conception of Israel, which he identified as the 'seed of Abraham' (41:8, זרע אברהם).[86] In light of these similarities, it is difficult to imagine that Deutero-Isaiah's vision of a servant to the nations was unrelated to the blessing mentioned in Gen 12:3. Just as the blessing of Genesis 12 takes on universal and international proportion, Deutero-Isaiah's "light to the nations" implies something more than Yahweh's victory over Babylon. As S. R. Driver has concluded, the mission of the servant was "to teach the world true religion."[87]

The third piece of evidence that clarifies Deutero-Isaiah's program for the nations is the text of Isa 44:5, which most commentators interpret as a reference to the assimilating proselyte:[88]

> This one will say, "I am the Lord's," another will call himself by the name of Jacob, and another will write on his hand, "The Lord's" and surname himself by the name of Israel.

It is curious that such unanimity exists when, as Grimm concludes, the entire context of vv. 1–4 addresses the Israelites. But this context none-

---

83. As Westermann points out, the term גוי is a political designation (see his *Genesis*, 2.149).

84. My discussion here depends on the work of Van Seters, *Prologue to History*, 252–57.

85. See 2 Sam 7:9, 8:13; 1 Kgs 1:47; Ps 21:4; and Psalm 72.

86. For this reason it has sometimes been suggested that the servant in Isaiah's "servant songs" was none other then King Cyrus himself. For a recent discussion, see A. Laato, *The Servant of YHWH and Cyrus: A Reinterpretation of the Exilic Messianic Programme in Isaiah 40–55* (ConBOT 35; Stockholm: Almqvist & Wiksell, 1992).

87. Driver, *Introduction to the Literature of the Old Testament*, 232.

88. Westermann, *Isaiah 40–66*, 137–38; Whybray, *Isaiah 40–66*, 95. But see Grimm, who associates the reference with the Israelites mentioned in vv. 1–4 (*Deuterojesaja*, 219–21).

theless lends support to the proselyte interpretation of v. 5, because the oracle predicts rapid multiplication of the Israelite people upon return to their land. Part of this growth would come from the ethnic foreigners who: (1) joined themselves to Israel (יקרא שם־יעקב/בשם ישׂראל יכנה) and (2) confessed Yahweh as God (יאמר ליהוה/יכתב ידו ליהוה), two steps that Deutero-Isaiah no doubt saw as one process. Although Deutero-Isaiah's familiarity with the ethnic traditions of Abraham and Jacob cannot be doubted, it is curious that the conversion process outlined in v. 5 barely touches on the issue of ethnic identity. Contrary to the Holiness Code, here there is no rhetorical distance between the foreigner and the proselyte or between the proselyte and the Israelite. Assimilation to the Israelite people is virtually synonymous with the acceptance of Yahweh, which confirms one's status, not as a גר, but as a member of the Jacob (יעקב) community itself. In other words, for Deutero-Isaiah, a change in one's religious identity *was* ethnic assimilation. This evidence supports the conclusion that Deutero-Isaiah did envision the spiritual restoration of foreigners as a part of his ministry program.

The pressing problem that remains for us in these "servant songs" is the servant figure himself, who has been variously identified as Cyrus, corporate Israel, pious Israel, Deutero-Isaiah, anonymous figures, the prophetic minority, Hezekiah, Zerubbabel, and various kinds of messianic figures.[89] Qohelet's words "there is nothing new under the sun" apply most pointedly to the scholarly discussion of the topic. Although I have no desire to add to the growing menagerie of interpretations, the servant figure raises an important issue for my work, primarily because almost every approach to "the servant" sees in the background a conflict between two or more ideological factions. This means that the servant songs are very important texts in any discussion of identity in the late exilic period. In certain respects, I have attempted to uncover what these songs can tell us about ethnicity and identity apart from a clear identification of the servant figure. This seems necessary to me, because none of the approaches to the servant figure seem to be much more probable than others that have been suggested. If we

89. The best summaries of the history of the discussion are dated but very helpful. See C. R. North, *The Suffering Servant in Deutero-Isaiah* (Oxford: Oxford University Press, 1950) 1–116; H. H. Rowley, *The Servant of the Lord and Other Essays on the Old Testament* (Oxford: Blackwell, 1965) 3–60. For a more recent bibliography, see Soggin, *Introduction to the Old Testament,* 368–71, 376–78.

suppose, for instance, that the servant should be associated with a minority position within the exilic community, in what sense would Deutero-Isaiah's perspective on Israelite ethnic identity be representative of the whole? And what if his position was with the majority? Or suppose that Duhm was correct and that we should distinguish the "servant songs" from the prophetic corpus itself.[90] As one can see, I have no firm convictions about the servant figure, apart from the fact that he should in some way be connected with corporate Israel, at least in the text's present form.[91] In spite of this impasse, however, the servant texts that I have discussed here make it possible to summarize some of the important changes in ethnicity and identity that took place between the early exile as represented by Ezekiel/HC and the late exile as represented by Deutero-Isaiah.

Summary:
Ethnicity and Identity in the Exilic Period and Beyond

The early exilic sources, Ezekiel and the Holiness Code, demonstrate that ethnic sentiments and the boundaries associated with them intensified for the Golah community after they settled in Babylon. These sentiments took shape in response to two different threats to their corporate identity. The first threat was the threat of cultural assimilation in the Babylonian context.[92] This was met by an effort to develop a new set of ethnic indicia that included, among other things, an emphasis on sabbath-keeping (Ezekiel 20), a concern for ritual purity (the Holiness Code), and participation in the assembly activities of the community.[93] These indicia "marked" a person as a member of the

90. B. Duhm, *Das Buch Jesaia* (5th ed.; Göttingen: Vandenhoeck & Ruprecht, 1968) 311–411.

91. On this there is at least partial agreement.

92. As Blenkinsopp points out, the enticements of Mesopotamian economic prosperity during the Neo-Babylonian and Achaemenid periods were considerable. Assimilation was therefore much more than a passive threat. Perhaps instructive in this regard are the "Murashu documents" (J. Blenkinsopp, "Temple and Society in Achaemenid Judah," in *Second Temple Studies* [ed. P. R. Davies; JSOTSup 117; Sheffield: JSOT Press, 1991] 50–53). See also G. Cardascia, *Les archives des Murašû* (Paris: Imprimerie Nationale, 1951); E. M. Yamauchi, *Persia and the Bible* (Grand Rapids, Mich.: Baker, 1990) 243–44.

93. On the development of new leadership and community structures in the exilic period, see Smith, *The Religion of the Landless*, 93–126.

ethnic community and so established the kind of social discourse possible within these parameters. However, serious efforts to establish and preserve ethnic distinctions also required adjustments in the criteria used to decide who was "in" and who was not, and this effort was particularly evident in the development of the term תושב. This term was employed rhetorically by the Holiness Code (and was probably coined by HC) to distinguish more clearly between the assimilating foreigner (גר) and the nonassimilating foreigner (תושב). We should assume that this was designed to place greater social distance between the Israelites and the foreigners who were not interested in assimilation and therefore represented an ideological threat to the community.

The second threat that faced the exiles was the potential loss of the ethnic homeland to the Judean remnant community, a community that had adopted (or produced) a forefather tradition in which they, like the ancient patriarch Abraham, were the proper heirs to the homeland properties. The response of the exilic community to this circumstance was threefold. First, it added to its set of ethnic criteria the most important criterion of all: group membership required participation in the exile experience itself (Ezek 11:14–21).[94] Second, it adopted the Abraham tradition as its own and then adapted it to the exilic situation. And third, in an effort to preserve ancestral property rights, the exiles compiled and documented the family land holdings as they were in Palestine prior to the exile. It appears that over the course of the exile these documents gradually came to be viewed not only as one's property records but also as a means of verifying one's status as an ethnic Israelite.

On the other hand, in spite of first appearances, the strong ethnic sentiments of the exiles did not prevent them from embracing the non-Israelites who desired to join their community. This was especially evident in the very supportive attitude that both the Holiness Code and Ezekiel had toward the גר. The exiles seem to have feared only those foreigners who came into frequent contact with the Israelites but who showed no signs of openness to assimilation. So with respect to ethnic

---

94. At face value, this seems to preclude the notion of ethnic assimilation, since it is hard to see how neighboring foreigners could ever be viewed as having experienced the exile. But Schramm has pointed out that a similar issue was faced by Ezra in the postexilic period, and his community apparently had no problem identifying assimilated foreigners as בני גולה 'sons of the exile' (B. Schramm, *The Opponents of Third Isaiah*, 60–61).

inclusiveness, there is a great deal of continuity between our early exilic sources and Deutero-Isaiah. However, complete ideological continuity does not exist here. In the Holiness Code, the foreigners (גוים) continued to stand apart from Israel as a social category (Lev 18:24) and were closely associated with the nonassimilating foreigner, the תושב (Lev 25:44–45), who was also kept at arm's length. By comparison, the linguistic and semantic boundaries found in the Holiness Code have totally collapsed when we get to Deutero-Isaiah. Not only were the culturally assimilating foreigners welcomed, but even the foreigner from a distant land, the גוי, was invited to accept Yahweh and to "call himself by the name of Jacob." In this respect, the outlook of Deutero-Isaiah represented something of a revolution, in which religious identity had almost totally supplanted the role of ethnicity in defining group identity. We must wonder if the influence of the Yahwist was felt here, since his "table of nations" in Genesis 10 suggested that all peoples—including the Hebrews (עבר, 10:21–25)—were ethnically related, to a greater or lesser extent.[95]

There is another very important and essential difference between Deutero-Isaiah and his early exilic predecessors, and it can be appreciated only when care is taken to distinguish between ethnic boundaries and the intensity of ethnic boundaries. With regard to ethnic sentiments and group definition, Deutero-Isaiah reflects a much greater familiarity with Israel's ethnic traditions—Abraham, Isaac, Jacob, the Exodus—than does any other prophetic source that we have examined. In this respect it has much in common with the most comprehensive and detailed explication of Israel's ethnic history, the pentateuchal J narrative. From this we should conclude that, during the late exilic period, Israelite ethnicity and identity was founded on a well-integrated history of its ancestors and its corporate life. In this sense, ethnic sentiments and their associated boundaries became more complex and detailed during the course of the exile. But nothing in Deutero-Isaiah suggests that the increasing detail of these ethnic traditions made its ethnic sentiments more intense or its ethnic boundaries become less permeable during the progress of the exile. The semantic and rhetorical distinctions that played such an important role in the early-exilic

95. See the discussion of Van Seters, *Prologue to History*, 174–87; see also F. Crüsemann, "Human Solidarity and Ethnic Identity: Israel's Self-Definition in the Genealogical System of Genesis," in *Ethnicity and the Bible* (ed. M. G. Brett; Biblical Interpretation Series 19; Leiden: Brill, 1996) 57–76.

Holiness Code are not found in Deutero-Isaiah. Even when גוי is employed to describe foreigners, it is used only as a means of inviting their religious and cultural assimilation to the Israelite community. In Deutero-Isaiah, the assimilating foreigner was not distinguished as a גר but was associated with Israel and with its forefather, Jacob (Isa 44:5). Deutero-Isaiah therefore reflects a marked abatement in the intensity of ethnic boundaries over the course of the exile. This fact demonstrates that there is no ready connection between ethnic sentiments, which were quite pronounced in Isaiah and in the pentateuchal J document, and the intensity of the ethnic boundaries that circumscribed them. Rather, like almost every source prior to his time, Deutero-Isaiah's emphasis on religious identity was very strong, and these religious sentiments preempted and overshadowed the ethnic components of Israelite identity.

Was Deutero-Isaiah a typical representative of the late-exilic Golah community? In certain respects I think that he certainly was not. We are able to trace two different lines of tradition that passed from the exile into the postexilic period. The first runs from Ezekiel and the Holiness Code to the postexilic Priestly Code and Ezra/Nehemiah. All of these sources reflect rather intense ethnic boundaries, and it is difficult to imagine Deutero-Isaiah playing a significant role in that tradition. The other line of tradition runs from Deutero-Isaiah to the postexilic Trito-Isaiah and features less rigid ethnic boundaries. A brief comparison of the two traditions in their postexilic garb displays the ideological rift that separates them:

> Let not the foreigner (נכר) who has joined himself to the Lord say, "The Lord will surely separate me from his people. . . . And the foreigners (נכר) who join themselves to the Lord, to minister to him, to love the name of the Lord, and to be his servants, every one who keeps the sabbath, and does not profane it, and holds fast my covenant—these I will bring to my holy mountain, and make them joyful in my house of prayer; their burnt offerings and their sacrifices will be accepted on my altar; for my house shall be called a house of prayer for all peoples. (Isa 56:3–7)

> After these things had been done, the officials approached me and said, "The people of Israel and the priests and the Levites have not separated themselves from the peoples of the lands with their abominations, from the Canaanites, the Hittites, the Perizzites, the Jebusites, the Ammonites, the Moabites, the Egyptians, and the

Amorites. For they have taken some of their daughters to be wives
for themselves and for their sons; so that the holy race has mixed itself with the peoples of the lands. And in this faithlessness the hand
of the officials and chief men has been foremost." (Ezra 9:1–2)

While the first tradition traced its heritage back to Deutero-Isaiah and
embraced the foreigner (נכר), the priestly Ezra tradition, which had its
roots in the Holiness Code, rejected them. From this evidence we must
assume that in Deutero-Isaiah we have only one side of the quite ener-
getic debate that absorbed the attention of the late-exilic Golah community and also of the postexilic Judean community.[96] But to stop
here makes the issues too simple. Like Trito-Isaiah, Ezra's community
also welcomed the assimilation of foreigners to the ethnic community:

> On the fourteenth day of the first month the returned exiles kept the
> Passover. For the priests and the Levites had purified themselves to-
> gether; all of them were clean. So they killed the passover lamb for all
> the returned exiles, for their fellow priests, and for themselves; it was
> eaten by the people of Israel who had returned from exile, *and also by
> every one who had joined them and separated himself from the pollu-
> tions of the peoples of the land to worship the Lord, the God of Israel.*
> (Ezra 6:19–21, italics mine)

These passages show that Deutero-Isaiah and Ezra shared both a devotion to Yahweh and an interest in foreigners who wanted to accept him
as their deity. The difference was in certain respects polemical and
shows that the community of Deutero-Isaiah felt less threatened by the
surrounding foreign populations than Ezra's party did. In my view, the
core of this debate was the theology of Deutero-Isaiah and his followers, which was so fixed on the religious status of one's heart toward
Yahweh that a preoccupation with one's ethnic origins seemed unimportant. This should be contrasted with the stance of Ezra's community, which is best understood in the light of the legal tradition that it

96. There are several recent studies of Israelite identity in its sociological context
in the postexilic period. See T. C. Eskenazi and E. P. Judd, "Marriage to a Stranger in
Ezra 9–10," in *Second Temple Studies* (ed. P. R. Davies; JSOTSup 175; Sheffield: JSOT
Press, 1994) 266–85; Schramm, *The Opponents of Third Isaiah*; D. L. Smith-Christopher, "The Mixed Marriage Crisis in Ezra 9–10 and Nehemiah 13: A Study of the Sociology of the Post-Exilic Judean Community," in *Second Temple Studies*, 243–65; also
by Smith-Christopher, "Between Ezra and Isaiah: Exclusion, Transformation, and Inclusion of the Foreigner in Post-Exilic Biblical Theology," in *Ethnicity and the Bible*
(ed. M. G. Brett; Biblical Interpretation Series 19; Leiden: Brill, 1996) 117–42.

had inherited and to which it was loyally dedicated. This tradition on the one hand was very open to religious assimilation and, on the other hand, contained numerous warnings about the dangers of foreign influence to the Israelite community. This means that, as we have reiterated time and again during our discussion, religious identity rather than ethnic identity turns out to be the most important issue for the authors of the Hebrew Bible.

In the course of this chapter, we also examined two other topics that are closely related to the question of ethnic identity. Regarding the biblical "tribal-list" tradition, it was determined that the lists in Ezekiel 48 represent the last stage in the tradition of the Hebrew Bible and that these lists correspond to the ones cited by the Chronicler and especially by the Tetrateuchal sources, which should now be associated with exilic or postexilic contexts. Regarding the biblical "tribal-settlement" tradition in Ezekiel 47–48, it was determined that this represents the first effort in the Hebrew Bible to depict the settlement of the tribes in their corresponding lands. This record was highly schematic and made no attempt to achieve geographical precision. But later descriptions of the settlement, influenced by an emerging Israelite historiographical tradition (Dtr and J), would attempt a more detailed description of the tribes and of their associated territories.

Chapter Seven

Summary and Conclusions

The History of Israelite Ethnicity

When the results of the present study are weighed against common scholarly ideas about Israelite ethnicity, it becomes clear that the two views stand quite apart from each other. Scholarship has tended to date the J and E sources of the Pentateuch rather early, and these are the Hebrew sources that offer some of the clearest explications of Israelite ethnic distinctiveness. But I have argued to the contrary that an inquiry that is based largely on our most datable sources—the prophetic corpus and Deuteronomy—provides a quite different picture of Israelite identity and of the history of its ethnic sentiments. The difference is that one can discern a development of Israelite ethnicity from the more simple to the more complex, with the most complete explications of Israelite ethnicity emerging rather late in Israel's history. This implies, of course, that the ethnic traditions of the Pentateuch are perhaps later than we have previously supposed.

If we are willing to confess that it is somewhat speculative, our history of Israelite ethnicity can begin with Merneptah's late-thirteenth-century stele. This source represents our earliest tangible contact with a people called *Israel* and suggests a context in which this sociocultural entity stood alongside other groups, specifically alongside the people of Canaan. There is evidence, though slim, that the identity of the people Israel included a pronounced emphasis on the deity El, as seen in the theophoric character of the name *Israel,* and in certain ways this reminds us of the biblical depiction of the Israelites. But there are many interpretive ambiguities in the text, and a rather long time-span separates Merneptah from our earliest biblical sources. In light of these problems, I do not believe that this is the only possible interpretation of the text, nor would I suggest that it is a highly probable reading of the stele. But it does seem to me a more probable reading than the others that have been offered and therefore provides us with the first context in which Israelite ethnicity might have either emerged or intensified.

Like Merneptah's Stele, the Song of Deborah also presents us with many interpretive problems, both in terms of its date and in terms of how its content ought to be construed. The final form of the song probably dates no later than the ninth century, but its contents do not fit that context and thus attest to a tradition that is somewhat older. How much older is hard to say. It shares with the Merneptah text a reference to people called *Israel*, a contrast between Israelites and Canaanites, and an emphasis on the shared religious identity of the Israelites. The song preserves the memory that Israel was composed of ten separate units, each associated with a particular geographical environ, and that these units were associated with each other by virtue of a common devotion to the god Yahweh. Just how this list of tribal units relates to other lists in the Hebrew Bible will be discussed below. But there are several points at which the text hints at ethnic identity, and the context of ecological and military competition is of the type that promotes the development and intensification of ethnic sentiments. On the basis of this evidence, it seems to me very likely that the song presumes an ethnic context and that the origins of Israelite ethnicity should be assigned a date no later than the ninth century B.C.E.

Given that both the Merneptah and Deborah texts present us with certain problems, our earliest substantive sources in the study were eighth-century prophetic collections. These sources seem to indicate that, although ethnicity was common among the smaller Levantine states in this period, ethnic boundaries were not particularly intense and played a rather secondary role in defining national identity. On the other hand, one should not conclude from this that ethnicity was an unimportant sentiment in the region, since the polemic of both Hosea and Amos presupposes a certain allegiance to an ethnic tradition. These ethnic ancestral traditions were common in the Greek materials as well, and it is possible that the Levantine traditions borrowed the conception from the Greeks via Phoenician influence or, perhaps more likely, that all of the parties involved inherited these ethnic models from the Phoenicians. The eighth century would have been the proper context for such a cultural transaction, since this period featured an accelerated exchange of ideas between the east and west. This date is also consonant with the evidence from the ninth-century Song of Deborah, which failed to mention ancestral origin traditions that could have lent support to its message of Yahwistic solidarity. On the other hand, we cannot categorically attribute Israel's ethnic traditions to Greek influences, because both the anthropological data and the Old Babylonian data show that there are other possible explanations for the emergence of Israelite ethnicity. These sources demonstrate the very natural tendency for any culture to exhibit ethnic behaviors under the proper conditions. Thus there is no obligation to attribute the origins of Israelite ethnicity to a process of cultural diffusion.

Although popular ethnic sentiments were well established by the late eighth century, when Hosea, Amos, and Isaiah did their work, it was the task of Hosea and his proto-Deuteronomic community to take these preexisting ethnic sentiments and to intensify them in support of a national mono-Yahwist agenda, which rejected all other deities as "foreign." This suggests that we should understand the intense Israelite ethnic sentiments of Hosea's community as a development of very intense religious sentiments, and not vice versa. The prophet's preference for the exodus migration tradition over the Jacob tradition was also based on this ethnic agenda, since a major reason for his rejection of Jacob was the patriarch's marriage to foreign women. Hosea's brand of ethnicity was a uniquely Northern tradition, as is implied by his failure to include the Judeans in his mono-Yahwist program and as is suggested by the fact that the eighth-century Southern prophets never applied the Israelite ethnic traditions to the Judean people.

Although it is clear that Amos and Isaiah were aware of the Israelite ethnic origin traditions, they employed no "foreign" polemic, as did their Northern counterparts. In fact, the polemic of Amos tended to stress the similarity between Israel and foreigners rather than to point out the distinctions between them. Instead of an intense ethnicity, the Southerners embraced an intense Yahwistic universalism, which probably explains why they were more interested in promoting Yahwistic unity between the Northern and Southern monarchies than was Hosea. The contexts that created the specific concerns of Hosea, on the one hand, and Isaiah, on the other, were quite different. Hosea responded to a perceived threat from within, particularly in the form of non-Yahwistic religious influences in Israel, while the external threat that confronted Isaiah was the Assyrian monarch, who claimed to be the "king of the universe." In response to the core/periphery situation created by Assyrian imperialism, Isaiah formulated a theology that stressed the universal kingship of Yahweh. That this was a common theological perspective in Southern prophetic circles seems confirmed by the similar perspective of his Southern cohort, Amos.

Chronologically, the next important literary witness in the history of Israelite ethnicity was Deuteronomy. In my view, the older, pre-Josianic core of Deuteronomy was composed after the fall of Samaria, when scores of Northern refugees moved South into Judah (although it is rather obvious that this pre-Josianic edition was informed at points by even older legal materials). Two of the primary purposes of this effort were: first, to preserve the mono-Yahwist agenda of the proto-Deuteronomic movement, and second, to employ its ethnic sentiment in support of Northern and Southern unity, especially with regard to the integration of the North's refugees. The first goal was accomplished by focusing on the exclusive covenant relationship between Yahweh and his people and by enumerating a number of features that were and were not characteristic of the Yahwistic faith. These features became ethnic markers in the sense that they clearly delineated authentic Yahwism in contrast to "foreign" religious activities. The second goal was accomplished with the creation of Deuteronomic "brother theology," which stressed the essential ethnic brotherhood of Northern and Southern Yahwists and their common ethnohistorical heritage in the exodus event. Also important in this effort to protect the Northern refugees was a new Deuteronomic emphasis on the 'sojourner' (גר), an emphasis that was prompted by the many Northerners who now lived in the South as a part of this sociological niche. But because many of the sojourners in Judah were not Israelite refugees, the effort to promote support for the Northern sojourners inevitably resulted in support for non-Israelites as well, which explains why Deuteronomy embraced the sociologically disadvantaged foreign sojourner and at the same time employed such a strong "foreign" polemic. With regard to this polemic, it is important to notice that Deuteronomy was much more opposed to foreignness—either non-Yahwism or "corrupted" Yahwism—than it was to foreigners in particular. That this was the case is confirmed by two features. First, Deuteronomy provided little in the way of ethnic markers that could serve in making ready distinctions between foreigners and native Israelites. And second, the foreigners that provoked the ire of Deuteronomy—the Canaanites, Hittites, Amorites, and so on—were rhetorical "others" rather than actual peoples on the seventh-century social periphery.

The book of Jeremiah brings us to the end of the Judean monarchy and serves as a bridge into the early exilic period. Like Deuteronomy, Jeremiah shows little evidence of intense ethnic competition with concrete foreign populations, and the prophet seems to have followed the Deuteronomic pattern of condemning supposedly foreign religious influences rather than assailing foreign peoples. Practices that have often been labeled *ethnic*, such as circumcision and sabbath-keeping, were not employed within an ethnic paradigm by Jeremiah, and circumcision at least was not viewed as a distinctively Israelite practice but rather as a ritual common to its neighbors. However, during the early exile, all of this changed. In the book of Ezekiel and in the Holiness Code, sabbath-keeping, circumcision, and ritual cleanliness became important ethnic distinctives for the exilic community. The Holiness Code established more stable ethnic criteria by distinguishing between the foreigners who were assimilating to the Golah community (גר) and those who were not (תושׁב). All of this reflects a marked intensification of ethnic sentiments among the exiles, which arose, no doubt, from an effort to preserve community identity in the midst of a foreign context.

The struggle of the exilic community was not only against the tide of Mesopotamian culture but also against the Judean remnant community, which had annexed the exiles' family properties. One consequence of this was that the exiles quickly organized themselves for a return to their ancestral lands and initiated a program to record the names and family holdings of the disinherited. Essentially, the end result of this process—as seen in Ezra and Nehemiah—was that the exilic community came to view itself as the true ethnic Israel. Another consequence of this conflict centered on the Abraham tradition, which appears to have originated in the Judean context and featured a patriarchal forefather who took possession of the empty land. But the exile community viewed themselves as the land's future inhabitants and eventually adopted the tradition, so that in Deutero-Isaiah it applied to themselves.

Although the distinctiveness of the exiles in contrast to the Judean remnant community was preserved throughout the exilic experience, it seems clear that the intense ethnic distinctiveness evidenced in Ezekiel and the Holiness Code dissipated during the course of the exile, at least among some of the Israelites. While the early-exilic Holiness Code went to great lengths to distinguish assimilating foreigners from non-assimilating foreigners, Deutero-Isaiah skipped the category altogether and identified assimilating foreigners as a part of "Jacob." This prophet of the late exile embraced a highly universalistic vision that joined all peoples under the kingship of Yahweh, and such a vision necessarily precluded very intense ethnic sentiments. From this we should conclude that, in contrast to the early-exilic community, the late-exilic community of Deutero-Isaiah no longer viewed the exilic context as a threat to the survival of the Israelite people. This should not be misconstrued to mean that Deutero-Isaiah was blind to the sense of Israelite ethnicity. On the contrary, his theoretical sense of ethnicity was highly developed, as revealed by his intimate familiarity with the exodus, Jacob, Isaac, and Abraham traditions. But Deutero-Isaiah was unique precisely because this well-developed sense of ethnicity was not linked to the intense ethnic separatism that characterized the early exile. Even after the exile, Deutero-Isaiah's highly universalistic perspective found some support among the returning exiles (see Trito-Isaiah). However, the stiff competition for land and resources naturally intensified Jewish ethnic sentiments, and the postexilic ethnic separatists (Ezra–Nehemiah) seem to have won the day over the Isaiah school. But in light of all of this discussion, there are two predominant themes. First, as it is presented in the biblical sources, throughout the period that we have examined, ethnicity seems to have played a secondary role to Israelite and Judean concerns about religious identity. And second, even in the most rhetorically ethnic sources, such as Deuteronomy and Ezra–Nehemiah, the Israelites tended nevertheless to have a keen interest in the assimilation of foreigners to their religious community.

Tribal Organization in Ancient Israel

As we pointed out in chapter one, the idea that Israel's twelve-tribe league developed along the lines of ancient Greek amphictyonies has been thoroughly discredited, and there remains very little conclusive evidence that Israel originated as a religious confederation centered around a central cult shrine. On the other hand, our analysis of the sources revealed that the earliest Israelite tribal list, the Song of Deborah, provides evidence that by the ninth century Israel did conceive of its early history as a religious confederation of tribes that shared common obligations to their god, Yahweh. The ninth-century date that we

assigned to this source represents a terminus ad quem; the tradition of
the confederation may be older. The tribal list contained in the song
shares a numerological similarity with the Greek amphictyonies in that
it contains ten tribal units, a similarity that I will address below.

The eighth-century tribal list from the Blessing of Moses (Deuteronomy 33) was also a ten-tribe list, but a comparison of this list with
the older Song of Deborah shows that some tribal groups have been
added and others removed. Moreover, the eighth-century prophetic
sources reveal that only some of the tribal names in the blessing can be
associated with functioning tribal units during that period (Ephraim,
Manasseh, and Gad, for instance). From this we should probably conclude that this list—and most likely the ninth-century list before it—
followed a literary convention that portrayed early national history according to ten-tribe schemes, and this is all the more attractive in light
of the ten-tribe amphictyonies described in the Greek materials. Although there is no way to prove it at this point, the obvious differences
between the Greek amphictyonies and the early Israelite confederation
tradition should not preclude the possibility that the numerological
similarity between them is no coincidence.

During the seventh century the tribal list of Deuteronomy 33 was
edited to include Levi, but because the tribal-list convention required
either ten or twelve tribes, the previously united Joseph tribe was re-
conceived as two tribes, Ephraim and Manasseh, thus preserving a
twelve-tribe scheme. The sixth-century appearance of Simeon within
the tribal lists introduced a new problem for the tribal-list tradition because it appeared to create thirteen tribes. However, we saw in Ezekiel
that the twelve-tribe model was easily preserved in one of two ways:
(1) by setting aside Levi as a special tribe or (2) by reuniting Ephraim
and Manasseh as a Joseph tribe. All of this is similar to the aggregative
tendencies of the Greek ethnic traditions and testifies to the fact that
the tribal configurations of the Tetrateuch correspond most closely to
the lists that are associated with the end of this aggregative process, that
is, to the sixth-century milieu or later.

The Forefather Traditions of Ancient Israel

The development of the patriarchal tradition as it appeared in this
study was quite different from the development suggested by the
present arrangement of the biblical materials. The earliest patriarchal

tradition that we meet in the sources is that of Jacob, who probably originated in the Northern Kingdom as an epic hero and was subsequently adopted as the Israelite forefather, an adoption that occurred prior to the eighth-century ministry of Hosea. That this adoption may have occurred during the early eighth century is suggested first by the patriarch's absence from the ninth-century Song of Deborah, second by the fact that he first appears in the eighth-century prophets, and third because similar traditions appear to have circulated in the Levant during that period. This ethnic conception of national origin may have originated in either Greece or Phoenicia, but this is not something that can be easily proved, as we have already pointed out. Other important forefathers known to the eighth-century Israelite prophets included Isaac, Joseph, and Ephraim/Manasseh. When joined to the Jacob tradition, they created four generations of forefathers, with the middle generations (Jacob and Joseph) associated with substantial traditions and the first and last generations (Isaac and Ephraim/Manasseh) associated with very minor traditions. This suggests that the primary role of the Isaac figure was to serve as the father of Jacob and makes it unlikely that the Abraham tradition, if it did at that point exist, had been integrated with the other patriarchal stories by the eighth century.

The Abraham figure first appeared in the book of Ezekiel as the forefather of the Judean remnant community. This tradition existed alongside the Exodus origin tradition and was quickly appropriated by the exilic community, which transformed Abraham into an exile returning to Palestine and integrated him into the previously existing patriarchal and exodus origin traditions. As was the case with the Israelite tribal traditions, so too in the case of the forefather traditions, we see that the Tetrateuchal sources seem to presume certain traditions and processes that date to the sixth century or later.

We can add one more observation to our summary of the historical development of Israel's ancestral traditions. On the basis of the eighth-century Blessing of Moses in Deuteronomy 33 we concluded that the various tribes in the list were very likely associated with other patriarchal characters that did not figure prominently in our prophetic sources. This is more evidence that we should not suppose that our eighth-century prophetic sources are exhaustive windows into that period of Israel's history. They are able to help us see what was there, but they are not very useful for disclosing to us what was not there.

Implications for Ethnicity Studies

A number of the generally accepted predictions made by ethnicity studies were sustained by our examination of the biblical data. Barth's notion of "ethnic boundaries" was particularly useful in our analysis of Hosea, Deuteronomy, and Ezekiel, and the idea that competition intensifies ethnic sentiments was supported by several contexts, including the proto- and classical Deuteronomic periods and also the early exilic period. The relationship predicted between various modes of identity was also confirmed, especially by the dynamic interplay between ethnic and religious modes of identity. On the other hand, the most common markers of ethnic identity—language and phenotypical appearance—played no vital role in Israelite ethnicity. Thus one must be careful to appreciate the uniqueness of Israelite ethnicity and its development, particularly in its dependence on religious sentiments and in its highly rhetorical nature.

On the theoretical level, two models of ethnic identity—Wallerstein's core/periphery model and van den Berghe's kinship model—were, with some modification, especially useful predictors of social behavior. Wallerstein's theory predicted that ethnic sentiments appear and intensify when peripheral social modalities fall under the domination of a core imperialist power, and the prophetic work of Hosea seems to bear this out. On the other hand, although the Assyrian threat probably contributed to it, Hosea's ethnic intensity seems to have been prompted more by his location on the periphery of his own society than by any imperialist pressures on his community. The case of Judea and its domination by Assyria raises still more questions because, contrary to Wallerstein's predictions, Isaiah displayed an intensification not of ethnic identity but of religious identity. In this case Wallerstein is correct to suppose that the peripheral experience intensifies identity but is wrong that it tends to create ethnic sentiments. So we can see that, although Wallerstein's theories have their merits, they are also plagued by a preoccupation with the effects of western expansion over the last few centuries and the many ethnic groups that have been victims of it.

Van den Berghe's theory, that ethnicity is a natural extension of kinship, finds particularly strong support in the biblical materials, especially in Deuteronomy. Deuteronomic "brother theology" was a deliberate attempt to extend the natural affiliations of kinship beyond the immediate family to fellow Judeans and Israelites. The presumption in Deuteronomy and elsewhere is that the notion of common ancestral origins would heighten one's sense of commonality with others in the community. This evidence seems to confirm what is intuitively appealing in my view: that ethnicity is primarily an extension of either real or fictive kinship affiliations. On the other hand, there is a slightly different situation that is involved in abstract uses of ethnicity to explain the origins of out-groups, as in the case of the Greek theory that the Scythians were sons of a fellow named Scythus (Herodotus *Histories* 4.10). Here the purpose of ethnicity is not to extend one's family and kinship affiliations to the broader group in which one participates but rather to explain the origins of another group, which seems to me a very different motive and process. So in the case of both Van den Berghe and Wallerstein, the alternating success and failure of the theories underscores the difficulties associated with using simplistic schematic models for describing and predicting highly complex human behaviors. Because of this, although I believe that ethnicity as a field of study will continue to raise valuable questions and make important observations relating to social organization and behavior, it is perhaps wise to bring the search for a single and fundamental theory of the ethnic process to a halt.

The Task That Remains

The present work is only a prolegomenon to the study of ethnicity in ancient Israel, and this means that many tasks remain for us in this avenue of research.

First, I have attempted to provide a general history of Israelite ethnic sentiments, and this reconstruction has been based on the most datable sources of the Hebrew Bible, namely, the prophetic corpus and Deuteronomy. Other biblical materials that are outside of the immediate purview of this monograph can now be evaluated against this chronological backdrop. I am thinking foremost, of course, about the pentateuchal materials and the Deuteronomistic History, as well as about the various form-critical and literary units that scholars see embedded within them.

Second, historically speaking my work has only touched on the postexilic period and the biblical sources that disclose it to us. This means that much remains to be done with Ezra/Nehemiah, the Chronicler, and the postexilic prophets, as well as in the area of postbiblical Judaism.

Third, here we have concluded that at certain points Israelite ethnic sentiments share many similarities with ethnicity as expressed elsewhere, particularly in Greece. Was this a case of ideological diffusion? And, if so, how and why did ethnic modes of identity arise in Greece? And to follow up on this question, how was this notion transmitted to the Israelite traditions? All of this needs to be examined more closely. Perhaps the most pressing questions that remain for us, however, are the many issues that my own study implies but leaves unaddressed and unresolved. Thoughtful readers will find in every chapter important questions that are not addressed explicitly, questions that I continue to find myself. Nevertheless, it is my hope that this monograph has helped in some small way to point the study of Israelite ethnicity in the right direction.

*   *   *   *   *

Theological Reflections

As R. P. Knierim has pointed out, the Hebrew Bible presents us with a diversity of theological perspectives,[1] and in the case of ethnicity these variations have been recognized even by rather conservative scholars.[2] But in the midst of these perspectives, there are important ideas that appear in all of the biblical sources that we have examined. This theological coherence appears in the form of three key themes, two of them explicit and the other implicit.

First, our biblical sources are, from a religious perspective, unabashedly particularistic and Yahwistic. The common focus in each text, from the Song of Deborah to the postexilic period, was religious identity centered in the person of Yahweh. Participation in the community of the text required exclusive commitment to him as God, along with a careful abstention from practices that appeared to place this allegiance elsewhere. It can be averred that there were many other perspectives in ancient Israel, but here our concern is with biblical the-

1. R. P. Knierim, *The Task of Old Testament Theology: Substance, Method, and Cases* (Grand Rapids: Eerdmans, 1995) 1–7.
2. On the very different ethnic spirit that separates the Chronicles from Ezra/Nehemiah, see R. B. Dillard, *2 Chronicles* (WBC; Waco, Tex.: Word, 1987) 50.

ology rather than with the ideologies that competed with it. So, while religious pluralism finds a home in some modern readings of the Hebrew Bible, those readings are entirely foreign to the communities that composed these texts.

Second, even in their most rigid form (i.e., Ezra), the ethnic boundaries of these Yahwistic communities made room for the assimilation of outsiders. This reflects the important place that religious assimilation had for their God, who desired that all human beings enjoy the benefits of covenant life. These theological perspectives are not alone the parlance of the Hebrew Bible but also appear, no doubt because of its influence, in New Testament theology at many points, as is so visible in Rom 3:6–7: "Consider Abraham: 'He believed God, and it was credited to him as righteousness.' Understand, then, that those who believe are children of Abraham."

Finally, the supposed theological diversity that one observes in the sources with respect to ethnic boundaries actually reflects, in a certain sense, a kind of theological coherence. It supports the theological legitimacy of efforts to adjust the character and intensity of community boundaries in response to both the threats and the opportunities that are presented to the community of faith. But such efforts must necessarily be circumscribed, as they were in all of our sources, by an unyielding allegiance to Yahweh and by a community life that reflects a commitment to his revealed word. This reminds us again that theological diversity is frequently a product of the more general and pervasive truths that gave shape to the biblical materials. Although these general truths implicitly guided the biblical authors, we are sometimes fortunate, from our later theological and biblical purview, to lay them out explicitly.

Index of Authors

Index of Scripture

Scripture is indexed according to Hebrew chapter and verse divisions.